D1753877

Life as a Man

Cover vignette of Mohonk mountain silhouette
courtesy of the Publications Office, State
University College, New Paltz, New York.

Studies in Modern German Literature

Peter D.G. Brown
General Editor

Vol. 34

PETER LANG
New York • Bern • Frankfurt am Main • Paris

Claus Reschke

Life as a Man

Contemporary Male-Female Relationships
in the Novels of Max Frisch

PETER LANG
New York • Bern • Frankfurt am Main • Paris

Library of Congress Cataloging-in-Publication Data

Reschke, Claus
   Life as a man : contemporary male-female
relationships in the novels of Max Frisch / Claus Reschke.
      p. cm. — (Studies in modern German literature ;
vol. 34)
   Includes bibliographical references.
   1. Frisch, Max, 1911- —Criticism and interpretation.
2. Love in literature.   3. Sex in literature.   4. Marriage
in literature.   5. Sex differences (Psychology) in literature.
I. Title.   II. Series.
PT2611.R814Z786   1990   833'.912—dc20   89-39785
ISBN 0-8204-1163-9   CIP
ISSN 0888-3904

CIP-Titelaufnahme der Deutschen Bibliothek

Reschke, Claus:
Life as a man : contemporary male-female
relationships in the novels of Max Frisch /
Claus Reschke. — New York; Bern; Frankfurt
am Main; Paris: Lang, 1990.
  (Studies in Modern German Literature; Vol. 34)
  ISBN 0-8204-1163-9

NE: GT

Back cover photo by Foto Krottmaier.

© Peter Lang Publishing, Inc., New York 1990

All rights reserved.
Reprint or reproduction, even partially, in all forms such as microfilm,
xerography, microfiche, microcard, offset strictly prohibited.

Printed by Weihert-Druck GmbH, Darmstadt, West Germany

In memory of

Seth Wallace Heartfield

CONTENTS

Acknowledgments xi

A Note on Texts and Translations xiii

Introduction xvii

1. In Search of "das wirkliche Leben" 1

2. *Die Schwierigen*: Uneasy Compromises
   Introduction 17
   Jürg-Yvonne: A Road Not Taken 21
   Jürg-Hortense: Two Worlds Confront Each Other ... 35
   Jürg's Suicide: An Ironic Misperception 45

3. *Stiller*: A Tale of Two Marriages
   Introduction 51
   Marriage as a Test: Stiller and Julika 54
   Interlude 1: Stiller and Sibylle 71
   An Endangered Marriage: Rolf and Sibylle 80
   Interlude 2: Stiller's Escape 94
   A Difficult Courtship: Stiller/White and Julika 100
   A Marriage Resumed: Stiller and Julika 110

4. *Homo faber*: A Glimpse at "das wirkliche Leben"
   Introduction 125
   An Erratic Relationship: Faber and Ivy 127
   The Miracle of Love: Faber and Sabeth 133
     The Voyage Begins 133
     At Sea 136
     Paris 152
     Italy and Greece 155
     Denouement 167
   Transgression and Guilt: Faber and Hanna 169
   Redemption 181

5. *Mein Name sei Gantenbein*: A Look through the Prism
   Introduction 191
   The Narrator: Puppeteer of the Self 197
   Enderlin: The Problematic Lover 204
   Svoboda: The Deceived Husband 218
   Gantenbein: The Seeing Blind Husband 230
      Setting the Stage 230
      Version 1: A Tolerable Marriage 236
      Version 2: An Intolerable Marriage 242
   The Narrator: End of a Long Journey 253

6. *Montauk*: Life as a Man
   Introduction 267
   Author versus Narrator: An Intimate Relationship .. 270
   Käte: The Foreign Student 276
   Constanze: The Mother of His Children 278
   Ingeborg: The Fellow Writer 283
   Marianne: The Editor 291
   Lynn: Undine and Nurse 298
   Max: Women, Aging, and Immediacy 305

7. *Der Mensch erscheint im Holozän* and *Blaubart*: Old Age and the Question of Guilt
   Introduction 315
   The Final Stage of Transient Time: *Der Mensch erscheint im Holozän* 316
   The Labyrinth of Guilt: *Blaubart* 321
   Conclusion 325

8. **Final Considerations**
   Introduction 327
   Frisch's Men: Common Characteristics 330
      Isolation 331
      Loneliness 333
      Creativity 335
      Chauvinism 336
      Agnosticism 339
   Frisch's Men: Similar Responses 341
      Love 342

>   Jealousy 343
>   A Graven Image 345
>   Repetition 348
>   Marriage 350
>   Transient Time 355
> Epilogue 361

Works Cited 367

Index 371

ACKNOWLEDGMENTS

This project could not have been started without the generous support of the University of Houston, which awarded me a Faculty Development Leave (sabbatic) for the academic year 1985-1986 during which I was able to do the necessary research for this study and to write the first draft. I am deeply grateful to the university and my colleagues there for providing me with the opportunity to get the project well under way during that year away from the campus.

I also thank my colleagues Gertrud B. Pickar, for reading an early draft of several chapters, and Barry A. Brown, for his much appreciated technical assistance in preparing this manuscript for publication. Special thanks go to Lore Feldman, who read the entire manuscript and provided invaluable suggestions.

Finally, I thank my wife Barbara, an editor by profession, whose encouragement and contributions at every stage of this project have inspired me to complete it.

Claus Reschke

A NOTE ON TEXTS AND TRANSLATIONS

All citations in German from the works of Max Frisch are taken from Max Frisch, *Gesammelte Werke in zeitlicher Folge*, vols. 1-7, Frankfurt: Suhrkamp, 1976-1986. (The pagination of the thirteen-volume soft-cover *Werkausgabe* of Frisch's works [Suhrkamp, 1976-1986] is identical to that of the hard-cover *Gesammelte Werke*.) Individual volumes of the seven-volume edition are identified in this study only by Roman numerals. They contain the following works that are dealt with herein:

I. *Jürg Reinhart: Eine sommerliche Schicksalsfahrt;*
    Die Schwierigen oder J'adore ce qui me brûle;
    Bin oder die Reise nach Peking.
II. *Tagebuch 1946-1949.*
III. *Don Juan oder Die Liebe zur Geometrie;*
    Stiller.
IV. *Homo faber.*
V. *Mein Name sei Gantenbein;*
    Kleine Prosaschriften (1964-1971);
    Zürich-Transit.
VI. *Tagebuch 1966-1971;*
    Montauk.
VII. *Der Mensch erscheint im Holozän;*
    Blaubart.

A few words about the English translations used in this study seem appropriate. For practical reasons of reference and usefulness to the reader, these translations are quoted from the published English translations of Frisch's works by Michael Bullock and Geoffrey Skelton. (Exceptions are *Jürg Reinhart, Die Schwierigen, Bin oder die Reise nach Peking*, and excerpts from a few short works, none of which has been published in translation.) Citations from the published translations appear in italics and are identified by either a page number alone or a short form of the title plus a page number. The English translations used, and the short titles used to identify them in the text, are:

Homo Faber, trans. Michael Bullock, 1959.
Sketchbook 1966-1971, trans. Geoffrey Skelton, 1974 (*Sketch II*).
Montauk, trans. Geoffrey Skelton, 1976.
Sketchbook 1946-1949, trans. Geoffrey Skelton, 1977 (*Sketch I*).
Man in the Holocene, trans. Geoffrey Skelton, 1980 (*Holocene*).
Gantenbein, trans. Michael Bullock, 1982.
I'm Not Stiller, trans. Michael Bullock, 1982.
Bluebeard, trans. Geoffrey Skelton, 1983.

All other English translations of Frisch's works and those of other authors quoted in this study are mine; they are easily identifiable, as they are not followed by a page number.

For the reader who is thoroughly familiar with German, the occasional awkwardness of the translations will be a minor annoyance. Such a reader will be inclined to read the primary quotations and to pass over the English translations that follow. My concern, however, is for the reader less than fluent in, or lacking any knowledge of, German. This reader has to rely on the English translations as a blind man does on his Seeing-Eye dog to guide him safely through the maze of ideas and characters present in Frisch's novels.

Some of the translations quoted here, because they are necessarily taken out of context, do not correspond very closely to the original text and thus will displease those readers who insist on linguistic purity in all translation. I have no quarrel with them or their demands, but I do beg their indulgence, especially for the approved translators of Frisch's works. These men's task was not to translate only a few lines of text, but to translate an entire creative work. This is a much more challenging and difficult task than translating a few isolated passages; it is a task that requires a broad, thematically focused perspective on the entire work. This broader orientation is what accounts for the occasional nonparallel translations from German into English of various passages quoted here.

When the original German and its approved English translation are too far apart in meaning, or where a translator has been obviously wrong, based on the larger context in which a particular passage occurs, I have substituted my own translation of the original German.

INTRODUCTION

Since the publication of *Stiller* (1954) and *Homo faber* (1957), much has been written about the problem of identity in the novels of the Swiss author Max Frisch. Indeed, the protagonist's search for himself, for an identity freed from the role he either chose for himself or that society forced on him, is a theme, perhaps the most dominant leitmotif, that emerges from all of Frisch's novels and plays. This theme overshadows all other topics and themes in the numerous critical interpretations devoted to Frisch's novels over the past thirty years. Many other themes, however, are as essential to a Frisch protagonist's development and as important to understanding Max Frisch's oeuvre. These other themes often illuminate the process by which the characters pursue their task of self-discovery; they also illustrate how the protagonist, always a man, finally confronts his own peculiar dilemma.

One such neglected major topic in Max Frisch's novels is the character of man-woman relationships, specifically the protagonist's relationships with women. Although a number of essays have dealt with this topic in the context of a single Frisch novel or play—most prominently *Stiller*—and one broader-based, longer study examines the portrait of the woman that emerges from Frisch's novels and plays (Merrifield 1971), no detailed study has focused on the protagonist's relationship to women in all of Frisch's novels, from *Jürg Reinhart: Eine sommerliche Schicksalsfahrt* (1934) to *Blaubart* (1982). My purpose here is to provide such a comprehensive study.

None of the protagonist's relationships with women—with the possible exception of Walter Faber's to Sabeth in *Homo faber*—leads directly to the protagonist's primary task: to discover and accept his true identity. Yet all of these relationships assist him in his search for himself, facilitate the process, and push him forward along the path. Underlying each relationship the protagonist enters into—except, perhaps, the one Max establishes with Lynn in *Montauk*—is the hope that this bond will help him to experience "das wirkliche Leben," "*the real life*," which he believes exists just beyond his reach.

This neoromantic longing for "the real life," a longing never completely satisfied, is a theme common to twentieth-century authors. It dominates the novels of Max Frisch and links them with those of Franz Kafka. Kafka's protagonists, who seek purpose and meaning in their lives in the realm of either the family (*Die Verwandlung, Das Urteil*) or the bureaucratic state (*Der Prozess, Das Schloss*), insist that man has a goal to reach but, paradoxically, no way to reach it nor the possibility of discovering a way; but the way must be found, Kafka's protagonists assert as they continue their hopeless quest.

Frisch's protagonists, in contrast, are not merely certain that their goal—"das wirkliche Leben"—exists, but also that they can reach it. Their personal tragedy, as they see it, is that this life is just beyond their grasp. Although they do not come up empty-handed, what they hold is less than or different from the life they expected and hoped for. "Das *wirkliche* Leben" seems forever to elude them. Is that goal, then, an illusion, or is the cause of their failure to seize it a basic human frailty, the inability to recognize that what we experience—alone or in a relationship—*is* the real life, that there is no other, more intensely "real" life for us to experience? And if this higher-order real life existed, would it not be too intoxicating, too rarified for mere mortals? Perhaps.

Nevertheless, the protagonists in Frisch's novels rarely abandon their quest for the real life. In their search, however, they misjudge and misinterpret the role and needs of every partner, never fully appreciating, accepting, or understanding either the partner or themselves, always longing for something or someone just out of reach. Instead of seizing what lies within their grasp and holding on to it, they chase a phantom, or so it seems, thus depriving themselves of the contentment and joie de vivre that could be theirs. The ability to see and to experience life and love nearly always comes too late.

At times, the protagonist's search for self-knowledge, forced on him either by unexplained circumstances and events as in *Mein Name sei Gantenbein* or by fate as in *Homo faber*, ends disastrously, as in *Die Schwierigen*. At other times the protagonist's valiant struggle against great odds seems puzzling, as in *Stiller*, or futile, as in *Homo faber*, especially since, in the latter novel, the protagonist dies soon after learning to accept himself and a different kind of life. In general, though, the p? through a loving relationship with a woman, gains at ... temporary insight. The relationship also gives him periods of joy in being alive, despite the anguish and pain of the search. These periods of happiness, long or short, allow him to approach his ultimate goal, the discovery and acceptance of his true identity.

The actual outcome of the protagonist's relationship to any of the women he loves can, for this reason, be viewed as generally positive. The narrator's comment at the conclusion of *Mein Name sei Gantenbein* supports this interpretation. After a painful investigation into his own nature and relationship with one woman, a relationship that has failed, the narrator exclaims: "Leben gefällt mir" (V 320), "*Living pleases me.*" Having followed this novel's narrator-protagonist through torturous self-analysis, the reader is tempted to believe him.

A study of the relationship between men and women in the novels of Max Frisch would be incomplete if it were limited only to the protagonists and the women they love. Since many of these women go on to other male-female relationships, including marriage, after their relationship with the protagonist has ended, the investigation needs to be expanded to include all major characters of a particular novel, men and women. This broader perspective allows us to discover if, to what extent, and why these various characters may arrive at insights and conclusions about themselves, their identities and their lives that differ from those reached by the novel's protagonist.

In a relationship with a woman, the major male characters frequently cling to outdated, stereotyped role models to hide their own insecurities and inadequacies. In every loving relationship the man lacks commitment to the woman and to the relationship itself, making a true partnership impossible. Egocentricity and a roster of failings, shortcomings, and insecurities, all rooted in the perception of self as an inadequate man, lead these men to a kind of obsessive behavior that gradually destroys the relationship.

In short, vis-à-vis the woman he loves, contemporary man—as his image emerges from Frisch's novels—frequently feels uncomfortable and insecure. Are these feelings rooted merely in contemporary man's identity problem, or are they also related to his ambivalent relationship to time? And is not the fear of repetition, which all Frisch's protagonists suffer, directly related to their confusion about the functions of the two kinds of time, transient and measured, in their lives? This study investigates these issues and many related questions about contemporary man as his composite picture emerges from the novels Frisch has written over the past fifty years.

In the general discussion in Chapter One I have two purposes, to identify the major themes linking Frisch's novels and to develop the premise on which this study is based: that characterizing the protagonist's relationship to women is vitally important to understanding Frisch's novels fully, since in that relationship the protagonist reveals himself more thoroughly than in any other circumstance. This premise is investigated in detail in Chapters Two through Six, in which five major Frisch novels—*Die Schwierigen, Stiller, Homo faber, Mein Name sei Gantenbein*, and *Montauk*—spanning a thirty-year period of the author's career are analyzed. In Chapter Seven I take a brief look at the two most recently published novels, *Der Mensch erscheint im Holozän* and *Blaubart*, to see what either may contribute to this thesis. The concluding Chapter Eight is a summation of those findings.

The intended audience for this study comprises students of German literature, literary scholars, and informed general readers. For the convenience of the first two, I have added a note section after each chapter and a list of works cited and an index at the end of the book.

Houston, Texas   Claus Reschke
August 1989

CHAPTER ONE

IN SEARCH OF "DAS WIRKLICHE LEBEN"

A close reading of Max Frisch's novels reveals many similarities as well as obvious differences. For one thing, a cluster of significant themes and topics recurs again and again as Frisch continues to investigate such problems as man's search for identity and self-acceptance, the relationship between the individual and society, the difficulties and rewards of marriage, and the problem of aging. For another, in every one of Frisch's novels the protagonist is a man and, with few exceptions, the novel's first-person narrator and the person through whose eyes all other characters and events are seen.

The result of this approach is anything but static. Although each novel's central character is confronted by many of the same issues and problems, each one changes and develops in his own way in response to the particular challenges posed in the novel. Similarly, Frisch changes his perspective and investigative focus from one novel to the next, so that his various protagonists mirror the author's own development from the earliest to the most recent of his published novels, spanning a period of fifty years.

At the core of most of Frisch's creative work is a human being's search for identity. Frisch's characters usually are unsure who they are or where they belong. But identity does not exist in a vacuum: human beings test and validate themselves in relationship to something or someone else—to their environment and, especially, to society. Thus the protagonists in Frisch's novels search not only for their own identity but also, and perhaps more significantly, for "das wirkliche Leben," the real, the meaningful life. Each of these protagonists—and in fact most of Frisch's characters, men and women, major and minor—is engaged in this search. They seek a life that is more complete than the one they are leading. The protagonist, especially, yearns for a life in which he might understand himself better, a life less tense, less filled with struggle, and more comprehensible than his present life. He perceives this potential existence dimly; it seems always to lie just beyond his reach. If he can grasp it, he may be able to live in greater harmony with himself and others.

Frisch's description of the central elements of mankind's longing for "das wirkliche Leben" is clearest in a little parable he published in 1945: *Bin oder die Reise nach Peking* (*Bin or the Journey to Peking*). It is a fragile, lyrical narrative in which Kilian, an architect (as Frisch was at the time), leaves his family and home to satisfy a deep-seated, inexpressible, yet irresistible longing for change from the reality of his present life. This indefinable nostalgia overcomes the successful architect every spring; it is a powerful longing, something like the restless urge that prompted Chaucer, in the opening stanza of his *Canterbury Tales*, to comment,

> Thanne longen folk to goon on pilgrimages,
> And palmeres for to seken straunge strondes,
> To ferne halwes, kowthe in sondry londes.
> (Chaucer 17)

Frisch describes it as

> ein märzliches Heimweh nach neuen Menschen, denen man selber noch einmal neu wäre, so, daß es sich auf eine wohlige Weise lohnte zu reden, zu denken über viele Dinge, ja, sich zu begeistern. . . . (I 604)
>
> *a springlike longing for new people, for whom one would once more oneself be new, so that it would be worthwhile in a relaxed manner to talk, to think about many things, even to be enthusiastic . . . .*

This nostalgia, Kilian explains, is similar to the powerful longing one might experience periodically for a long conversation with a woman, perhaps a lover-to-be, when the acquaintanceship is new. Kilian realizes that, although his life is half over, he has not yet fulfilled his own expectations. He is beginning to feel ashamed to face the youthful self-image he holds. The boredom Kilian finds so depressing is born of his daily professional routine and his marriage. In an effort to escape the ordinary, the habitual, and the repetitive, Kilian sets off on an imaginary journey to the Chinese capital, Peking, a code name for the happiness one may have missed or is missing in life.[1] His travel companion is *Bin*, the alter ego of the *Ich* (I). Together these two form a whole, expressing the core of human existence in the succint statement of personal identity: *Ich bin* (I am). If the *Bin* is repressed and not allowed to join the *Ich* at least occasionally, Kilian recognizes, life holds only the grayness of daily routine. Yet to follow the lure of the *Bin*, its promise of eternally fulfilling the *Ich*'s yearning for excitement and variety, without balance from the routine of daily activity would produce perpetual instability, also an unsatisfactory condition. Kilian discovers this in the course of his travels.

At the end of his journey through the dreams and longings of his internal world, Kilian comes home to his wife, Rapunzel, and their child. Although Kilian realizes that his journey to the exotic interior of his being did not satisfy his longings as he hoped it would, he is now more comfortable with himself and his conventional life, because he recognizes that here at home, where we love, we really listen to one another, we hear one another with the heart. Only in this manner, Kilian now knows, are we able to transcend feelings of being torn; only when we comprehend this can we build bridges of real understanding between ourselves and our beloved, the *Du* (you) of our existence.

In the Peking of Frisch's story, where past and future are one with the present, man lives in harmony with himself, his dreams, his friends, his spouse, his children, the universe and all its creatures. Neither the protagonist in *Bin* nor anyone else can ever reach Peking, however, for "man's life is short and Peking so far away!" (I 649). But if we start on the road to Peking, we will achieve more contentment than if we never begin that journey. We should be grateful, Frisch's protagonist implies, for the insights we gain along the way.

Picking up his child and looking at him carefully, Kilian decides the child most resembles *Bin*, his guide on the road to

4   LIFE AS A MAN

Peking (I 658). Thus the child, by its existence, manifests the nostalgia, the fervent longing for "das wirkliche Leben" that seems to lie just beyond Kilian's grasp, but for which all of Frisch's protagonists yearn.

Kilian's poignant experience is either reflected or repeated in each of the five novels that are the focus of this study—merely as a suggestion in *Die Schwierigen*, which preceded *Bin oder die Reise nach Peking*, and most prominently in *Homo faber*, which followed it. In the latter work Walter Faber, more subconsciously than consciously, gropes for an experientially richer existence than he knows in his career as an engineer. At an involuntary, yet fateful, stopover in a Mexican desert begins the quest that eventually leads him to his past and his future. Later, on board a ship crossing the Atlantic, he meets Sabeth, a strangely appealing young woman. In her company, especially after they become lovers, he experiences the beauty and love that are possible in life. Unknown to him, it is his own daughter who has introduced him to "das wirkliche Leben."

In *Stiller* the protagonist's search for the more complete life is subordinated to his search for identity, although neither one seems possible without the other. In *Mein Name sei Gantenbein* the protagonist's search for wholeness requires that he first fragment himself. Then, as he examines his nature and his relationship to a woman, he tries to discover, first, under what conditions he can maintain a long-term relationship with a woman and, second, what went wrong in his life and marriage. In *Montauk*, the protagonist's search for "das wirkliche Leben" emerges as the dominant theme once more, this time treated reflectively, as the aging writer Max attempts to come to terms with himself and his past.

Almost always Frisch shows his protagonists in two kinds of essential relationships: a broad one, in which the mores and expectations of society come under scrutiny and are tested, and a close personal one with the woman or women he loves. The second type of relationship is the one Frisch explores most fully in most of his novels. The exceptions are *Der Mensch erscheint im Holozän* (1979) (*Man in the Holocene*), which concentrates on the problems of aging, and Frisch's first novel, *Jürg Reinhart* (1934). Even in this earliest novel of an immature writer, however, Frisch laid the groundwork for his later concerns, especially the protagonist's preoccupation with male-female relationships and his effort to find a way to self-realization in these relationships. Subtitled *Eine sommerliche Schicksalsfahrt* (*A Fateful Summer's Journey*), this early novel contains little that is actually "fateful." It describes the conflicts the twenty-one-year-old protagonist feels between his natural longing for a woman's sexual love and his scruples about accepting that love. Instead of solving his problem Jürg represses it, replacing his desire for a sexual relationship with the desire to perform a meaningful, manly deed that would serve as his initiation into maturity (I 305).

The novel contains a cast of lively characters, most of the important ones women. As early as page one (I 227) the reader meets Marga, a thirty-nine-year-old Dutch baroness who, married to a sixty-year-old man, would like nothing better than to seduce the attractive, sexually still innocent Jürg Reinhart, irrespective of how comical her single-minded pursuit of that goal appears to the world. And then there is Hilde, a far less scheming and less complicated woman, eighteen years old, who works at the *Pension* in which Jürg is a guest. She understands Jürg's desires and encourages him when Jürg becomes temporarily infatuated with her. Although she clearly indicates her interest in Jürg and her willingness to satisfy his sexual longing, he cannot overcome his scruples and take advantage of the opportunity Hilde offers so freely.

Two other women, the mother and daughter who own the *Pension*—the elder an aristocratic but impoverished German widow—are equally interesting characters created by the young Max Frisch. The mother is a strong, practical woman who tries to make a living as an innkeeper without becoming involved in the lives of her guests. Her daughter Inge, thirty years old, is the novel's major female character, the one Jürg comes to love, although his sexual ethics prevent their relationship from progressing beyond that of good friends. Toward the end of the novel Inge is near death from cancer. When there is no hope of her recovery and she is in great pain, Jürg administers to her the overdose of morphine that ends her suffering. This mercy killing, which Inge's mother had attempted but could not carry out, ironically is the manly deed Jürg has been seeking to mark his full maturity, qualifying him to join the fellowship of men. Motivated by his love for Inge, he accepts not only the difficulty of the task but also the moral responsibility for the deed.

Euthanasia was an unusual topic for the literature of the 1930s, and it was as controversial then as it is today. The theme of "becoming," however, of achieving maturity through commitment to and performance of a significant deed, is easily recognized as a Goethian theme the young Swiss author borrowed from the old master. Not a poor choice of mentor for a young writer, although Frisch's handling of the theme of "becoming" in this early novel is, not surprisingly, immature and unsatisfactory.

Frisch's second novel, *Die Schwierigen* (*The Difficult Ones*), first published in 1943 and extensively revised in 1957, again concerns a protagonist named Jürg Reinhart. However, in the revised version of the novel, which is the basis for this study, he shares only his name with his predecessor. Frisch confronts this other Jürg with a host of themes and issues that are related, as always, to the protagonist's search for self-knowledge and his role in society, but here for the first time the protagonist's relationships with women become significant. Through Jürg, Frisch examines the artist's role in a bourgeois society and the ambiguous social position he occupies. Jürg struggles with a number of issues: how to reconcile his carefree artist's life and a stifling middle-class routine complete with the prospect of a traditional marriage to Hortense, one of the two women he loves; and how to assess the validity of his artistic calling as a painter, which, with some provocation from Hortense, he comes to doubt seriously. In addition, he must face the unusual problem of his perceived social and genetic inferiority. Why, in the end, Jürg rejects both the bourgeois and the artistic life, becomes a gardener, and eventually removes himself completely by committing suicide, will be dealt with in detail in the next chapter.

Die Schwierigen has weaknesses one might reasonably expect from a relatively inexperienced novelist. Its structure is much simpler than that of later works. The characters are not as sharply delineated and their often abrupt, dramatic actions are less clearly motivated than they will be as Frisch matures. The philosophical statements are facile, the style highly derivative. In addition, the direct autobiographical link between Jürg Reinhart and the author is too obvious. While he was writing this novel Frisch, like Jürg, was torn between two opposing worlds, that of the imagination and that of practical reality. Specifically, Frisch was torn between the demands of his budding career as an architect, with which he supported himself and his growing family, and his love for writing, which, even after a self-imposed abstention, would no longer be repressed (II 588; Jurgensen 1976,47; Stine 71-78). Frisch succeeded in reconciling the demands of society with his personal needs as an artist, eventually turning from part-time to full-time writing, but Jürg Reinhart fails, essentially because he lacks the confidence and faith in himself and his calling as an artist that sustained Max Frisch.

In Frisch's next novel, *Stiller* (1954), the protagonist, sculptor Anatol Ludwig Stiller, also attempts to end his struggles by committing suicide, but this attempt fails. Although Stiller, in the process of his unsuccessful suicide attempt, discovers and accepts his new identity, he cannot convince the people closest to him—his wife, family, and friends—or society at large, as symbolized by the court, that he is no longer the person he was seven years earlier when he suddenly abandoned wife, friends, and profession to find out who he really was and to discover "das wirkliche Leben." Stiller never comes close to it.

Homo faber, published three years later, was acclaimed quickly, perhaps because its theme, man's dilemma in a modern, technological society, touched readers' lives. Through his love for a woman, Sabeth, the protagonist discovers a more complete self and embraces a richer life, although soon thereafter he dies during an operation for cancer. In the next novel, *Mein Name sei Gantenbein* (1964) (translated into English as *Gantenbein* in a new edition with the author's consent in 1982), the protagonist, the unnamed first-person narrator, uses the tools of analysis to investigate in great detail his attitudes about and relationships with women. Like his two predecessors, this protagonist eventually reaches a more complete understanding of himself and, as the novel ends, accepts his life and himself, despite his frailties and inadequacies.

This ultimate self-acceptance is also the position of the protagonist at the end of *Montauk*. Max gains this new, more positive view of himself during a weekend spent in reflection and conversation with his current young lover in a small resort town on Long Island, New York.

One significant aspect of the five novels, from *Die Schwierigen* to *Montauk*, with which I am most concerned is that in all of them the protagonist's relationship with women, and the women themselves, are vitally important to the man's search for "das wirkliche Leben." A woman who loves and is loved by the man can defeat and destroy him or, more often, can serve as the mirror and nurturer of his dormant abilities that, once awakened, enable him to live in greater harmony with himself and others.

In an early *Tagebuch* entry from 1946 Frisch wrote:

> Wir wissen, daß jeder Mensch, wenn man ihn liebt, sich wie verwandelt fühlt, wie entfaltet, und daß auch dem Liebenden sich alles entfaltet, das Nächste, das lange Bekannte. . . . So wie das All, wie Gottes unerschöpfliche Geräumigkeit, schrankenlos, alles Möglichen voll, aller Geheimnisse voll, unfaßbar ist der Mensch, den man liebt —
> Nur die Liebe erträgt ihn so. (II 369)

> *We know that every person who is loved feels transformed, unfolded, and he unfolds everything, the most intimate as well as the most familiar, to the one who loves him as well as to himself. . . . Because the person one loves is as ungraspable as the universe, as God's infinite space, he is boundless, full of possibilities, full of secrets —*
> *Only when one loves can one bear it.* (Sketch I 16-17)

In a truly loving relationship, then, both partners are extremely vulnerable to each other. However, only in such a fragile relationship can the mystery of human beings become somewhat more fathomable, to both the lover and the beloved. That is why relationships between women and the male protagonists in Frisch's novels are so important. That, too, is why a thorough understanding of the relationships these women weave and maintain with the men, even if only briefly, is essential to a complete understanding of the novels.

Although the women beloved of Frisch's protagonists are as different as their various relationships, they have some common characteristics. All of the women, for example, are well educated and from middle- or upper-middle-class families. Most have some professional or vocational training and can therefore support themselves if necessary. Each is endowed with an intelligent, independent mind as well as a strong and temperamental nature. All are basically self-reliant characters who make their own decisions. Generally, they strive to be equal partners in their relationship with the protagonist. Knowingly or not, each contributes directly to the success or failure of the protagonist's quest.

For most adult human beings, the closest relationship possible with another person is marriage. The possibilities and problems of marriage are of enduring interest to Max Frisch, as he demonstrates in all his novels and in his *Tagebücher* (*Sketchbooks*), his literary diaries.

To Frisch, marriage seems to be the most difficult and perhaps the most necessary of human institutions. It combines an abstract concept and a shared, lived experience. As two individuals shape and define a marriage, so the marriage itself shapes and defines them. Marriage holds more promise than any other relationship between a man and a woman, Frisch believes: it can be either rewarding or disastrous. In *Die Schwierigen*, Yvonne, one of the major woman characters, reaches these conclusions:

> Ein Wunderbares ist um die Ehe. Sie ist möglich, sobald man nichts Unmögliches von ihr fordert, sobald man über den Wahn hinauswächst, man könne sich verstehen, müsse sich verstehen; sobald man aufhört, die Ehe anzusehen als ein Mittel wider die Einsamkeit. (I 551)

> *There is something marvelous about marriage. It is possible as soon as one does not demand anything impossible of it, as*

soon as one grows beyond the delusion one could understand the other, had to understand the other; as soon as one stops looking upon marriage as a means against loneliness.

Whether one should take this statement at face value is a matter I shall investigate in the following chapters. Suffice it here to note that Yvonne needed two marriages to gain this perspective.

Stiller, more than any other of Frisch's novels, may be seen as a study of the institution of marriage. Frisch contrasts here the marriages of two couples, the sculptor Anatol Ludwig Stiller and his wife Julika, and the prosecutor Rolf and his wife Sibylle. All four are closely linked by plot and theme, but they look at marriage differently. To Sibylle, marriage means an independent decision to live one's life in a given, freely chosen partnership, to shape one's life and the marriage with the partner's help, to grow in and through this special partnership, and to enrich one's own and the partner's life and the partnership. Rolf is far less certain about the significance of marriage, although he seems to have considered the subject at length, since as a lawyer he has often had to deal with failed marriages. In the process Rolf has developed a self-serving theory about modern marriage that is intended to keep it interesting and viable by allowing both partners brief extramarital affairs. But when Sibylle accepts his repeated challenge and tests his theory, thereby threatening their marriage, Rolf is as helpless and confused as she. Sibylle, frustrated by her inability to communicate with her husband, calls him "a married bachelor" (III 639), which may be an overstatement but pinpoints one problem of their troubled marriage.

The marriage of Julika and Stiller is in trouble for other reasons. Both partners chose marriage, not because of love and shared social interests, but because of individual weaknesses. For Julika, marriage to Stiller was a convenient escape from the troublesome attention and implied sexual demands of other men, while Stiller regarded Julika as a personal challenge through whom he could prove himself as a man.

The yardstick by which Frisch measures the success or failure of a marriage is stated in the title of an essay he wrote in 1946: "Du sollst Dir kein Bildnis machen" (II 369), *"Thou shalt not make unto thee any graven image"* (Sketch I 16; Exodus 20:4).

Clearly, Frisch is referring to the Second Commandment, applying it to human relationships. Frisch is certain that one should not form and cling to an image of another person, for such an image contains preconceptions and prevents the other from changing. Judged by this dictum, the marriage of Stiller and Julika is a failure, mainly because Julika clings to her fixed image of Stiller. Stiller, for a while at least, sees changes in Julika when he returns after a seven-year absence, but he cannot persuade her to take a fresh look at him. That is why their second attempt at marriage ends in failure. Rolf and Sibylle, by contrast, eventually succeed in their marriage, because Rolf manages to modify his image of his wife and therefore his attitude and behavior toward her.

In *Mein Name sei Gantenbein*, Frisch externalizes this human tendency of forming an image of one's partner, carrying it to its extreme. He makes this figurative blindness concrete in the character of the ostensibly blind Theo Gantenbein, who enters the dressing room of the well-known actress Lila, his future wife, outfitted with armband and cane. From that first meeting she mistakenly accepts him as the person he pretends to be, a blind man. Gantenbein's assumed blindness is the key in the protagonist-narrator's careful analysis of the relationship and marriage as well as its failure.

In *Montauk* the "graven image" theme is less dominant, as the protagonist reflects on his past and his four important long-term relationships, two of them marriages. The relationships themselves are central in his reflections during the long weekend he shares with Lynn, his current lover, at a beach on Long Island. Like other protagonists in Frisch novels, Max has been guilty of a misdeed. Max learns of it when Marianne, his second wife, tells him in desperation that he "in zehn Jahren nichts zu ihrer Selbstverwirklichung beigetragen habe" (VI 679), *"in ten years . . . had done nothing to help her develop her potentialities"* (*Montauk* 63). Max's error: to have treated his wife as if he were Adam and she Eve, made of his rib, telling her, "Come, follow, and I will lead!" (VI 679; *Montauk* 63). Max's crime: male chauvinism. Slowly Max begins to understand the nature of his wife's accusation and to accept the enormity of the charge.

12   LIFE AS A MAN

Marriages, seven of them, also are important in *Blaubart* (1982) (translated in 1983 as *Bluebeard*), Frisch's most recently published and in some ways most unusual novel. The book reveals only a few selected aspects of the life of the physician protagonist, Dr. Felix Schaad, and his relationships with his seven wives, as these relationships might help the court decide his innocence or guilt of the murder of one of them, of which he stands accused. Since the protagonist's relationships with his wives are presented from an extremely limited perspective, only those that pertain directly to the central theme of this study will be considered in Chapter Seven.

Another concept, that of time and man's relationship to it, has interested Max Frisch for many years. In a *Tagebuch* entry as early as 1946 he observes:

> Wir leben auf einem laufenden Band, und es gibt keine Hoffnung, daß wir uns selber nachholen und einen Augenblick unseres Lebens verbessern können. Wir sind das Damals, auch wenn wir es verwerfen, nicht minder als das Heute—
> Die Zeit verwandelt uns nicht.
> Sie entfaltet uns nur. (II 360-61)

> *We live on a conveyer belt and have no hope of ever catching up with ourselves and improving a moment in our life. We are Then, even when we spurn it, just as much as Now—*
> *Time does not change us.*
> *It only unfolds us. (Sketch I 12)*

And what is time, he wonders.

> ... ein Zaubermittel, das unser Wesen auseinanderzieht und sichtbar macht, indem sie [die Zeit] das Leben, das eine Allgegenwart alles Möglichen ist, in ein Nacheinander zerlegt; allein dadurch erscheint es als Verwandlung, und darum drängt es uns immer wieder zur Vermutung, daß die Zeit, das Nacheinander, nicht

wesentlich ist, sondern scheinbar, ein Hilfsmittel unsrer Vorstellung. . . . (II 361)

. . . a magic device which separates out our nature and makes it visible by laying out life, an omnipresence of all possibilities, as a series. That alone is what makes it seem transitory, and that is why we always tend to suppose that time, the one-thing-after-another, is not actual, but apparent: it is an aid to visualization . . . . (Sketch I 12)

A year later, in 1947, Frisch returns in his *Tagebuch* to the subject of time and distinguishes between measured clock time and that other omnipresence that moves us inexorably toward death. He writes:

Vielleicht müßte man unterscheiden zwischen Zeit und Vergängnis: die Zeit, was die Uhren zeigen, und Vergängnis als unser Erlebnis davon, daß unserem Dasein stets ein anderes gegenübersteht, ein Nichtsein, das wir als Tod bezeichnen. (II 499)

Perhaps one should make a distinction between time and transience; time as that which the clock shows, and transience as our experience [that our existence is confronted by] something else, . . . a nonexistence which we call death. (Sketch I 116)

Unfortunately, Frisch does not always differentiate in his novels as clearly between these two kinds of time as he does here. In *Homo faber*, for example, he uses the word "time" to mean sometimes *clock time* and sometimes *transience* or *transient time*. The concept of measured or clock time embraces the notion of repetition, the repetition of events and actions that is observable in nature: the daily rising and setting of the sun, the recurring cycle of the seasons, the continuous revolution of the earth around the sun. Mankind is part of this endless process of periodic repetition, this rhythm of nature. Any human effort to break out of this cyclical pattern only illustrates the degree to which a human being's life is out of tune with the natural order of things.

The concept of transient time is more complex, since it seems to preclude the periodic repetition germane to measured time. Because transient time is closely associated with the chronology of human life, from birth to death, any action or event, even if its nature is repetitive, is always experienced against the backdrop of the particular stage in life at which it occurs. This characteristic of transient time guarantees that every human experience or action is unique. At the same time, this transience prevents us from ever repeating exactly any experience or action, no matter how repetitive its nature, either to enjoy it again or to correct or improve it. Thus any point in life that we have passed, either ten minutes or ten years ago, is gone forever.

From the perspective of an individual's life, transient time embraces measured time. Efforts to escape the confinement of either of these two time concepts that affect life simultaneously are doomed, as Walter Faber and Anatol Ludwig Stiller illustrate vividly. Faber, who lives by measured time and dreads repetition, finally becomes attuned to transient time late in his life—although soon enough to glimpse "das wirkliche Leben" and to sense the joy of being alive. Stiller also changes his appreciation of time in the course of the novel. Earlier in life he, too, had feared repetition and ignored transient time. After his rebirth, however, he becomes aware of the role of time in life; he understands the cycles of life and the inevitability of death—at the proper time. Content to live a quiet life, he attempts to correct his past errors in his reestablished marriage with Julika and learns to live alone after her death. Stiller now wants to live within the limits of transience, of omnipresent time, at peace until "a real death" will come to him.

Felix Enderlin, in *Mein Name sei Gantenbein*, tries to ignore the passage of time altogether. In his relationships with women he wants to avoid repetition, to live without a past or a future, to focus only on the present. He fails. In contrast, Max in *Montauk* seems, at least temporarily, comfortable and at peace with transience. He seeks neither to repeat nor to forget, seeing life not only as a sum of events, but as a complex relationship with time. The inevitability of aging as a part of that process Max seems to accept as well.[2]

IN SEARCH OF "DAS WIRKLICHE LEBEN"   15

The degree to which each of the major male characters in these novels is alert to the function of time in his life affects his view of himself and his relationships to the women he loves. Just as each protagonist seeks "das wirkliche Leben," so each is challenged to come to terms with the realities of time, aging, and death. Subsequent chapters will explore this concept further.

A reader of the early *Jürg Reinhart*, or even of *Die Schwierigen*, could scarcely suspect that the young Max Frisch would develop into one of the twentieth century's most important novelists. Nevertheless, the antecedents are there: the protagonist's search for himself; his need to love and be loved by a woman; his vulnerability, naive blindness, and destructive jealousy; his sense of guilt when a relationship fails, and his progress toward a more complete life when it succeeds. How these early seeds wax and blossom in such complex environments as *Stiller, Homo faber, Mein Name sei Gantenbein, Montauk, Der Mensch erscheint im Holozän,* and *Blaubart* will be explored in the chapters that follow.

NOTES

[1] Petersen observes that Frisch here employs the city of Peking to symbolize the externalized goal of his protagonist's longing and journey in much the same way as the writers of German Romanticism 150 years earlier used "die blaue Blume" (*the blue flower*) to symbolize the internalized goal of their heroes, men like the protagonist in Novalis' *Heinrich von Ofterdingen* (Petersen 1978a 39).

[2] Frisch's nearly compulsive preoccupation with the process of dying is well known. In his second *Tagebuch*, in which the protagonist becomes one of the founders and an official of an organization called "Vereinigung Freitod" (Suicide Association), he addresses his concern about age and aging at length, both ironically and cynically (VI 90 ff.). He deals with the topic more sympathetically in his novel *Der Mensch erscheint im Holozän* (1979) (*Man in the Holocene*).

CHAPTER TWO

DIE SCHWIERIGEN: UNEASY COMPROMISES

In Max Frisch's first major novel, *Die Schwierigen*, the protagonist, Jürg Reinhart, maintains an important relationship with two women: Yvonne, the daughter of a well-to-do merchant, and Hortense, the daughter of an "Oberst" (colonel) and a member of the landed gentry. Jürg is a thirty-year-old artist, a fairly unsuccessful painter, whose relationships with these two women force him to face a serious problem: how to reconcile his life as an artist with the conventional life of a married man and, by extension, to reconcile the artist's carefree, bohemian life-style with the conventional pattern society expects of its burghers.

Unlike most of Max Frisch's later novels, which employ first-person narrators, this one is written in the more conventional third person. When it was published for the first time in 1943 its title was *J'adore ce qui me brûle oder Die Schwierigen*; it included portions of earlier Frisch works, particularly sections from the novel *Jürg Reinhart: Eine sommerliche Schicksalsfahrt* (1934), (*Jürg Reinhart: A Fateful Summer's Journey*), and *Blätter aus dem Brotsack* (1940), (*Leaves from the Haversack*). In 1957 Frisch revised the novel, deleted from it the earlier material, and republished it with the title now reversed: *Die Schwierigen oder J'adore ce qui me brûle*.

Frisch's decision to reverse the title was appropriate for two reasons. First, the earlier *Jürg Reinhart* ends on a positive note: Jürg concludes his maturing process and achieves a sense of meaning in his life. To think of the second novel as a continuation of the first would pose a contradiction, because the second Jürg is quite different from the first; he has no sense of accomplishment and eventually ends his life by suicide.

Second, none of the major characters in the second novel—Jürg, Yvonne, or Hortense—ever loves anyone or anything fervently enough to be set aflame by it, as the placement of the phrase "J'adore ce qui me brûle" in the first title suggests. Actually, the two women eventually seek, if not happiness, at least contentment in a secure, conventional marriage appropriate to their social station after they end their somewhat bohemian relationships with Jürg. As for Jürg himself, the fire that consumes him is not kindled by either of the two women or even by his commitment to art. It is his own misperception of his value to himself, to art, and to others that leads him to end his own life.[1]

Reversing the novel's title—thus switching its focus in the revised version—made good sense, therefore. The reversal places the emphasis where it ought to be, on the major characters. Jürg, Yvonne, and Hortense are "die Schwierigen" (the difficult ones) (Petersen 1978a 34-35). The revised version is the one that serves as the basis for the following discussion.

The basic plot is quickly told. Jürg Reinhart once again encounters Yvonne, years after their first casual meeting in Greece. Her father has died meanwhile, and Yvonne has moved back to Switzerland, where she lives on a small inheritance. Jürg and Yvonne eventually fall in love. Months later, during an extended vacation in the Tessin, Yvonne decides to leave Jürg and marry her former boss, Hauswirt, a businessman, although she still loves Jürg and is pregnant with his child. Jürg, who does not know about the child, is desolate. Eventually he consoles himself with his only student, Hortense, whose father, the colonel, is a pillar of society who "values the secure, the sound, and the unequivocal" (I 481). He regards honor as an absolute, especially as it concerns his own social class and family. He tells Jürg who his real parents are—something Jürg has not known—and persuades him and his daughter that a marriage between them would be inappropriate, since they come from two completely different social backgrounds and genetic stocks.

Years later, Jürg and Hortense meet again. She is now married to an architect, has two children, and comes with them to spend part of the summer on a friend's estate. Jürg, who is no longer painting and has assumed a different name, now works as a gardener on the estate (I 560 ff). During a long conversation (I 585-92), Jürg tries to convince Hortense, who recognizes him at once, that his life is useless, and he implies that he ought to end it. A few years later he does. Alone, isolated from society, he dies in his room while, ironically, outside his open window, the people celebrate the harvest with food, drink, music, and dance.

All major characters in this novel are "Schwierige," difficult people. The work's subtitle, *J'adore ce qui me brûle*,[2] applies most specifically to Jürg, the protagonist, because his tragic misperception of his social and genetic value leads him to eventual self-destruction. The subtitle may also be applied to Yvonne, who is attracted to and in love with Jürg but finds her dreams of a happy life with him impossible to fulfill, and to Hortense, though only superficially, during the early part of her affair with Jürg.

All of Jürg's relationships are difficult. Yvonne, the first woman he loves, eventually rejects him as a suitable husband and as father of the child she is carrying because he does not meet her preconceived notion of what a husband and father should be. She believes Jürg to be an irresponsible artist, incapable of providing for her and the child. Hortense rejects him as a suitable husband because, once she learns the truth about his origin, she realizes that, according to her family's and society's standards, he is an unacceptable mate. Since this second rejection throws Jürg into a socially inferior role, he begins to think of himself as an outcast, a homeless and rootless man.

Die Schwierigen has four other male characters: Hinkelmann, an archeologist and Yvonne's first husband; Hauswirt, the businessman she later marries; Ammann, a soldier and later an architect whom Hortense marries; and Jürg's biological father, a butcher. As a character, Jürg's father is relatively unimportant, although his role in the plot is essential. He is not an admirable person; he impregnates Jürg's mother, then refuses to marry her or share responsibility for the child; and when he marries a servant girl later and fathers two more children, he turns out to be a cowardly, irresponsible, narrow-minded, and sometimes domineering father.

The other three men are important to the story because they love and marry the two women, but none is developed fully. Hinkelmann, an immature young German scientist, kills himself early in the novel, soon after Yvonne leaves him. Frisch leaves no doubt that Hinkelmann is too immature to be a real partner in a creative, meaningful marriage. Hauswirt, in contrast, is a practical, no-nonsense businessman, "a man who knows what he wants—and how he wants it" (I 429); he is a good provider and generous father, even when he learns that the child Yvonne has borne is not his own. Ammann, a dashing Swiss officer from an upper-middle-class family, is a stereotypically insecure, spoiled rich boy who, surprisingly, becomes a capable architect and an adequate, though not enriching, husband for Hortense.

Although Yvonne and Hortense are very different, both fascinate Jürg Reinhart equally. Hortense is physically attractive; Yvonne is not. Both are intelligent and capable. Although they are not economically independent in the same sense as are the women in Frisch's subsequent novels, women like Sibylle or Julika in *Stiller*, Hanna in *Homo faber*, Lila in *Mein Name sei Gantenbein*, or Lynn, Marianne, Ingeborg, or Constanze in *Montauk*, they share essential characteristics with these later women, such as a strong will and a fierce sense of independence. Both Yvonne and Hortense appear to have been educated to the extent then fashionable for young ladies of the middle class, but only Hortense has received formal schooling, not necessarily because her parents believe it to be in her best interest but because they hope to end her relationship with Jürg, her bohemian art teacher, by sending her to Paris to attend the Sorbonne.

Neither woman is particularly interested in financial independence. Yvonne supplements her small inheritance for a while by giving violin lessons and later by working as a secretary, typing letters in English (I 427-30). But when her employer becomes interested in more than her typing and linguistic skills and proposes marriage, her moral principles force her to choose between accepting his proposal or quitting her job. She chooses to quit. Hortense seems never to have held a job, even though her knowledge of languages and her painting skills might have allowed her to earn a small income.

This chapter examines in detail the relationships between Jürg and Yvonne and Jürg and Hortense. One might wonder, for example, why Jürg falls in love with either of these so very different women, or why either is attracted to him, comes to love him, yet leaves him finally to marry a completely different kind of man. One might also ask what Jürg hopes to accomplish by taking his own life, believing that with his death nothing of him remains in the world. Finally, one might ask what picture of the *man* Jürg Reinhart emerges—this early in Frisch's career—from his relationships with these two women.

Considered as an independent work, *Die Schwierigen* is probably less interesting today than any of Frisch's later novels. The characters lack the depth and subtle motivation for their often dramatic actions that one finds in Frisch's more mature works. The philosophy they expound is facile. The novel's style is highly derivative and contains strong echoes of Thomas Mann in its depiction of Jürg as an artist with a bad conscience vis-à-vis society and "normal" people; of Gottfried Keller in the self-doubting, skeptical stance of the protagonist toward the artist's existence; and of Albin Zollinger in its long lyrical passages and its expansive evocations of landscapes and moods (Petersen 1978a 34-38). Nevertheless, *Die Schwierigen* is important to this study because, through Jürg Reinhart and his relationships with the women he loves, it explores for the first time many of the concepts that recur in Frisch's later novels: his ideas about the source of strain in the relationships of men and women; the protagonist's search for identity; the man's need to be loved by a woman; his vulnerability in love; and the problems of marriage, blindness, and jealousy.

JÜRG-YVONNE: A ROAD NOT TAKEN

When Jürg accidentally encounters Yvonne on a street of the small Swiss city in which they both now live, years after their first meeting in Athens, he has no idea that his acceptance of her invitation to a cup of tea at her apartment will be the start of a complex, intimate relationship whose sudden end will cause him immeasurable pain.

When they first met Jürg was not yet a painter, although at that time Yvonne introduced him to her other guests all evening long as a painter and a fellow countryman just passing through (I 393). A fellow countryman he is, a young Swiss traveling through southern Europe without any specific goal except to see the world. He is a self-assured young man of about twenty at this time, not at all troubled by being the only guest at the party not formally attired in a tuxedo: he feels comfortable in his white linen slacks. In this role of the untroubled, carefree, and alert young man, Jürg is vividly reminiscent not only of his not-accidental namesake in the earlier *Jürg Reinhart: Eine sommerliche Schicksalsfahrt*, but also of the young Max Frisch who, in 1933 when in his early twenties, roamed the Balkans for several months as an independent journalist (II 586-87). Jürg's lyrical perception of nature, as well as some of his experiences, have been identified by several critics as autobiographical (Jurgensen 1976 47).

Yvonne is immediately attracted to this young man by his unconventional behavior and his dream-like attitude toward reality as well as by the strange mixture of romantic melancholy and vigorous optimism he presents—qualities that will compel her, ten years later when they meet again, to commit herself to an emotional-sexual relationship with Jürg, only to end it abruptly after nine months for reasons involving essentially the same qualities that attracted her.

When Jürg first meets Yvonne she is twenty-five years old and the wife of Dr. Hinkelmann, a successful German archeologist nine years her senior. She had been an only and unwanted child, ugly and very thin, defects for which her parents never forgave her. Her mother, who was beautiful, told her from early childhood how ugly she was. Her father, during her teenage years, was insensitive enough to point out frequently that she looked like an ironing board or a fence post; he never seemed to tire of comparing her with other, pretty, girls her age. Yvonne's most unattractive feature was her high forehead, which her mother tried to hide by combing her hair in an ingenious style.

Unloved by her parents, Yvonne grew up with a profound craving to be accepted and loved; she had an existential fear of living and an even greater fear that some day she, too, would be a mother. At age twenty-one, when she first met Dr. Hinkelmann,[3] she had a terrible view of her life and herself:

> ein nichtsnutziges Dasein, ein Mißgeschick von Tochter, überflüssig von Geburt an, eine rettungslose Gans. (I 405)

a good-for-nothing existence, a misfortune of a daughter, superfluous from the moment of birth, an irrevocably silly goose.

This low self-concept, combined with her craving to be loved, make Yvonne enter an unsatisfactory, unfulfilling marriage, hoping that, as a woman and a human being, she can be of use to someone.

Jürg sees Yvonne differently. He thinks she may be a painter, a physician, or perhaps a sculptress (I 392). He is intrigued by this woman who seems simultaneously fragile and strong, casual and direct, relaxed and intense. Slightly exasperated after trying unsuccessfully to guess her profession, he asks her: "My God, what are you then?" to which, surprised, she replies simply: "I'm twenty-five . . . married . . . ." (I 392).

This is the first time any man has asked Yvonne directly about herself and has, without hesitating, accepted her simple answer. Most men, Yvonne tells Jürg during this first conversation, are vain and cannot bear entertaining the thought that the person they believe understands them is really very simple and direct. Men feel hurt if a woman tells them that, Yvonne comments, and then adds:

Alle sagen, man sei klug, man sei begabt—nur weil man ihnen überlegen ist, und im Grunde will man es nicht einmal, glauben Sie. Immer so lächerlich, wenn die Frau überlegen ist, so aufreibend auch, wissen Sie. Was kommt dabei heraus? Und dann, mein Gott, immer das gleiche Lied, man sei keine Frau—weil sie nicht aufkommen, weil es einfach keine Männer mehr gibt . . . . (I 393)

They all say one is intelligent, one is talented, only because one is superior to them, and strictly speaking one doesn't even want to be, believe me. It is always so ridiculous when the woman is superior, also so exhausting, you know. What comes of it? And then, my God, always the same song: one is not a real woman—because they can't cope [with it], because there simply are no more real men. . . .

In these few lines, Yvonne expresses her awareness not only of the conventionality of her life but also of its contradiction:

while she thinks of herself as an uncomplicated, direct, and simple woman, a "silly goose," to use her favorite phrase, the people around her, especially men, think of her as someone highly intelligent and clever. They treat her benevolently as someone peculiar but, simultaneously, as less of a woman. Men, according to Yvonne, are unable to accept and cope with a woman who is intellectually superior to them, because "real men" no longer exist. The question is, what does Yvonne mean by "real men"? Do she and Jürg agree that modern men are ill equipped to satisfy the needs of a woman, that they must once again "become men," as he tells Ammann at the conclusion of the Nietzschean version of the story of Turandot with which he tries to console them both after they are abandoned by the women they profess to love (I 478-80)?

Indeed, this phrase of Yvonne's, "real men," is problematic. What does she mean? Certainly men who live their own lives, not bound by the social restrictions that bind *her*; men who, unencumbered by convention, search for a meaningful life. Men like the young, carefree, self-assured Jürg Reinhart, for example, whose optimism and enthusiasm are infectious and whose romantic melancholy, which, in Jürg, she identifies at once as that of a painter, makes them especially attractive to her. Meeting Jürg at that party in her parents' house in Athens makes Yvonne realize all the more clearly the lie she is living, a lie fabricated of other people's perceptions and expectations of her, unrelated to what she really feels and thinks, what she really wants from life, how she yearns to find love and acceptance. Intuitively she seems to know that Jürg and the life he lives are much more real, much more vibrant than her own.

Yvonne never really loves Hinkelmann, her first husband. When they meet she is drawn to him by compassion and by the belief that, as a scholar, he surely is more intelligent than she. During his first visit to her parents' house he clumsily drops an expensive teacup to the floor, pouring tea all over his new slacks, while he describes what the ancient Asians thought about death. Feeling compassion for this somewhat awkward man, the ugly and unloved Yvonne, who bears a striking resemblance to Adalbert Stifter's Brigitta, as Merrifield points out (Merrifield 41), visits his room that same night and allows him to make love to her, justifying her action by thinking: "If it really makes him happy!" (I 405). Her comment suggests, and she later confirms (I 467), that she herself received no pleasure in their sexual union.

A year later she agrees to marry Hinkelmann, believing that she can respect and perhaps come to love him for what she perceives to be his greater intellect. Yvonne, the ugly duckling, only smiles when her fiancé suggests that his parents accompany them on their honeymoon. She "left it completely up to him to decide, for he, after all, was the man" (I 401), although the narrator makes clear that Hinkelmann would have welcomed her enthusiastic approval. And when his parents leave for home, Yvonne quietly assumes the role of the departing mother, accommodating herself and her needs to the requirements of her husband's career, caring for him as if she were, indeed, his mother.

Disillusion sets in gradually. Once, listening to Hinkelmann talk about his archeological work, she is reminded of "a landscape as on the moon, so without air, without fish and bird, without a shepherd, without a single living goat" (I 395). She realizes that Hinkelmann never talks about living things, never about people, neither his colleagues nor the people with whom he comes in contact during his work on the Greek islands. Indirectly, cleverly, he talks only about himself, his importance.

Yet she continues to care for him, until she learns she is pregnant. When she shares this happy news with Hinkelmann she is startled by his frightened reaction. Repeatedly he asks, "What will we do now?" (I 404). Yvonne responds decisively. She abandons her submissive role and takes charge of her life and that of the unborn child. Without asking her husband's advice she decides to leave a marriage based on pity, not love, and to abort the child whose father is spineless and egocentric. Hinkelmann's helpless reaction to her dual resolve only reinforces her determination, for, as she twice explains to him: "Man bekommt kein Kind von seinem Sohn" (I 402,405), *"One doesn't have a child with one's son."* Hinkelmann, devastated by the failure of his marriage and unable to cope with the loss of Yvonne, eventually kills himself.

Courageously, Yvonne has escaped from a life that, because of its artificiality, its conventionality, has threatened to suffocate her. In an effort to find real meaning in her life she resolutely turns her back on past failures, determined to make a new start.

However, when she accidentally meets Jürg again in the street, years later, and invites him to a cup of tea, her new life, in substance, has grown to be much like her old one: marked by the same duality, that same tension between "Schein und Sein" (seeming and being). Her few friends see her as self-sufficient and independent. Selfishly, they look on her as their pillar of support and assurance, "a secure axis in the whole confusion" of life (I 427), without noticing that she, too, is lost and bewildered (Butler 31), still yearning to be accepted and loved.

The men in her life include a young physician and a lawyer, but her relationships with them are intellectual and platonic because Yvonne ends a relationship the moment a man becomes interested in her as a woman. Her close friendship with Merline, a young violin student, although it has strong sexual overtones, satisfies some of Yvonne's maternal needs. She serves as a substitute and loving mother to the young woman whose own mother neither listens to nor cares about her daughter's feelings and thoughts. From her own youth Yvonne is well acquainted with this tragic situation.

Knowing, however, that her new life has become as artificial and empty of meaning as her previous one, Yvonne realizes that the essential ingredient lacking is a total commitment to a relationship with a man. By her unwillingness to make such a commitment, Yvonne has shut herself off from the meaningful life experiences she seeks. Thus her accidentally meeting Jürg once more seems almost fateful. She sees it as her last chance to find meaning in life outside herself, provided she can make the necessary emotional commitment to Jürg. She does, for a time.

Jürg is essentially the same man Yvonne met ten years earlier: with a dreamlike attitude toward reality, carefree and happy in his bohemian existence, an artist not subject to society's conventions. Unlike Yvonne, he welcomes uncertainty as an essential part of life. As a painter, accustomed to looking beyond appearances and beneath surfaces, Jürg knows that there is no social or religious structure onto which a man can hang his life. Only the structure one creates for oneself, based on one's own perceptions and insights, has any validity. "All existence," Jürg tells Yvonne during their first long walk through the countryside, "flows into infinity" (I 435). Man's task, especially if he is a painter, Jürg explains, is to show the limitless reality of the human soul. Jürg sees his life as a painter suspended between two poles, work and atonement. Work is the joy, the excitement that does not let one sleep, a rejoicing for hours and days. It results in a state of happiness that wins people over without wanting to. His work teaches Jürg to be happy in solitude; it grants him the freedom of spirit to escape the routine conventionality of ordinary human patterns. Atonement, the other pole that supports Jürg's life, is the inevitable result of the sudden, repeated attacks of melancholy that plague him, brought on by living too intensely, by straining too hard to experience the beauty of life, and, ironically, by making too great an effort to forge relationships that might restrict freedom and individuality (Butler 33).

Yvonne listens, fascinated, and surrenders willingly to Jürg's enthusiasm. She begins to share his penchant for an uncertainty of living that one must accept, Jürg tells her. He is certain that one must embrace "das Ewig-Unsichere, das unser Leben in der Schwebe hält wie eine glühende Kugel" (I 435), *"the eternal uncertainty that holds our life suspended like a glowing sphere,"* in order to experience "das wirkliche Leben." Life then, according to Jürg, is a continuous encounter with the present. Transient time, which governs all life and accompanies it from beginning to end, is of no importance to him, as he views the uniqueness of existence taking place only in the present.

During this first walk in the country and their first long talk about life and living—actually a monologue delivered by Jürg—Yvonne experiences feelings she thought long dead. Considerate of her comfort and wise about the conditions of the meadows in early spring, Jürg had advised Yvonne to put on "good shoes and proper stockings" (I 432). This kindness had moved her "with the secret shudder of a hope that Yvonne actually believed buried a long time ago" (I 432), the hope of being accepted, of being loved for herself.

A few weeks after this first outing, during which they visit each other several times, Jürg and Yvonne enter into what, for all practical purposes, is a marriage. Twice, the narrator refers to their relationship as such (I 460,476). The union ends abruptly when Yvonne realizes two things simultaneously: that she is pregnant with Jürg's child and that Jürg is unsuited to be her husband and a father to the child, for he is incapable of providing for them. Decisively, as she acted once before in her marriage to Hinkelmann, Yvonne takes control of her life and changes its direction.

The happiness Jürg and Yvonne enjoy for only nine months is a fictitious one right from the start. Yvonne hopes to find love in a relationship to which she is totally committed. But she is deaf to what Jürg reveals about himself in that long monologue during their first walk in the country—that for him, Jürg Reinhart the painter, his work and his independence will always come before any relationship.

In part it is economic necessity that forces Jürg and Yvonne to share their limited resources. Yvonne's small inheritance is nearly gone, and she is without a job because she left hers when Hauswirt proposed marriage to her. Jürg can no longer rely on his mother as he used to; he has recently moved from her home and now lives in his studio. Income from the sale of his paintings is sporadic and too small to support even one person adequately. Jürg seems unconcerned, but Yvonne waits patiently for something to happen, hiding behind a calmness that belies her anxiety. Fatalistically she tells herself, "Something . . . always happens" (I 460).

In an art supply store, "smiling like a mother at her son" (I 446), Yvonne indulgently watches Jürg choose from the wide selection of paints on display the few tubes he can afford; occasionally she buys him a tube. In that same store one day, Yvonne witnesses from a distance how, in a grand manner, Jürg solicits his first and only drawing student, Hortense, who came in to ask the salesclerk to recommend a teacher. Jürg's sales pitch succeeds, and since he has also just been commissioned to paint the portrait of a young army officer, Ammann, happier times seem to await the lovers. Through a number of symbolic images, however, the narrator indicates that Jürg and Yvonne's happiness is false. The end is inevitable, as indicated by the image of an advancing scythe that is heard but not seen by the lovers as they sit behind a green wall of grass in a meadow (I 445).

When Yvonne finally musters enough courage to tell Jürg about her past life, especially the abortion of her child, the occasion provides the first sign of their inability to communicate effectively about important matters. Yvonne is still deeply disturbed about the abortion, which causes her profound pangs of guilt, for, as she explains, "unborn, it [the child] is more real, more present than everything born" (I 430). Unexplainably, Jürg is incapable of responding to the confession of this deeply troubled woman, his lover. Her plea for sympathy and understanding meets with silence; he asks no questions, nor does he ask for details. She has risked everything by confessing, and he acts as if her confession bears no relationship to him. A gulf of silence and physical distance separates the lovers: the narrator observes, "Reinhart sat on the window sill" (I 457).

Why does he not comfort her? He, the painter, who experiences the world, life, reality through his eyes, is blind to the anxiety mirrored in her face and deaf to the fear echoed in her voice. Jürg does not understand that Yvonne is looking up at him like a condemned woman, drowning in her feelings of remorse, guilt, and shame, waiting for the moment of grace that will save her when Jürg, through a compassionate word or gesture, will show that he understands her feelings, loves her, and therefore accepts her actions.

Jürg never offers that compassionate understanding. At this time in his life he has no relationship to anyone's past, including his own. He believes only in the present. Jürg is able to accept the uncertainty of a future, but with the burden of a past he can do nothing; he faces it uncomprehending and without interest. That attitude will change dramatically in less than a year, but too late to help Yvonne.

Signs of trouble in their relationship increase during their prolonged vacation in the Tessin. There is, for example, the incident of the cart. On their way to town one day to pick up a suitcase, Jürg—carefree and in high spirits, like a child on vacation—jumps onto their little wagon as soon as the road slopes enough, steering it presumably with his feet, as children are wont to do. To keep pace with the accelerating cart, Yvonne has to jump onto it too. When the wagon turns over accidentally, the two of them land on their backs in the town square, neither seriously hurt. Jürg laughs, but Yvonne is indignant; she feels publicly humiliated by Jürg's childish behavior. The very first day Yvonne and Jürg arrived in the Tessin, she knew that she ought to leave, that "it didn't work; not with Reinhart, either" (I 461). But she stays.

Another problem concerns 300 Swiss francs, which Hauswirt, Yvonne's former boss and still her suitor, has offered Yvonne to help finance her vacation. Not an altruist, Hauswirt made this gesture in an attempt to buy Yvonne's affection. Knowing this, Yvonne cannot understand why it does not bother Jürg, who sees no problem in accepting the money from "a man with 800 employees and a blue car" (I 462). He wants her to accept so they can stay longer in the Tessin.

For Yvonne, however, the matter is so serious that it threatens her relationship with Jürg very fundamentally. If Jürg really wants her to accept Hauswirt's offer, she is sure he can not really love her, does not intend to assume economic responsibility for their relationship, and is a social parasite who will sell even her, the woman he claims to love, for a miserly 300 Swiss francs to a businessman who believes in supply and demand, even in matters of human relations, and who is willing to pay the price for what he wants.

Jürg fails to understand Yvonne's aversion to accepting Hauswirt's offer; her attitude seems to him like an obsession with middle-class conventions. He sees himself as far above such petty notions.

This issue and the cart episode deepen Yvonne's doubts about the possibility of a permanent relationship with Jürg. She tells herself that Jürg's conduct and attitudes are unmanly, no matter how happy he seems to be with her and she, at times, with him. She believes that "nowhere did one have to be more honest than where one loved" (I 461).

The final issue is that of the child. Having a child with Jürg has become an irresistible longing, an obsession. It is also, as Yvonne admits to herself while posing in the nude for Jürg, her only motivation for staying on with him in the Tessin. Aware of her advancing age, she fears "that she would miss what all the others had, what all other [women] described as life's highest possession" (I 467). As her relationship with Jürg grows more and more troubled, and as he begins to experience increasing doubts about his artistic ability, her longing for Jürg's child grows stronger. "A child with him she could have loved, probably more than she loved him" (I 467), she thinks as she sits for him.

The problem is that Yvonne cannot see Jürg supporting her and the child. To expect that of him, as he has already shown her, is as useless as to expect him to protect them; the careless cart accident demonstrated this vividly. No, the very child she wants with Jürg prohibits her from sharing her life with him.

Jürg does not know that Yvonne is already pregnant when she tests his love by writing Hauswirt, accepting his offer of 300 francs. She wants to give Jürg one last chance, hoping he will decide not to mail the letter. He fails. After reading it over casually and commenting that she has expressed herself well, without really understanding what she means by the words she has written, he pockets the letter to mail it in town on his way to another day in the country, loaded like a donkey with painting paraphernalia (I 470). When he returns in the evening, Yvonne is gone. He searches for her through the Tessin for two days, haunted by the fear that something terrible has happened to her, that she has fallen off a cliff in the dark. Unable to find any trace of her, he returns home and is surprised to find Yvonne in her apartment, "upright and neatly combed, without a wrinkle in her face, her lips lightly touched up, Yvonne, the lady, granting a short interview" (I 471). She counters Jürg's request to talk about her sudden departure and their current situation with the phrase she used years earlier in response to Hinkelmann's pleas for them to talk: "Explanations don't change anything" (I 402,471).

The realization that Jürg is unsuitable as a husband and father has shocked Yvonne. By implication, she is guilty of what Frisch believes to be *the* cardinal sin in human relationships: she has formed "a graven image" of her lover. She decided in advance how he ought to behave as a man, as a lover, and as a potential husband and father. She has formed an image of Jürg and frozen him in it. Then, without giving Jürg a chance to prove her wrong and without being willing to help him change, grow, and develop his innate abilities, she decides that he is inadequate and walks out of his life.

The concept of forming "a graven image" of one's partner will be explored in detail in Chapters Three and Five, as Frisch makes more direct use of it in subsequent novels. The significant fact here is that this concept is already in evidence, though indirectly stated, in this early novel.

Yvonne comes to a second, equally important realization before she leaves Jürg. Both as a man and an artist, she realizes, he merely professes theoretical principles about life but does not live by them, nor does he recognize or accept their practical consequences. Pregnant, and disappointed in her final attempt to find meaning in life outside herself, Yvonne retreats to the conventional world she has known all her life, as her decision to marry Hauswirt makes clear.

As Yvonne refuses in stony silence to explain her behavior, Jürg realizes that their relationship is over. In his confusion and sense of loss, however, he is plagued by fierce jealousy. He lies in wait for Hauswirt, not knowing whether he wants to congratulate him on his new happiness or to shoot him; he spends hours in the courtyard of Yvonne's apartment building, in the chilly dampness of early winter, watching through curtained windows as the shadows of Yvonne and Hauswirt move to and fro. One night he receives a crushing blow: Hauswirt does not go home. Way past midnight he sees them turn off the lights in the apartment. Jürg is now convinced that he has lost Yvonne to the rival who will give her economic security. Too late, he recognizes that a personal relationship can become a central, integrating force in the lives of two people only in proportion to each partner's commitment to the other and to the partnership.

Yvonne, for her part, finds she can enjoy the economic security she craves—and for which she envied Merline, her young friend—only if she is willing to relinquish her yearning for a better-than-conventional life, for "das wirkliche Leben." Although that real life may exist, if she can believe Jürg, her attempts to find it have failed. Thus she returns to the values of her childhood and youth, settling into marriage with Hauswirt and choosing for herself and Jürg's child the safe life defined entirely by bourgeois values of money and property. By choosing to marry Hauswirt for the sake of stability and security, Yvonne makes the same decision her mother once made, a decision for which Yvonne has never forgiven her.

Yvonne's marriage to Hauswirt succeeds mainly because she is able to substitute "respect" for "love," something she tried unsuccessfully to do in her earlier marriage to Hinkelmann. Frisch portrays Hauswirt as a stereotype and somewhat of a caricature of the hard-headed, money-conscious businessman who is made, unwittingly, to accept the child of a penniless painter as his own, only to discover years later that he is biologically unable to father a child.[4]

Ironically, though, Yvonne's marriage to Hauswirt reduces the closest relationship of a man and a woman to a mechanistic life process based on the partners' economic and biological, not spiritual and psychological, needs. Theirs is a relationship in which they do not advance each other's growth or help each other to achieve "das wirkliche Leben." Yvonne settles for far less than she had once hoped for—but far less by whose standards? Jürg's? Her own? Max Frisch's? Her choice is, after all, not merely acceptable to her, but also seemingly appropriate. This the narrator subtly suggests by describing a scene in which Yvonne, in the dim light of her apartment, approvingly compares the features of the man before her, Hauswirt, with those of the man she once dreamed about; both bear a resemblance to her deceased father (I 472).

Yvonne has made a compromise, but she has not deceived herself. She is aware of a lack of integration with her environment; she knows "she does not belong in this place" (I 550), "an apartment with elevator, garden, refrigerator, terrace, nanny, and a view to the lake" (I 537). Although these symbolize an outwardly stable, secure life and marriage, Yvonne finds herself dreadfully bored. This the narrator, with a touch of irony, indicates in describing how Yvonne and Hauswirt spend their evenings together:

Er [Hauswirt] saß und las, er trank sein Glas voll Wein, und Yvonne rauchte, manchmal legte sie eine Patience— wie am Abend, als sie von Reinhart erfuhr, von seinem Tode—ihre Ehe war durch nichts mehr zu erschüttern. (I 597)

He sat and read, he drank his glass of wine, and Yvonne smoked; sometimes she played Patience—as she did the evening she heard about Reinhart, about his death—her marriage could no longer be affected by anything.

The last conversation Jürg has with Yvonne before her marriage takes place during the winter on the street, where Jürg has waited for Yvonne to come out of a store. Looking unkempt and pale, he blocks her path, scolds her for hanging up on him when he telephones, then, recognizing her impatience and anger, he forgets what he wants to tell her, says "goodbye," and leaves her at a street corner.

By the act of turning her affection to another man, Yvonne seems to have cast a spell over Jürg, a spell that in his perception of reality ties his existence far more closely to hers than when they were united in love. If once she was an object of admiration and wonder to him, during the weeks their relationship disintegrates she gradually becomes an obsession. With astute insight, Frisch not only portrays here a rejected lover, but also illustrates a basic truth in human relationships: that we never cherish anything more deeply, are never hurt more painfully, than when the object of our love has moved beyond our reach, either of his or her own volition or through death. Max in *Montauk*, in his relationship with Ingeborg; Anatol Ludwig Stiller and Rolf in *Stiller*, in their relationship with Sibylle; and Walter Faber in *Homo faber*, in his relationship with Sabeth, share Jürg's misery in their own ways.

After Yvonne has been married for some time, Jürg's painful memories force him to confront her once more. In a scene that clearly depicts an emotionally disturbed man, he forcibly enters Yvonne's apartment and nearly attacks her physically to relieve his anguish. When he tries to make her look at him just once more, Yvonne closes her eyes. "He held her like a defenseless bundle, like a corpse," while she pleaded: "'Reinhart, . . . I am alone at home—I can't defend myself. . .'" (I 552). Jürg slowly releases her, turns and leaves, furious. He never sees his son, who is already in bed.

Jürg does not arrive at any useful conclusions as a result of his relationship with Yvonne or its traumatic ending except that he decides not to kill himself but to retreat into his world of imagination. Once again he feels free to enjoy unrestrictedly, self-indulgently, his bohemian existence on the fringe of society, without obligation. Once more he escapes the world of reality into which his relationship with Yvonne had almost forced him.

Yvonne, die Wirkliche, die Leibhaftige. . . was geht sie ihn an? . . . Wie eine Wolke umfängt ihn der Wahn. . . es könne ihm nichts mehr geschehen von dieser Gestalt, nichts mehr. (I 477)

Yvonne, the real one, the living one . . . what does she matter to him? . . . Like a cloud the illusion envelops him . . . [that] nothing could ever again happen to him from this person, nothing.

Nevertheless, the irrevocable loss of Yvonne to Hauswirt eventually drives Jürg to look at his carefree, artistic existence more carefully. For a while he makes a deliberate effort to reject his near-parasitic life and to become a more participatory member of society, someone willing to share in the daily routine of the majority. Economic stability becomes his primary goal, at least temporarily, in the aftermath of his loss. He even seems to look at personal relationships from a new perspective, one in which total commitment to a partner and the relationship is a primary and integrating force. These lessons, at least temporarily learned from his failed relationship with Yvonne, will be subjected to a vigorous test in Jürg's next relationship with a woman, Hortense.

JÜRG-HORTENSE: TWO WORLDS CONFRONT EACH OTHER

Hortense is the young woman Jürg recruited in the art supply store as his first and only student. Their relationship has two phases. The first, marked by a certain casualness of attitude and tone, lasts almost two months. It is primarily a student-teacher relationship, and it fascinates both parties—but Hortense more than Jürg, because at the time he is still in love with Yvonne. The second phase is separated from the first by more than six months, during which Jürg and Yvonne vacation in the Tessin and finally separate. In the meantime, to Hortense's great surprise, Jürg has made a conscious but ultimately futile attempt to become a fully accepted, conventional member of society. Although Jürg and Hortense grow much closer during the second phase, the relationship proves even less enduring and less satisfactory than that of Jürg and Yvonne.

To understand the full extent of the difficulties Jürg and Hortense encounter during the second phase of their relationship, one must look first at some key elements of the first. Hortense was born into an old, socially established family, one somewhat more affluent than Yvonne's. She is about ten years younger than Jürg, about fifteen years younger than Yvonne; she is also prettier than Yvonne and, Jürg thinks at the time, more like a child—which attracts and delights him. Jürg does not really examine his feelings for her, intrigued as he is by her comparative inexperience and naiveté, by her exuberance. Perhaps feeling a bit reckless on an outing, he kisses her spontaneously. He also goes sailing with her one summer afternoon, pretending to know more about the sport than he does, only to discover that Hortense is an excellent sailor. Jürg tries to intrigue Hortense with his knowledge of the world, and he chastizes her for her childish ideas.

In the relationship's early phase, Jürg's part is mostly play; he is far too occupied with Yvonne to take serious notice of Hortense. "She was his student, a minute source of income" (I 488), the narrator observes laconically.

Hortense looks at the situation quite differently. She sees in Jürg's world the possibility of escaping the restrictions of her family and social class, represented most graphically by the formidable figure of the colonel, her father. Hortense yearns to establish her own identity, free from the conventions of her class; she wants to discover a life of her own—"das wirkliche Leben"—richer and more exciting than the life she sees around her. Amidst the smell of paint and the half-finished paintings at Jürg's studio, Hortense breathes the fresh air of personal freedom. When her father learns of her liaison with Jürg—a liaison that, at the time, exists only in her head—he forbids her to see Jürg again. Hortense, predictably, continues to visit Jürg's studio in secret. Discovered, she defies her parents, insisting she will do as she pleases, which is to see the painter, her teacher, whenever she chooses.

Inexperienced in her feelings for a man, Hortense is far less sure of herself and the freedom Jürg's carefree life promises than she appears to be. After Jürg's first exuberant kiss, which she receives with tightly closed lips, she is plagued by the fear that she may never see him again. She is afraid of losing him and, alternately, wants to escape him. "J'adore ce qui me brûle,"— that phrase embossed on a coin in her father's collection seems to apply to Hortense at this stage. Jürg, however, takes little notice. "He did not even know her jealousy," the narrator observes (I 490).

In Jürg's world, as Hortense imagines it, all things are possible, even those one can barely imagine or is not allowed to do. Hortense believes that whatever Jürg does is right—unorthodox perhaps, but right. Yet her natural instincts are to be careful and not to follow any suggestion of his too quickly. One night, as she returns from a concert, they meet accidentally on the street. She has forgotten her house key, and he casually suggests they wander through the moonlit night into the new day. As Hortense hesitates a little too long, Jürg observes: "There are things one does easily and at once . . . or not at all" (I 490).

Hortense's hesitation, the narrator comments, was caused by a single thought: "Oh . . . if he were to force me!" (I 490). Force her to do what? Walk with him? Love him? Sleep with him? Whatever she wants him to force her to do, the opportunity has passed. Jürg suggests she spend the night at a hotel and walks away.

Before the first phase of their relationship ends abruptly, as Jürg leaves for the Tessin with Yvonne, an important scene takes place in Jürg's studio. When Hortense comes for her lesson Jürg mentions casually that he accidentally almost burned down his studio the previous day. Hortense dares him to do just that: to burn all his paintings and start anew. She recalls having read that Heinrich von Kleist did that, burned all his writings and started fresh.

Hortense's challenge is clear: if Jürg is secure in his artistic calling, confident in his talent, he will accept her dare and, like Kleist, burn all his creative work. Jürg falls silent, and Hortense asks: "What would be lost?" (I 491). This time he responds, vehemently: "You know . . . you are a little devil, Hortense.

Devil with a family brooch on the collar" (I 491). He accuses her of demanding a lot, nearly everything, from a person—and then he suddenly breaks off. This is the first suggestion that Jürg is not sure of himself as an artist. His doubts, once tentatively mentioned in conversation with Yvonne (I 451), will become more evident during his stay in the Tessin (I 464,466).

Jürg quickly recovers from being forced to face his doubts. He asks Hortense what she would do if someone were to accept her dares, then finishes scornfully: "I see you standing there, Miss Hortense—frightened out of your wits!" (I 491).

When Hortense and Jürg meet again half a year later, Jürg has done exactly what Hortense challenged him to do: he burned all his paintings—the canvasses, that is; he sold the frames.[5] He gave up his studio and has taken his first regular job, as a draftsman in an architect's office. Hortense cannot decide whether he is joking or has lost his mind.

But Jürg is serious; the changes are the result of his loss of Yvonne and his new focus on economic security. Amazed, Hortense hears him admit that never before has he grasped the reality of life: "I have never yet really worked in my life," he tells her; "I've always done only what I liked, what enticed me. . . . I have enjoyed my life, but I haven't lived" (I 497). As Hortense remains silent, Jürg asks rhetorically:

> Was bin ich denn? Ein Mann von dreißig Jahren, der just sein eigenes Brot verdient. Hälfte des Lebens, Menschenskind, Hälfte des Lebens! . . . Wann kommt die Reife, die man als Jüngling in jedem Erwachsenen neidvoll vermutete? Wann fängt es denn an, das wirkliche, das sinnvolle, wesentliche Leben? (I 497)

> *What am I? A man of thirty who barely earns his living. Half of my life is gone, for heaven's sake, half of my life! . . . When does that maturity come which, as a youth, one enviously thought every adult had? When does it begin—the real, the meaningful, the essential life?*

Hortense is stunned to learn that Jürg has turned his back on nine years of artistic existence. She cannot believe that he has abandoned the life that, only a few months ago, was for her the "quintessence of distant blue skies and freedom" (I 500). Jürg's world had awakened in her

> eine Ahnung . . . , die nicht mehr wegzudenken war, Ahnung eines täglichen Lebens, das habloser und härter, aber freier, rücksichtsloser und großzügiger ausfallen könnte, leichter, unheimlicher auch, voll Bekenntnis zum Ewig-Unsicheren, das unser Leben in der Schwebe hält wie eine glühende Kugel. (I 500)

a presentiment she could not forget, the presentiment of a daily life that could turn out to be less material and harder but freer, more reckless and more generous, easier, also more eerie, filled with a commitment to the eternal uncertainty that holds our life suspended like a glowing sphere.

Clearly, Jürg's artistic world appears to Hortense to contain the adventure she seeks. But the adventure Jürg now seeks is different. For him now the greatest adventure of all is marriage, "the risk of a total commitment, commitment to a riddle that outlasts us" (I 500).

Jürg and Hortense are moving in opposite directions. While he seeks to begin a "normal," conventional life, using a conventional marriage as his entrée to society, Hortense wants to shed her social conventions and seek a new life in Jürg's artistic world. This contradiction overshadows the entire second phase of their relationship. The harder Jürg tries to live conventionally, the more carefully he plans the details of their marriage, the more clearly Hortense sees that this is not the kind of life she wants to share with him.

Jürg proposes marriage; she does not reply. Yet he goes ahead to plan their life together, as if she had already accepted his proposal: he imagines where they will live, what their daily life will be like, and the child—a boy, of course—they will have. He even buys wedding rings without telling Hortense, wears one to see how it feels, and is promptly ridiculed by the artist Alois, his friend.

Meanwhile, Jürg and Hortense encounter problems with themselves. Jürg has difficulty fitting smoothly into the eight-to-five office routine; he is frequently late to work, daydreams on the job, and has already become annoyed about the pettiness of his coworkers, the dull routine and mediocrity of their lives, and their shallow thoughts. Most of Hortense's problems are related to Jürg. The more deeply she thinks she is in love with him, the more confused she becomes. The bourgeois life he asks her to share, void of spontaneity and adventure, is not the life she wants.

Jürg grows impatient with Hortense's delay in accepting his marriage proposal. Like Hortense, he suffers from the increased tension of their relationship and begins to suspect her family of trying to separate them. Unable to meet in Hortense's home or in Jürg's room, the lovers must meet in cafés, on park benches, on street corners. "Obdachlose Liebe" (love without a roof over its head), Max Frisch calls this situation in his next novel, *Stiller*, in which the protagonist and his lover experience the same situation.

To sort out her feelings, Hortense decides to spend some time at the estate of a close friend, Gerda. About twice Hortense's age, Gerda is married and has two children, but she cannot help Hortense solve her problems. She listens attentively, however, and points out that, if Hortense decides to marry Jürg, she will have to deal with the social pressure her family will exert, because his social background is very different from hers and his profession, painting, does not fit her father's definition of an acceptable son-in-law. Not only does Hortense not know if she can withstand that pressure, she is not even sure she really loves Jürg. Many small things about him—the way he eats, for example—bother her. Why should she marry *him*, why not some other attractive, healthy man, she muses. Gerda sympathizes with her troubled friend but has no advice for her. If she does marry Jürg, Hortense eventually concludes, it may be only to avoid dreaming about him all her life.

One cold February morning when Hortense and her father are driving to one of their estates, Hortense realizes that her father will resist forever accepting Jürg as a son-in-law. Her father believes in order, honor, and duty and will not tolerate a smudge on his family's honor, he tells her. That morning he found a letter for Hortense from Jürg in the day's mail and uses the opportunity of their drive to talk extensively about social responsibility and heredity. He points out that pride in one's genetic heritage is inborn. Keeping that heritage pure is a duty, sometimes an unpleasant one, for each member of the group, he believes, but from this social consciousness arises a pride that serves as a sixth sense when one is choosing a mate. Just as one does not crossbreed bulldogs, greyhounds, and poodles, even though one loves all of them, because each breed would be destroyed by the creation of mongrels, so too the crossbreeding of people of different social classes produces mongrels. And mongrels, even if brilliant and successful, are exceptions to the norm, the colonel asserts. They lack the right to propagate, for the propagation of mongrels violates the natural order. The colonel recognizes that young people may want to rebel against this order, but he insists they must subjugate their desires to it, for, he concludes, like Icarus, all men are blinded by the same sun and plunge to their extinction if they get too close to it and burn. "J'adore ce qui me brûle" (I 504).

To illustrate his comments about heredity, social pride, and responsibility, the colonel tells Hortense the story of a governess and her lover, a butcher's apprentice. The young woman, from a good family, was employed by Hortense's grandfather. When the grandfather, who valued honor and virtue, called the governess to account for her affair with the butcher's apprentice, she essentially told him to mind his own business. But the governess became pregnant. The incident was swiftly dealt with; the governess was dismissed, and her child, a boy, was given to foster parents to raise, since his father denied parentage and refused to marry the woman. She eventually drowned herself.

The colonel believes the bastard's existence is the most miserable of all, for he has to go through life without the inner strength and pride that come from one's heritage. Free of meaningful social ties, the bastard may seem to be leading a carefree life, but in truth, the colonel tells his daughter, his life is very lonely. He has no inherited social function, so he must choose his own, without guidance from his forebears.

Hortense listens somewhat absentmindedly to her father's sermon. His social philosophy seems inflexible and dated, his concept of breeding rigid. She does not think of it again.

While Hortense is in the country visiting Gerda, Jürg is not idle. His new attitude toward life forces him to think about the past and the future. He is ready, he believes, to say farewell forever to the life of the artist and to accept a bourgeois life. His marriage plans cause him to wonder for the first time about his own background. He hardly knows his relatives, who are simple folk—craftsmen, storekeepers, low-echelon civil servants. He has never cared much for them; that attitude will have to change, he tells himself. He remembers that his father, who died some years earlier, became something of a drunkard during his last years, and this recollection troubles him. Had his father been a drunk all his life? Might he, Jürg, have inherited that tendency?

To find out the truth, Jürg visits his mother, who lives in a small apartment in a neighborhood he does not like. Jürg admits to her that he is plagued by an indefinable, existential fear, which has even forced him to stop painting, he tells her. Something is terribly wrong with him and his life. So as not to live in fear all his life, he wants to find out what it is.

Jürg tells his mother about a recurring dream that haunts him. He is in a butcher shop, where the butcher, dressed partly as an executioner, partly as a priest, hands him a package wrapped in newspaper. It contains the ashes of his father, the butcher tells Jürg. But when Jürg opens the package, he finds "only a small upper and lower jaw, which one could open and close, ridiculous to look at" (I 531-32). The teeth in the jaws fall out with every movement; signs of depravity and decay are everywhere.[6] Jürg does not know what the dream means.

His mother remains silent on that topic, but she assures him that his fears about his father's drinking are unfounded. By all that is sacred to her, she tells him, she is positive he cannot have inherited his father's tendency to drink. Her statement is so positive that it becomes ominous and raises more questions than it answers. When Jürg keeps insisting his mother tell him truthfully if his father was always a drunk, even before Jürg was born, she implores him: "Stop it! Nothing will be gained by it" (I 532). His mother has not really answered his questions, and Jürg's visit is less reassuring than he had hoped. Ironically, he learns the truth from Hortense's father, and it is a very different truth from what he suspects. Determined to reach an understanding with the colonel, Jürg requests a meeting with him while Hortense is still visiting Gerda. His action surprises Hortense, and she is even more surprised to learn that her father grants Jürg's request. The meeting takes place on Pentecost, and the colonel does all the talking. He tells Jürg he is the illegitimate child of a now deceased, attractive young German governess from a good, middle-class family who was employed by the colonel's family, the same governess the colonel told Hortense about a few months earlier. Jürg's real father is the butcher's apprentice who delivered meat to the house several times a week. The colonel describes him as an unattractive fellow who at the time was about twenty-one. Today he has his own butcher shop in a nearby village. Jürg, then, is a bastard and thus socially unacceptable to the colonel and his family.

Strangely, the night before the interview with the colonel, Jürg has an experience that foreshadows the news he is to learn. He has gone out to the cemetery to visit his father's (actually his foster father's) grave and decides to spend the rest of the night walking in the woods. Abruptly he comes upon a couple copulating behind the branches of some young trees. "As if compelled, he watched the couple, holding his breath, as they moved, no particular couple, entangled in the ecstasy of procreation . . . " (I 543). The primal scene is symbolic. Jürg stands barefoot, holding his shoes in his hands, mesmerized, afraid to make a sound. The explanation comes the next day: Jürg is the issue of such an act—a careless, irresponsible act, the colonel would call it. A marriage between his daughter and Jürg is out of the question.

Once more, Jürg's relationship with a woman he loves has ended. After losing Yvonne, Jürg tried to become an integral part of society, to lead a conventional life, and to commit himself to a woman in marriage. This time he is willing to support the relationship economically by holding a steady job. His best intentions fail, not so much because of Hortense's father's intervention or their different social backgrounds, but because he and Hortense were set on an opposite course when phase two of their relationship began.

Moreover Hortense, like Yvonne earlier, is guilty of the sin that inevitably destroys most relationships of Frisch's characters: she, too, formed a graven image of her partner. Hortense sees Jürg as the carefree artist in pursuit of the *real* life, a life full of excitement and adventure, and that is how she freezes him in her mind. She is neither willing nor able to give up that image when she learns that Jürg has changed and that the great adventure in his life is no longer the pursuit of "das wirkliche Leben" in an artistic environment, but a conventional marriage, complete with a conventional job.

Not even after their relationship ends does Hortense give up her image of Jürg. Years later, when they meet unexpectedly, she tells him how, through all those intervening years, she has thought of him in a special way: "You always walking in the distance of a life more real . . . you painting again, you wandering along shores I shall never reach" (I 585). After they separate, however, their lives undergo another drastic change of direction.

Like Yvonne before her, but not entirely for the same reasons, Hortense compromises: she withdraws into the social environment she has always known. To punish Jürg (according to the narrator [I 558]), she marries Ammann, an attractive young man appropriate to her social class, a budding architect who a few years earlier had commissioned Jürg to paint his portrait. They have two children, Annemarie and Peter. From Hortense's final conversation with Jürg it is clear, however, that her life with Ammann, not unhappy but filled with the obligations of a wife and mother, lacks spontaneity, excitement, and adventure.

Jürg, after his relationship with Hortense has ended, withdraws once more to the fringe of society, not to his previous artist's existence but to that of a homeless, rootless transient. When he and Hortense meet again, Jürg has served time in prison for attempting to kill his real father while in a state of distress and depression. He has also learned that he has a younger, worthless half-brother and a half-sister, Jenny. She is the young woman, it turns out, who modelled for him on several occasions and who earns her living as a waitress in the

DIE SCHWIERIGEN   45

bar Jürg and his artist friends once frequented. Jürg's father threw her out of the house when he learned that she modelled nude for young artists. Hypocrite that he is, Jürg's father, the butcher, considered such "immoral" behavior by a family member unsuitable to his mercantile status in the community—a nice touch of social criticism by Max Frisch, one inviting comparison between the butcher's moral values and social stance with those of the colonel.

Each of the women Jürg loves ends her relationship with him for, from her perspective, the same reason: each is disappointed in Jürg. Each sees that Jürg is unable to act according to the principles of living that he professes to hold. Neither woman tells Jürg what both know intuitively; Hortense expresses it succintly: "Man heiratet keine Worte" (I 548); *"One does not marry words."*

JÜRG'S SUICIDE: AN IRONIC MISPERCEPTION

Jürg's suicide at the end of the novel seems, at first glance, to be related only marginally to his problems of relationships with the two women he loved. Clearly it is related to his concept of identity and his perception of himself in society. But because the ideas of his role in society after he and Hortense separate arise in part from his failed relationships with Yvonne and Hortense, a few comments about his self-inflicted death are appropriate.

When Jürg returns from prison for the attempted murder of his father, he changes his name to Anton and serves as gardener on the estate of Hortense's friend Gerda, who has died. His withdrawal from society and from any human relationship that demands commitment could not be more complete. He is content to tend the shrubbery and flowers, observe life from the sidelines, and, if asked, give advice. He is willing to advise Hortense's adolescent daughter, Annemarie, when she questions the principle of a child's obedience to her parents, in this case her father. Jürg also enjoys building a toy for Annemarie's younger brother, Peter, and watches the boy's delight in it. Behind this outwardly peaceful existence, however, Jürg hides his sense of failure.

For Yvonne, Jürg was the last chance of rescue from spiritual isolation. He was able to describe to her vividly the creative relationship that was possible with him as a mate—a relationship that would give her life the meaning she yearned for. In the same sense, Hortense represented for Jürg his last chance to enter into a creative relationship with life that, during the first phase of their relationship, she thought he already possessed. Jürg, however, has given up the hope he once expressed to Hortense: "That another person believes in us when our faith in ourselves has been destroyed and gives it back to us, that I thought would be love, the miracle of love, the grace, inexplicable, like the drawing near of an angel"[7] (I 545).

Having learned his origin from the colonel, Jürg has adopted the colonel's restrictive social creed and constructed for himself a model of obligation and fulfillment in which the choices are limited. According to Jürg's model, human beings have three choices. The first two are positive: they can either use their inherited gifts and talents to make a magnificent mark in life—through a single act, a single, momentous achievement, irrespective of the consequences; or they can settle for a healthy, conventional existence, a bourgeois marriage, through which they pass on their gifts, talents, and ethics to the next generation.

In his relationship with Yvonne, Jürg tried to exercise the first choice; in his planned marriage to Hortense, he chose the second. Both ended in failure. Jürg has only one choice left, he believes, a self-denying, negative one: to end his life. He believes that the life he inherited from his parents is so flawed and deficient that it must not be transmitted in any form.

Is this what became of Jürg's desire for "das wirkliche Leben?" He now sees himself as one of the colonel's social and genetic mongrels, as less than a whole person. He defines "a whole person" for Hortense during their last long conversation as someone whose life "is rooted in a fearless, cheerful, natural self-confidence" (I 588). Hortense cannot argue with this. But it seems an error to her to think that the lack of this kind of self-confidence makes one deficient.

Hortense recognizes that in his thinking Jürg has entered a dead-end street, but she cannot help him find a way out. Jürg's neurotic obsession with being a mongrel and the world not needing any more "Halblinge" (I 591) has gone so far that he no longer listens to reason. He interprets his death wish as a noble mission, a willingness to serve humanity, not by fathering a child and adding to the world's "halfness," but by killing himself. The irony could not be more complete, since the reader knows what Jürg does not: he has indeed fathered a child, Hanswalter, who is courting Hortense's daughter Annemarie.

While people outside Jürg's window celebrate the harvest with speeches and laughter, wine, song, and dance, Jürg ends his life (I 592-95). Frisch's attitude here is clear. He does not approve of Jürg's solution to his life's problems; Jürg's analysis of himself and his life is mistaken, and so is the conclusion he draws from that analysis.

Central to the novels of Max Frisch is the problem of marriage, the possibility of creating a lasting bond between a man and a woman (Butler 50). Frisch has in mind a fundamental union of two people, not merely its conventional expression as a useful social institution. In his relationships with Yvonne and Hortense, Jürg confuses these two aspects. Although he recognizes eventually what Hortense and Yvonne already know intuitively—that "das wirkliche Leben" can only be lived instinctively and not by reflecting about it or by merely adhering to social convention—he comes by this insight too late. If there is one specific reason why Jürg's relationship with the two women he loves does not succeed, it is that neither he nor they are willing to commit themselves, without preconceptions or expectations, to each other and their relationship. Instead, all three compromise eventually, each in his own way and uneasily. As a result, "das wirkliche Leben" slips out of reach for all of them. Jürg, as an artist, perhaps came closest to it in his youth. Hortense, always aware of it but in her marriage to Ammann permanently out of touch with it, imagines Jürg to have achieved "das wirkliche Leben." Yvonne is the only one who consciously seems to turn her back on it as the price for her compromise in marrying Hauswirt. Farthest removed from "das wirkliche Leben," she returns to the spiritual isolation and artificiality of her early life. Only occasionally does she feel a deep inner discomfort about her existence which, at those moments, she finds like an upset stomach, "zum Kotzen," *"nauseating"* (I 550).

The picture of contemporary man that emerges from *Die Schwierigen* is less than positive. With the focus primarily, but not exclusively, on Jürg Reinhart, the picture is that of a man who at times is confused about himself and his true nature, one who often yearns for the impossible, "das wirkliche Leben," without identifying what he longs for or measuring his ability to achieve it. At other times he settles, more or less contentedly, for the obtainable and for an ordered, structured life. Overall, the image that emerges gradually in the course of the novel is that of an emotionally scarred man. He seems less capable of surviving life than his counterpart, woman. Although the women are often as confused as the man, they are more closely attuned to their nature and thus better able to make use of their intuition. The women are more flexible and in general more whole than the man.

In short, the picture of contemporary man emerging from *Die Schwierigen* is that of a human being inadequately equipped to engage successfully in the enterprise of living.

NOTES

[1] If anything in particular qualifies as a cause for Jürg's suicide it is the discovery of his own social and genetic background. This discovery leads him to the misperception of his own social and genetic inferiority, which burns and destroys him, as the title to Part III of the revised novel, "J'adore ce qui me brûle oder Die Entdeckung," implies (I 481).

[2] This sentence was engraved on a bronze coin Hortense's father discovered on a trip through Provence. Actually it is a modified version of the text the Archbishop of Rheims, St. Rémy, caused Clovis, then King of France, to repeat on the occasion of his baptism on Christmas day in 496 A.D.: "Courbe la tête, fier Sicambre; adore ce que tu as brûlé, brûle ce que tu as adoré" (Grégoire de Tours, *Histoire des Francs* II 23).

[3] The text contains inconsistencies about Yvonne's age when she first meets Hinkelmann and, possibly, about the duration of their marriage. The narrator states: "Yvonne married at twenty-one" (I 390). That would place her age between nineteen and twenty when she and Hinkelmann first met, since the narrator continues: "Only a year later the son announced . . . his engagement to Yvonne, the odd young woman whom he had mentioned in his letters on occasion" (I 399). But Yvonne, later recalling that meeting, reports that she was twenty-one (I 405).

The narrator also states that Yvonne was twenty-five when she first met Jürg Reinhart (I 390), a fact Yvonne herself confirms (I 392), and that she knew then that she was pregnant (I 390). That would put her pregnancy at least into the fourth year of her marriage to Hinkelmann. However, the narrator later records: "Three whole years she did not contradict [him]. . . . She played the mother for three years, until those summer days when she became aware that she was pregnant—three years she had left every decision up to him, since he, after all, . . . was the man" (I 401). With this statement the narrator implies that Yvonne was twenty-two, not twenty-one, when she married Hinkelmann, thus contradicting himself. It is a puzzle, but not one of great importance.

⁴The reader may discover a problem in the chronology of Yvonne's second pregnancy. The novel does not clarify it. Since Yvonne knows she is pregnant in the fall and her baby is born in the spring, and since we know she did not marry Hauswirt until at least early winter, one wonders that the practical, no-nonsense Hauswirt never realized that this very slender woman was already several months pregnant before their wedding and never questioned the paternity of a child born six months afterwards. As with the discrepancy about Yvonne's age, one must simply accept that this is what happened.

⁵The autobiographical reference to Frisch himself is clear. Once, in his late twenties, Frisch had bundled up all his writings, including his sketchbooks, and burned them. Like Jürg, he was surprised how much creative outpouring there was to be burned. Frisch had so many bundles of writings that he had to make two trips up into the forest to burn them all (II 588; *Sketch I* 195).

⁶The dream seems to come straight from a Kafka story. The psychological insights of the young Max Frisch are surprising. Since the butcher handing Jürg the package represents his real father, as Jürg will soon learn, the significance of his dress—half executioner, half priest—suggests the archetypal father-son conflict that, in this case, ends with the son's attempted murder of the father.

⁷The figure of the angel as a guide to the protagonist recurs dramatically in Frisch's next novel, *Stiller* (1954). Here only hinted at, it is an essential element in Frisch's first *Tagebuch* entries from 1946, where it is associated with the puppeteer Marion (II 359; not included in the translation, *Sketch I*).

CHAPTER THREE

STILLER: A TALE OF TWO MARRIAGES

In their search for a meaningful life, all the main characters in Frisch's novels face a set of problems, the central one being the creation of a lasting bond with a member of the opposite sex. Since marriage offers the ultimate opportunity for this bonding, it is not surprising that marriage, with its problems and its possibilities, is examined repeatedly. In *Stiller* (1954), marriage is a dominant concern and is closely linked to the novel's primary theme, the protagonist's search for acceptance of his new identity.

Stiller brought Max Frisch praise from literary critics soon after its publication, but acceptance by general readers came slowly (Petersen 1978a 129). The story is about a Swiss sculptor, Anatol Ludwig Stiller, who abruptly leaves his wife, mistress, friends, profession, and country to search for himself. He discovers who he is, if we are to believe him, after a series of remarkable adventures in the United States and Mexico that conclude with an unsuccessful suicide attempt and his rebirth. Secure in his new identity, he returns to Switzerland, only to discover that his countrymen, including his wife, refuse to see that he is now another person, even though he looks and in many respects behaves much like the missing Stiller.

"I am not Stiller!" are the novel's first words, the protagonist's plea to be accepted as the man he has so painfully become. The rest of the novel deals with his struggle to remain true to his new identity, for which he chose the name James Larkin White, an American of German descent. Despite his protestations, however, and his efforts to legitimize this identity through a string of stories he tells to various people in various versions while he is held in a Zurich jail, he cannot persuade anyone that he is indeed Jim White. Society has no context for this Jim White, whereas a ready frame of reference waits for Anatol

Ludwig Stiller. Thus society, in the persons of lawyers, friends, and family, carefully informs the self-proclaimed White about the details of Stiller's life before his disappearance.

Stiller/White loses the confrontation.[1] Eventually he is forced to accept the name and past of the person he claims *not* to be. Defeated, he resumes the life of the sculptor Stiller. In his marriage, the relationship he considers most important, however, he remains true to his new self. Until the night before his wife, Julika, dies, he continues trying to convince her that he is not Stiller.

The story is told in two parts. Part I consists of seven notebooks written in jail by the prisoner at the request of his public defender, Dr. Bohnenblust; Part II is a postscript written by the public prosecutor, Rolf. In the seven notebooks, the protagonist not only records the adventures of Jim White and significant events in the life of the missing Anatol Ludwig Stiller as they are told to him by his various visitors, but he also notes his thoughts and observations and describes his life in jail, including conversations with inmates, the warden, his defense lawyer, the prosecutor, and visitors. The prosecutor's postscript may justifiably be viewed as an eighth notebook, as Butler asserts, because it reports Stiller's life after his release from jail. It does not provide the objective, quasi-legal summary one might expect but is a highly selective description of Stiller's life, as Butler demonstrates in his analysis (Butler 82-87).

In this novel Max Frisch shows marriage to be the shared living experience of a man and a woman who in that relationship can grow either closer or apart. He tells of two marriages, one of Stiller and Julika and one of Rolf and Sibylle. These marriages are markedly different yet contain similarities. For example, each marriage goes through two phases separated by a crisis during which one of the partners leaves for a prolonged period. Both escaping partners travel to the United States, where Stiller discovers himself and where Sibylle proves her strength and puts her life in order. Although the second phase of Rolf and Sibylle's marriage is happily marked by the birth of their second child, an indication that their resumed marriage is working, the second phase of Stiller and Julika's marriage leads to the couple's withdrawal from society, the partners' almost complete isolation from each other, and Julika's death.

Frisch, who once wrote, "Time does not change us. It just unfolds us" (II 361/*Sketch I 12*), seems to regard marriage as an opportunity for the partners to expand their activities and to develop their potential strengths, to unfold. It is pertinent, therefore, to ask what the characters in this novel say about the possibilities and limitations of marriage. Why do both marriages in *Stiller* undergo a period of severe crisis, and why are the two marriages resumed? Why does one resumed marriage succeed and the other fail? Most important, what does the protagonist reveal about himself in his marriage to Julika and in his love affair with Sibylle?

To answer these questions I shall examine each marriage in both its phases and also the relationship of Stiller and Sibylle, proceeding chronologically when possible and basing the study on the notebook entries of Stiller/White. One must keep in mind that often several characters talk to the protagonist about an incident, and that their perceptions and recollections of it contain discrepancies. Furthermore, Stiller/White himself is the recorder of these conversations, not verbatim but as he recalls them. To those recollections he adds his own comments about events in the life of Stiller, the man he claims not to know. That the life he is thus recording is his own former life becomes evident as the novel progresses. It is always possible, therefore, that in writing it down Stiller/White deliberately or naively distorts what has been told to him, influenced perhaps by his own recollections of that past event. In other words, Stiller/White is not necessarily a reliable narrator.

The possibility of distortion by a subjective narrator is common in Frisch's novels. I deal with it here only to the extent that it impinges on my central concern: the marriages and love affair that reveal the nature of relationships between the men and women in the novel. Similarly, matters of structure, style, and language; social commentary on Swiss and American life; the protagonist's adventures in the United States and Mexico; and the protagonist's search for identity—all topics that reflect Frisch's interests and skill—will be dealt with only as they bear directly on marriage and, particularly, the protagonist's relationship with the women he loves.

MARRIAGE AS A TEST: STILLER AND JULIKA

Anatol Ludwig Stiller, sculptor, nearly thirty years old, meets the beautiful Julika Tschudy, ballerina, age twenty-three, unexpectedly one evening, when a group of his friends with the admired ballerina in tow storms Stiller's studio—according to the second notebook in which Stiller/White records the details of their courtship and marriage until the day Stiller disappears. Stiller's friends have been celebrating after a performance of Tchaikovsky's *Nutcracker* in which Julika, then the acknowledged future prima ballerina of the Zurich Ballet, has danced. Seeing the lights still burning in Stiller's studio, they continue their celebration there, since all the bars and cafés have closed.

During the ensuing party Stiller is asked to tell once more his "story of Toledo," an experience he had while fighting on the side of the communists in the Spanish Civil War from which he recently returned. Stiller does not want to tell the story, but when his friend Sturzenegger begins to tell it, Stiller takes over. Julika does not pay much attention to the story but watches Stiller, whose fingers are constantly moving as he talks, while his face remains lifeless. For some reason she feels pity for him. The story no longer seems to be a vivid memory, but rather an anecdote about a soldier who, one morning at dawn at the river Tajo, is confronted by four enemy soldiers. He does not fire at them as he should, because he suddenly sees the four fascist soldiers as people, and "he found it impossible to shoot at human beings, he couldn't do it" (III 491/122). Instead of shooting at the enemy, Stiller found himself being disarmed, beaten, and tied up by his captors, then left lying in the brush. His friends interpret this failure of a soldier's courage as humanitarianism and celebrate it as such. Stiller, ill at ease, wants to end the matter and escapes into the role of attentive host.

Like a leitmotif, Stiller's Spanish Civil War story keeps resurfacing throughout the first part of the novel. The contrast between Stiller's lifeless face and his constantly moving fingers as he tells it hints at discrepancies between the story he tells and what really happened that morning in Spain; he may be omitting facts, or perhaps changing them to suit his purpose. But why? Julika does not ask; she only notices the outward signs of Stiller's inner tension while he talks. The cause of Stiller's anxiety is revealed later: his feeling of personal inadequacy, which he believes the incident in Spain proves. His specific fear is that he is less than a courageous, virile man.

Julika has comparable fears, based on her feelings of inadequacy, of not being a complete woman. Her life is devoted entirely to dance. Any nonartistic intrusion, among which she includes men and their romantic interest in her, is an unwelcome distraction.

The courtship of these two is strange from the beginning. Stiller does not know much about the ballet, which makes him feel somewhat uneasy. Nevertheless, after a performance he waits patiently in front of the theater for almost an hour for the beautiful ballerina, apologizes for his persistence in waiting so long, fears bothering her with his presence, yet never asks what has kept her. Julika likes his behavior, as she likes listening to his stories and watching his embarrassment and fear of not being taken seriously when she responds only with a little smile. When she refuses to walk arm-in-arm with him on the street, he reacts with dismay and apologizes profusely for his forwardness, which he himself now finds repellent. Julika likes that about Stiller, too, his tendency quickly to see himself in the wrong. In fact, she likes him better than any other man, because she knows not only how much he desires her but also that he will never take her by force; he lacks the necessary assertiveness. Julika especially likes that about Stiller.

They take short walks in the country, during which Stiller is never bothered that Julika talks exclusively about ballet, colleagues, conductors, stage designers, hair dressers, and ballet masters. Although he knows little about these matters, he listens patiently. Other men have complained that she seems to think and talk of nothing else, but not Stiller. Julika likes that. Once, in March, during their first stroll in the country, when Stiller insists they walk across a still-muddy field, one of her shoes becomes stuck in the mud and he has to help her. Julika feels as if Stiller were a brother; she likes that feeling, too. For the first time, Julika has met a man she does not feel threatened by, a man she is not afraid of.

The sexual tension between Julika and Stiller manifests itself in her fear of frigidity and his fear of impotence. Julika's fear is reflected in her attitude toward the ballet. Only up on the stage, with the curtain raised, the sound of the orchestra filling the theater, the lights bathing her slender body, and with the audience out front does Julika feel whole. Then she feels herself at the center of a magic circle no one can penetrate. The space around her is hers, to be filled by her movement. On the stage Julika feels what "otherwise she never feels anywhere, bliss, an unutterable bliss" (III 478/111). This voluptuous pleasure on stage, when she is the center of attention, protected by the music like "a spell cast around Julika, whom all could see but could not grasp" (III 478/111), illustrates a narcissism that is part of Julika's nature and reflects the strong egocentricity of her character.

Stiller's fear of impotence grows out of the experience in Spain that has fundamentally affected his self-image; it is supported by his comparative lack of success as a sculptor. He needs to prove himself, he believes, and more as a man than as an artist. This he hopes to accomplish with Julika, this frail-looking, beautiful woman. But, Stiller/White observes in his notebook: "Any reasonably experienced man . . . would immediately have recognized in this fascinating little person a case of extreme frigidity" (III 437/74). Stiller evidently does not recognize this characteristic in Julika. He approaches her shyly, constantly afraid of being a bother to her.

When Stiller is sentenced to a few months in jail for his participation in the Spanish Civil War, Julika is not troubled by his absence. She writes to him several times. Her letters, she later claims, show her sincerity about and love for Stiller. True to her shy nature and her inability to convey her feelings in anything but dance, however, she never expresses those feelings directly. Stiller constantly has to guess at what she feels for him.

A year after they meet, they marry. One wonders why. What drew these two people together? Their interest in each other's profession is minimal—although Stiller enjoys attending ballet rehearsals and sketching the dancers. Their cultural and social backgrounds are very different. Stiller comes from a lower-middle-class background, "eigentlich überhaupt aus keinem Milieu" (III 444), *"in fact he had hardly any background at all"* (80). His mother is the daughter of a railroad worker, his father is never mentioned; his stepfather spends his days somewhere in an old-people's home. Julika, in contrast, comes from a well-to-do family, not rich but cultured; her mother, a Hungarian, was a lady of the best circles, "somehow an aristocrat" (III 444/80); her father was the Swiss ambassador in Budapest. Both her parents are dead; she became an orphan at eighteen.

When Stiller and Julika make love, Julika never feels blissful and voluptuous. She never experiences the abandon of orgasm and, although she does not want to hurt Stiller, she refuses to simulate it, to pretend to share his sensuality and lust, only to make him believe she loves him physically and, above all, to give him confidence in his masculinity.

What a relief it is for Julika, therefore, to escape this nagging problem and to stand on stage alone:

Tausend fremde Blicke auf ihrem Körper zu fühlen, Blicke so unterschiedlicher Art, Blicke von Gymnasiasten und verheirateten Biedermännern, Blicke, die alles eher als die tänzerische Leistung erfaßten, in der Tat, es machte Julika weniger aus, als wenn Stiller, ihr Mann, seine harte und von der Bildhauerei etwas rauhe Hand auf ihren Körper legte. (III 451)

To feel thousands of strange eyes on her body, eyes of so many different kinds, the eyes of schoolboys and respectable married men, eyes that took in anything rather than her skill as a dancer; as a matter of fact this worried Julika less than when Stiller, her husband, laid his roughened sculptor's hands on her body. (87)

The secret fear among the two partners, their fear of sexual inadequacy, weakens their marriage from the start. Stiller/White observes in his notebook:

Als Fremder hat man den Eindruck, daß diese zwei Menschen . . . auf eine unselige Weise zueinander paßten. Sie brauchten einander von ihrer Angst her. . . . Jedenfalls hatte die schöne Julika eine heimliche Angst, keine Frau zu sein. Und auch Stiller . . . stand damals unter einer steten Angst, in irgendeinem Sinn nicht zu genügen. (III 440)

> Looking at these two people from the outside, one has the impression that Julika and the vanished Stiller were suited to one another in an unfortunate manner. They needed each other because of their fear. . . . The beautiful Julika harboured a secret fear that she was not a woman. And Stiller too . . . was at that time perpetually afraid of being somehow inadequate. (77)

In addition, Julika's careless, yet seemingly harmless, remark on their wedding night, a remark never disclosed in the course of the novel yet never forgotten by Stiller, leads him to think of himself from that moment on as "a greasy, stinking fisherman" married to "a crystal water-fairy" (III 449/85).[2] Whatever that remark was, it illustrates Julika's strong distaste for the sexual act and Stiller's sensitivity and extremely defensive reaction to any remark reflecting on his sexuality. He expresses his perception of Julika artistically when he fashions out of plaster a statue of her, "a head on a long, columnar neck, more of a vase than a woman" (III 604/223). The sexual symbolism is obvious; so is the frigidity of the material and the object's shape. Julika, it seems, is perceptually a strange, beautiful, inanimate object for Stiller.

Similarly, the relationship between Stiller and Julika is sterile. Right from the outset of their marriage, Julika's behavior demonstrates a lack of personal commitment to her partner and to the relationship. Her fragile health—she suffers from a mild case of tuberculosis—and the demands of her career as a dancer make it impossible for the couple to have children. Instead, they acquire Foxli, a dog, which Stiller scornfully refers to as "the Sacred Beast" (III 456/91) and which Julika treats as a substitute child; Stiller believes the dog is treated better than he is. The dog accompanies them to restaurants (as is customary in Europe) and is allowed to sit on a chair just like Stiller, not (as is also customary) under the table. But then, no waiter can refuse the beautiful ballerina anything. Besides, what will they do with half the filet mignon that Julika, who eats little, leaves on her plate?

Stiller is actually jealous of the little dog, the center of attention everywhere, and he cannot refrain from making nasty comments about it. When someone remarks to Julika about her sweet little dog, he responds, "Yes, very sweet, we'll make jam of him before long" (III 457/91).

Julika uses her marriage to Stiller to shield herself from the unwanted attention of other men, although she is aware of Stiller's self-doubts and fear of masculine inadequacy. Playing the role of the physically weak, not-very-healthy woman, Julika believes "she could only hold Stiller through his bad conscience, through his fear of failure" (III 440-41/77). Lacking the confidence that she, as a woman, can satisfy the needs of a free, emotionally healthy man so he will stay with her, she chooses a weak, unfree man, one plagued by self-doubt and secret fears, because she is only able to exist in a relationship with a man "by having a husband whom she could continually forgive" (III 441/77).

Stiller, in turn, clings to Julika's weakness. Any healthy woman would demand certainty and strength from him or she would leave him. But Julika, in spite of her charming exterior, is so emotionally closed up that she can express herself and her feelings only in dance. To Stiller she appears "like a marine creature whose glorious colours are only visible under water" (III 438/75).

Stiller, the insecure man, sees himself as Julika's redeemer. The challenge he sets for himself in his courtship and marriage is to set Julika free: to rescue her from her emotional prison offstage and to add to her life as a woman the beauty she evokes and experiences onstage. By succeeding in this task, Stiller feels, he will conquer forever his own secret fears of inadequacy and incompetence.

Stiller and Julika are guilty of the cardinal sin in human relationships, as Max Frisch defined it. They have formed a "graven image" of each other. Neither is aware of fixing on this image, but neither can look beyond it, either. One of several dreams Stiller/White has in his jail cell presents their relationship symbolically. Julika and Stiller raise their hands to each other, displaying the stigmata that appear in the palms. This act evokes the unsettled question: "Who is the cross and who the crucified?" (III 415/54). The question is central to both phases of their marriage.

In Frisch's *Sketchbook* essay "Thou shalt not make unto thee any graven image," he elaborates on his application of the Biblical concept to human relationships. He writes:

> Wir wissen, daß jeder Mensch, wenn man ihn liebt, sich wie verwandelt fühlt, wie entfaltet, und daß auch dem Liebenden sich alles entfaltet, das Nächste, das lange Bekannte. . . .
> Unsere Meinung, daß wir das andere kennen, ist das Ende der Liebe . . .—nicht weil wir das andere kennen, geht unsere Liebe zu Ende, sondern umgekehrt: weil unsere Liebe zu Ende geht, weil ihre Kraft sich erschöpft hat, darum ist der Mensch fertig für uns. . . . Wir künden ihm die Bereitschaft, auf weitere Verwandlungen einzugehen. Wir verweigern ihm den Anspruch alles Lebendigen, das unfaßbar bleibt, und zugleich sind wir verwundert und enttäuscht, daß unser Verhältnis nicht mehr lebendig sei.
> "Du bist nicht", sagt der Enttäuschte oder die Enttäuschte: "wofür ich dich gehalten habe."
> Und wofür hat man sich denn gehalten?
> Für ein Geheimnis, das der Mensch ja immerhin ist, ein erregendes Rätsel, das auszuhalten wir müde geworden sind. Man macht sich ein Bildnis. Das ist das Lieblose, der Verrat. (II 369-70)

We know that every person who is loved feels transformed, unfolded, and he unfolds everything, the most intimate as well as the most familiar, to the one who loves him as well as to himself . . . .
Once we feel we know the other, love is at an end every time. . . . It is not because we know the other that we cease to love, but vice versa: because our love has come to an end, because its power is expended, that person is finished for us. . . . We withdraw from him our willingness to participate in further manifestations. We refuse him the right that belongs to all living things to remain ungraspable, and then we are both surprised and disappointed that the relationship has ceased to exist.

"You are not," says he or she who has been disappointed, "what I took you for." And what was that? For a mystery—which after all is what a human being is—for an exciting puzzle of which one has become tired. And so one creates for oneself an image. That is the loveless act, the betrayal. (Sketch I 16-17)

Herein lies a part of Stiller's problem with Julika. She has made a "graven image" of him as an insecure man, full of self-doubt in his abilities as an artist and in his virility as a sexual being, ready to apologize at any time for any of his behavior, a trait of character that meets Julika's need to forgive. However, in casting this frozen, inflexible image, Julika overlooks the reality of Stiller's character; she does not see his deep craving to overcome his fears, his craving to change. Julika's frozen image of him does not allow for change. Stiller's "graven image" of Julika, however, embraces the idea of change, makes it a necessity. Nevertheless, his image of himself in that relationship is fixed—as Julika's redeemer, through whose power she will be saved, and as a consequence he will be saved in turn. These are the widely separated poles from which they approach their marriage.

Whether Stiller is capable of producing the desired change in Julika is another matter; he seems ill equipped to succeed. Once more, Stiller has over-challenged himself, as he did when he enlisted to fight in the Spanish Civil War. He is an artist, not a soldier. Sibylle recognizes that at once when she hears him tell his Spanish Civil War story.

Even before he meets Julika, Stiller's self-doubt is expressed in many ways, including his inability to be alone. He admits this explicitly: "in the hour of inability to be alone, it was never with anyone but a woman, with the memory or the hope of a woman, that I escaped from my loneliness" (III 683/294). Raised without the influence of a father by a loving, understanding mother—according to Stiller/White's notebook entries that contrast sharply with his younger stepbrother Wilfried's recollections of their mother (III 672-74)—Stiller turns out quite different from the practical Wilfried, who is a bit rough and dull, the manager of the fruit section at a farm cooperative. Stiller becomes a sculptor and a malleable, charming man but one unable to take a firm position on anything. He seldom lives in the present, dwelling either in the past of his memories or in the future of his hopes. Like Rip van Winkle, with whom he shares other character traits, "he was always a bit afraid of the world and badly needed to be liked" (424/62). As a young man he is not happy with himself because he expects more of himself than he fears he can deliver. In a way, Stiller is similar to his one-time friend Alex, the pianist, a homosexual man who was unable to bear his deviance from the norm and eventually killed himself. Alex's distraught parents visit Stiller/White in jail, hoping to derive some comfort from talking with him about their son.

Although Stiller is radically egocentric, concerned only with himself, his feelings and his actions, he too is unable to accept himself. "He feels he has no will power, and in a certain sense has too much," Stiller/White observes, then adds: "he employs it in willing not to be himself" (III 600/219). He becomes more and more dependent on the judgment of the people around him. In his studio, Stiller/White comments in his notebooks, one had the exciting feeling that the occupant would "jederzeit aufbrechen und ein ganz anderes Leben beginnen . . . können" (III 603), *"depart at any time and start a completely different life"* (222). Stiller's sketches and drawings show talent, but they promise more than he is able to achieve in his finished statues. Whether he is really a talented sculptor remains uncertain throughout the novel, although some of his statues have been bought by the city of Zurich and are on public display, as Julika points out to Stiller/White on one of their walks in the city (III 431).

When Stiller was a young man, he read one day in a newspaper, in a discussion of his works, that the world had expectations of him. Suddenly he represented a publicly recognized artistic hope for the future, which frightened him. He concluded from the article that the world expected him to live a life dedicated to impassioned work, which would lead to fame. That is the image of himself that he cannot live up to. His talent is not adequate to meet these expectations.

Fortunately, in a way, the Spanish Civil War provides him a temporary escape from his artistic responsibilities. As a somewhat "naive Communist, more corectly: a romantic Socialist" (III

592/212), Stiller enlists in the army. But his experience in Spain shakes his self-confidence further, handicapping him more severely than any artistic defeat would have done. He returns to Switzerland, convinced that he is an impotent, cowardly man.

Eventually Sibylle tells him that his failure in Spain has nothing to do with virility, but that as an artist he was simply not meant to be a soldier. At the time, Stiller wants to hear none of this because it suits his masochistic stance to think of himself as less than a man. Nevertheless, Sibylle is correct. Stiller overestimated his ability and his nature when he expected to perform like a soldier. When once again he follows that same pattern, assigning himself the impossible challenge of being Julika's "redeemer," the results are grievous.

As the marriage of Stiller and Julika progresses, Stiller gradually grows more frustrated about his inability to change Julika, to awaken her and turn her into the woman he believes she really is. Initially thoughtful of her frail health, he now alternates between concerned overprotection and angry frustration. Genuine concern induces him to press her continually to see her doctor again. Julika resents any interference in her life and refuses, growing more stubborn the more Stiller persists. At the theater everyone admires Julika's courage in continuing to dance despite her failing health. Julika, ironically, needs the environment of the theater with its dust-filled air to feel whole and breathe freely, to escape for hours from the stifling hold her marriage and Stiller have on her. Stiller, meanwhile, finds it idiotic that she wears herself out for the ballet. When, without her knowledge, he calls the theater to cancel her performance one evening because she is running a high fever, Julika considers this an interference she, as an artist, cannot condone. She counters by calling a taxi to take her to the theater anyway; Stiller, enraged, screams after her as she walks down the stairs. His public display of fury shocks Julika.

Although Stiller tries to make amends for his outbursts with especially thoughtful behavior and small gifts for Julika, the gulf between them widens with each incident and the silence between them grows deeper. Their own perceptions of their life together diverge more and more. Julika, for example, claims to be quite content; Stiller is not. He continues to worry about her health and fears she is exhausting her limited energies unwisely. His concern for her welfare alternately pleases and infuriates Julika. As it did for the young Jürg Reinhart in *Die Schwierigen*, art comes first in her life. If she comes home exhausted from a performance, too tired to be the charming wife and exciting lover, she expects Stiller always to be understanding. He interprets her constant fatigue in terms of himself, seeing it as a way of evading his attention. He vents his resulting frustration either in sudden emotional outbursts or in lengthy speeches about trivial issues, like Julika's failure to return empty dishes to the kitchen.

The lack of effective communication between Stiller and Julika takes its toll, as Julika withdraws more completely into her world of theater and dance and Stiller into his work as a sculptor. Eventually, both have an extramarital affair. Julika's, with a young advertising consultant, a friend of Stiller's known for his virility, is brief. Stiller knows the man has been in love with the ballerina for some time, yet it is Stiller who introduces them. Perhaps he wants to know whether Julika can be tempted, whether she will respond to this virile man differently than she responds to him. When she does—Julika visits the young man in Ascona for about a week—Stiller nearly goes out of his mind with jealousy. Barricaded in his studio, he swallows enough sedative pills to sleep for days.

Julika returns, but Stiller believes for a long time that she is hiding her happiness from him. For months afterward he remains alert for any sign that the affair may have started again. Once he even searches through her purse for some evidence—a letter, a train ticket to Ascona, or an entry in her pocket calendar—to confirm his suspicions. He discovers nothing. Whether Stiller feels jealous primarily because he loves Julika or because he fears the other man has succeeded sexually where he could not is difficult to assess.

Another time Stiller asks Julika point-blank what the advertising consultant means to her and is surprised when she answers: "You brought me to despair, Stiller, let's say no more about it, I've come back, but you mustn't drive me to despair" (III 454/*89*). For a while after that, their relationship improves a bit.

Stiller is thoughtful and considerate of her, cooks her favorite dishes, and is mindful of her frail health in what he asks of her. Stiller's affair, which follows Julika's, is with Sibylle, an attorney's young wife whom he meets at a masked ball. Their liaison lasts nearly seven months, much longer than Julika's with the advertising expert. For Stiller, however, the advertising consultant remains always "the great man who was able to make Julika happy" (III 454/89). Stiller is blind to the fact that Julika, after her week-long affair in Ascona, returned to him unchanged, which suggests that her fear of being less than a complete woman is still intact. By comparison, Stiller's fear of sexual inadequacy recedes substantially during his affair with Sibylle. He even fathers a child with her, although at the time he does not know it.

Julika's tuberculosis is growing more severe. Diagnosed several years earlier, it was then not a cause for alarm; the doctor merely advised Julika to spend summers at a sanatorium in the mountains. She never told Stiller about the doctor's recommendation, believing they cannot afford to lose her earnings for three months. Hers is the couple's only regular income, 620 Swiss francs per month; Stiller's sculptures earn them some money, but only occasionally. Julika does not resent this, but she asks him in return to be considerate in his demands of her.

What does he ask of her? To be more sensible in pursuing her career, to conserve her precious energies, and to allow them to live more like a conventional couple. Her persistently poor health worries him more and more.

Sometimes they talk about children. Stiller wants a child, not because he feels a compelling need to become a father but because he believes "a child might have fulfilled Julika as a woman in a way that he was unable to do" (III 442/78). He keeps pressing the issue, will not listen to her protestation that she is perfectly satisfied with her life as it is and that, besides, they cannot afford a child. Finally, as her last line of defense, Julika fires off her strongest argument, asking Stiller: "Why have a child by a mother with T.B.?" (III 442/79). That settles the issue of children. Using her illness, Julika for the first time denies Stiller a fundamental component of marriage: children.

When Julika arrives at Stiller's studio, unannounced, one morning, she ostensibly has come to tell him that she has finally seen her doctor. Actually, she saw the doctor a week earlier but never told him. However, she has grown suspicious of Stiller, whose behavior has seemed odd lately: suddenly he is no longer worried about her fever and seems to think his profession is as important as hers; he no longer attends ballet rehearsals; and he has spent several days and nights in a row at his studio. Julika finds him washing wine glasses from the previous evening, whistling. There is a black hair on his light-colored slacks and a hairpin on the floor, which she picks up without comment. Julika tells Stiller the results of her medical checkup: her tuberculosis has progressed alarmingly and, as soon as possible, she must go to a sanatorium at Davos, in the mountains. Surprised, Stiller asks: "Is it [the diagnosis] true?" (III 446/82). She misunderstands, thinking he questions the truth of what she has said, becomes hysterically upset, and orders him out of the room. Stiller responds quietly that this is his studio, not her dressing room at the theater.

Julika is furious also because Stiller has never bothered to find out whether her sanatorium stay would be covered by medical insurance, in which case, she says, she would have gone years ago and might now be well. In view of their fractured communication pattern and her failure to tell him her doctor's earlier recommendation, it is difficult to see how he could have thought of doing this. Julika's accusation seems unfair and her fury misdirected.

To Stiller the whole chain of events—Julika's deteriorating physical condition and imminent departure for Davos—is upsetting. As always when frustrated, he reacts with violence and hurls the wine glass he has been drying into the kitchen alcove, apologizes, and later, angered by their continuing failure to communicate, smashes an empty gin bottle in the same corner. True to his established pattern of alternating concern and anger, he then overreacts in the opposite direction, accepting complete responsibility for Julika's illness and for the fact that she now has to go away, leaving him behind. Stiller/White records in his notebook that Julika's husband seemed to consider himself responsible for everything concerning her, something she could never understand about him. Julika does not seem to know about the "graven image" Stiller has formed of her or about the task he took on, that of proving his manliness by making her a happy woman, freeing her imprisoned feelings, and making her love him.

Julika dances her last two premiere performances for the season and goes to Davos. She seldom answers Stiller's regular letters, believing she simply cannot write. Nor can Stiller bring himself to visit her. Another impasse.

One of the patients at Davos is a young, well-educated Jesuit seminarian with whom Julika spends many hours in animated conversation. She feels safe with him; he treats her as he might treat a nun, that is, like an asexual being. Beyond handshakes, they have no physical contact. At the same time, the more Julika's graceful body surrenders to the fever of her illness, the more she feels a confusing, hitherto unknown longing for a man. She dreams about sex, but not sex with her husband—sex with "head physicians, baker's boys, and men whom she had never seen" (III 482/115). And she knows her husband is betraying her with another woman.

Julika and her new friend talk easily about many things: from Eros to communism, Thomas Aquinas to Albert Einstein. The young man is interested in a wide range of topics. An astute observer, he tells Julika, without mincing words:

> Ich habe . . . das Gefühl, meine liebe und verehrte Julika, Sie wollen nicht erwachsen werden, nicht verantwortlich werden für Ihr eigenes Leben, und das ist schade . . . .
> Wer sich selbst nur immerzu als Opfer sieht . . . kommt sich selbst nie auf die Schliche, und das ist nicht gesund. Ursache und Wirkung sind nie in zwei Personen getrennt, schon gar nicht in Mann und Frau, selbst wenn es zuweilen so aussehen mag, Julika, weil die Frau scheinbar nicht handelt. Es fällt mir nur auf: eigentlich alles, was Sie tun oder nicht tun, begründen Sie mit etwas, was beispielsweise Ihr Mann nicht getan oder getan hat. Das ist doch . . . infantil. (III 483-84)

> *I have the feeling, my dear and respected Julika, that you don't want to grow up, you don't want to be responsible for your own life, and that's a pity. . . .*

Anyone who is always seeing himself as a victim . . . never gets wise to himself, and that's not healthy. Cause and effect are never divided between two people, certainly not between a husband and wife, even though it may sometimes look like it, Julika, because the wife apparently doesn't act. It just strikes me that you explain everything you do or don't do by something your husband has or has not done. That . . . is infantile. (115-16)

Julika is stunned, and a bit angered, by the young Jesuit's assessment of her and her attitude toward life and marriage. But she hides her reaction behind casual conversation, teasing the young man about the wisdom of his pronouncements that far exceeds his age. "My wise one!" she comments (III 484), a phrase that offends him slightly. Their relationship never regains its lighthearted tone and casualness. The young man's sudden death a few weeks later surprises and shocks Julika.

Through this Jesuit seminarian Julika becomes acquainted with the Second Commandment, "Thou shalt not make unto thee any graven image"—or rather with Frisch's application of it to human relationships. But because she does not understand the young man's assessment of her attitude toward her marriage, she also misses the point of his comments about a "finished image" and does not apply them to herself, only to Stiller.

Stiller first visits Julika in August, after she has been in the sanatorium for several months. The chief physician tells him that Julika's illness is far more serious than Stiller has realized, but Stiller manages to get permission to take her for a short walk so they can talk. Julika is very weak, but she is absorbed in the beauty of her surroundings during this first walk outside since arriving at Davos. Stiller, for his part, is absorbed in Julika. At one point he asks her the question that will continue to concern him for a long time: "Did you ever really love me?" (III 472/105). Julika, who never understood the importance of that question, does not reply. Verbal communication between these two is as impossible as ever.

They sit on the grass to rest. Impulsively Stiller embraces Julika, kisses her passionately, and throws his arms around her hips. Then he bursts into tears and buries his head in her lap. Hoping to calm him, Julika puts her hand on his hair. But he becomes even more agitated and tries to bite through the thick cloth of her corduroy skirt into the skin of her abdomen. The sexual symbolism is obvious. Torn by his feelings of love, guilt, and helplessness, Stiller reacts as he always does when frustrated: dramatically.

Julika is deeply embarrassed. People are coming, she tells him, and he straightens up. A moment later, as he sits next to her, sadly looking out over the valley, all Julika can do is repeat the phrase she often used at home in Zurich when he was moody: "Jaja—bist ein Armer!" (III 463,475), "*Yes, yes—you're a poor fellow!*" *(97,108)*. Julika's only recourse for dealing with her husband in such a situation seems to be to soothe him, like a child.

When Stiller returns to Zurich he continues his affair with Sibylle. In November he visits Julika for the second and last time, to end his marriage to her. She is lying on the balcony when he arrives, her arms tucked under the warm blanket so that she looks like a mummy, with only her head moving. Stiller is pale, unshaven, and smells of garlic and alcohol. He tells her a dream he has had: he is trying to strangle her but fails because she is too elastic; all she does in the dream is smile at him.

Then he begins a long monologue recounting his and her sins, during which he attempts to come to terms with his entire life: his defeat during the Spanish Civil War; his love for Julika and her acceptance of his love—which she did, he believes, because she is covertly in love with his fear of inadequacy as a man, since she herself is afraid to be a healthy, normal woman, something he knows, he says, because she considered him unkind when he told her joyously one day that she had no fever; her excessive demands for consideration; her need to make sure that he always felt in the wrong and required forgiveness; her excessive need to forgive. But he knows too, he admits, that had he not thought of her as an invalid to make himself feel more powerful, not made her his personal test, not challenged himself to make her bloom into full womanhood, she would never have thought of shackling him with her illness, and they might have led a normal married life. In this marriage who, indeed, is the cross and who the crucified?

In response, Julika tells Stiller what her late Jesuit friend told her about forming a "graven image" of people in human relationships. She is, of course, thinking only of Stiller, not herself, as she repeats the Jesuit's words that "it is a sign of non-love, that is to say a sin, to form a finished image of one's neighbour or of any person" (III 467/100). Did Stiller not always carry with him a fixed image of her? She admonishes him about this as she continues to lecture him: "not for nothing does it say in the Commandments 'Thou shalt not make unto thee any image' . . . . Every image is a sin. All those things you've been saying are exactly the opposite of love, you know" (III 500/130).

Stiller is puzzled. This does not sound like Julika, so he asks: "Where did you get all that from?" (III 500/130). Julika does not answer.

It is ironic that Julika is the one to tell Stiller during their final meeting:

> Wenn man einen Menschen liebt, so läßt man ihm doch jede Möglichkeit offen und ist trotz allen Erinnerungen einfach bereit, zu staunen, immer wieder zu staunen, wie anders er ist, wie verschiedenartig und nicht einfach so, nicht ein fertiges Bildnis, wie du es dir da machst von deiner Julika. (III 500)

> *When you love someone you leave every possibility open to them, and in spite of all the memories of the past you are ready to be surprised. . . at how different they are, how various, not a finished image such as you have made of your Julika. (130)*

Julika is far less open than he, far less willing to modify the image that, from the beginning of their relationship, she has held of him. Both, however, are guilty of forming a "graven image" of each other, of holding on to it throughout their marriage, and thus suffocating each other with it, denying each other the space and possibility to grow. Although Stiller seems less guilty in this respect than Julika, the difference between them is small.

Before Stiller leaves Julika at Davos, he tells her brutally that her illness no longer makes any impression on him, that he can now look at her without feeling the need to apologize for something, that for the first time he is aware that it is not she nor her illness, but he himself, who has prevented him from living. Armed with this knowledge, Stiller is ready to take dramatic action. He bolts from Julika and their marriage. He has failed to redeem Julika and failed to prove his manhood. He disappears from Zurich in an effort to escape, and along the way he discovers who he really is.

INTERLUDE 1: STILLER AND SIBYLLE

Stiller's seven-month affair with Sibylle, the wife of a successful attorney, casts further light on his character and especially his difficulty in building a valid, lasting relationship with a woman. Although he gains perspective and sexual confidence through their relationship, he does not grow enough to match Sibylle's maturity.

The timing of their meeting is significant for both. Stiller, at the time, finds himself in an increasingly difficult situation in his marriage: Julika's brief affair with the advertising consultant has increased his self-doubt. Sibylle, who unlike Julika is a woman of normal sexual appetite, has a problem with her husband, Rolf, who has his own fixed image, if not of her, then of marriage. Frustrated by it, Sibylle attempts to break temporarily out of her relationship with Rolf to teach him what she considers a long-overdue lesson.

Equally significant is the make-believe environment in which Stiller and Sibylle meet, a masked ball, which allows them to hide their ordinary, socially accepted identities behind the mask of an assumed character. As someone else, they can permit neglected aspects of their personalities to surface. Stiller wears the costume of a Pierrot, a stock comic character of old French pantomime who reveals himself, usually awkwardly, through his actions that generally accomplish the opposite of what he intends. Stiller could not have chosen a more appropriate costume to focus attention on his character.

Sibylle is in many respects one of the most competent and lively women Max Frisch has created, honors she shares with Sabeth and Hanna in *Homo faber* and Marianne in *Montauk*. Like most of Frisch's women, her background is upper-middle-class—in her case with actual wealth. She is well educated, and although at the time she meets Stiller she is not working professionally, she has the knowledge and skills necessary to earn her own living. She and Rolf have a four-year-old son, Hannes.

Unlike Julika, Sibylle usually evaluates her emotions and actions with a healthy measure of self-criticism. She is one of those fortunate human beings in whom a mixture of reasonable judgment and sound intuition generally leads to appropriate action, which prevents her from being trapped in a foolish situation for any length of time. She is able to make difficult decisions and to carry them out unafraid, even when the decisions affect the people she most cares about. She is usually sensitive to others' feelings, but expects those she loves to be as realistic as she is. Still, although she is capable, intelligent, independent, and eminently interesting as a character, Frisch did not create her without frailties.

When they meet, Sibylle is twenty-eight and Stiller about thirty-two. Stiller, in his Pierrot costume, is comical and full of life. He charms Sibylle completely. Their free and easy enjoyment of each other's company leads to an exchange of caresses. After Stiller learns Sibylle's name from his friend Sturzenegger, they meet several times in town and discover they have many things to talk about. They can share ideas as well as covert caresses that, afterward, seem more like memories of a dream than actual happenings.

Sibylle is attracted by the romantic image of Stiller's world, by "the magic of the provisional" (III 603/222) in the atmosphere of his studio, where she appears one afternoon, seemingly on the spur of the moment, much to Stiller's delight and surprise. She plans to stay only a short while, or so she says, but her husband is out of town and she stays much longer. When they leave the studio around midnight, they follow Sibylle's suggestion and drive in her car to a small country inn where they spend the night making love.

Their first long evening together at the studio opens new vistas to both of them. Stiller offers to cook dinner, and while he is shopping Sibylle has time to look carefully at the things in the studio. Stiller's world, she realizes, is sharply different from the solid, bourgeois order of her own environment; the difference makes her feel enchanted and adventurous. During hours of frank conversation, Stiller tells Sibylle, at her request, of his experience in the Spanish Civil War, but this time he explains what the incident really means to him: it proved that he is a failure and a traitor. Although his charge was to guard a bridge, he found himself unable to pull the trigger and kill the four French soldiers who were approaching. Deeply shamed by his failure, he lied to his superiors, claiming his Russian-made machine gun malfunctioned.

Stiller does not specifically tell Sibylle, but his comments imply, that his love for Anja, a fellow revolutionary from Poland who called him "her German dreamer" (III 615/232)—a remark, Sibylle notices, that still hurts ten years later—was ultimately responsible for Stiller's sense of failure as a soldier. He had wanted to impress Anja with an act of courage, facing four armed enemy soldiers alone, but he missed his opportunity.

Once he returns from the war, his lie about the malfunctioning weapon changes: without objecting, he allows his friends to interpret his failure of courage as humanitarianism. That false interpretation caused the tension Julika noticed the first time she met Stiller. Thus Stiller, who enlisted in the war to escape society's challenge to him as an artist, returns to Zurich to find himself in an even greater dilemma, this time facing not merely public expectation of him as an artist, but a fait accompli, a false public image of himself as a man, which he helped to create by his silence. Sibylle has the feeling that Stiller has wanted to "confess" to her, and that he feels relieved afterwards.

The incident in Spain is obviously the most traumatic experience of Stiller's life so far. Understanding his dejection and wanting to comfort him, the warm-hearted Sibylle would like to put her arms around him. She thinks better of it, though, realizing that "Stiller would have felt himself misunderstood as all men do when their seriousness is countered by a different seriousness" (III 616/234). Instead, she suggests that he may be too demanding of himself if he expects to succeed in everything he undertakes. Perhaps, she suggests, by attempting to prove himself a soldier he chose a role for which he is completely unsuited. He is, after all, an artist. Stiller rejects the idea, commenting that a woman probably is not able to understand such matters. Sibylle disagrees but says nothing. Stiller tells her:

> Ich bin kein Mann. Jahrelang habe ich noch davon geträumt: ich möchte schießen, aber es schießt nicht—ich brauche dir nicht zu sagen, was das heißt, es ist der typische Traum der Impotenz. (III 617)

> *I'm not a man. I've dreamt about it for years: I want to shoot, but the gun doesn't go off—I don't need to tell you what that means, it's a typical impotence dream.* (234)

Sibylle concludes that Stiller likes himself in the role of the inadequate male, does not want to transcend the experience in Spain but prefers to hide behind it, and does not want to be loved because he is afraid of finding himself inadequate again. Her first reaction is to leave him, but she changes her mind. She suggests they spend the night in bed together, and it turns out to be a night of fulfillment for both of them. The next day Sibylle is full of energy and happiness, eager to share her joy with everyone.

Sibylle and Stiller are happy, although perhaps not as happy as their jealous spouses suspect, Stiller/White remarks in his notebook, because their love is "a love without a roof over its head" (III 624). Obviously they cannot meet at her home. They cannot be together in Stiller's studio either, for he claims that everything there reminds him of Julika. Since Julika hardly ever visits the studio, and only one object, the elongated vase (which could be put in a closet), can visually remind him of her, Stiller must have another reason for not spending in his studio the few hours he can share with Sibylle. Is he afraid Julika will surprise them? Embraces hidden from view in a field of tall wheat, making love in the forest at night—this is romantic, even exciting, but not a long-range solution. Extended walks in the country and long talks in country inns are no substitute for a secure love-nest, either. Stiller and Sibylle are reminiscent of another Frisch pair of lovers who have a similar problem, Jürg Reinhart and Hortense in *Die Schwierigen*.

Both, meanwhile, have really fallen in love and need to act. One day, on the spur of the moment, Sibylle suggests they go to Paris. She has enough money for the two of them—her husband's money, of course. Since Stiller has few financial resources, he can accompany her only if he is willing to accept her generosity.

Their planned trip to Paris in July ends at the Zurich railroad station. Both have last-minute hesitations, although Stiller tries to cover his by resolute action. Standing on the platform, luggage in hand, he seems ready to board the waiting train, but Sibylle remains sitting on the bench and watches the train leave without them. She has not really changed her mind about wanting to go to Paris with Stiller, but she is bothered by the grim determination with which he acts on their plan. Her intuition tells her that he is bringing the ghost of his wife along. Sibylle realizes that Stiller cannot just take off and forget Julika, even for a few days, and even though she is now cared for at Davos. In August, when he learns on that first visit to Julika that her condition has worsened, he again concludes that he cannot go away to Paris, at least not now.

Stiller's and Sibylle's happiness is complicated at best. In silence, their hands interlaced, they sit in a field, two adulterers, both chewing blades of grass. The only thing in the world that seems uncomplicated to them is marriage—to each other rather than to their respective spouses, as Stiller/White comments.

During the next few weeks Stiller and Sibylle meet almost daily; Rolf does not interfere, which infuriates Sibylle. She has not stopped loving Rolf—in fact, she loves both men—and Rolf's failure to take a stand seems inappropriate to her. She cannot continue both relationships; one has to end, and she hopes fate will determine which one it will be. Sibylle is emotionally unable to make the choice, because the two men satisfy two seemingly contradictory needs: Stiller represents adventure, excitement, the unpredictability of life, while Rolf represents security and order. Rolf, by nature, is a conquerer, she muses. Although that can be terrible at times, in some respects it is also simpler. He seems to her like a big Saint Bernard that one had better not hold on a leash unless one wants to be knocked down by him. Stiller, in contrast, is her confidant. Rolf is self-righteous, a man who never apologizes for any of his actions; Stiller is addicted to apology. One could fear for Stiller, Sibylle feels, but not for Rolf. Stiller seems like a brother to her, almost like a sister.

That Stiller accepts their use of Rolf's money without question begins to bother Sibylle, and she feels that spending her husband's money to buy new clothes to make herself look pretty for Stiller is wrong. Stiller might at least protest, she thinks.

They finally plan a trip to Paris in the fall, "maybe only [for] a few weeks, maybe longer" (III 627/243), as she tells her husband. Stiller is still unable to set a specific date because he is not yet comfortable about leaving Julika, whose condition requires her to avoid any kind of excitement.

In September, Stiller becomes deeply involved in preparing an exhibition of his sculptures in Zurich. He is so occupied with that project that Sibylle cannot find a time to share her own excitement with him: she has just learned that she is pregnant. Concerned with details of the upcoming show, however, and feeling alternately exhilarated and afraid because of it, Stiller seems to have neither eyes nor ears for anything else. When he takes an afternoon off and they go sailing, Sibylle could tell him about the baby—but she does not. She keeps thinking about the differences between the two men in her life, Rolf and Stiller. She is still in love with both of them. To merge them into one person would be ideal, Sibylle thinks, as she and Stiller sail across the lake and she watches "this man who was perhaps already the father of her second child" (III 631/247). She crosses the swaying deck to him, cradles his head in her hands, and kisses him again and again. To his surprised question: "What's the matter?" (III 632/248), she has no answer.

Soon thereafter Stiller telephones to say they are going to Paris after all, at once. Sibylle is thrilled. She cannot act immediately, however, as she has commitments for the whole day. But during a promised visit to the circus with her son, she reaches a decision to leave Rolf, go to Paris with Stiller, find work, and become an independent woman. She decides "for Paris, for Stiller, for the risk" (III 633/249). Since Sibylle makes that far-reaching choice during a circus performance, one might be tempted to question its validity; how stable is she emotionally, how able to make a rational decision just then?

When Sibylle finally arrives at Stiller's studio, he is packing his suitcase, contagiously happy and surprised that she has not brought hers. Suddenly she learns that this trip has come up because Stiller has to go to Paris anyway in conjunction with his upcoming exhibition and that he thinks this is the perfect time for them to go. He needs to be there, "and Julika has no excuse to excite herself and send her temperature curve up on account of this trip" (III 635/251).

Sibylle understands instantly. Her answer is "No"—she will not go to Paris feeling like Stiller's mistress. Stiller goes to Paris alone, but he is sure she will follow him in a few days. He is wrong.

In contrast to Stiller's indecisiveness about their relationship, Sibylle realizes quickly what she must do. She tells her husband that she is not going to Paris but will spend the next week with a girlfriend at St. Gallen. Next, she telephones a trusted doctor and schedules an abortion for that week.

After her release from the hospital and an unsuccessful attempt to communicate effectively with her husband, Sibylle goes on the spur of the moment to Pontresina, ostensibly to ski (III 637-38/253). She is confused and desperately lonely. Her marriage to Rolf seems to be over, and Stiller, whose child she has just aborted, obviously regards her as only his mistress.

Stiller, back from Paris, learns to his surprise that Sibylle has gone skiing. He calls her in Pontresina but finds out little: she chatters on about superficial things. He calls her so often that the concierge finally tells him Sibylle is out, even though she is standing in the hotel lobby at that moment.

Mystified, Stiller goes to Pontresina to find out what is happening. Carrying on a stream of small talk with him, Sibylle hides her feelings of disappointment about their relationship. She shows delight and interest in everything she knows Stiller despises, and he has no way of stopping her compulsive, somewhat hysterical behavior. Sibylle becomes more talkative as Stiller grows more silent. He starts to stutter a little, something Sibylle has not noticed in him before.

Their meal in an elegant restaurant, complete with Sibylle's favorite wine, is a farce. Sibylle acts ridiculous, knows it, but cannot stop. In her emotional pain she delights in deliberately wounding Stiller. Finally, on their way back to the hotel, Sibylle admits why she did not go to Paris with him:

Es war einfach ein solcher Schock für mich . . . jetzt plötzlich paßte es dir, jetzt wo du ohnehin nach Paris fahren mußtest, jetzt hattest du einen bequemen Vorwand, jetzt sollte ich kommen, jetzt war unser Paris auf einmal möglich. In diesem Augenblick, siehst du, kam ich mir wie deine Mätresse vor. (III 647)

It was simply too much of a shock for me . . . . All of a sudden it suited you, now that you had to go to Paris anyway, now you had a good excuse, now you wanted me to come, now our Paris was suddenly possible. At that moment I felt like your mistress. . . . (261)

Stiller is silent. Sibylle, apropos of nothing, wonders aloud where she might be a year from now; Stiller's friend Sturzenegger has asked her to come to California as his secretary, at one hundred dollars a week and her passage paid for. "He's in love with me" (III 646/261), she comments, possibly quoting Rolf, as there is no evidence in the novel to support this assertion. Perhaps, she muses, she will be in California by this time next year, then adds: "It's funny. . . with you one knows perfectly well. I don't believe you will ever change, not even in your outward life" (III 647/262).

Is Sibylle merely acknowledging that Stiller is predictable? Or is she making a mistake similar to Julika's, casting a "graven image" of Stiller as a never-changing, weak, indecisive, and somewhat irresponsible, egocentric man? If the latter, her attitude is the antithesis of love, as the Jesuit explained to Julika and as Frisch wrote in his *Tagebuch 1946-1949* (II 370-74). In her abrupt reaction, once she discovers Stiller's lack of commitment to her, Sibylle is reminiscent of Yvonne in *Die Schwierigen*. When Yvonne interpreted Jürg's willingness to accept Hauswirt's offered money as a demonstration of his lack of feeling for her, she too acted abruptly. Just as that relationship ended soon thereafter, so too does this one.

Stiller and Sibylle separate for the night, agreeing to meet the next morning for breakfast. Feeling powerless to stop the ending of their relationship, Sibylle confesses: "I really loved you—" (III 647). Her use of the past tense makes clear that their relationship is over.

Stiller never shows up for breakfast. When he reappears two days later, he is pale, tired, and unshaven. For a while he will not say where he has been, but finally tells Sibylle he has been to Davos and has separated from Julika. At last he did what Sibylle wished for all summer, but now it is too late for them. Unexpectedly, she is worried about Julika, who for her has changed suddenly from a ghostlike to a real person, an ill, unhappy, and deserted sister. "You shouldn't have done that . . ." she tells him, then corrects herself: "We have no right to do that . . . . It's madness, Stiller, it's murder" (III 649/263).

During Stiller's final visit to Julika, he tells her that not only is their marriage at an end, but also his affair with Sibylle. On what he bases the latter statement is unclear—Sibylle's behavior, his own inclination, or an intuitive perception—because neither has actually made such a statement.

Sibylle is frightened by Stiller's action, but he finally feels free. He has changed during the past forty-eight hours, become more decisive.

Sibylle is so subdued, however, that Stiller asks whether something is wrong. She admits only that she was angry with him for leaving her behind in Pontresina. Finally she adds ominously: "I did something stupid, I must tell you, something very stupid" (III 650-51/265). Stiller asks about it, but her answer is interrupted first by the innkeeper, who brings coffee, and then by Stiller's rambling report of his search for Sibylle's perfume in Paris. Sibylle meanwhile keeps thinking about the past two days. Feeling deserted, her self-image low, she took revenge on both men she once loved and slept with two men she hardly knows on two consecutive nights. Her behavior seems like that of a common whore. How will Stiller react to this monstrosity? "I know that," he responds after listening to her confession, then adds, "Only I never told anyone" (III 654/267), and tells her of a similar experience from his own past. Both feel at that moment that there is a chance for them to pull their lives together.

This proves to be a false hope. The next morning, after spending a wretched night together, they separate permanently at the Pontresina railroad station.

AN ENDANGERED MARRIAGE: ROLF AND SIBYLLE

The story of Rolf and Sibylle's marriage, as it emerges from Stiller/White's notebooks, serves as a comparison with and is parallel to that of Stiller and Julika's marriage. The latter is told to Stiller/White mainly by Julika, while the former is described by both participants from their own perspectives. As a result, the notebook entries concerning Rolf and Sibylle's marriage, in particular several important incidents, are full of discrepancies that reveal specific aspects of each partner's personality.

For example, Rolf's account of his wife's visit to his office before she leaves for Pontresina (III 580-81) and Sibylle's recollection of the same visit (III 636-41) show major disparities, to which I shall return. During that conversation, Sibylle reveals something important about Rolf: his ability to express himself lucidly. Sibylle tells him: "Du kannst dich nur besser ausdrükken als ich, drum habe ich dich stets reden lassen" (III 640), *"It's only that you can express yourself better than I can, that's why I always let you talk"* (255). The ability to state one's ideas succinctly requires control over one's emotions and thoughts. As a lawyer, Rolf has obviously developed this quality; it is virtually a requirement for success in his profession. Rolf tends, therefore, to omit from his account any detail that might show him out of control and, like all Frisch's men, occasionally given to violent emotional reactions. One of these omissions, seemingly unimportant, is his failure to recount what happened when Sibylle told him that, instead of going to Paris, she would go to visit a girlfriend in St. Gallen. Upset by her proposed absence because he had scheduled their move into a new house during that week, Rolf smashed his coffee cup against the kitchen wall. This he neglects to mention when describing the incident to Stiller/White.

Although Rolf can verbally hide his sense of frustration and anguish, his actions sometimes betray him. A few days before the cup-smashing incident, when Sibylle tells him at breakfast that she and Stiller plan to spend some time together in Paris later that fall and that she therefore will need quite a lot of money, Rolf's face reddens, his hand holding a cup shakes slightly, and he jams the buttons of his overcoat into the wrong buttonholes. This time Sibylle steps up and buttons his coat correctly before he leaves for the office.

That this occasional lack of control over his emotions is not new and not a direct result of Rolf's knowing about Sibylle's affair is shown by his behavior on the night he returns home from a business trip, before he learns his wife has a lover. When Sibylle ignores his overtures to lovemaking, he shatters his beer glass by throwing it into the sink. These violent displays of temper occur regularly in the marriage.

Stiller/White, in his notebooks, records two relevant observations about Rolf after their first meeting in jail: Rolf is a skeptic "who doesn't even believe everything he says himself" (III 383/26), and Rolf seems self-conscious, which leads Stiller/White to conclude, in surprise: "This man has some confession to make to me" (III 383/26). The confession Rolf ultimately makes is the story of his marriage. In ironic juxtaposition, Frisch manages here to have a prosecutor confessing to an inmate the misdeeds of his marital life.

In his work as an attorney, Rolf is concerned about problems of human interaction and relationship in which daily repetition may itself be the source of the problem. In a marriage, he has seen, routine and habit may eventually result in monotony and boredom. Rolf shares this awareness and concern with most of Frisch's men, who tend, like Kilian in *Bin oder die Reise nach Peking*, to contrast the dull routine of daily life with the adventure they perceive they are missing and which they believe could be theirs in "Peking."

To ensure that monotony does not threaten his own marriage, Rolf developed, after serious thought and research in several disciplines, he claims, a theoretical model for a marriage that allows enough personal freedom, including brief extramarital affairs, to keep the marriage alive and interesting for both partners. In such an arrangement, Rolf believes, the partners can live with dignity and without deception. He claims that his model is based on the absolute equality of men and women, and he expects his wife to accept it. When she finally does, he cannot tolerate the consequences.

Sibylle is fundamentally unable to accept Rolf's theory, no matter how often he expounds it. She calls it "eine Männer-Theorie" (III 557), *"a man's theory"* (181), and intuitively rebels against it. Although she cannot counter Rolf's views with logical arguments, she dismisses them, insisting "that life couldn't be solved with theories" (III 558/*181*). She always feels hurt when he has a brief affair with another woman or when she suspects he has slept with someone on one of his business trips, especially because, in conformity with his despised theory, he expects her to trust his love for her. She is certain that his theory is self-serving, arrogant, chauvinistic, and based on his supremely self-confident assumption that no one could ever replace him in her life.

Sibylle suspects that if his self-confidence were shaken only once, his theory about a viable modern marriage would soon collapse. Her flirtation with a British officer during a visit to Cairo was evidently not threatening enough. Perhaps a brief affair with the Pierrot she met at an artists' masked ball will frighten Rolf back to his senses.

Sibylle's affair with the "Maskenball Pierrot," as Rolf refers to Stiller, has the desired effect. Rolf thinks often about the rival. He decides suddenly to build his own house, which Sibylle has always wanted, and at the location they chose together years ago. Now he buys the lot even before telling her about his plans. Sibylle's reaction is less jubilant than he expects. Rolf is surprised. A week later he brings a young architect, Sturzenegger, to talk about the house and their special requirements—for example, a master bedroom or separate bedrooms? They are interrupted by a telephone call, which Sibylle answers strangely, so that Rolf surmises the caller is her masked-ball Pierrot. Afterward Sibylle seems jumpy. She studies the architect's plans dutifully and finds everything agreeable: one decision or another, it seems not to matter. Rolf is puzzled. She acts as if she would never live in the house.

Sibylle's affair with Stiller progresses and leads to the long evening at Stiller's studio and the night they spend together at an inn, while Rolf is in London at a legal conference. The next day, Sibylle is eager to share her happiness. Anticipating her husband's return, she is both excited and apprehensive about confessing her adultery. As she meets him at the airport, she is sure he will notice a change in her. He does not. In the car he talks about rough flying weather over the English Channel. He is tired and wants to be pampered a bit by Sibylle—as if he had returned from the front lines, she thinks, not a business trip.

Sibylle is surprised that she can now look at her husband without the fear that he is hiding something from her. Suddenly she feels free of the delusion of not being able to live without Rolf, of whom she is still fond, but now the feeling is mixed with compassion for his somewhat arrogant self-assurance. Sooner than Rolf, she notices a new tone in her own voice. She suggests they go to the movies; when he agrees, she drops the idea, ostensibly out of motherly concern for him; he said he is tired. Compassionately, she places a hand on his arm as she drives. He tells her she looks splendid, to which she responds noncommittally: "Es geht mir auch sehr gut" (III 621), "*Yes, I feel fine*" (238). She now believes that Rolf knows everything.

He does not, which Sibylle cannot understand. The more time that passes without his knowing about her adultery, the more thoroughly everything between her and Rolf will be poisoned, Sibylle thinks. She fears that, once Rolf knows what she has done, he will simply put his arm around her in a gesture of benevolent understanding, not taking her affair seriously and thereby making her feel like a traitor to Stiller; if that happens, she will hate Rolf, she is sure. When they arrive home everything there, the furniture, the books, the whole comfortable atmosphere of their apartment seems to be conspiring on Rolf's behalf, so that Sibylle for the present gives up her attempt to confess.

Rolf looked forward to a quiet, relaxing evening at home, but finds Sibylle uncooperative. She stays busy with chores, obviously avoiding him. Rolf believes that Sibylle is being difficult because she suspects once again that he was with another woman on his trip to London. He has had enough of her bourgeois, narrow-minded views on marriage. Besides, this time she is wrong: he has not been with anyone. Once more he launches, he hopes for the last time, into an explanation of his modern marriage theory.

Sibylle lets him talk without interruption, although she would like to tell him that she is not in the least jealous and that now she understands his ideas better than ever. She remains silent, finally kisses him on the forehead, and goes to her room, locking the door without thinking. When Rolf insists that she open the door, he is perplexed when he sees a happy, smiling face instead of the tearful one he expects. Suddenly the truth of what has occurred in his absence dawns on him. Clumsily, he asks, "You've been with a man?" (III 624/240), to which Sibylle replies simply, "Yes." Happy now that he knows the truth, she asks him to leave the room.

Rolf accepts the startling truth with what Sibylle takes to be a remarkable calm. He leaves the apartment abruptly, however, and stays away for several days—to give her some peace and freedom, Sibylle believes, and is grateful.

Rolf is anything but calm. He, his marriage, and his whole philosophy of marriage are about to be tested severely. He boards a night train without luggage or any idea where he is going, glad that at this late hour, midnight, a train is still leaving Zurich and that he does not have to face Sibylle in the morning. The greater the distance between them, the better, he thinks as the train crosses into Italy.

In the early morning hours he reaches Milan. As the train waits at the deserted station, childish plans of revenge race through Rolf's head. The delay makes him even more conscious of the aimlessness of his flight from Sibylle.

Rolf goes on to Genoa. Tired, unshaven, with nothing to carry except a superfluous coat, he walks through the city and stops at a corner bar filled with taxi drivers and porters, where he drinks a cup of black coffee. He keeps thinking of Sibylle and their last conversation. She does not know, she said, whether they will divorce or how they will go on. One of Sibylle's comments keeps running through his head. It makes him so angry that he talks to himself as he trudges aimlessly through the streets of Genoa. Sibylle said:

> Du hast mir keine Freiheit zu geben. Was soll denn das heißen? Ich nehme mir die Freiheit schon selbst, wenn ich sie brauche. (III 552)

> *You don't have to give me my freedom. What do you mean by that? I can take freedom for myself, if I need it.* (176)

After Sibylle's admission of her adultery—a conversation she, interestingly, does not mention to Stiller/White—Rolf must have indicated that he would agree to a divorce if she wanted one, using the common expression "jemanden freigeben," i.e., to give someone his or her freedom. Sibylle's furious reaction to his choice of words spotlights her strong independent streak, which in theory Rolf has been encouraging. Has he not told her, time and again, that she ought to embrace a more liberal concept of marriage, accepting his brief extramarital affairs? Now that the situation is reversed, Rolf reacts with anything but the broadmindedness he preached to Sibylle. As he walks through Genoa, he curses his wife on the other side of the Alps in language that makes him feel better the more vulgar it is. He has never behaved this way before. His lofty theory of a modern, liberal marriage has come crashing down on his head the first time it is tested.

In Genoa, Rolf has an experience of considerable significance that continues to haunt him, like an oppressive dream, for many years. This experience, which involves a parcel of flesh-colored material (sometimes translated as "pink"), has been the object of numerous speculations by interpreters of this Frisch novel. It begins when he is conned into lending an unknown Genoese 20,000 lire and accepting as temporary security the package of cloth. Then follow many fruitless attempts to find the Genoese and reclaim his 20,000 lire, eventually to sell the cloth, to give it away, even to abandon it. No matter how desperately he tries he cannot dispose of this flesh-colored burden until, just before boarding his Zurich-bound train, he stuffs it down a toilet at the railway station (III 553-557,559-566,570).

In my view, this episode is central to Rolf's theory of marriage and symbolizes the basic problem in his marriage to Sibylle. Rolf himself provides the clue for this view when he states:

> Die meisten von uns haben so ein Paket mit fleischfarbenem Stoff, nämlich Gefühle, die sie von ihrem intellektuellen Niveau aus nicht wahrhaben wollen. Es gibt zwei Auswege, die zu nichts führen; wir töten unsere primitiven und also unwürdigen Gefühle ab, soweit als möglich, auf die Gefahr hin, daß dadurch das Gefühlsleben überhaupt abgetötet wird, oder wir geben unseren unwürdigen Gefühlen einfach einen anderen Namen. Wir lügen sie

um. Wir etikettieren sie nach dem Wunsch unseres Bewußtseins. (III 668)

Most of us have [such] a parcel of [flesh-colored] cloth—namely, our feelings—that from our intellectual level we should like to ignore. There are two ways out of the difficulty that lead nowhere: either we kill our primitive and therefore unworthy feelings, as far as we can, at the risk of killing our emotional life altogether, or we simply give our unworthy feelings another name. We lie about them, disguise them as something else. We label them to satisfy the wishes of our consciousness. (281)

Rolf's use of the adjectives "flesh-colored," "primitive," and "unworthy" in this passage in association with human feelings makes it clear that he means sensual, sexual, primal feelings of lust that an individual denies harboring, even craving, the more formally educated he is and the higher his professional or social status.³ Repressing those feelings may lead to emotional suicide, as Rolf points out; the person involved gives them another, more easily acceptable name, such as "natural drive," without ever coming to terms with these feelings.

Rolf's name for these feelings is subsumed by the name "open marriage." His marriage theory allows room for sexual primitivism, adventure, and excitement in extramarital affairs. The immediate cost to the marriage is the absence of commitment; the long-term price is the gradual destruction of the marriage from within, so that eventually only its shell remains. Rolf's inability to rid himself of the parcel of flesh-colored cloth illustrates that he does not come to terms with those feelings but represses them.

Although this traumatic experience haunts Rolf, it also helps him to recognize that his theory of marriage is indeed a self-serving hoax, the "Männer-Theorie" that Sibylle always labelled it. He hides his fierce jealousy of Sibylle's affair, first by fleeing from Zurich and later by pretended indifference, but he clearly cannot accept the consequences of his marriage theory when his partner uses it. Neither he nor the young Jürg Reinhart in *Die Schwierigen* can accept the practical consequences of his theory about living. Jürg's theory costs him his "marriage" to Yvonne;

Rolf's almost costs him his marriage to Sibylle. It actually does, for a while.

During those four days in Genoa, Rolf realizes that he really loves Sibylle and does not want to lose her. Despite his chauvinism in considering women first as objects for sexual gratification, he believes he has been trying to share with Sibylle a "livable marriage" in which the partners maintain their dignity and exist without deceit. His life with Sibylle, he thinks now, may not be quite what she thought it might be when they married, but it is not a living hell, either. It is a marriage like many others, he believes, and for him "das wirkliche Leben," as he understands it.

Rolf returns from Genoa with his behavior unchanged. He seems to be in control of his emotions and his behavior. One fact, however, leaves him powerless: during those four days his love for Sibylle became the focal point of his life, but *her* focus was suddenly "umgebucht," "*rebooked*," as he puts it (III 566), to the other gentleman.

From the train station in Zurich Rolf takes a taxi to their apartment, then changes his mind, returns to town, and rents a hotel room for the night. The next day, a Sunday, he goes out to look at the house they are building. There he runs into the architect, Sturzenegger, the man Rolf has now decided to suspect as his wife's lover. Although he has not asked Sibylle her lover's name, he knows she likes the young architect; in fact, on recollection, he suspects they were lovers the first time Sturzenegger came to the house, because Sibylle went humming through the apartment after he had been there. Even Rolf could have known that his suspicion of Sturzenegger makes no sense, but the architect is a convenient target for his jealousy.

On this Sunday at the building site, Sturzenegger tells Rolf that he will leave soon for California to build a large factory there, something Sibylle already mentioned—except that Rolf then understood "Canada," not "California." The news confuses Rolf. Why is Sturzenegger going to California and leaving Sibylle, his beloved, in Zurich? Rolf is not concerned enough to pursue the question, however, nor does it puzzle him that Sturzenegger and Sibylle still address each other with the courtesy form of "you," "Sie." He is far more concerned that no one in Zurich ever see him as upset and jealous as he was in Genoa.

Rolf's decision not to let Sibylle know how he really feels about her turns out to be a serious mistake. Although Sibylle, the one in the wrong at the moment, desperately seeks a sign of his continued love for her, he decides to punish her by appearing at all times detached and composed, as if whatever she does is of no concern to him. All he has to do to hide his emotions is to recall the scornful, triumphant look on Sibylle's face before he left the apartment. His detachment and composure will force her to her knees, he is sure. Rolf demonstrates here how little he knows his wife.

For a whole harrowing spring and summer Rolf tries to pretend he can live by his theory of marriage when Sibylle practices it. He accords her complete independence. His consistent response to her is "Do as you like." During the summer he is appointed a public prosecutor; Sibylle, for social reasons, seems pleased. They appear arm in arm at social functions. Their behavior is a farce, but socially necessary, as both realize. For one of them to move out of the apartment and live alone would startle at least the relatives, so they continue to live together, giving the outward appearance of an unchanged relationship.

During the summer Rolf succeeds in convincing himself, without a doubt, that Sturzenegger is indeed his wife's lover. The architect, like Sibylle not yet thirty, enjoys her lively personality. Rolf is already forty-five. Feeling somewhat inadequate these days, Rolf thinks it natural that Sibylle and Sturzenegger should be attracted to each other.

One day in early fall Rolf, in a conversation that Sturzenegger must find peculiar, explains his theory of a modern, viable marriage. When Sturzenegger asks him: "Have you ever known a man ... who really could bear it, I mean, who didn't just pretend to —?" (III 576/197), Rolf smiles and replies: "I thought I was that man." He has finally admitted to himself that he cannot bear the implications of his theory.

This conversation takes place in Rolf's car, as he drives the young architect home. When Sturzenegger finds out that Rolf believes he and Sibylle are lovers, he is surprised and embarrassed. He will be leaving soon for his assignment in California, and so he does not deny the accusation. He invites Rolf inside for a glass of wine, which Rolf declines. Sturzenegger quickly disappears into his house.

Rolf's plan to punish Sibylle by remaining detached is partially successful. When she tells him that she needs money for her stay in Paris with Stiller, Rolf's nonverbal reaction is shaky but his verbal response is calm; he asks her how much she will need. Rolf does not answer when she tries to elicit his opinion of her decision, nor does he comment on her obvious regard for him and his reputation by going to Paris instead of pursuing the affair in Zurich. Her declaration that unless she and her lover were seriously in love they would not go off together—"I'm not irresponsible," she points out (III 628/244)— evokes from Rolf only the noncommittal response: "You must do what you think right" (III 628/244). Sibylle is dumbfounded. Does he not care that his wife is running off with another man? Does he no longer love her? Has he ever? Sibylle simply cannot understand him.

Rolf, of course, cares deeply, and he still loves her. He is shackled not only by his decision to hide his feelings, but also by his natural inability to share them. Exposing his emotions does not fit the stereotypical male image Rolf has of himself.

Rolf's theory of marriage almost crumbles when, with Sibylle away, he has to manage the move into their new home by himself; his self-control cracks, as his interactions with the movers illustrate (III 578). At the new house, Rolf has all of Sibylle's belongings stacked in her room; crates and boxes everywhere create a disorderly atmosphere that pleases only little Hannes. Suddenly Rolf, looking at the general confusion and not knowing whether his marriage will continue or end in divorce, asks himself: "What [do] independence and freedom in marriage really mean. . . ?" (III 578/200). He decides they mean common property and all kinds of utensils and appliances and a maid to keep things clean. And Hannes? Rolf does not want to think about Hannes, but he knows that the present situation cannot go on much longer.

Her abortion behind her, Sibylle returns at the end of the week. Hannes shows her around their new home. As she looks at the boxes and satchels stacked in her room, she decides they are "things, nothing but things, a pile to put a match to"

(III 637). When Hannes wants to show her his father's new room, Sibylle leaves the house abruptly. She has to see Rolf; they have to talk. She has to know whether he still loves her. Unexpectedly, she appears in Rolf's office. When he tells her that a certain Mr. Stiller, "your lover I suppose" (III 637/253), called in her absence, she picks up her purse, ready to leave. Rolf asks where she is going, and she blurts out "to Pontresina," recalling a poster advertising a winter vacation. However, it is only November, not real winter yet. Rolf responds laconically: "Do as you please" (III 638/253).

But Sibylle does not leave his office. Instead, she observes: "I think it's ridiculous . . . completely ridiculous, the way we are behaving, childish . . ." (III 638/253). Rolf remains silent. In the conversation that follows, these two characters' differences in personality become clear not only by *what* they report to Stiller/White about this stormy conversation but also by *how* they report it. Rolf's report—detached, thoughtful, and seemingly objective—covers one printed page (III 580-81/201-02); Sibylle's account—detailed, subjective, showing signs of emotional turmoil—lasts for five printed pages (III 636-41/251-56). This record is Sibylle's counterpart to what Rolf said about marriage when he reported the Genoa episode to Stiller/White (III 557-60/180-83).

Sibylle takes on the role of the injured party and launches into a long, somewhat disjointed discourse about their marriage, hoping all the while that Rolf will stop her with a gesture or a word that shows he still loves her. He does not. His only response is an occasional concise summary of her comments or a brief question to force her to express herself more precisely. What emerges from Sibylle's tour de force is not only the picture of an unhappy woman who loves her husband and is waiting desperately for him to tell her he loves her, too, but also the picture of a married couple never able to communicate effectively about anything of importance.

Marriage, the primary topic of Sibylle's comments, is for her a fate, not a legalized relationship. In her view, her husband is as vital in her life, as important and integral, as her father or her son; he is not just any man, interchangeable with the next. Sibylle believes in these ideas about marriage, she tells Rolf, even today. She does not know where she got these ideas, and she knows Rolf considers them bourgeois. His theory of marriage is "nonsense," she maintains; she never wanted any "playing room" in the marriage. She does not want to be just any woman in her husband's life, the one he just happens to be married to; she wants to be the only one. She imagined her marriage to be different from what it has turned out to be; she has listened to his "lectures on marriage" only because she thought his knowledge was based on experience, and she has let him continue to talk on the subject without having much faith in what he was saying because he could express himself so much better than she. Theirs, Sibylle insists, is just a legalized affair, not a marriage, entered into because she was pregnant at the time. Rolf is nothing but a married bachelor, she tells him. The fervor of her accusations illustrates how much she cares about the marriage. But although Rolf listens attentively, she is unable to penetrate his composure.

The major difference between Sibylle's and Rolf's views of their marriage is commitment. Rolf, Sibylle realizes, never made a total commitment to her or to their marriage. She did, because that is what marriage means to her: openness and sharing of each other's fears, hopes, joys, and sorrows; consideration for and support of each other. In her kind of marriage, divorce is not possible. She never expected she and Rolf would have to face that issue; it was something experienced by other people whose marriages constituted little more than legalized affairs performed for the sake of bourgeois tastes. Those marriages were invalid from the start, Sibylle believes. Now she recognizes that their marriage falls into the same category. Rolf does not want a wife, she tells him, he only wants to conquer her with his generosity, placing her into bondage so he can enjoy his freedom.

Sibylle stops suddenly and calls everything she has said "nonsense." Before she has a chance to answer Rolf's question about where she saw the *sense*, presumably in their relationship, the telephone interrupts them, calling Rolf away. The communicative gulf between them is apparent in their final exchange before they leave the office:

Rolf: I see ... you're disappointed that I didn't forbid you anything.

Sibylle: No . . . you're really not in a position to forbid me anything, Rolf, that's the miserable thing about it, from the beginning you merely had an affair with me, to be exact, and therefore no right to prevent me from having another affair—
Rolf: You must do what you think right. (III 641/256)

Rolf walks Sibylle to the elevator. Now, she realizes, she *has* to go to Pontresina.

There, feeling lonely and lost, Sibylle waits for Rolf to call her, telling her that he misses her, loves her, wants her to come back. Rolf never calls. Instead, Stiller turns up at the resort, and she ends her affair with him.

Sibylle cannot simply return to Rolf, even though she loves him, because he has given no sign that he loves her and that they might be able to continue their marriage, though under different conditions. She needs time to find her balance again before she can know where she belongs. If she allows Rolf to continue to support her, she will lose her personal freedom forever. Sturzenegger's invitation to come to Redwood City as his secretary seems to provide exactly the opportunity she needs to put herself and her life back in order.

On her return to Zurich she tells Rolf of her decision; he agrees to a divorce. Sibylle leaves it to him to start the process but asks him to let her take Hannes with her to the United States. After twenty-four hours' consideration, Rolf agrees.

Sibylle and her son never get farther west than New York, where she establishes a life of her own. When Sturzenegger comes from California to take her with him to be the secretary he really does not need, Sibylle decides not to go. She has already found a suitable position in Manhattan in which she can use her knowledge of foreign languages. In Pontresina, Sibylle learned that the path from wife to whore is short. Holding down a job at eighty dollars a week as a secretary-translator and being completely independent is therefore of utmost importance to her. For the first time she, daughter of a wealthy family, has to live like other people: lonely, responsible for herself and her child, dependent on no one, living by her own talents. She welcomes the challenge; meeting it restores her self-respect.

Although Sibylle loves her new life, her job, translating from English to German, French, and Italian business letters that always say the same things, is utterly boring; she wants to leave after six months, but her employer doubles her salary and she stays. Sometimes her monastic life is lonely, but she enjoys the freedom. Her first apartment is anything but luxurious: it is so dark, even during the day, that she can neither read nor sew without turning on the light; if she opens a window to let in fresh air, the soot in the air quickly covers everything; and to sleep at night she has to wear earplugs to shut out the noise from the street. After her salary raise she moves to an apartment on Riverside Drive with a view of the Hudson River, continues to rebuild her life, and adapts happily to a different society.

Once, in Central Park, she thinks for a moment that a passerby she sees only from the rear is Stiller. A few days later, going down a subway escalator, she believes she sees him again, going up. He stares at her, but gives no sign of recognition. As she turns around in the busy subway station, she sees him coming down the escalator again. He looks like Stiller and wears a GI overcoat like the one Stiller always wore. Is it he? Is he following her? In the confusion of the crowded station she involuntarily enters the next subway car. She never sees the man again.

After Sibylle has lived in New York for two and a half years, Rolf appears. He has come to New York, not on business, he tells her, but to see her, to ask her if she would be willing to resume their marriage. Still unable to express his feelings, Rolf makes Sibylle an either-or proposition: either they get a divorce, or they live together—"but once and for all," he adds (III 661/274). Neither has changed much, they discover, except both have grown a little older. As they look down on Manhattan at night from the Rainbow Room at Rockefeller Center, sipping martinis, they look at each other now and then in silence, smiling a bit mockingly as they realize they do not need to be separated by an ocean. Rolf's love for Sibylle, she notices, expresses itself in his eyes, not in words or touch; she feels there is no one in the world to whom she is closer than this man. She does not deny her feelings, but she asks for twenty-four hours' time to think about his proposal.

The resumed marriage, based this time on a mutual commitment to each other and to the marriage, must have worked. Stiller/White records in his notebooks that an elated Rolf one day announces that his second child, a girl, weighing nearly seven pounds, was born the night before (III 566).

INTERLUDE 2: STILLER'S ESCAPE

After Stiller breaks away from his marriage, his profession, and his home in Zurich, he eventually arrives in the United States. There and in Mexico he undergoes a series of experiences that change him profoundly. In the novel this change is signaled by his adopting a new name: Jim White.

This portion of Frisch's *Stiller* deals primarily with the protagonist's search for his identity, which is not my focus here. During this period, however, two females, one a mulatto woman, Florence, and the other a cat, Little Grey, who is strangely evocative of Julika, play important roles in Stiller's life. Although Stiller/White alludes in his notebooks to other relationships while he was away from Zurich, those with Florence and with Little Grey are the ones that reveal the most about his character and the inherent possibilities that lead him eventually to return to Switzerland as James Larkin White.

Jim White is the hero of the cave story that Stiller/White tells his jailer Knobel.[4] Based on a legend of the discovery and exploration of the Carlsbad (New Mexico) Caverns at the turn of the century by one James Larkin (Jim) White and his Mexican friend, "the other Jim," it *is* a story. Stiller/White makes this clear when Knobel, suddenly confused, asks him at the end of his tale: "—are you Jim White then?" (III 521/*148*), and Stiller/White answers with a laugh: "No, . . . not really! But what I've been through myself, you see, was exactly the same—exactly" (III 521/*148*).

This admission is as close as Stiller/White can come to putting into words the extraordinary nature of his own change. Through an analogous tale, with Jungian overtones, he relates the exploration of his inner self and the triumph and emergence of the new self from the cave. This tale of transformation from the old self to the new, from Stiller to White, is a specific example of what Stiller/White means when he writes in his notebook: "Man kann alles erzählen, nur nicht sein wirkliches Leben" (III 416), *"You can put anything into words, except your own life"* (55). To describe his own reality, Stiller/White admits, he has no language, no words. So he invents one story after another, some in multiple versions, to convey that reality.[5]

One of these stories is about Florence, a vivacious mulatto woman who was actually Stiller/White's next-door neighbor in Oakland, California. He told the first version of the story, a dramatic fictional account of their relationship, to Knobel (III 402-07). However, the final version of the story, which Stiller/White tells to no one in particular but simply records for himself in his notebook, is the important one.

According to the early version of the tale Knobel hears, Jim White, the adventurer, alias Stiller/White, rescues Florence from a fire in Oregon, kidnaps her, escapes with her to California, and kills her husband Joe who pursued them to Mexico. In truth, however, Stiller/White and Florence had a fragile relationship. It was never intimate in the traditional sense, and yet, because it accompanied the journey that led Stiller to become Jim White, it was indeed uniquely "intimate."

Florence is not one of his fictional characters, Stiller/White emphasizes; she really exists. She lives with her parents next door to the cottage where Stiller/White is living. He watches her whenever she is out in her yard, sometimes even talks to her. He admires her, is intrigued by her, even a little in love with her, he admits in his notebook.

In the final version of her story (III 537-40), Florence emerges as a particularly graceful woman, especially when she dances. Perhaps Florence's graceful dancing reminds him of Julika, the ballerina. As he watches Florence dance one evening, first with a tall black man, then with other partners, and finally alone, he recognizes the naturalness with which her whole being expresses itself in the dance and his own lack of physical grace that makes him feel like a cripple by comparison. Florence exhausts four partners without ever appearing tired herself, and then stops suddenly—exuberant, happy, and not at all embarrassed. Stiller has an opportunity to join in her dance but does not. He could not, he writes, perhaps because he was too self-conscious—not only because he lacked grace himself but also because he felt out of place, a white man in a bar filled with black people. He has actually been looking for Florence, going from bar to bar. When she notices him among the onlookers, she greets him politely. Stiller/White reacts with confusion; he feels he could never be an adequate man for this earthy woman, although she absolutely fascinates him.

One Sunday Stiller/White, from behind drawn curtains, watches a curious scene: Florence, her parents, and a large group of guests, all overdressed for a hot Sunday afternoon, are having a backyard party. The occasion, he discovers, is Florence's wedding: she has married Joe, the tall man he saw her dancing with. Joe is a sergeant stationed in Frankfurt and has only three weeks of leave left.

Stiller/White misses Florence a great deal during those three weeks. Hoping to see her at least from a distance, he goes to the nearby black Baptist church he knows she attends, but sees only her husband. While watching the people in the church, Stiller/White becomes acutely aware of a paradox. He, an outsider here because he is white, watches a church full of people who themselves are outsiders in a society in which he is an insider. These "outsiders" act, and some of them dress and deliberately look, like insiders—for example, the young woman who has applied a coat of white powder to her face and neck. The irony is not lost on Stiller/White. He thinks about the absurdity of man's lifelong yearning to be someone different, about how difficult it is to accept oneself as one is. That problem, of course, is Stiller's, too.

When Florence comes home after her husband has returned to his unit in Germany, one of her first questions to Stiller/White is about his cat, Little Grey. The story of Little Grey serves a function similar to that of the cave story: to externalize and illustrate Stiller's internal struggles.

Stiller/White acquired Little Grey along with the cottage in which he lives rent-free. In return for the living quarters, he is to feed the cottage-owner's cat, even though Stiller/White dislikes cats. This cat is accustomed to eating in the kitchen, but Stiller/White is determined she shall stay outdoors. The persistent cat sits on the sills outside closed windows and meows all night, wanting to be let in, wanting to share Stiller's life. Night after night she keeps him awake and simultaneously, he fears, gives him a reputation for cruelty among his neighbors, especially Florence. All attempts to keep the cat outside are futile. One night, furious at her, he grabs the four-legged tyrant and puts her, literally, on ice in the refrigerator—as Stiller once put Julika "on ice" after they started to grow apart by staying at his studio for days (III 445).

But Stiller demonstrated years ago that he cannot kill. He removes the cat from the refrigerator after a few hours and nurses her back to health, treating her as she wants to be treated. He realizes she is taking the same advantage of his guilty conscience, purring and rubbing against him to show she forgives him, that Julika always did—first making Stiller feel guilty about his conduct and then forgiving him for whatever she made him feel guilty about. Furious with himself and his failure to be firm even with a cat, he grabs Little Grey, the Julika stand-in that is terrorizing his life, and throws her out of the window as far as he can, putting as much physical distance between himself and the cat as possible, just as he did with Julika by leaving her in Davos and coming to the United States.

Alas, Stiller cannot escape his conscience, no matter how great the distance between himself and the creature that makes his life miserable. When Little Grey does not return, he searches for her nightly and asks his neighbors if they have seen her. When the cat finally jumps on the window sill after eleven days, she has "a gaping wound in her face dripping with blood, and [is] looking at me as though I had wounded her" (III 414/53-54). Again Stiller nurses her back to health and suffers because he has given in to her once more. One night, on impulse, he checks to be sure her wounds have healed and then carries her quietly into the garden. Thereupon the whole circus starts anew: Stiller refusing to let the cat into the house, the animal spending the night sitting at the cottage's closed window, meowing pitifully, preventing Stiller from sleeping and alerting the neighbors to his cruelty.

Although Stiller/White is adept at telling fantastic stories, there is little doubt that the cat, like Florence, really exists. Florence asks about her nearly every time she sees Stiller/White and once carries the cat, injured and bleeding, home to him in her arms. What is doubtful is that Stiller mistreated the cat as badly as Stiller/White claims he did. On the subconscious level, though, Little Grey and Julika are interchangeable: the cat is an externalization of the "mistreated" Julika whom Stiller left at Davos. Stiller/White specifically establishes that connection, writing, "And if it wasn't my graceful ballerina, it was Little Grey, the graceful beast of a cat, that kept jumping on to my window sill although it had nothing to say to me" (III 685-86/296). As the cat sits on the sill, looking accusingly at Stiller with its glowing green eyes, so Julika "sits" at the window sill of his subconscious, looking at him with the same accusing expression.

Stiller's prolonged battle with "[this] graceful beast of a cat" (III 685/296) has specific echoes of his marriage to Julika. In a dream, Stiller once tried to strangle Julika (III 494); he finally ran away from her, leaving her at Davos, in order *not* to kill her, although he is now certain that his flight from her is equal to murder. When he first tells the story of the cat to Dr. Bohnenblust, his defense counselor, Stiller/White admits: "I could not cope with this animal" (III 414). He could have been talking about Stiller's relationship with and marriage to Julika, which he could not cope with, either.

Subconsciously the returned Stiller, as Stiller/White, is still unable to come to terms with his past relationship with Julika who, like the matador in a bullfight in which grace opposes force, has hooked her barbs into him. Frisch laid the groundwork for this comparison by once describing the two barbed banderillas hanging crossed on Stiller's studio wall. Although Stiller does not take them off the wall when he pantomimes a bullfight for Sibylle (III 605-08)—Sibylle comments that he seems to be afraid of them—he demonstrates vividly how the banderillero, who sticks his barbs into the bull's neck, prepares the bull for the real fight with the matador. As Stiller describes in detail the plight of the wounded bull, who eventually has six barbed banderillas sticking in his bloodied neck, it seems to Sibylle as if, symbolically, Stiller has been similarly wounded. His obsessively detailed description of the final round between the matador and the bull resembles a confrontation between a graceful dancer and the brute force of an enraged animal, at the end of which grace and skill win over naked force. The parallel is clear. Like the bull, Stiller is wounded by the barbs of the banderillas the ballerina Julika stuck into him.

Believing his life to be useless, Stiller attempts suicide with a small-caliber pistol he finds in his rented cottage and for which he has only one bullet. Perhaps the old weapon, which he cleans carefully, does indeed fire prematurely, as Stiller/White later suspects. More likely, however, the man who already demonstrated that he cannot take another man's life, cannot even kill a cat, is not able to take his own life, either, no matter how firm his resolve. The bullet does not penetrate his brain but only grazes his skull. Only in his invented stories, not even in the dreams in which his frustrations and anger seek release in violent action, does Stiller succeed in killing any living creature.

Florence hears the shot and is the one to reach him first. She holds his battered head in her hands, trying her best to keep him conscious. She succeeds, although Stiller is close to death.[6] He remembers the experience of moving through a dark, narrow pipe at the end of which is a bright light. But he does not reach the end of the pipe; he does not die. Instead, he is given a chance to decide for himself to live once more, "jetzt aber so, daß ein wirklicher Tod zustande kommt" (III 727), *"but this time so that a real death [takes] place"* (334). A real death, however, can only take place after Stiller has lived a real life, "ein wirkliches Leben," which Stiller/White seems to indicate has not yet happened.

Stiller/White comments that he was never closer to the essence of grace than at that moment. He later refers to this encounter with death as a meeting with "his angel." He is unable to explain the experience more precisely, for language fails him in his written account as it fails him again when he tries to define his angel to Rolf. "As soon as I try to describe it," he says, "it leaves me, then I can't see it any more myself" (III 702/311).

At the moment of experiencing that special grace, Stiller chooses life. Afterward he has the distinct feeling of having just been born. He is unconditionally ready to be nothing else but the person he is born—reborn—to be, to seek no other life than the one he has just received and which he cannot throw away.

That reborn person is *not* the old Stiller, whose decisive

psychological experience occurred in the Spanish Civil War. There he tried to prove himself something he is not: a soldier who carries out orders without questioning them, a man who can pull the trigger as ordered. Stiller, the artist, although sympathetic to social and political causes, is not the man to force either social or political change with a gun in his hand. Thus, what Stiller thought of as treachery and as demonstrating his failure as a man is instead only an error in judgement arising from insecurity and lack of knowledge of his true identity.

To demonstrate that the new, reborn Stiller is a different person, he chooses for his new identity the name of Jim White, the man whose cave experience and existential murder of "the other Jim," his alter ego, symbolizes Stiller's own rebirth. Both men, forced to make a choice, have chosen to live. The "new" Stiller, as Jim White, accepts himself as he is, acquires an American passport, and returns to Zurich, expecting his associates also to accept him as the person he is now. At the Swiss border, however, a fellow traveler, reading a magazine, recognizes him from a picture as the sculptor Anatol Ludwig Stiller, who disappeared from Zurich seven years earlier. He notifies the border officials, who arrest Stiller/White on a number of charges, among them punching a border guard who refused to let go of his arm.

A DIFFICULT COURTSHIP: STILLER/WHITE AND JULIKA

Jim White meets Julika Stiller-Tschudy, who lives in Paris, for the first time in his jail cell in Zurich, where he landed as a result of the border incident. The Swiss authorities sent her a series of photographs of the man they arrested, whom she recognizes as her missing husband, Anatol Ludwig Stiller.

Their first meeting begins with Julika's casual greeting, "How are you?" (III 408/48), which signals that she recognizes and accepts him as her lost husband; it ends violently with Jim White losing his temper. Frustrated by Julika's insistence on seeing only her missing husband before her, Stiller/White throws her onto his bunk, kneels above her, holds her down with one hand and, with the other, grabs her chin to keep her from speaking. Had Knobel not entered the cell at that moment, no telling what might have happened.

Stiller/White breaks off his notebook entry at that point, leaving the possibilities open. Might he have tried to strangle her? Based on Stiller's dreams about strangling his wife, this is conceivable. That violent outburst, which, like his earlier one against the border guard, was caused by frustration, becomes in retrospect an early clue that Jim White and Anatol Ludwig Stiller are the same man.

After Julika leaves, Stiller/White writes down his first impression of her at length:

> Ihre Haare sind rot, der gegenwärtigen Mode entsprechend sogar sehr rot, jedoch nicht wie Hagebutten-Konfitüre, eher wie trockenes Menning-Pulver. Sehr eigenartig. Und dazu ein sehr feiner Teint; Alabaster mit Sommersprossen. Ebenfalls sehr eigenartig, aber schön. Und die Augen? Ich würde sagen: glänzend, sozusagen wässerig . . . und bläulich-grün wie die Ränder von farblosem Fensterglas, dabei natürlich beseelt und also undurchsichtig. Leider hat sie die Augenbrauen zu einem dünnen Strich zusammenrasiert, was ihrem Gesicht eine graziöse Härte gibt, aber auch etwas Maskenartiges, eine fixierte Mimik von Erstauntheit. Sehr edel wirkt die Nase zumal von der Seite, viel unwillkürlicher Ausdruck in den Nüstern. Ihre Lippen sind für meinem Geschmack etwas zu schmal, nicht ohne Sinnlichkeit, doch muß sie zuerst erweckt werden, und ihre Figur . . . hat etwas Knappes, etwas Knabenhaftes auch, man glaubt ihr die Tänzerin. . . . Sie raucht sehr viel. Ihre sehr schmale Hand . . . ist keineswegs ohne Kraft, keineswegs ohne eine beträchtliche Dosis unbewußter Gewalttätigkeit, wobei sie sich selbst . . . ganz und gar zerbrechlich vorkommt. Sie spricht sehr leise, damit der Partner nicht brüllt. Sie spekuliert auf Schonung. (III 407-08)

Her hair is red, very red in fact, in keeping with the new fashion, not like rose-hip jam, however, but like dry minium powder. Very curious. And with it a very fine complexion— alabaster with freckles. Also very curious, but beautiful. And

*her eyes? I should say they are glittering, somehow watery
. . . bluish-green like the edges of colourless window-glass, and
at the same time, of course, full of soul and therefore opaque.
Unfortunately her eyebrows have been plucked to a thin line,
which gives her face a graceful hardness, but also a slightly
masklike appearance, as though perpetually miming surprise.
Her nose looks very aristocratic, especially from the side; there
is a great deal of involuntary expression in her nostrils. Her
lips are rather thin for my taste, not without sensuality, but
they must first be roused; and her figure . . . has something
spare and also boyish about it; it's easy to see she's a dancer
. . . . She smokes a great deal. Her very slender hand . . . is
by no means lacking in strength and a considerable measure of
forcefulness, although she seems to see herself as completely
fragile. She speaks very softly, to prevent her interlocutor from
shouting. She banks on being protected.* (47-48)

A large portion of this description recurs almost verbatim near the end of Rolf's postscript, after Julika's death (III 779). Rolf combines with it a partial repetition of Stiller/White's further description of Julika after his attack—lying on his bunk, breathing heavily, her eyes closed. Stiller/White writes:

Ihre offenen Haare sind köstlich, duftig, seiden leicht. . . .
Ihre Schneidezähne sind vortrefflich, nicht ohne Plomben,
sonst aber von einem schönen Perlmutterglanz. . . . Ich
betrachtete sie wie einen Gegenstand . . . ein Weib, ein
fremdes, irgendein Weib. (III 412)

*Her loose hair was gloriously silky and as light as gossamer. . . .
Her front teeth were splendid, not without fillings, but otherwise
gleaming like mother of pearl. . . . I looked at her as though she
were an object . . . as though she were just any unknown
woman.* (51)

The composite picture of the beautiful Julika that emerges from these two descriptions is impressive. It is also startlingly mixed, partly substantiating and partly contradicting the image that emerges from Stiller/White's notebook entries of the younger Julika who was Stiller's wife before he disappeared.

That Julika, although a gifted dancer, appears to be frail, an image she deliberately cultivates and seems to believe; she is very beautiful but fragile, and she suffers from tuberculosis. Stiller/White's description of the woman who visits his cell affirms that image through such details as her tendency to speak softly so the other person does not dare raise his voice against her and her constant expectation, indicated by appearance and actions, that others should be especially considerate of her. Yet other details seem incongruous. She is now a heavy smoker, after years of having tuberculosis; her small hand is not lacking strength or "eine beträchtliche Dosis unbewußter Gewalttätigkeit," *"a considerable measure of unconscious violence;"* and, although she seems to consider herself fragile—yet is dramatic with her flaming red hair and masklike facial expression emphasized by thin, plucked eyebrows—she now appears to be a healthy, vivacious, and self-reliant woman. Her appearance today is considerably different from the "other" Julika after her seven years of living without Stiller.

Stiller/White has planned to tell Julika a story when they meet. It is a parable he invented about Isidor, a bourgeois pharmacist with a wife and five children who lives a normal, ordered life, troubled only by his wife, who constantly asks nagging questions. One day, while they are on vacation in the south of France, he abruptly leaves his family and joins, not quite voluntarily, the Foreign Legion, where he lives a life far more adventurous and exciting than his old one and becomes "a real man."[7] Seven years later he returns home. When his wife responds to his sexual advances by asking where he has been all those years and why he never sent a postcard, he leaves again. First, though, he fires his revolver three times into his wife's untouched birthday cake, splattering her morning coat with cake from top to bottom, an action clearly symbolic of sexual frustration. He returns a year later, but when his wife begins her nagging questions again, he leaves once more, this time without firing into the cake, and never returns.

Stiller/White intends the story as a warning to Julika. But the story he actually tells her is different in several respects, especially in the figure of Isidor, who is no longer a vigorous legionnaire but a passive sufferer and whose virile, symbolic warning has been changed to mute pleading. In changing the story, Stiller/White interpolates a recent dream (III 415), the one about the confrontation of Julika and Stiller in which both hold out their hands, revealing the stigmata in their palms. The question, "who is the cross and who the crucified?" (III 415/54) remains unanswered.

Julika does not take Stiller/White's story seriously. Making the same mistake as Isidor's wife, she asks almost the identical reproachful questions. She refuses to recognize in the man before her anyone different from the man she is married to, the man who, like Isidor, has been missing for almost seven years. This inflexible attitude is what eventually provokes Stiller/White's physical attack. Alone again in his cell after Julika leaves, Stiller/White recognizes the impossibility of being able to tell someone else about one's life. This inability, he writes, condemns us to remain

> wie unsere Gefährten uns sehen und spiegeln, sie, die vorgeben, mich zu kennen, sie, die sich als meine Freunde bezeichnen und nimmer gestatten, daß ich mich wandle, und jedes Wunder (was ich nicht erzählen kann, das Unaussprechliche, was ich nicht beweisen kann) zuschanden machen—nur um sagen zu können: "Ich kenne dich." (III 416)

> *as our companions see and mirror us, those who claim to know me, those who call themselves my friends, and never allow me to change, and discredit every miracle (which I cannot put into words, the inexpressible, which I cannot prove)—simply so that they can say:*
> *"I know you."* (55)

In these few lines, Stiller/White states the tragedy of his life: neither Julika nor Sibylle nor the authorities nor his friends are able to recognize that the man who has returned is not identical with the one who left almost seven years ago. As Siegfried Lenz once observed about Stiller: "All of them crucify him onto the picture that represented him in his past [and] do not want to recognize that he, in order to be able to continue living, had to change into a different person" (Lenz 132; translation mine).

Stiller/White is the victim of that cardinal sin of human relationships: the formation by Julika and the others of an unalterable, "graven" image they refuse to part with. His explanation when Julika asks him about the scar over his right ear is revealing in this respect, as it shows how much he thinks of himself as a different entity from Stiller. He tells her, rather casually: "Somebody tried to shoot me" (III 420/59), and then, since she doubts the truth, he tells her a story.

The more often Stiller/White sees Julika, the more she fascinates him. He notices moments of unexpected grace, especially when they are alone; a disarming innocence, the sudden blossoming of girlhood, a facial expression of just-awakening womanhood. To Stiller/White she sometimes seems like an innocent girl hiding in the shape of a mature woman. He concludes: "There is nothing womanly this woman does not possess, at least potentially, smothered over perhaps, and her eyes alone . . . have a gleam of frank anticipation that makes you jealous of the man who will one day awaken her" (III 420-21/59).

Stiller/White is beginning to fall in love with Julika, and for the same reason that caused Stiller to fall in love with her years earlier: he wants to be the one to awaken her to the full womanhood he perceives to be slumbering within her. Although Stiller/White repeatedly states that he fears repetition, he repeats Stiller's most crucial decision in accepting the challenge to awaken Julika. For the second time he believes that he is the man to do this, and he makes that challenge the basis of his strengthening relationship with her. Intellectually he knows that "everything depends on whether one succeeds in ceasing to wait for life outside repetition;" instead, one needs repetition "of one's free will (in spite of [coercion]) . . . (III 421/59). This view does not conquer Stiller/White's ever-present fear of repetition, but it provides him with a means of combatting it.

Thanks to Julika's generously posted bond, they are able to explore Zurich together during his weekly few hours of freedom from jail. During those excursions, Stiller/White falls more deeply in love with Julika. Once he kisses her spontaneously in public (III 429), which prompts Julika, convinced as she has been from their first meeting that she is speaking to her husband—here indicated by her use of the familiar form of "you," "du"—to caution him, teasingly: "This is Zurich" (III 429/67), where proper public behavior is expected, and of them, too.

During one of their excursions, while they are sitting in a Zurich café, Julika hands Stiller/White a piece of paper containing a brief note Stiller sent to her at Davos. Stiller/White responds by telling her, "I love you." He repeats his declaration of love and wants to tell her more—how he feels at that moment, how he feels about their meeting, their relationship, about his hopes for the future—but Julika no longer hears him. In her thoughts she is back at Davos (III 433-34).

This moment summarizes the problem between these two: Stiller/White wants to live in the present, Julika in the past. A shot of whiskey now and then helps him to remain true to his new identity, "for experience has taught me that without whisky I'm not myself, I'm open to all sorts of good influences and liable to play the part they want me to play, although it is not me at all" (III 361/7), as he explains at the beginning of his first notebook. He is drinking whiskey now (III 432), aware of the threat Julika and her fascination with the past pose.

Is she happy in Paris, Stiller/White asks as he sips his whiskey, trying to bring her back to the present. She, however, uses his question as an opportunity for another excursion into the past, describing for him once more her misery at Davos. Stiller/White waits anxiously "for her to come out of her past, which she wanted to forgive and in order to forgive had to describe in detail, into the present of our short afternoon" (III 433/70). He reaches for her and turns her face so she has to look at him, takes her hand to bring her back to the present, and repeats his declaration of love once more. She, looking at him, only sees Stiller, and listening to him only hears what Stiller might have said in such a situation. In short, Stiller/White's courtship of Julika is a disaster.

Feeling suddenly depressed and hopeless, Stiller/White believes:

> Jedes Gespräch zwischen dieser Frau und mir . . . ist fertig, bevor wir's anfangen, und jede Handlung, die mir jemals einfallen mag, ist schon im voraus gedeutet,

meinem augenblicklichen Wesen entfremdet, indem sie in jedem Fall nur als eine angemessene oder unangemessene, eine erwartete oder unerwartete Handlung des verschollenen Stillers erscheinen wird, nie als die meine. Nie als die meine! (III 434-35)

Every conversation between this woman and myself . . . was finished before it began, and any action it might occur to me to take was interpreted in advance, alienated from my present being, because it would in any case appear as an appropriate or inappropriate, an expected or unexpected action on the part of the missing Stiller, never as my action. Never as my action. (71)

Stiller/White motions to the waiter that he wants to pay. Believing he wants to order another whiskey, Julika cautions him in a wifely fashion not to drink so much. Stiller/White is tempted to order another out of spite: as if she could treat him as she might have treated her lost Stiller! Their ability to communicate seems to decrease in proportion to the time their troubled courtship lasts. Sadly he observes: "Her whole behaviour did not relate to me, but to a phantom, and once confused with her phantom . . . one was simply defenceless" (III 435/72). Stiller/White can find no way to proceed. He has no language to express reality, to prove once and for all who he really is, *now*.

Julika has never doubted that this man is her husband. She is incapable of thinking anything else, no matter how often he tells her his name is White. She calls it his "idée fixe." On his part, Stiller/White labels as her idée fixe the belief that they, as the two people they are *now*, have ever been married. This is a fine but very important distinction, but Julika does not understand it. Since Stiller/White claims to have murdered his wife, he cannot be the man whom, in her "need to forgive everything," she has waited for. Nor can she be the woman he murdered, she who stands before him "in so blühender Manier" (III 410), *"in such full bloom,"* who survived the unhappy marriage she keeps telling him about. He knows less and less what she wants of him.

The crisis of communication between Stiller/White and Julika deepens, as both seem gradually to revert back to the people they were before Stiller disappeared. This is shockingly evident in the studio scene, Stiller/White's last chance before the court announces its verdict in his case to persuade at least Julika that he is Jim White or to agree voluntarily that he is Anatol Ludwig Stiller. Stiller/White does neither.

Julika has been in Paris, where she has put her affairs in order before resuming her life with her returned husband. During her absence, Stiller/White realizes how much he misses her. He dreams about her and, to pass the time waiting for her return, he tries to visualize her in the new fall coat she plans to buy in Paris. Beyond the externals of her beauty and charm, which everyone can see, Stiller/White is certain that Julika is a grand woman. Perhaps she is not an easy woman to love, he muses, but then, he still sees her as a woman who never before has been loved or has loved. He would like to be the one to love her and to be loved by her. He knows that she is his only hope of proving himself as a human being, provided she recognizes the changes in him and stops clinging to the frozen image of her missing Stiller.

Stiller/White imagines an exhaustive conversation with Julika in which he admits, indirectly, to be her missing husband. Then he tells her that they must try to live with each other, knowing the risk of their situation:

> Entweder machen wir uns am andern kaputt oder es gelingt uns, einander zu lieben. (III 688)

> *Either we destroy one another or we succeed in loving one another.*[8]

This insight is almost prophetic. Essential for the success of their resumed relationship and marriage is that Julika accept Stiller as the man he is, not was; that they make a real commitment to their marriage; and that they accept the fact that they never before loved each other. That, he believes, is the real reason they cannot separate. Couples who have once been happy in their own way and thus at least once realized their potential together can get divorced, Stiller/White reasons, and concludes that he and Julika cannot divorce because "we were never through with one another" (III 689/299).

Stiller/White knows that to make their resumed marriage succeed may be as difficult as trying to walk on water—while the water keeps rising, threatening to drown them.[9] He is willing to accept, if necessary, his friends' and society's rejection of him as Jim White, because they lack and are unwilling to construct a frame of reference into which to fit him. But he is not willing to accept Julika's rejection of him as Jim White for these same reasons. If she loves him, Julika should be able to find out who Jim White really is and to accept that reality. Only in an act of faith, here synonymous with an act of love, lies any hope for their marriage. And only if the marriage succeeds can either of them experience "das wirkliche Leben." But they must cross that threshold *together*: "neither of us can cross it alone" (III 689/299).[10]

Unfortunately, Stiller/White never gets a chance to have that conversation with Julika. They meet next during a site hearing at Stiller's former studio, accompanied by Rolf, the prosecutor, Dr. Bohnenblust, the defense attorney, and Knobel, the warden. When Stiller/White asks Julika the only question that really matters to him: "Do you love me?" (III 713/321), he believes everything depends on her answer; his future is in her hands. Julika does not understand the question and remains silent. Stiller/White tries to explain: If she really loves him, a confession that he is her missing husband becomes superfluous. Nothing seems more logical to him. Julika's answer is still silence. She cannot take what Stiller/White is asking of her, the existential leap of faith into nothingness. She, like everyone else in that studio, is waiting for Stiller/White to confess that he is indeed Anatol Ludwig Stiller. But all he is willing to admit publicly is "daß ich ein Verhältnis habe mit dieser Dame —" (III 716), *"I'm having an affair with this lady"* (323).

Julika, during her absence, has reverted back to her former self. She has even brought along a dog, a new "Foxli." Stiller/White is deeply agitated, believing that the entire world seems to have conspired against him to reject his new, true identity; even Julika has betrayed him. He explodes into a display of violence that has strong orgasmic overtones. He smashes and throws out of the window everything in sight reminiscent of the missing Stiller—sculptures, plaster casts, bits of modeling material, his spatulas, an African mask, a Celtic axe, and the two Spanish banderillas. None of these things has anything to do with Jim White.

Then, as if awakening from a trance, exhausted and sweaty from physical exertion, Stiller/White laughs and then falls silent. Characteristically, Julika's response to this violent outbreak is the question: "What now?" (III 723/330), the same question she twice asked her husband after his verbal assault during his last visit to Davos. Like her husband then, Stiller/White now looks at her silently. Soon thereafter, he accepts defeat through the court. Jim White resumes the life and the marriage of Anatol Ludwig Stiller.

A MARRIAGE RESUMED: STILLER AND JULIKA

The picture of Stiller and Julika's marriage after his release from jail emerges from the postscript that follows the seven notebooks. Rolf, its author, is the Swiss prosecutor who was assigned to determine Stiller's identity and who, during many conversations with the prisoner, became his friend. To assume that because the author is a lawyer the postscript is a factual, objectively written summation of *Switzerland v. Stiller* would be an error, however. The postscript is as subjective and limited in perspective as Stiller/White's notebooks, and Rolf turns out to be as unreliable a narrator as Stiller/White has been.

The postscript can be divided into four sections, two short ones—III 730, 749-53 (English translation *339, 356-60)*—and two long ones—III 730-49, 754-80 (English translation *339-56, 360-84)*. The two long sections, each containing an important conversation—the first between Rolf and Julika, the second between Rolf and Stiller—reveal the most pertinent details of Julika and Stiller's lives and resumed marriage.

In these two separate conversations, Julika and Stiller show that the dilemma of their entire relationship is unchanged; they are still unable to communicate with each other effectively. Rolf is familiar with this problem from his marriage to Sibylle. But he and Sibylle have achieved at least a workable solution to their problem in their resumed marriage, symbolized by the birth of their baby girl, while Julika and Stiller have not. Just as their lack of honest communication destroyed their original marriage, it now leads to the failure of the resumed marriage, symbolized by Julika's recurring and increasingly serious tuberculosis and her death.

After Stiller's release from jail in the fall, he and Julika leave Zurich and live for several months in a small hotel in Territet on Lake Geneva. When Rolf and Sibylle visit them there in February, they are shocked to find that the Stillers have practically withdrawn from the world. They live in a single room and subsist on a meager diet of cold snacks, except for the daily warm breakfast that is included with the room. They have few possessions—not even a hot plate to heat water for tea until Rolf and Sibylle lend them one—and their limited finances are dwindling fast. Stiller, in a jovial mood, introduces himself and Julika to his guests as "a couple of Swiss inland emigrants" (III 732/340). To Rolf and Sibylle, sitting in the Stillers' small room crowded with trunks, they seem more like Russians living in Paris or, as Sibylle comments, like newly arrived German Jews living in New York: nothing belongs to them. To Sibylle and Rolf the Stillers seem like aliens in their own country. They seem to be getting along with each other well enough under the circumstances, Rolf observes, like "two people in chains who had the good sense to put up with one another" (III 733/341).

After their visit, Rolf and Sibylle do not keep in touch with the Stillers, who do not write to them either. Rolf feels guilty about neglecting Stiller, a feeling he is to experience more than once during the next two years.

Six months after their visit, Rolf and Sibylle receive a letter in which a happy Stiller announces that they have found, rented, and moved into their dream house in Glion, near Montreux. In later letters, Stiller describes the former farmhouse enthusiastically and in great but ever-changing detail, supplementing his descriptions now and then with a few sketches. He has turned to pottery, he writes, and seems to find a ready market for his "Swiss pots" (complete with American Indian patterns), especially among American tourists.

Usually Stiller's letters are filled with lighthearted banter, but once he comments seriously that not past, but present, reality matters most to him now. He writes: "I cling to life as never before, you see I always have the feeling death is on my heels—that's quite natural, you know, a sign of life" (III 735/ 343). In each letter Stiller invites Rolf and Sibylle to come and take a look for themselves.

Stiller writes about Julika, too—that, for example, she had a part-time job for a while, working in a grocery store, and later that she is teaching dance classes at a nearby girls' school. Rolf notices, however, that Stiller never writes about how his marriage is faring. Nevertheless, compared with those months in Territet, their lives seem to have improved dramatically in Glion.

Sibylle visits them first, en route to the south of France with her two children. When Rolf asks her afterward about the Stillers' dream house, Sibylle laughs and tells him he has to go and see it himself.

In truth, the Stillers are not doing as well as Stiller's letters indicate. Julika's tuberculosis has recurred, periodically forcing her to go to the mountains for treatment. At those times, Stiller frequently telephones Rolf, usually late at night, ostensibly to discuss weighty topics such as the philosophy of Kierkegaard as contained in a book (*Either-Or*) Rolf sent him, but really because Stiller is lonely, Rolf believes. Since his own telephone has been disconnected for nonpayment of bills, Stiller calls Rolf from a tavern, often slightly drunk, accompanied by background noise that makes it difficult for Rolf to understand him. At the end of these late-night conversations, Stiller's behavior is peculiar. He never says "good-bye" and hangs up, but simply stops talking and waits for Rolf to break the connection. This strange behavior of Stiller's may be related to his stated inability to be alone (III 681); once he has reached out to another person, he wants to maintain the contact as long as possible, even in silence, forcing his conversation partner to choose the moment to break contact and throw Stiller back on to himself.

Rolf finally goes to Glion, a year and a half after visiting the Stillers in Territet. It is October when he arrives in Montreux by train. Stiller meets him but, Rolf notices, acts somewhat odd at first: he does not take a single step toward his friend, just stands motionless on the platform, letting Rolf approach him. After a few awkward minutes, however, their conversation flows easily once again. Stiller looks unchanged, Rolf notices; he is wearing a former suit of Rolf's with sleeves too short for him, giving him a youthful appearance, and his hair is a little grayer and thinner. Although Rolf has been somewhat nervous about this reunion, afraid their friendship may have become outdated, he is quickly reassured.

Rolf and Stiller climb up the steep hills to Glion, stopping on the way for Stiller to pick up a few bottles of wine. They talk animatedly of wine-growing, the concept of culture, leisure as its prerequisite, and the relationship between luxury and dignity. Once at Stiller's house, Rolf can see why the rent is so affordable: neglect and decay are evident everywhere. The house is overgrown with ivy, only its upper part clearly visible—a little stone tower with firing holes. "A Swiss chalet distantly related to a Scottish castle" (III 740/347), as Rolf comments ironically.

Stiller does not seem even to notice that the place is badly run down. His pottery workshop is in a former laundry shed. As Rolf listens to Stiller assessing his less-than-spectacular skill and future as a potter and to his comments about the pottery of different eras and nations, Rolf observes that Stiller has indeed changed. He used to talk only about himself, or about topics like marriage, racial groups, volcanos, and gangsters. Now his mind seems to focus more precisely on objects: his pottery, his flywheel, his glaze.

When Julika comes home from her job at the girls' school, Rolf discovers that she has changed, too. Unlike Stiller, she has aged noticeably, but she still is unusually attractive. He feels sympathetic toward her but has never known what to talk to her about. He has always thought of her as aloof. She probably has no idea, he conjectures, watching her, how little she conveys about her thoughts and feelings to others, and then cannot understand when someone does not just sense her liking for him, her pleasure over a visit, or her delight in a gift. Accepting the hand-printed scarf Rolf has brought her, she says: "You can't get anything like that round here" (III 742/349-50), then quickly puts it aside. She has a deep-seated shyness, Rolf believes, that keeps her from expressing herself in words, but the abruptness of her manners makes others, including him, feel uncomfortable.

Rolf remembers that the inability to tell each other how they really feel was a basic problem in Stiller and Julika's earlier marriage. It worries him to see that the problem remains. Stiller's casual manner barely hides the compulsiveness of his efforts to be attentive to Julika, as if he constantly feels the need to atone for something. The more he tries, stubbornly, the more his unsuccessful efforts seem to tire Julika. She merely tolerates them, eventually gives in to them, Rolf notices. Julika does not seem to want all this attention. She seems not to want to be entertained, either. Any attempt to make her laugh is doomed to failure, Rolf discovers; one feels quite stupid afterward. Apparently Julika has no real laughter, none that originates inside her; her laughter remains forever on the surface. It seems to Rolf that she finds it as difficult to laugh heartily as to understand that people, especially Stiller, cannot interpret through her masklike facial expression her silent approval of them or of the things they do for her.

Casually, in the course of the conversation, Stiller suggests that Julika ought to start her own ballet school in Lausanne. The idea does not seem to be new to them, but Julika rejects the suggestion with a vehemence that surprises Rolf.

When Rolf and Julika talk about Stiller, who has left to buy more wine, Rolf discovers that she is proud of what Stiller has accomplished over the past two years. But when he encourages her to keep telling Stiller so, since, like every normal man, he needs to be appreciated by the one he loves, she insists that she has told him. Significantly, she adds: "I don't know . . . what he expects of me. Haven't I told him? Can I help it if he doesn't listen?" (III 743/350).

This phrase, "I don't know what he expects of me," or, slightly changed to the question, "What does he want of me?" (III 746/353) has become Julika's leitmotif in her resumed marriage. She has never known the answer. Before Stiller's disappearance she often asked the same question. Her repeating it now indicates the state of their relationship, its regression since those carefree days in Zurich when she took the jailed Stiller out on the town once a week.

Julika is obviously at a loss. Rolf realizes that she sees herself as a finished, completed being when she tells him, "I am as I am. Why does Stiller always want to change me?" (III 748/354). Julika seems to carry in her heart a "graven image" not only of Stiller but also of herself. She does not allow either of them the opportunity to grow or to change as individuals or as marriage partners. She admits that perhaps Stiller means well, that he is sure he loves her. But when Rolf asks if she loves Stiller in return, she responds, after a moment of thoughtful silence: "I understand him less and less" (III 748/355). Never, in the course of the novel, does Julika ever say she loves Stiller. She probably believes she does, but hers is a strange sort of love that rejects growth and change.

Julika takes advantage of Stiller's brief absence to urge Rolf to talk her husband out of his idea about a ballet school, because "it is impossible, believe me." She adds, ominously, "Of course, he can't know—" (III 746/353).

What Stiller can't know is that Julika's tuberculosis, which was considered cured during his absence, has not only recurred, which all of them know, but has reached such an advanced stage that her whole left lung must be removed as soon as possible (III 747). Since Julika is no longer associated with the theater and its constant, unavoidable dust that may have contributed to her initial tuberculosis infection, the cause of her illness seems to be more psychosomatic than physical. It becomes progressively worse the longer she and Stiller are married, is alleviated when they are separated, recurs as they resume their marriage, and becomes so severe that only extirpative surgery can limit its further spread. As Julika did once before, she is keeping her doctor's advice a secret from Stiller.

Rolf believes he has never seen a person more lonely than Julika. Between her anguish and the world stands an impenetrable wall: an old, helpless, and incurable certainty of not being heard, not being listened to, least of all by her partner who, she seems to feel, hears only himself. Rolf wonders, as Stiller did when he looked at her in his jail cell: Has this woman ever been loved by anyone? Has she ever loved someone? Only moments earlier, while Stiller was chatting away, Julika's face appeared to Rolf like a permanently frozen mask (III 743). Stiller paid no attention to it, according to Rolf, who finds it difficult to believe that any human being's face can be so expressionless while she suffers such agony.

How different is his own resumed marriage with Sibylle! How much more open, more vital than it used to be—so full of life! And their daughter, already more than two years old, is filling their lives with joy.

As Rolf looks up he sees, startled, that Julika has undergone a silent transformation; he looks into a completely disfigured face. Her mouth is open, as it is in masks of antiquity; she is unsuccessfully trying to bite her lip; her mouth, trembling, remains open as if paralyzed. Julika is crying without making a sound, her eyes open but unfocused and swimming in tears; her two small hands clenched into fists in her lap, her whole body shaking. Sitting in her chair Julika has become a different person, unrecognizable, unreachable, with no personal characteristic left. She has been reduced to a despairing, trembling body, to flesh screaming in the terror of death, without making a sound.

When Stiller returns, Julika gets up quickly to compose herself. He is not to know how matters really stand with her; he is not to know of the impending operation to be performed as soon as she is no longer afraid, or of how much she fears dying. She has extracted a promise from Rolf that he will keep her secret safe. In this atmosphere of conspiracy, Stiller's well-meant inquiry of how she is feeling has a chilling effect, and his question to Rolf: "Isn't she looking splendid?" (III 749/356) is deeply ironic.

Indeed, when Julika rejoins them, she does look splendid. Seeing a completely different person from the one he saw a few moments ago, Rolf begins to wonder if he has dreamed rather than experienced the previous scene. Since Stiller and Julika behave as normally with each other as they did earlier, their interaction indicates vividly their absolute lack of communication, the depth of their isolation, and the complete failure of their resumed marriage. This scene is surpassed only by what happens the day Julika leaves Glion to have her lung operation. Her things are packed, she and Stiller have to leave for the hospital in an hour, and Stiller goes off to find some flowers for Julika, attempting to show her his love. While he is away she leaves for the hospital (III 770); Stiller returns to an empty house. The two partners are as far apart as they have ever been.

After his visit to Glion, Rolf for the first time reads the seven notebooks Stiller/White wrote in jail. He has known they exist, but never bothered to look into them. He is shocked by the picture of Julika that emerges from their pages. He believes that Stiller's subjective portrait of his wife does violence to her and says more about himself than about Julika. However, since Rolf is not an objective observer of Stiller or Julika or a reliable narrator of the events he experiences with them, his judgments and his postscript reflect his own perceptions.

After reading the notebooks, Rolf concludes that Stiller's task should be not to escape his past, sterile relationship with Julika but to integrate that experience into a living present. Rolf is wrong. The opposite is true, as Stiller's comments about his suicide attempt and rebirth and the insights he expresses during his imagined conversation with Julika before his release from jail clearly indicate: he hopes to leave the past behind, hopes that he and Julika, in spite of that past, will be able to experience "das wirkliche Leben" together, without suffocating each other.

Rolf and Stiller keep up a sporadic correspondence over the next six months. Rolf is concerned about Julika, but except for one letter in which she implores him not to tell Stiller about their conversation at Glion, he hears nothing about her condition. Perhaps the operation has proved unnecessary after all.

The following spring Rolf and Sibylle accept the Stillers' invitation to stay at Glion for a few days over the Easter holiday. They look forward to spending some time in the country. When they arrive, they find an empty and apparently hastily deserted house. Unknowingly, they have arrived on the day of Julika's long-postponed lung operation, as Stiller explains when he returns more than an hour later. Although he is terribly worried about Julika, he pulls himself together to welcome his friends.

Except for everyone's concern about Julika, the next day, Easter Sunday, is almost idyllic. Stiller visits the hospital early, returning with the good news that Julika is doing well, as well as can be expected. Somewhat relieved, Stiller and his guests set off on a long walk through the countryside, returning in the late afternoon.

This weekend provides the one opportunity to see Rolf and Sibylle's resumed marriage at work—seen, of course, through Rolf's eyes. As they spend a happy Sunday in the country, one senses a peacefulness, relaxation, and understanding between them. Their communication, nonverbal as well as verbal, seems to flow smoothly. Sibylle is so relaxed that she takes a long nap by the lake after lunch, snug in a bed of dry grass Stiller has made for her.

That evening Stiller goes again to the hospital, but this time the doctor will not let him see Julika; she is resting and should not be disturbed, he says. Rolf finds this worrisome, but keeps quiet. Stiller rushes busily into preparations for an evening of conversation with his friends at home. When Rolf and Sibylle finally start up the stairs to bed, Stiller reverts to his behavior on the telephone—he seems unable to break contact, to respond to their "Good night," and stands looking up at them.

Around one o'clock in the morning Rolf, unable to sleep, goes downstairs in his pajamas and finds his friend in front of the fireplace. The fire has died. Sitting motionless, Stiller is not asleep but fairly drunk. Instead of heeding Rolf's admonition to stop drinking, Stiller refills his glass. This is the occasion, with Rolf shivering in his pajamas and Stiller with his guard down as a result of the alcohol, on which the second of the two significant conversations reported in the postscript takes place.

Stiller admits to Rolf that he is terrified of losing Julika. He cannot imagine facing life without her, even though their life together is less than ideal. If Julika should die—without first recognizing Stiller as the reborn man he is and without herself learning to truly love him—his whole life's work will be a failure.

Not every marriage turns into an absolute, existential challenge, but Stiller and Julika's has. Rolf has difficulty comprehending this. His nature and his marriage, in which each partner does not rely for acceptance only on the other, demonstrate clearly the difference between him and Stiller. Rolf, the attorney, is a conformist: he prefers order and convention, for they make his life in society both possible and tolerable. Stiller, the artist, after his rebirth is essentially a free man; he does not need structure and order, nor are the conventions of society essential for him to live a meaningful life; he even welcomes being an outsider, like the young Jürg Reinhart in *Die Schwierigen*, as long as—and this is crucial for Stiller—he has Julika's acceptance of him *as he is*, with all his faults and idiosyncracies (Butler 85, Petersen 1978a 126-28).

Stiller's need for validation and acceptance by someone or something outside himself is not unusual; it is part of the human condition. Since his rebirth he has had no trouble accepting himself, does not want to be "anyone different from the person I was just born to be" and does not want "to seek any other life than this one, which I cannot throw away" (III 727). His problem is that Julika is the only person he has chosen to validate him. Rolf suggests that Stiller and Julika reach beyond each other and turn to God, that they learn to pray for each other. But Stiller replies, "One has to know how to pray!" (III 772/377). In jail he wrote in his notebook: "If I could pray, I should have to pray that all hope of escaping from myself should be taken from me" (III 690/300). But Stiller cannot pray. Although he read the Bible in jail, his inability to pray indicates that he is not a believer but an agnostic. He cannot turn to God for validation, although toward the end of his long conversation with Rolf on that night, he asks him to "Pray for me that she shall not die!" (III 777/380).

Rolf, because of his religious belief, has more resources in his marriage than Stiller does. His marriage to Sibylle is successful, not only because they accept and love one another, but also because they do not depend only on their marriage to validate their existence. As important as it is to them, their marriage is only a part of their complete relationship with God. Stiller, lacking belief in a Supreme Being, has only his present life in which to complete himself. In a conversation with Dr. Bohnenblust, Stiller once defined "das wirkliche Leben" as the period during which he can become identical with himself. During that conversation Stiller also insisted that a real life leaves a deposit, "eine Ablagerung," in the shape of something alive, then added:

> Ablagerung ist auch nur ein Wort, ich weiß. . . . Gott ist eine Ablagerung! Er ist die Summe wirklichen Lebens. (III 418)

Deposit is [also] only a word, I know. . . . God is a deposit! He is the sum of real life. (57)

For Stiller, the "Ablagerung" of his life is his marriage: it represents the totality of his existence, both in its suffering and its happiness. In other words, Rolf's life is metaphysically anchored; Stiller's is not. Julika represents, therefore, a kind of substitute God to Stiller, the only reference point of his existence (Petersen 1978a 126-27). No wonder he struggles to achieve her acceptance and love until the very night she dies.

Nine years earlier, at Davos, when Stiller and Julika separated, Stiller realized that he alone, and no one else, prevented him from experiencing "das wirkliche Leben." This insight gave him the courage to leave Julika and to set out in search of his real self. After discovering it and accepting his second chance to live "ein wirkliches Leben," he has come back to Julika, for he realizes that only in his relationship with her can he experience that life. As he explains to Rolf:

Wenn du dein halbes Leben lang vor einer Tür gestanden und geklopft hast, Herrgott nochmal, erfolglos wie ich vor dieser Frau, vollkommen erfolglos, Herrgott nochmal—und dann geh du weiter! Vergiß sie, so eine Tür, die dich zehn Jahre versäumt hat! . . . Ich habe sie nicht vergessen können. . . . Weil's einen Punkt gibt, wo sich das Aufgeben nicht mehr lohnt. (III 768)

When you've stood half a lifetime knocking at a door, great God, unsuccessfully as I stood before this woman, absolutely without success, great God—then see if you can pass on! . . . I could not forget her. . . . Because there comes a point when it simply isn't worth while giving up. (373)

Even now, Stiller has not given up. He admits he may have chosen the wrong partner, even that the task he set for himself may have been too large, but since he has accepted the challenge of Julika, he will not abandon the task.

Rolf accuses Stiller of wanting to be Julika's redeemer (III 765). Although this accusation is partly true, it is too simple.

Rolf never understands that Stiller, in turn, needs Julika to be *his* redeemer, too.

During this nocturnal conversation with Rolf, while he fears for Julika's life, Stiller gains a second important insight: he realizes that we, not others, are responsible for our guilt, that we *are* the guilt. That insight sets Stiller free. Only hours before Julika's death he is permanently freed from his dependence on her acceptance and love. Finally he has the courage to do what he was never before able to do: to be alone. In his conversation with Dr. Bohnenblust about "das wirkliche Leben," Stiller may have had a premonition when he observed: "Vielleicht ist das Leben, das wirkliche, einfach stumm—" (III 418), "*perhaps life, real life, is simply mute—*" (57).

Stiller's insight that we *are* the guilt explains, probably better than any particular philosophical system (Butler 77-82, Petersen 1978a 125-28), his unexpected behavior and the change that Rolf observes the morning after their long night of conversation. Then, Stiller was in agony over the possibility of Julika's death. This morning he seems calm and secure. He does not go to the hospital early, as he planned; he does not even call the hospital to find out how Julika is. Instead, when Rolf and Sibylle come down to breakfast they find him in his studio, working on his pottery. When Rolf goes to the hospital to visit Julika, Stiller does not accompany him; when Rolf returns, Stiller seems already to know that Julika has died. Eventually Rolf drives him to the hospital but observes that Stiller goes more as a formality than to meet any inner need. He does not stay long. Rolf observes that Stiller seems far removed from the events around him; his behavior is distant, dreamlike.

After Julika's death, Stiller, the man who by his own admission cannot live alone, who needs to be around a woman to escape feelings of self-doubt and loneliness, and who has craved from his youth the approval and acceptance of others, continues living in isolation at Glion, only occasionally keeping in touch with Rolf. A second suicide attempt is out of the question; that would not bring about the real death he had in mind at the moment of his rebirth.

"Who does violence to whom?" in this marriage, Rolf had asked earlier (III 750). The question may be restated, using the symbolism of Stiller/White's dream: Who is the cross, who the crucified? If Rolf's opinion, expressed as he looks at the dead Julika's face and recalls Stiller/White's description of her in his notebook (III 407-08,412), were to be taken as the answer, the crucified would have to be Julika. However, since Rolf has shown that his grasp of the facts is less than complete, the question remains open.

As a protagonist, Stiller is a modern antihero who fails, despite valiant efforts, to achieve "das wirkliche Leben" in his relationships with several women and in his marriage to one. As his resumed marriage progresses, his life, as his name suggests, turns "stiller," more quiet, until—after Julika's death—he accepts his failure and his life without further struggle and fades into almost utter silence at the end of the novel.

The tale of two marriages, as told in *Stiller* by a superb storyteller, explores the problems and possibilities of marriage. Max Frisch, who sees his function as author to be posing, not answering, questions (II 467), offers in *Stiller* few and only tentative suggestions of how this perhaps most essential of human institutions may be lived. Some of the requisites he proposes are that the partners be truly committed to each other and the relationship, that the partners share openly their thoughts and feelings, their hopes and joys, and that they have the courage to remain true to themselves throughout the relationship. In Frisch's view, a successful marriage provides the partners with the opportunity to grow and realize their potential—to unfold. Rolf and Sibylle seized that opportunity once their marriage had run into difficulty; as a couple, Stiller and Julika never did. The image of contemporary man as he relates to women is at best ambivalent in this novel. The two men have certain character traits in common such as egocentricity, chauvinism, possessiveness, insecurity, and an inability to communicate with their partner. However, whereas Rolf is at least partially able to change his view of himself and his partner, Stiller remains obsessed by his idée fixe, his mission.

NOTES

[1] Since the central issue in Part I of *Stiller* is whether or not Jim White is indeed the missing Anatol Ludwig Stiller, I elected to call the person jailed by the Swiss authorities "Stiller/White" until the issue is resolved in the novel.

[2] Stiller's negative self-image extends to normal, uncontrollable bodily functions, as his comment about sweating indicates (III 459). In this respect, his attitude parallels that of Walter Faber in *Homo faber*, who comments frequently about sweating and taking showers (IV 29,34,37,51-52,134) as well as growing a beard and shaving (IV 10,41,63,152,182). Obviously, both men are almost pathologically self-conscious about the body and its functions.

[3] Butler is in error when he interprets this episode as illustrating Rolf's belief that he, like Stiller, is guilty of making excessive demands on himself. Rolf's laborious attempts to rid himself of the parcel are not analogous to Stiller's labyrinthine experience in the Carlsbad Caverns, although the comparison is interesting (Butler 84).

[4] Unfortunately, the entire cave story, plus other significant portions of the text, were omitted in Michael Bullock's 1958 English translation, *I'm Not Stiller*, that became popular in the United States in the Penguin Books edition (1961). A whole generation of English-speaking students who have read this text have missed a key episode of the novel. The omitted sections were restored in the second English translation, published by Methuen, London, in 1982.

[5] Butler notes that these stories "occur predominantly in the first Notebook, in which Stiller's attempt to escape his identity is still possible. . . ." After the third notebook these stories cease because their function, "the gradual revelation of Stiller's personality culminating in his 'experience with his angel,'" is taken over by the stories that other characters tell Stiller/White about Stiller, until, at the end of the seventh notebook, the two seemingly disparate identities emerge as one, at least to the satisfaction of society and the court (Butler 56).

⁶Although death from a superficial skull wound would be unusual, this is what the text says.

⁷Stiller/White simply borrows the idea of the Foreign Legion from Knobel, who in an earlier conversation mentioned that three hundred Swiss per year join the Foreign Legion because "it gets on their nerves here" (III 370/14).

⁸This quotation is important, even prophetic. I substituted my own translation of the German text because the published translation, "Either we smash ourselves to pieces on one another or we love one another" (298) seems too violent and physical.

⁹Frisch first refers to the Biblical image of walking on water, like the image of the angel, in his story of Marion, the puppeteer, in the first *Tagebuch*. The angel challenges Marion to realize his full potential through self-knowledge, which Marion longs for. The faith required for this process is compared with the faith required to walk on water (II 359,500-01).

¹⁰At the conclusion of his first notebook, Stiller/White records a recurring feeling: having an urge to fly, to jump off a window sill into the nothingness of space, with no possibility of surviving unless he really can fly, which, at the moment of jumping, he is unaware of (III 436). This is the existential leap that Stiller/White refers to here.

CHAPTER FOUR

HOMO FABER: A GLIMPSE AT "DAS WIRKLICHE LEBEN"

The protagonist in Max Frisch's *Homo faber* (1957), which followed *Stiller* by three years, is an engineer, Walter Faber. He is fifty years old, older than the protagonists in Frisch's first two novels, but like the others is Swiss. He works for UNESCO, is based in New York, and travels widely to provide technical expertise to developing countries. He is trained to solve problems through observation, enumeration, and assessment of technical data; whenever a project is concluded, he presents a factual report to his superiors. This novel is one of Faber's reports, as its subtitle, *Ein Bericht* (*A Report*), makes clear.

In one of Frisch's earliest *Tagebuch* entries, from 1946, he wrote: "Schreiben heißt: sich selber lesen" (II 361), *"To write is to read one's own self"* (*Sketch I* 12). In a very specific sense, this is true of this report of Faber's, the last he ever writes. It differs from his usual reports in that its subject is his own life rather than a technical problem and its "audience" is not someone in a head office but Faber himself and, ultimately, his friend and former fiancée, Hanna. He writes it in the first person and in two installments, beginning in Caracas, where a stomach ailment confines him to his hotel room for several weeks, and completing it in his hospital room in Athens moments before he is to undergo an operation for stomach cancer that he does not survive (IV 203). The report concerns events in his life at three different time periods: the present, in the Athens hospital; the recent past, the period leading up to and following the death of his daughter; and the distant past, as far back as twenty-three years when he and Hanna were lovers.

Walter Faber, because of his engineering training and perhaps his own turn of mind, believes in the supremacy of the rational. All forces in nature are ultimately controllable, he is convinced.

He believes that the human mind is superior to the power of nature, and therefore man, by employing technology, will subjugate nature in the foreseeable future. As one would expect from a man who respects facts and reason and is trained to pay attention to details, his report contains many objective references to specific dates, times, places, and events. As one might not expect, however, the report is also deeply subjective. Not only does Faber intermingle topics and time levels freely, returning many times to significant events in his life—such as his relationship to Hanna twenty-three years ago—but he also presents a given topic from several perspectives (each validly his own) in an effort to come to terms with it.

Faber's report is more than a self-revelation; it chronicles a process of self-awareness, the protagonist's growing consciousness of his own life and of the possibility of "das wirkliche Leben." At its center stands a shocking event that violates a powerful social taboo: a father, unwittingly, has taken his own daughter as a lover. The novel's focus is not on the incest per se but on how it could have come about. What factors, what kind of mental attitude, what special "blindness," what omissions of fact, and what kind of wishful thinking could have led to this love affair between the father, a respected professional—a symbol of modern, technical man who sees himself as soon to be master of the universe—and his daughter, an intelligent, self-reliant woman thirty years his junior?

Two incongruities in this rational engineer's personality are already evident on the first page. Faber feels unexpectedly uneasy about a natural phenomenon, the vibrations caused by the Superconstellation's engines as they are revved up for a flight from New York to Mexico City via Houston. Moreover, he is uncomfortable with people in general, which seems odd for a man who travels much and constantly deals with people of many countries as part of his job. His uneasiness is manifested by his reaction to his seatmate who, like Faber, is waiting for liftoff. The vibrations and the passenger make Faber "nervous," he writes, and continues on the next page: "Menschen sind anstrengend" (IV 8), *"People are tiring"* (4).

His strange reactions are highlighted by many other details Faber reports in the first part of the novel. His uneasiness about natural forces is reiterated immediately by the blinding snowstorm

HOMO FABER 127

during takeoff. As Faber comments: "Man kam sich wie ein Blinder vor" (IV 7), "*I felt like a blind man*" (4). The narrative technique Frisch employs in *Homo faber*—an account written by the protagonist and arranged according to the dictates of his associative thinking rather than chronologically—is familiar from *Stiller*. Its development is worth pursuing, along with the examination of other issues old and new: identity; coincidence, providence, and fate; and man's desire to master nature. However, since my focus in this study is the relationship of contemporary man to women as Max Frisch pictures it, I shall deal with other aspects of this novel only as they relate to Faber's experience with three women: Ivy, a model; Sabeth, Faber's twenty-year-old daughter; and Hanna, Sabeth's mother, to whom Faber was engaged more than twenty years earlier.

AN ERRATIC RELATIONSHIP: FABER AND IVY

Nowhere does Faber's view of life, the assumption that man should control nature, clash more dramatically with reality than in his relationship with Ivy, an attractive, twenty-six-year-old model. He describes her as having watery blue eyes, a boyish figure, full breasts, and narrow hips—an appropriate figure for a model, he observes. Ivy is married, but that does not stop her from badgering Faber to marry her as they wait three hours at a New York airport for his delayed departure for Mexico City. Faber tells her unmistakably, and apparently not for the first time, that he has no intention, ever, of getting married.

Faber is glad finally to be aboard the plane and to have escaped Ivy. Later, when engine trouble forces the plane to make an emergency landing in the Mexican Tamaulipas desert within view of the Sierra Madre Oriental mountain range, and while the rescue helicopter is waiting to take letters from the passengers to their loved ones, assuring them they are safe, Faber types a letter to Ivy on his portable typewriter (with a carbon for his files!) in which he ends their relationship. The circumstances are interesting: in the arid desert, away from civilization and in a potentially life-threatening situation that usually causes people to reach out to those they care about,

Faber gets up the courage to break off a sexual relationship that he has been unable to control.

Faber's refusal to marry Ivy on principle, a statement made on the first page of his report, suggests a fundamental flaw in his character: he is afraid of commitment to another human being, and as a result he avoids any serious involvement with people. He hides this fear in his work, carrying on the technological profession that keeps him moving from place to place. Faber feels secure only at the lonely periphery of life. His uninvolvement is reminiscent of that of Jürg Reinhart in *Die Schwierigen* after he chooses to be a gardener. Jürg is determined to withdraw from life because he considers himself an unworthy bastard. What motivates Walter Faber's emotional isolation?

Faber has already provided a clue: his nervousness in a situation that he cannot control. He thinks of himself as a practical man, and he experiences the world through his intellect, not his feelings, as he states repeatedly in the first part of his report. Women, he believes, are different: unpredictable, moody, emotional, and requiring one to respond with feelings. He has little use for these characteristics. He feels extremely uncomfortable, in fact helpless, when facing women. In these situations he is not in control.

For the same reason, lack of control, Faber is bothered by natural physical functions. Like Stiller, he is hypersensitive about sweating. His reaction to a growing beard is almost pathological, and he is compulsive about being clean-shaven. He feels freer, more secure, once he has had a shave.

Sexuality is another concern Faber shares with Stiller, although Stiller's sexual maladjustment early in his marriage arose from Julika's disgust with sexual intercourse, which made Stiller feel guilty for asking it of her. In Faber's sexual relations *he* is the one who is disgusted. He always has been, except when Hanna was his partner. His first sexual experience at eighteen was with the forty-year-old wife of his teacher. That experience left him feeling guilty and ashamed of himself and the sexual act. The pattern he established with the teacher's wife (IV 99-100) became permanent: he craved intercourse, tried to suppress the urge, and then tried to forget the act as soon as it was over. The craving has never left Faber, but neither has the fear, that of surrender of the self.

The basis for Faber's obsessive reaction to involuntary bodily functions, including sex, is that they contradict most persuasively his cherished belief that man can and eventually will master nature. Nowhere does his repugnance of uncontrolled, teeming nature become more evident than in his reaction to the Guatemalan jungle, through which he travels in search of Joachim Hencke, an old friend from his student days in Zurich. In the jungle, Faber is appalled by the uncontrolled, overabundant procreation he observes everywhere. "Wherever you spat, it germinated" (IV 51/51), he writes. After describing the burial of Joachim, whom he found hanging from the rafters of his cabin, a suicide, Faber records his impression of nature in the jungle:

Verwesung voller Keime, glitschig wie Vaseline, Tümpel im Morgenrot wie Tümpel von schmutzigem Blut, Monatsblut, Tümpel voller Molche, nichts als schwarze Köpfe mit zuckenden Schwänzchen, wie ein Gewimmel von Spermatozoen, genau so—grauenhaft. (IV 68)

decay filled with seed, as slippery as vaseline, pools in the red of dawn like pools of filthy blood, menstrual blood, pools full of newts, nothing but black heads with jerking tails like a seething mass of spermatozoa, just like that—horrible. (69)

What disgusts Faber is the rampant sexuality he observes everywhere; the intensification of the life-death cycle in the jungle disturbs him to such an extent that he sees himself literally watching life springing instantly from death; even more deeply disturbing is the utter lack of control he observes in the jungle. It challenges his view of the world in which man stands at the center, controlling nature. Any evidence to the contrary is a threat not merely to Faber's world view but also to his existence, both as an engineer charged with harnessing the powers of nature to make them serve humanity and as a man who believes he has learned to master his own nature.

Faber finds his mechanistic view of the world challenged on both fronts repeatedly, though at first subtly, after he boards that plane for Mexico City. At first only the vibration, which Faber, the engineer, knows ought to be controllable, and the blizzard, which has delayed the flight, demonstrate man's lack of control over nature. Later, as engine failure forces the plane to land in the Mexican desert, the passengers, most of them with urgent business elsewhere, are stranded for four days. Faber's lack of control over his own life becomes apparent when his past unexpectedly catches up with him: his seatmate turns out to be his old friend Joachim's brother. Spontaneously, Faber interrupts his business trip to Caracas for a few days, without official clearance, to accompany the brother on a visit to Joachim in Guatemala.

Returning to New York, Faber finds that Ivy ignored his farewell letter, which she carries in her purse, and is waiting for him at the airport. In the face of that persistence, Faber makes a second spontaneous decision within a few weeks: he picks up the telephone, calls a travel agency, and books passage to France on a ship leaving the next day.

Ivy is furious. Although she knows that his next trip will be to Paris, she also knows that he is not expected there for another week, enough time for her to change his mind about ending their relationship. What follows is hilarious comedy. First Faber convinces Ivy that, although he has flown more than 100,000 miles, his last experience made him afraid to fly. He supports his assertion of danger so graphically with probability theory and facts and figures about plane crashes that Ivy finally begs him never to fly again; she can already see his charred remains among the plane's wreckage.

During that scene Faber also promises Ivy to consult a doctor about his abdominal pain, which occurred several times during his last trip, even causing him to faint during a brief stopover in Houston. The recurring stomach pain is further evidence that Faber is not in control of himself or his life. He ignores the clue.

Ivy is not easily discouraged and is determined that Faber not break off their relationship. She knows his vulnerability in sexual matters and that she can seduce him almost at will. Faber knows it, too. Always afterwards, he reports, he hates her for this and hates himself for succumbing to her.

Ivy seems obsessed with triviality. She has, for example, persuaded Faber to buy a red car that matches her lipstick, something between tomato and raspberry red, and she pays excessive attention to her makeup, in Faber's opinion. She visits her psychiatrist regularly, which is fashionable; has a sadomasochistic need to experience pain, Faber believes; and has moods that fluctuate widely—from furious, temperamental outbursts when Faber shows less than gentle, loving concern for her or upsets her carefully laid plans, to a seemingly genuine, though overly dramatic, concern for his welfare. Most of her actions seem calculated for effect. Perhaps Ivy really loves Faber, but he is not sure. Obviously she does not want to lose him.

Although Ivy frightens him sometimes, he admits, Faber repeatedly refers to her as "a nice kid" or "a good kid" (IV 30,31,65,68/28,29,65,68). She is "tough" (IV 64/65), as he knows from experience. He also knows that she considers him an egotist, a barbarian in matters of taste, and in general a brute in his dealings with women. All this she has told him repeatedly in fits of temper during their quarrels. She accuses him of a lack of feelings, an accusation that does not disturb him. Faber knows perfectly well that he occasionally allows himself the luxury of feelings, but he prefers to think of these episodes as fatigue phenomena, as happens to steel, nothing more.

Of Ivy's personal life Faber knows surprisingly little, considering the duration of their relationship. He knows that she is Catholic and a model, although sometimes he is not sure about the latter, and that she tolerates jokes on almost any topic except the Pope. Her husband, a civil servant in Washington, D.C., loves her and has no intention of divorcing her. Faber does not know if this is Ivy's first marriage, which he seems to doubt, nor does he know whether she is currently involved with any other men besides her husband and him. He knows nothing about her parents, but she has told him that she grew up in the Bronx and thinks of herself as "just a dead-end kid" (IV 67/68), a remark Faber finds odd.[1] His fragmentary, casual knowledge of her is strange until one recalls that Faber finds people in general "a strain."

That Ivy may be lesbian, or frigid, as Faber conjectures, is as doubtful as his notion that her need to seduce him is perverse and stems from a desire to humiliate him, which, he thinks, is the only way she derives pleasure from their relationship. Faber, however, is the one who has a sexual problem, as his description of their coupling makes clear; he has difficulty concentrating on what he is doing and is tempted to solve a chess problem while Ivy is approaching orgasm. When he closes his eyes to concentrate more effectively on her and the task, he kisses not Ivy, whom he holds in his arms, but his own elbow. Besides being very funny, the incident underscores Faber's egocentricity and narcissism.

After Faber persuades Ivy that he would probably crash if he flew to France, their caresses lead to sexual arousal and the two wind up in bed. A few hours later, after another comic scene between them, Ivy seduces him a second time, Faber claims. To avoid a possible third seduction in one night by this sensuous woman, Faber telephones his friend and chess partner, Dick, and invites him and his friends over for a party, way past midnight. When they arrive, most of them already drunk, their antics do not amuse Faber, who, Ivy claims, lacks a sense of humor. At one point in the night Faber, by now also drunk, screams at his guests:

> In eurer Gesellschaft könnte man sterben. . . ohne daß ihr es merkt, von Freundschaft keine Spur . . . ! (IV 67)
>
> *In your company a man could die . . . and you wouldn't even notice, there's no trace of friendship . . . ! (67-68)*

Like Stiller, who always needed a whiskey or two to remain true to himself and to withstand the pressures of others (III 361-68,432,435), Faber understands a particular situation most clearly, frighteningly so at times, when he is slightly drunk. Alcohol releases his inhibitions and lowers his customary defenses against the power of intuition, which, as an engineer, he rejects because it cannot be observed, measured, and verified.

His indictment of his guests contains a clue to the real reason Faber has suddenly chosen to leave for France by ship, rather than wait in New York for his planned trip by plane. He is fed up with this empty life, its routine, its arid quality, its shallowness. When he returned from Guatemala and Caracas, he thought his relationship with Ivy had ended, yet he finds himself back in it again, once again waiting for Ivy to finish her interminable dressing routine. Although in New York nothing seems to have changed, much has changed for Faber. He has gone through an emergency landing in the desert and a drive through the Guatemalan jungle teeming with uncontrollable life, and he discovered Joachim's body hanging on a thin wire from the ceiling of his cabin. He cannot forget the sight or the stink of his friend's decaying corpse turning slowly in the breeze like a scarecrow, his face black, his tongue blue, arms grey, hands white like sponges, and his fingernails purple (IV 84/85). Faber cannot talk to Ivy about these experiences, even though they have left a lasting impression.

Returning from the travel agency to his apartment and Ivy, Faber has the distinct feeling of beginning a new life—not merely of escaping Ivy and her sensual, sexual hold over him, but also of escaping his way of life in the United States. He explains the feeling of elation to himself as anticipation of his first ocean crossing. But it is more than that. As a result of his recent experiences in Central America and the activation of powerful memories from a past that lay buried for twenty years, Faber is starting his European journey in an unstable psychological condition. His conflicting emotions, which he can normally repress by keeping a fast pace in his life, will now, during this leisurely cruise across the Atlantic, have a chance to surface and demand attention.

Ivy helps Faber pack and drives him to the harbor. As the ship leaves the pier, Faber gazes at the receding Manhattan skyline and Ivy standing on the pier waving to him, her little feathered hat easily noticed in the crowd. Faber films the departure from New York harbor through his new telescopic lense. Overcome by the emotion of departure, Faber does not yet know how true was his premonition of the previous night. A new chapter of his life has begun.

THE MIRACLE OF LOVE: FABER AND SABETH

The Voyage Begins

As Faber stands in line to receive his dining table assignment, soon after the ship has left port, he sees dangling in front of him a red ponytail belonging to a slender young woman dressed in black jeans and a black turtleneck sweater. The line moves slowly, so Faber has half an hour with nothing better to do than to look closely at the woman; although he cannot see her face, he notes those details of her body and movements he can observe from the rear. He speculates about her face.

It is indicative of Faber's psychological instability at this time and of his readiness for new experiences that he takes such interest in this woman. The veneer of his rationalistic shield is cracked, his latent sensuality aroused.

The young woman does not notice Faber at all, as is evident a little later when he sees her again, this time playing Ping-Pong with a young man. She has changed into an olive-green corduroy skirt that looks much better on her than the jeans, Faber thinks. He nods discreetly at her, but she gives no indication of recognizing him. This causes Faber to wonder for a moment whether she is a different woman. When she chases a wayward ball, she nearly collides with him and still gives no sign of recognition.

Faber's assumption that the woman should have noticed him, which is without reason, illustrates not only his self-centeredness, which he shares with other Frisch male characters, but also the degree to which, after only a few hours on board ship, he has become mentally involved with this young woman.

The two actually meet for the first time a few moments later when Faber picks up a Ping-Pong ball that has bounced away from her and hands it to her silently. She thanks him, in English. Reporting the incident, Faber adds in parentheses: "In general she spoke German" (IV 72/73), illustrating how closely he has been observing her and also that she does not know him and believes him to be an American, like most of the ship's passengers.

Faber continues to watch the woman and the Ping-Pong, until eventually he plays one game with her. Her name, he finds out, is Elisabeth—Elisabeth Piper, he discovers later. Immediately he shortens her first name to Sabeth, "because Elisabeth seemed to me an impossible name" (IV 74/75). The name change illustrates the proprietary interest he has already taken in her and his attempt to lift her out of the anonymity of the passengers and of her common first name.

Throughout his report, especially its first section, Walter Faber claims repeatedly that he did not pursue Sabeth. The assertion represents his effort to explain and justify what happened and to establish his innocence. His personalization of her name is an early signal that Faber's words and actions frequently contradict each other.

The next morning, while Faber stands at the ship's rail, Sabeth stops by and initiates their first conversation. As Faber reports the meeting, he has the impression that she wants to be nice to him because she thinks he is lonely. She tries to get Faber to talk about whatever he is interested in, and he obliges. Enthusiastically he tells her about navigation, radar, earth curvature, electricity, and entropy; the latter Sabeth has never heard of. Faber notices that she has a quick, agile mind and easily follows his explanations about the so-called Maxwellian demon, the topic of his dissertation a long time ago.

He goes on to tell her his ideas about robots and their superiority to human beings. Sabeth remains skeptical and eventually laughs at his assertion that human actions are merely reflex responses to specific impulses or information and therefore removed from our will. A machine, Faber insists, can perform as well as, if not better than, a human being.

He must be joking, Sabeth thinks; perhaps he is teasing her. Man is not a machine, she argues. Faber cites scientific sources in support of his assertions, talking, he remembers, like a college sophomore. A machine, he continues, does not experience anything; it knows neither fear nor hope, which interferes with a task; it has no wishes of its own with regard to the outcome of its functions. It works according to the pure logic of probability; therefore, Faber declares:

Der Roboter erkennt genauer als der Mensch, er weiß mehr von der Zukunft als wir, denn er errechnet sie, er spekuliert nicht und träumt nicht, sondern wird von seinen eigenen Ergebnissen gesteuert (feed back) und kann sich nicht irren; der Roboter braucht keine Ahnungen— (IV 75)

The robot perceives more accurately than man, it knows more about the future, for it calculates it, it neither speculates nor dreams, but is controlled by its own findings (the feedback) and cannot make mistakes; the robot has no need of intuition. . . (76)

Sabeth thinks Faber is funny.

She does not know, of course, about Faber's strong aversion to uncontrolled nature and its perpetual cycle of propagation, birth, decay, and death, nor that this aversion led him to adopt the creed of the engineer: technology, as a science, can explain and divide the world of phenomena into its definable parts (Petersen 1978a 134). For its support this creed relies heavily on the mathematical principles of addition and probability. Faber, especially in the first part of his report, makes extensive use of both to explain to himself the many coincidences of his life since the night he boarded a plane in New York to fly to Caracas.

Faber's creed extends to human relationships, too, including his relationships with women, of whom Ivy stands as representative for all. But something is amiss in Faber's view of life, as his uncomfortable relationship with Ivy indicates. Sabeth puts her finger on it with her objection that humans beings are not machines; they have feelings—exactly what Faber has been trying to avoid.

Their first conversation is curious: a learned excursion into the world of robots and modern technology instead of the conventional, casual banter one might expect when two strangers meet aboard a transatlantic liner. From this beginning, however, the relationship between Sabeth and Faber develops, albeit awkwardly, into one much more meaningful than either expects. As a result, when the ship reaches Southampton, Sabeth bids farewell to her boyfriend, "who made a sour face" (IV 94/96) because his and Sabeth's joint travel plans have suddenly changed. Sabeth continues her voyage to France in the company of Faber, while he, the man who wants nothing to do with marriage, spontaneously proposes to her—presumably the first marriage proposal he has made since his wedding plans with Hanna, years ago, failed to materialize.

A close examination of events that lead up to this unexpected proposal helps to illuminate Walter Faber, the man he was before he met Sabeth and the man he becomes under her uninhibited tutelage and guidance.

At Sea

Faber's shipboard relationship with Sabeth is marked by barely concealed jealousies, at the root of which lie his feelings of inferiority about his age—at fifty, he is more than twice

Sabeth's age—and his ignorance of anything not related to engineering and technology, especially art.

Faber's feelings of inferiority about his age are shown most clearly in his jealousy of Sabeth's boyfriend, a young graphic artist and fellow Swiss, as Faber eventually discovers, and, as he grudgingly has to admit, a very able young man. Faber has watched the young man carefully many times, but they first meet in Sabeth's cabin. She is suffering from a touch of seasickness and, instead of going on deck for fresh air, she goes to her cabin. Faber accompanies her there. Sabeth's "Schnäuzchen-Freund" (IV 81), *"mustached friend" (82),* as Faber condescendingly refers to him on several occasions, puts her down on the bed—as if he were her husband. Faber can barely hide his resentment that the young man, not he himself, is touching Sabeth, as he opens the porthole for some fresh air and brings Sabeth some water. The young man (Faber never tells his name) unfastens Sabeth's sandals to make her more comfortable, an action Faber nastily interprets as "playing the Good Samaritan" (IV 81/82), then adds, condescendingly and in exasperation, "as though her sickness came from her feet!" (IV 81/82).

As Sabeth lies on the bunk "in a limp heap with her legs spread out and her face as pale as china clay" (IV 81/82), he notices that her red belt is much too tight. Loosening it would be sensible, but Faber considers such action inappropriate for either him or Sabeth's young friend. To suggest that Sabeth do it herself seems not to have occurred to him, or if it has, he remains silent lest the young man hear his suggestion and rush to assist Sabeth once more, touching her body even more intimately, something Faber's jealousy will not permit.

Although Faber is not sure of the two young people's relationship, he acknowledges that the man sitting on the bunk next to Sabeth may be her lover. Faber's sexually oriented jealousy is evident as he observes: "Sabeth was already a real woman, when she lay like that, not a child" (IV 81/82). Quickly, he pulls a blanket down from the upper bunk to cover her body, perhaps to squelch his rising sexual feelings, but telling himself she may be cold.

Neither man can do much more for Sabeth at the moment, so Faber manipulates the conversation so that both agree to leave her cabin together. To prevent the young man from returning,

Faber challenges him to a game of Ping-Pong (IV 81). All tables are occupied, so Faber engages him instead in a conversation about turbines, graphic art, and the business aspects of the young man's profession.

Although Faber likes the young artist well enough, he cannot understand what Sabeth sees in him. Faber most resents the fact that the young man talks only about himself, his dreams and his future, without showing any interest in Faber. After all, he is "a man in an important position" (IV 82), and the young man could show some interest in "what someone like him had already achieved in this world" (IV 82). Annoyed, Faber concludes young whippersnappers like this friend of Sabeth's have no respect for the accomplishments of their elders, a complaint he will repeat later in reference to Sabeth. The young only smile politely, Faber observes, if one tells them about one's accomplishments. Of course, he quickly assures himself, there is no reason why he, Walter Faber, engineer, working for UNESCO, should feel inferior to this young man.

But jealousy compels Faber to tell Sabeth's friend about his accomplishments anyway. Faber is jealous of the young man's profession, which is artistic, and of his plans, hopes, and dreams for the future. Compared with Faber's own, they seem so vital, so forward-looking and creative. The young man's confident outlook, his exuberance, and his energy—all of which Faber also observed in Sabeth's Ping-Pong game—make Faber feel envious and inferior, for he can no longer match any of them. Besides, Faber fears that his future may be limited. Although he tries to ignore the problem as soon as his stomach pains stop, he fears that he may be seriously ill.

Later in the day, when Faber takes Sabeth some pills he promised her earlier, perhaps some medication for motion sickness, which once helped him in a similar situation, Sabeth does not let him in even though she is fully dressed; instead, she accepts the medicine through the door she opens only a crack. Faber wonders if the young man is there. Again he feels jealous and insecure, masking his emotional reaction once more with a condescending observation: "Holding hands and taking off her [espadrilles] hadn't helped her" (IV 82/83).

Max Frisch has always been interested in jealousy, one of the most powerful and destructive emotions. In his first *Tagebuch* he defines it as "the fear of comparisons" (II 713; *Sketch I 268*), a definition appropriate for many of the male characters in his novels, from Jürg Reinhart in *Die Schwierigen* to Max in *Montauk*. Men who are confident and sure "of their power and glory" (II 714; *Sketch I 269*), Frisch continues, are seldom plagued by this devastating emotion. The effects of jealousy will be examined in more detail in Chapter Five. Here I shall only note that Faber's jealousy does arise from his fear of Sabeth's comparing him, first, with her youthful, artistic boyfriend, and second, with some of the culturally more knowledgeable passengers aboard, particularly the jovial Baptist minister from Chicago.

This gentleman shares Sabeth's interest in the arts, something Faber has never been interested in; in fact, his interests include little outside the realm of technology. As he listens to the congenial conversation of Sabeth and the Chicago minister, Faber is suddenly appalled by his own ignorance. Particularly in the visual arts, Sabeth and the minister obviously share a great deal of pleasure, much to Faber's jealous dismay.

Their conversation is part of one of the funniest scenes in the novel, during which Faber's jealousy of another man and his envy of someone's artistic knowledge merge. The scene takes place, if we are to believe the sequence in which Faber reports it, after Sabeth's first long conversation with Faber but before she becomes seasick, at a time, therefore, when they know still very little about each other.

Faber and the minister are eating breakfast when Sabeth joins them, which Faber immediately interprets as indicating that Sabeth really likes him, since she could have sat at one of the many empty tables. Casually, she and the minister begin to talk about the Louvre, a topic of which Faber is ignorant. But when he tells Sabeth that he has never been there, she can hardly believe that anyone can be so disinterested in one of this civilization's major art collections. Her reaction feeds Faber's insecurity and his sense of ignorance. His unspoken response is condescending amazement that Sabeth should assume that he *should* be interested in the arts. But it is really the Baptist minister who annoys him, not so much with his silly jokes about engineers, but with his flirtatious behavior toward Sabeth.

The form of the minister's flirtation is what irritates him particularly, as the minister constantly paws Sabeth, as Faber sees it, placing his fleshy hand on her arm, her shoulder, then back on her arm, all the while chatting enthusiastically about art, artists, and the Louvre and interrupting his speech periodically with exclamations of "Listen . . . listen!", to which Sabeth simply replies: "Yes, I'm listening—" (IV 77). The minister is a nuisance, Faber thinks, and goes so far as to accuse him, silently, of pursuing the topic of the Louvre only to be able to continue pawing Sabeth. Faber calls the minister's behavior "eine Altherren-Manier" (IV 77), *"an old-gentleman's mannerism."* One is tempted to respond, as one is so often when Faber jealously criticizes the conduct of other people, with the truism: it takes one to know one. Faber is also, much to his own surprise, given to grabbing people by the arm (IV 17,19).

If one adds to the minister's "repulsive pawing behavior" his smiling and apparently tolerant comments about engineers, comments Faber takes personally, one can understand the basis for the furor of emotions slowly coming to a boil in Faber. Sabeth seems to sense his irritation and tries to get him to talk about robots, but, like a stubborn child, Faber refuses.

Seldom are Faber's feelings of jealousy, insecurity, and inferiority resolved as happily as at the conclusion of this incident. Faber's cabin mate, Lewin, a hulking Israeli farmer on his way home from California, joins the trio. As he does so, two conversation groups form: Sabeth and the minister continue to talk about art and the Louvre, and Lewin and Faber discuss diesel engines, because Lewin has recently visited the ship's engine room. Faber, however, never takes his eyes off Sabeth. As he watches jealously, he sees her, still listening attentively, remove the Baptist's hand from her arm and place it, like a napkin, beside her arm on the table. Faber's inner tension dissolves in laughter, which puts the somewhat embarrassed minister on the defensive. Sabeth rescues the poor fellow by commenting admiringly: "He really knows a lot" (IV 78/79).

If Faber's statements can be believed verbatim, it is Sabeth who asks him, not the other way around, to show her the ship's engine room. Soon it is clear, however, that Faber has subtly suggested the visit, perhaps to get even with the minister, whose knowledge about the arts, Faber believes, has impressed

Sabeth deeply. Well, if it is knowledge that impresses this young lady, he, Walter Faber, engineer, travelling on behalf of UNESCO, certainly has lots of technical knowledge he can put on display for her benefit.

The visit to the ship's engine room figures significantly in Faber's relationship with Sabeth. It symbolizes his cautious descent into the depths of his own being. On the surface, the tone and language with which Faber describes their visit seem objective, almost nonchalant. Frisch has, however, chosen a rhythmic pattern and vocabulary that reveal Faber's excitement. In the bowels of the ship, the inner vibrations Faber feels in Sabeth's presence merge with those produced externally by the powerful engines driving the ship. The effect on him is sensual, if not sexual. The rapidly alternating technical and nontechnical detail and objective and subjective statements with which Faber describes his observations, sensations, and reactions as he and Sabeth climb down a series of iron ladders to the engine room floor vividly demonstrate Frisch's skill in communicating psychological insights.

As Sabeth climbs catlike down the ladders, the watching crew, who believe her to be Faber's daughter, respond with calls, whistles, and lecherous leers—at least that is how Faber perceives their encouraging comments and interested stares. Sabeth, seemingly oblivious to what Faber labels the crew's overtly sexual attention, finds them to be friendly and bemoans the fact that they have to travel the ocean their entire lives without ever seeing it. Her sympathies are obviously with them, as they are later with the fish outside the ship's hull, while Faber is explaining technical details.

That Faber's mind is not exclusively on technical data is illustrated by his detailed description of Sabeth climbing down the ladder in front of him:

> Sabeth in ihren schwarzen Cowboy-Hosen mit den ehemals weißen Nähten, der grüne Kamm in ihrer Hintertasche, ihr rötlicher Roßschwanz, der über den Rücken baumelt, unter ihrem Pullover die zwei Schulterblätter, die Kerbe in ihrem straffen und schlanken Rücken, dann ihre Hüften, die jugendlichen Schenkel in der schwarzen Hose, die bei den

Waden aufgekrempelt sind, ihre Knöchel—ich fand sie schön, aber nicht aufreizend. Nur sehr schön! (IV 86-87)

Sabeth in her black jeans with the once white seams, the green comb in her back pocket, the reddish pony-tail dangling over her back, the two shoulder blades under her black pullover, the groove in her taut, slim back, then her hips, her youthful thighs in the black trousers that were [rolled up to] the calves, her ankles—I found her beautiful, but not provocative. Just very beautiful. (88)

Faber's use of vividly descriptive language that evokes sensual images and his insistence that he does not find Sabeth provocative, only beautiful—even his choice of "provocative"— belie the objective impression he tries to create and behind which he wants to hide. They expose his deep infatuation, his growing obsession with this young woman. This is the first time in his report that Faber has called anything "beautiful." That it is a human body, that of a woman, intensifies the dichotomy of feelings Faber harbors about both.

A moment later Faber assists Sabeth down the last few rungs of the ship's ladder—unnecessarily, it seems, since she was in no real danger of falling. He describes their first physical contact, brief and opportunistically initiated by him, as follows:

Ihre Hüften waren merkwürdig leicht, zugleich stark, anzufassen wie das Steuerrad meines Studebakers, graziös, im Durchmesser genau so—eine Sekunde lang, dann stand sie auf dem Podest aus gelochtem Blech, ohne im mindesten zu erröten, sie dankte für die unnötige Hilfe und wischte sich ihre Hände an einem Bündel bunter Putzfäden. Auch für mich war nichts Aufreizendes dabei gewesen. . . . (IV 87)

Her hips were remarkably light and at the same time strong, gripping them was like gripping the steering wheel of my Studebaker, the same slenderness, exactly the same diameter—just for a second, then she was standing on the landing of perforated sheet metal; she didn't blush in the least, but thanked me for my unnecessary help and wiped her hands on a bundle of brightly colored cotton waste. I hadn't felt stirred by the contact either. . . . (88)

Again, Faber's description of this incident seems to be, on the surface, factual and objective. Its sensuality does not escape Faber, however, as is illustrated by his unusual and somewhat daring comparison between the tactical experiences of holding Sabeth by the hips and holding the steering wheel of his car between his hands, especially not when this analogy is followed by Faber's insistence that the event he has just described contained nothing provocative for him, *either*. The statement is presumptious, because it assumes that Sabeth might have felt or was expected to experience his touch as provocative, which is doubtful; it is also a veiled admission that Faber expected touching Sabeth to be provocative—and that, for him, it was.

To reinforce the supposed casualness of his first physical contact with Sabeth, which Faber craved for some time, he cleverly follows this description by reporting his technically oriented observations, which he merely thought about but did not bother to explain to Sabeth, problems of torsion, friction coefficient, and metal fatigue that she would not have been interested in. Of course Faber is right. Sabeth, a layperson, is not particularly interested in technical explanations. Not surprisingly, therefore, her thoughts are already outside with the fish, with living things, while he is still pointing out construction features of the ship's hull. When Faber takes Sabeth's hand and places it over one of the huge rivets holding the ship's hull together, she wonders aloud about sharks on the other side of it, or at least, over the noise of the engines, that is what Faber thinks she is saying. He concludes his report of their visit to the engine room with the casual remark: "Ich hatte ihr etwas bieten wollen" (IV 87), *"I had wanted to give her something [special]"* (89).

What does Faber know about this young woman into whose orbit he is willingly drawn more and more? He knows that she received a one-semester scholarship to study at Yale (the English translation erroneously states "a year"; IV 82/83) and that she is presently on her way home to Athens, where her mother lives. He also knows that she believes her stepfather, a certain Mr. Piper who lives in East Berlin, is a dedicated Communist, and that Sabeth is worried about finding an inexpensive hotel room in Paris,

144   LIFE AS A MAN

where she plans to stay for a few days to revisit the Louvre. Later she plans to hitchhike to Rome, a plan Faber, in a parenthetic comment, labels "Wahnsinn" (IV 82), *"crazy"* (84). Sabeth does not yet know what she will do at home. Interested in both the natural sciences and the arts, she is thinking of studying either pediatrics or visual arts. She likes to travel and toys with the idea of becoming a stewardess, which Faber forbids her outright, on what basis is unclear. Whatever turn her life takes, Sabeth wants to visit China and India some day. While they chat on deck, Sabeth often lies on her deck chair clad in a bathing suit and he stands at the railing. He feels self-conscious about his age and intimidated by her youth. He is uncomfortable in his role—that of either Sabeth's uncle or her peer.

Faber, who during the fast pace of his normal life is able to avoid involvement in other people's lives, is shown to be extremely vulnerable once that routine is broken. That was so during the emergency landing in the Mexican desert, where his past caught up with him in the person of Herbert Hencke; it was so on his trip through the Guatemalan jungle, where teeming, uncontrolled nature confronted his rigid, controlled attitude toward bodily natural functions, life, and death; and it is so now on this transatlantic voyage during which, unprotected by his usual routine, he finds himself vulnerable to human impulses, his own and Sabeth's.

In the past Faber has always been able to persuade himself that the factors affecting human lives—time, aging, and death, for example—do not concern him; technology placed him beyond their reach. As he explained to Sabeth and the Baptist minister in proposing that ancient statues are the ancestors of today's robots:

Die Primitiven versuchten den Tod zu annullieren, indem sie den Menschenleib abbilden—wir, indem wir den Menschenleib ersetzen. Technik statt Mystik! (IV 77)

Primitive peoples tried to annul death by portraying the human body—we do it by finding substitutes for the human body. Technology instead of mysticism! (78)

Thus, while the ancients attempted to annul death by portraying the human body in time, Faber, the technologist, wants to annul death by replacing the human body with something (robots) existing outside the restrictions of time.

As long as he stays busy and keeps moving, Faber can ignore the knowledge that time is transitory, that our existence is always confronted by another, "a nonexistence, which we call death" (II 499; *Sketch I* 116). Just as his response to the challenge of nature is that technological man shall ultimately control it, so his response to the challenge of time is that humans shall somehow transcend it, exist outside its restrictions. This is, perhaps, Faber's fundamental error: ignoring the need to shape his life according to the contours prescribed by time, limits signaled by the natural cycle of youth, middle age, and old age (Butler 105). Had Faber not indulged in hubris by considering himself outside the controls nature places on human life, he might at least have questioned the propriety of his relationship with Sabeth, a woman thirty years younger than he, on this basis alone.

Faber does not. Despite his discomfort about his age when he is with Sabeth, despite his impatience with the thoughtlessness of youth and his jealousy of its seemingly limitless future, and despite his abdominal pain, he persists in ignoring the realities of time as diligently as he has rejected the realities of nature.

Faber would like technology, something rational and measurable, to replace the invisible controls of nature, which he labels "mysticism." Mythology is a part of mysticism, and so is intuition; he denies the existence of both. Ironically, the two things Faber prizes most highly in his life—the theory of electromagnetic forces in nature that he refers to as the Maxwellian demon and his portable typewriter, Baby Hermes—bear names that combine mysticism and technology, not replace one with the other.

From mysticism and mythology it is not a long step to chance, *Zufall*, which Faber acknowledges as a component of the law of probability. As an engineer, however, he might have noted how many chance encounters and spontaneous decisions have occurred in his usually stable, regulated life since the night he boarded the plane to Mexico City. Could they be more than *zufällige* (chance) occurrences? Could they be providence; could they be fate? "I don't believe in providence and fate," Faber explains:

als Techniker bin ich gewohnt mit den Formeln der Wahrscheinlichkeit zu rechnen. . . . Ich bestreite nicht: Es war mehr als ein Zufall, daß alles so gekommen ist, es war eine ganze Kette von Zufällen. Aber wieso Fügung? Ich brauche, um das Unwahrscheinliche als Erfahrungstatsache gelten zu lassen, keinerlei Mystik; Mathematik genügt mir.
  Mathematisch gesprochen:
    Das Wahrscheinliche . . . und das Unwahrscheinliche . . . unterscheiden sich nicht dem Wesen nach, sondern nur der Häufigkeit nach. . . . Indem wir vom Wahrscheinlichen sprechen, ist ja das Unwahrscheinliche immer schon inbegriffen und zwar als Grenzfall des Möglichen, und wenn es einmal eintritt, das Unwahrscheinliche, so besteht für unsereinen keinerlei Grund zur Verwunderung, zur Erschütterung, zur Mystifikation. (IV 22)

as a technologist I am used to reckoning with the formulas of probability. . . . I don't deny it was more than a coincidence which made things turn out as they did, it was a whole train of coincidences. But what has providence to do with it? I don't need any mystical explanation for the occurrence of the improbable; mathematics explains it adequately, as far as I'm concerned.
  Mathematically speaking, the probable . . . and the improbable . . . are not different in kind, but only in frequency . . . . The term "probability" includes improbability at the extreme limits of probability, and when the improbable does occur this is no cause for surprise, bewilderment, or mystification. (19-20)

However, if Faber looked carefully enough at the series of chance occurrences in his life since that snowy lift-off in New York, he might well question whether their frequency does not exceed the limits of the law of probability. The improbable, chance, may not be cause for bewilderment, but in Faber's case it seems to form a pattern of its own.
  Max Frisch has definite opinions about the role of *Zufall* (chance) in human life, which he recorded in the last entry of his first *Tagebuch* (II 749-50/*Sketch I 300-01*). "Der Zufall," Frisch writes there, "[ist] was uns zufällt, ohne unsere Voraussicht, ohne unseren bewußten Willen" (II 749), *"chance [is] what comes*

our way without our preknowledge, with no conscious use of will power" (Sketch I 300). Frisch continues:

> Das Verblüffende, das Erregende jedes Zufalls besteht darin, daß wir unser eigenes Gesicht erkennen; der Zufall zeigt mir, wofür ich zur Zeit ein Auge habe, und ich höre, wofür ich eine Antenne habe. . . . Wir erleben keine [Zufälle], die nicht zu uns gehören. Am Ende ist es immer das Fälligste, was uns zufällt. (II 750)

> *The amazing and startling thing about every chance happening is that it brings us face to face with ourselves; chance shows me the things for which I now have an eye, which I am at this moment attuned to hear. . . . We experience none that are not relevant to us. In the final count it is always the most fitting thing that befalls us.* (Sketch I 301)

The *Zufälle* that occur in Faber's life after he boards the plane for Mexico City begin with the engine defect that leads to the plane's emergency landing and his discovery that his seatmate happens to be Joachim Hencke's brother; from Herbert Hencke he learns that Joachim married Hanna twenty years earlier, that they had a daughter, and that they were later divorced. This chance reawakening of his past leads Faber to the unreasoned, spontaneous decision to accompany Herbert through the Guatemalan jungle to visit Joachim, who is dead when they arrive. Back in New York, circumstances lead Faber to sail instead of fly to France. He is accidentally delayed in his apartment, when the travel agency phones him to say that he can begin his voyage the next day. Finally, he meets on board, by chance, a woman who is his daughter, because she happens to be waiting in line in front of him, her reddish ponytail dangling in front of him, attracting his attention.

A lot of *Zufälle* occurring in a short time provoke Faber to uncharacteristically spontaneous actions. In Houston, feeling extremely ill during a stopover on his trip to Caracas, he tried to interrupt the trip. Hiding first in a bar, then in a restroom, he wandered back into the airport lobby when the announcements urging him to reboard the plane had stopped and he thought that the plane had taken off. He was speechless when a flight attendant accosted him and promptly escorted him back onto the plane. This incident, which occurs early in the novel, seems to indicate that a force stronger than mere chance and spontaneity has entered Faber's life. Based on the information he received later from Herbert Hencke about Joachim and Hanna and the information he receives piecemeal from Sabeth about her life, he, as a student of mathematics, ought to have been warned that the improbable, which is also accounted for by the theory of probability, might have become a reality in his case. This possibility seems to him an impossibility, however, as he states repeatedly in his report. The improbable does not fit into his view of a reasonable, ordered, and calculable world. For once, he ignores the full implications of the theory of probability (Lüthi 29), as he ignores the factual, scientific implications of his stomach pains.

However much Faber would like to ignore the operation of chance and however strongly he would like to reject the natural forces of time, sexuality, and death, he becomes more deeply enmeshed in all of them on this ocean voyage. In describing the Guatemalan jungle in his report, he juxtaposes such images as "stinkende Fruchtbarkeit" and "blühende Verwesung" (IV 51), *"stench of fertility"* and *"blossoming decay" (51)*, to mirror his confused reaction to the rampant procreation he sees. His reaction to human sexuality contains the same confusion: though he wants to repress it, he is almost compulsively alert to it. His thoughts about Sabeth and his jealousy of any man near her cause him to react more like a hypersensitive, sexually repressed teenager than a fifty-year-old man.

He films Sabeth compulsively. Recording on film what he sees is a habit: he filmed the desert scene, the ship's departure from New York, and now he records on film what he sees on shipboard, but especially Sabeth. She does not approve. Once his photography so angers her that she demands he explain what he wants from her. Her anger startles Faber and makes him feel insecure. Another time, when he is observing Sabeth from a distance, she tells him: "You keep watching me all the time, Mister Faber, I don't like it" (IV 85/86). Faber's silent reaction, again insecure, is: "She doesn't like me" (IV 85).

He wants to capture her, to possess her, at least on film. If she knew it, she would not like that, either. Sabeth is perfectly capable of taking care of herself, as her handling of the Baptist minister demonstrated to Faber. She gives the impression of a woman at ease and at peace with herself most of the time, basically—an unusual state for a person only twenty years old. At the same time, Faber has observed, she has a healthy curiosity about people and her environment.

During their last evening on board, Sabeth senses Faber's loneliness. He has not danced all evening. Even Lewin, the Israeli farmer, has danced with her once, but not Faber. Is he sad, she wonders, as she leaves the dance floor to look for him. He is on deck, and when she joins him there he lends her his jacket so she will not catch cold, dressed in a thin evening dress and standing in the strong wind.

No, he isn't sad, he tells her; he simply cannot do these modern dances, these "existentialist jigs" (IV 89/91) in which everyone dances by himself. That this day is his birthday, his fiftieth, he does not tell her, perhaps out of vanity, because Sabeth once guessed, in answer to his question, that he is forty. Always open to new experiences, Sabeth finds exciting "a night like this on deck, with the wind whistling through the ropes and flapping the canvas of the lifeboats" (IV 90/91). Faber, not to sound sentimental, escapes in a description of the night sky, fully aware that focusing on a comet is mainly an attempt to control his confused emotions.[2] He tells Sabeth he has two wishes: that she will not become a stewardess (which he had already "forbidden" her), and that she will not hitchhike to Rome. He offers to pay for her transportation, but Sabeth responds with a peal of laughter. Disappointed, he concludes: "She misunderstood me" (IV 90/92).

Such comments in Faber's report may indicate that Sabeth really does not understand him, but her actions indicate otherwise. This is already evident after their first Ping-Pong game. Late that evening, while walking on deck, he encounters her and her boyfriend promenading arm in arm. According to Faber, "she pretended not to notice me; as though I wasn't under any circumstances to know she was in love" (IV 74/74). More accurately, Sabeth later identifies Faber's perception to be motivated by jealousy. Despite his denials, she is aware of his deep loneliness.

Faber is still irritated, this last evening of their voyage, by Sabeth's suspicion that he is sad because of loneliness. He explains to her that living alone is the only possible condition for a man. Again, Sabeth's response is laughter. Faber quickly adds details of why sharing his life with a woman on a day-to-day basis is not for him; the mere thought of it drives him to think about joining the Foreign Legion.[3] His description of women in the morning and at breakfast time is meant to be funny but earns him only Sabeth's rebuke. She calls him a cynic. Faber objects, but says nothing.

When Sabeth is asked by someone to dance, Faber remains at the table to continue, in a silent monologue, his self-justifying tirade against living with a woman, something he cannot stand for any longer than three weeks, he claims. He starts by weighing the pros and cons of marriage, but it soon becomes apparent that, despite the strain human associations are for him and his view of feelings as "fatigue phenomena," Walter Faber's existence is desolate. Neither writing letters nor drinking alcohol is a comfort at times when he is especially aware of his empty, sterile life. He admits: "Sometimes I just fall asleep, the newspaper on my lap and my cigarette on the carpet" (IV 92/94). Once he awakens, he pulls himself together and turns on the radio: an all-night classical station, broadcasting symphonies; he turns it off and stands quietly in the apartment, holding the glass of gin that he really does not like, not moving so as not to hear his own footsteps. The picture is that of a deeply lonely man. He concludes, however, that his situation is not tragic, only tiresome: "You can't wish yourself 'good-night'. . . ," he observes, but adds quickly: "Is that a reason for marrying?" (IV 93/94).

His real reason for not marrying has become transparent by now: he is afraid to commit himself to any woman, afraid to open up, to let anyone know him and his vulnerabilities. Taking such a chance might prove his view of life wrong.

Nevertheless, marrying is exactly what he proposes before he and Sabeth part at Le Havre. Only once before has he proposed marriage to anyone, and that was to Hanna.

Sabeth introduces the topic during the shipboard party. Returning to the table after a dance and finding Faber deep in thought, she asks what he is thinking about. He claims not to know. Seemingly out of the blue she suggests, "You ought to get married, Mister Faber!" (IV 93/95). Before he can reply, her artist friend has whisked her off to the dance floor again, leaving Faber holding her purse. While he waits for her return, he admits to himself that he knew exactly what he was thinking about: how men and women copulate, the actual process. The specifics seem absurd to him, the idea of it perverse—if only one were not forced by one's own instinctual, sexual drive to join in "the dance." Raw, uncontrolled nature stares at Faber again. At no time during this voyage is the difference between Sabeth and Faber more obvious: she is primarily the actor, he the observer and contemplator.

Faber believes his thinking is logical. He seems unaware that it is also associative and becoming more so during this voyage. Once Sabeth has introduced the subject of marriage, she reminds him increasingly of Hanna; but rather than asking her logical questions based on what he already knows about her life, he performs his third spontaneous act: he proposes marriage to Sabeth. She has just—much to Faber's surprise—bidden her graphic-artist boyfriend farewell at Southampton. She turns crimson, but neither accepts nor rejects his proposal. She asks whether he is serious. Faber's response, as is his habit, is a counter question, disguised as an exclamation: "Why not!" (IV 95).

Somewhat uncomfortably, they go on deck to watch the disembarking passengers, among them Sabeth's friend. They stand silently next to each other at the rail, "without touching" (IV 95/97), as Faber states in his report, adding dramatically: "My life was in her hands. . ." (IV 95/97).

When Sabeth quietly asks him a second time if he is serious about his marriage proposal, he kisses her—her forehead, her cold, flickering eyelids, then her mouth, "which startled me," he adds (IV 95). At that moment, Sabeth seems to Faber more of a stranger than any woman he has ever known. He kisses her tears away, as if she were a child, notices her half open mouth, and finds the entire situation impossible. Clearly, this conclusion is erotically associative. Earlier, as Lajser Lewin, his cabin mate, slept with his head down on the dining table, his half-open mouth—"like the red mouth of a fish against the green aquarium glass" (IV 93/95)—reminded Faber, by association, of Ivy and her "epileptically happy mouth" (IV 94/95) at the moment of orgasm. Sabeth's mouth again forces an association with Ivy, illustrating that Faber is still trapped by his earlier thoughts of human sexuality and human copulation.

Sabeth and Faber remain standing on deck, close to each other, she trembling, whether from the early morning chill or from emotion is not clear. The following day they arrive in Le Havre, where they separate.

Paris

Although both are headed for Paris, Faber and Sabeth do not travel there together, nor have they agreed to meet again. Faber knows exactly where to find her, however: in the Louvre. At first his search for her is unsuccessful. He makes his way through the vast museum complex on several visits, and Sabeth, without giving any sign of recognition, as she later admits, notices him a few days before they actually meet. Faber, however, flatters himself into believing that Sabeth thinks their meeting was really chance, because that is what he wants to believe. Their separation lasted a week.

They sit in the Tuileries Gardens while it is snowing, rush across the Place de la Concorde where Faber loses his hat to the Parisian traffic, and walk on arm in arm, Faber "hatless, like a boy in the flurrying snow" (IV 101/103). Faber is probably not aware of the metaphoric implication of his observation. The simile is not only a reminder of the blinding snowstorm during which he began his flight to Caracas from New York a little over a month ago, but also an illustration of his tumultuous emotional state, which, in Sabeth's presence, blinds him to the facts of his life.

Twice before he acted spontaneously in her presence. First, slightly drunk, he told her the grisly details of discovering Joachim's body in Guatemala, although he never mentioned his friend's name. The second occasion was his marriage proposal, about a week earlier. Now he reacts spontaneously for the third time, inviting her to the opera that evening. Faber has never been to the Paris Opera, an environment he would normally shy away from, since many operas are driven by passion and powerful emotions that on occasion burst into the open, amplified many times by the *crescendi* from the orchestra. Having found Sabeth again, however, he does not want to lose her. He manipulates her into accepting his invitation by asking her to buy the tickets for him. She accepts the invitation, and they arrange to meet at seven that evening.

By attending the opera, Faber is willingly subjecting himself to art and to emotion in an activity that is likely to please Sabeth. Something is happening to the man who attempts to rationalize every experience, but Walter Faber is not aware of it.

He arrives much too early to take Sabeth to the opera. Instead of waiting in the café where they agreed to meet, he sits in the glassed-in veranda of the café next door and, once more playing the secret observer, watches for Sabeth. She, too, is early and waits for him in the designated place. Faber drinks his Pernod without haste as he follows her every move through the glass. "I was happier than I had ever been in Paris" (IV 104/107), he writes. And why not? No one is competing with him for Sabeth's attention. Possessively proud that this young woman is waiting for *him*, he savors his feelings as long as he can, observing: "I could never be happier than [now]" (IV 105/107).

He is not always happy during his Paris visit: the old Walter Faber is having difficulties with the new one. When he reports to his boss, Williams, he feels guilty about having interrupted his Caracas trip to visit Joachim and even about having traveled to Paris by ship instead of the customary plane. These actions now seem irresponsible to him, especially the delay of his Caracas trip. After all, his is the reputation of a man who takes his job seriously, is always on time, always conscientious. Rattled by Williams' frequent interruption of his report with the phrase, "That's okay"—what is he really thinking? Faber wonders—he gratuitously adds a brief report of Joachim's suicide. Williams suggests Faber take some time off. At first Faber refuses. But a few days later, after he has linked up with Sabeth again and learned that she is still determined to hitchhike to Rome, he changes his mind. He now plans a leisurely trip of two weeks or more through southern France and Italy and accepts Williams' offer of his car.

How Faber persuades Sabeth to travel to Rome with him is open to speculation. His offer and her acceptance of it, though apparently only an arrangement of convenience, actually demonstrate the voluntary decision of both to enter into a closer relationship, one that will become far more personal and intimate than either may have thought possible. Frisch makes clear how intimate their relationship is to become by interrupting the flow of Faber's report at this point. Frisch uses this technique in this novel whenever he wants to call attention to a specific important topic, one that has been introduced but so far has not been dealt with adequately. This device allows Frisch also to expose a character's basic attitude about a given topic.

This time the subject is abortion. In a lengthy single-paragraph tirade (more than 80 printed lines), Faber justifies abortion (IV 105-07). He begins quietly, but soon introduces an extraordinary staccato rhythm; his argument passes through non sequitur, cliché, wild generalization, and primitive fear to an impressive finale in which he states forcefully his opposition to the idea of fate. He concludes that anyone in this technical age who opposes abortion is completely irrational and might as well abandon civilization:

> Wir leben technisch, der Mensch als Beherrscher der Natur, der Mensch als Ingenieur, und wer dagegen redet, der soll auch keine Brücke benutzen, die nicht die Natur gebaut hat. Dann müßte man schon konsequent sein und jeden Eingriff ablehnen, das heißt: sterben an jeder Blinddarmentzündung. Weil Schicksal! Dann auch keine Glühbirne, keinen Motor, keine Atom-Energie, keine Rechenmaschine, keine Narkose—dann los in den Dschungel! (IV 107)
>
> *We live technologically, with man as the master of nature, man as the engineer, and let anyone who raises his voice against it stop using bridges not built by nature. To be consistent, they would have to reject any kind of operation; that would mean people dying every time they had appendicitis. [Because that's fate!] No electric-light bulbs, no engines, no atomic energy, no adding machines, no anesthetics—[straight] back to the jungle!* (109-10)

The eruptive quality and orgasmic rhythm of this passage are startling. They reveal Faber's undissipated guilt about the abortion he and Hanna agreed to twenty years ago when they decided not to marry. Better and more effectively than any other passage in the novel, this soliloquy unmasks Faber as an intellectual and moral hypocrite. His linguistic tour de force cannot conceal the real reason behind his defense of abortion: his fear of commitment to his then fiancée, Hanna, and his refusal then to accept responsibility for his actions, including the child he fathered. Walter Faber, engineer and self-proclaimed spokesman of the modern, technological society, asserts in this remarkable interlude that abortion is ethically justified in the name of a humanity that no longer accepts nature as an idol to be revered, but that sees itself as the controller and eventual master of nature.

Italy and Greece

When Faber resumes the report of their travels, he and Sabeth are already in Italy. Both are happy, Faber reports, "in spite of the difference of our ages" (IV 107/110). When they talk to each other, they now use the familiar form of "you," "du." Today such usage may seem natural, since Sabeth and Faber are spending a lot of time together. During the 1950s, the period of this novel, however, social conventions still dictated the formal usage, especially in view of the differences in their ages and professional positions. That it has not been maintained indicates that their relationship has changed: Sabeth and Faber are no longer "acquaintances" but now consider each other "close friends." Sabeth seems to prefer the company of this older, more mature man, as her scornful evaluation of men her own age shows:

"Buben! . . . Das kannst du dir gar nicht vorstellen—man kommt sich wie ihre Mutter vor, und das ist furchtbar!" (IV 107)

"Boys! . . . You can't imagine what they're like—they think you're their mother, and that's frightful!" (110)

The implication is clear: these young men do not know how to treat her as a woman. Does that mean Faber treats her as one? It does.

During the first night of their trip to Rome, in Avignon, Sabeth and Faber became lovers. Faber recalls the date clearly: "It was the night (May 13th) of the eclipse of the moon" (IV 124/127). They have been sitting outside, at a café, when the spectacle in the sky starts. Faber pays quickly, and they walk to their hotel terrace where, standing arm in arm, they watch the eclipse for an hour. Faber explains the phenomenon in scientific detail to Sabeth who is deeply affected by the majestic event and "kissed me as never before" (IV 124/128).

Faber, too, is affected by the spectacle. He, who in the Mexican desert described the moon as "a calculable mass circling round our planet, an example of gravitation, interesting, but in what way an experience?" (IV 24/22), all at once feels the impact of the eclipse. The moon, formerly a peaceful, undisturbing entity, suddenly acquires the unsettling, mysterious aspect of "an enormous mass drifting, or hurtling, through space" (IV 124/128). Comparing his two reactions to the moon, the second less than six weeks after the first, one notes that Faber's powers of perception, although still dominated by his rationalism, have been growing during the past weeks.

The shared experience of watching the eclipse, which moves them deeply, causes Sabeth and Faber to share their thoughts and feelings, making them vulnerable to each other. As Faber comments: "I spoke about death and life . . . in quite general terms, and we were both excited. . . " (IV 124-25/128). Sabeth, Faber observes, "felt for the first time that I took us both seriously" (IV 124/128). Her response is instinctive: she kisses him "as never before."

It is she, the younger of the two and the woman, who comes to Faber's room later, to share her love and herself with him. Faber accepts her gift of love, having neither the courage nor the desire to send her away. From that night on, his life is not to be the same.

There is no question of Faber's guilt, of his deliberate failure to pursue the truth of Sabeth's identity simply by asking her, before they become lovers, who her parents are. The incestuous nature of their relationship is not, however, central to this study. The central issue is rather the quality of their relationship and how it contributes to Faber's growth so that he may eventually glimpse "das wirkliche Leben."

Faber's love for Sabeth has changed him in many ways. He feels neither guilt nor shame after their sexual union, as he did with all other women except Hanna. He and Sabeth, he points out, are happy as they continue their journey through Italy. Through Sabeth's love, Faber gains a degree of self-acceptance he has not known before. He discovers joy in being alive, joy in a given moment, and joy in their sexual relationship. Through Sabeth he begins to see what, subconsciously, he has been aware all along was missing from his life: the pure joy of living, of seeing, and of wonderment; an appreciation for the visual arts; a love for all living creatures, for their beauty and their enormous potential; the joy of reaching beyond one's own selfish desires to experience someone else's happiness. With Sabeth as guide, he begins to understand a different, more complete view of life than he has known, although he is never able to integrate it completely into his own. Not only does Sabeth guide him to the richness and beauty that life has to offer; she also, like a female Hermes, leads him back to Greece, the cradle of civilization, back to Hanna, and, symbolically, to Hades, for it is in Greece that both Sabeth and Faber die.[4]

Faber's learning process is by no means smooth. As he points out, their trip through Italy is not always easy for either of them: "I bored her with my experience of life, [and] she made me [feel] old by waiting from morning to evening, wherever we were, for my enthusiasm. . ." (IV 110/112-13).

Like most people, Sabeth is enthusiastic about things she is interested in. When Faber tries to explain something technical or to tell her of *his* experiences, *his* achievements, Sabeth listens politely, Faber comments, "as one listens to an old man" (IV 109/112), without interrupting him. Now and then she anticipates a detail, indicating that she has heard this story from him before, which embarrasses him. At the same time, Sabeth has boundless confidence in Faber, "merely because one is thirty years older" (IV 109/111). She even believes him capable— because "You're a man!" (IV 114)—of chasing away a group of American tourists who, to her dismay, stop to picnic near the ancient Roman burial mound she and Faber chose temporarily as their resting place.[5]

Faber does not lose his sense of insecurity easily. He is sure, for instance, that Sabeth has no respect for him or his experience, which annoys him. Faber believes that only the future and a bit of the present are important to Sabeth. She, in fact, demonstrates vividly that she lives in the present, anticipates the future with joy, and has a genuine interest in the past, because, after all, her mother is an archeologist. Sabeth expresses her thirst for knowledge in her devoted study of the art objects in the museums and of the history of the towns and churches she and Faber visit on their way to Rome, her faithful Baedeker their guide.

Despite the changes Sabeth may have encouraged in Faber since they met, she still considers him cynical and ironic about opinions he does not like. Her attitude to life differs greatly from his. Sabeth looks forward to everything that has not yet happened in her young life, both concrete and indefinite: a visit to Tivoli Gardens in Rome, having children of her own someday, and even tomorrow morning's breakfast. Faber envies this joyous expectation, partly because he senses limitations on his own future and partly because his ability to enjoy life is so much more limited. In his defense he points out: "I took pleasure in every moment that was in any real sense pleasurable" (IV 109/112).

Feelings of jealousy, like those of insecurity, never leave Faber completely. Although he observes, "I saw no reason to be jealous" (IV 108/110), he also admits, "Something kept making me jealous" (IV 108/111). Faber is envious of Sabeth's youth and optimism; jealous of men who may be his rivals for her attention; and envious of her genuine interest in the visual arts, of her insatiable hunger to know the facts about the objects she is looking at and the places they are visiting, and most of all of her ability to experience uninhibitedly the joy that she sometimes expresses in song. Faber occasionally feels like an imposter, pretending to share Sabeth's enthusiasm when in fact he really does not; often he would rather sit in a café with a glass of Campari instead of trudging along with Sabeth through old churches and a seemingly endless number of museums.

Nevertheless, in an effort to please Sabeth, to be near her and to share more fully her life and interests, Faber is willing to learn new things, although not without a tough struggle to overcome his reluctance to accept anything that cannot be explained rationally. Faber, in fact, takes major steps to learn about art, such as defiantly stepping in front of a statue to test whether Sabeth's mother is right in saying that every person can experience a work of art. The assertion fails the test; Faber "was merely bored" (IV 110/*113*). A passing Italian couple, the father carrying the sleeping child, is far more interesting, he finds, than all the statues in the museum. But he does not stop trying to reach outside himself to learn.

His curiosity is perhaps getting the better of him when he approaches a tour group and listens to its guide, a priest, explain a bas-relief depicting the birth of Venus; then, almost like a first-grader, which in matters of art he still is, he immediately has to show off his just-acquired knowledge to Sabeth, commenting that the young flutist standing off to one side is "entzückend" (IV 111), "*charming*" (*113*). This immediately earns him Sabeth's rebuke. "Entzückend," she exclaims in youthful exuberance, is a totally inappropriate word to describe such a work of art. She reels off a whole string of even less appropriate adjectives, chosen helter-skelter from the adolescent's vocabulary she returns to when she is excited, suggesting "fantastic, absolutely insane, super, brilliant, terrific" instead (IV 111). Perhaps her emotional response is triggered by her recognition that, for the first time, Faber has expressed an opinion of his own about a work of art. His reaction to Sabeth's apparent criticism is a feeling of injury: he cannot stand it, he writes, when someone tells him what he has to feel, adding with annoyance: "I feel like a blind man" (IV 111/*113*).

But Faber does not give up his effort to learn more about the things that interest Sabeth. A short time later he is the one who discovers, without help, as he points out proudly, the head of a sleeping Erinys. Tentatively he tries out some adjectives to describe his reaction to this young Fury's sleeping head. Finally he decides to use a simile to describe the statue properly:

> Es war ein steinerner Mädchenkopf, so gelegt, daß man drauf blickt wie auf das Gesicht einer schlafenden Frau, wenn man sich auf die Ellbogen stützt. (IV 111)

> *It was the stone head of a girl, so placed that when you leaned forward on your elbows you looked down upon it as though upon the face of a sleeping woman.* (*114*)

Then he wonders what the Erinys might be dreaming about, a question that to him is far more interesting than knowing from what century the statue dates. This is a curious turnabout for Walter Faber, the engineer. Suddenly, his interest in facts yields to an interest in the dreams of a statue, although he grants that may be "no way to look at art" (IV 111/114). The engineer who declared at the start of his report, "Novels don't interest me. Nor do dreams" (IV 15/12), seems to have come a long way since the night he took off from New York for Mexico City.

A moment later, unintentionally, Faber provides Sabeth with a perceptional experience that they share, like children playing a game. Faber has walked away from the head of the sleeping Erinys, where Sabeth is still standing, to look once more at the birth-of-Venus bas-relief. As he stands facing Venus, his body casts a shadow upon the Erinys, changing the light on the statue and making her face appear "far more wide awake, more lively, positively wild" (IV 111/114). Sabeth and Faber change places, so he can watch the transformation himself. Although he explains the change as merely a matter of lighting, he, too, is delighted with the effect.

Neither Sabeth nor Faber indicate that they understand the symbolic significance of their discovery, as Max Frisch, of course, does. Their observation is a warning, provided one is able to understand its language. Faber does not mention in his report that the Venus bas-relief they are looking at contains actually three figures: on one side the flute-playing girl, nude; then Venus, the goddess of love; and on the other side and opposite the girl, a somewhat older, matronly woman carrying a ceremonial vase. Thus Venus is placed literally between the older and the younger woman.[6] As Faber gazes up at the work, his attention is naturally drawn to the younger woman, whom he earlier called "charming," while his shadow awakens the Erinys to give her an expression of wild fury. If we substitute Hanna for the older, veiled woman to the Venus' right and Sabeth for the young one on her left, the meaning of the awakening Fury becomes clear.

Erinyes, in antiquity, were goddesses who avenged any transgression against natural order in the world, especially offenses against the foundations of human society. They punished mercilessly all violations of filial duty, regardless of the circumstances. Thus they pursued Orestes for slaying his mother, even though he was merely avenging his father's murder by his mother and her lover, as the social code of the time demanded;

they also pursued Oedipus for marrying his mother, even though he believed he was acting in accordance with the law and the message he had received from the oracle. The Erinyes' principle was consistent and like that of the Old Testament God: an eye for an eye, a tooth for a tooth.[7] Neither Faber nor Sabeth could have grasped the mythological or real implications of this symbolism and its relevance to their own lives when they made their discovery at the museum in Rome.

As Faber and Sabeth continue their trip through Italy, which he once refers to as a "Hochzeitsreise" (IV 113), "honeymoon" (116), Faber also learns, step by step, more about Sabeth and her family, specifically her mother. He learns from Sabeth—"a child I was treating like a woman, or a woman I was treating like a child, I didn't know myself which it was" (IV 114/*117*)—that her mother works at an archeological institute in Athens because, as Sabeth explains nonchalantly, "she had to earn a living, because she was divorced from Herr Piper" (IV 112/*115*). He also learns that Sabeth's mother majored in philology, not archeology, at the university; that Sabeth does not seem to like her stepfather, Herr Piper, the East German Communist who apparently adopted her; that her mother's first name is Hanna and her maiden name Landsberg, information to which Faber reacts by feeling faint, falling silent, and letting go of Sabeth's arm; and details about their life in Paris, London, and East Berlin during and after World War II.

When Sabeth discovers that Faber once knew her mother, and even Joachim, whom she believes is her father, she thinks it "fantastic, simply fantastic" (IV 118/*121*). She can't imagine her mother as a typical university student "living in a garret" (IV 119/*123*) because Hanna never told her about that part of her life.

Perhaps prompted by his memory of her mother, perhaps by his steadily growing subconscious knowledge that Sabeth may not be Joachim's daughter, Faber expresses concern that she may become pregnant. He learns then that he need not worry, and that he is her third lover. The first was Hardy, "teaching at Yale" (IV 120,153/*123,158*), and the second the graphic artist on the ship, who wants to marry her, but, as Sabeth points out, "that was a mistake on my part, . . . I don't like him at all" (IV 120/*124*).

After she tells Faber, though, Sabeth is worried. "Do you think I'm bad?" (IV 121/124), she asks him. Faber's response shows his increasing confusion and concern. "That's okay . . . that's okay" (IV 121/124), he tells her, using the same meaningless phrase his boss, Williams, used in response to his troubled report about his trip to Caracas and Paris. His confusion is not related to Sabeth's confession per se, but to the accumulating facts that suggest strongly that Sabeth might be his daughter. Faber needs time to think. Therefore, when Sabeth repeats her question, "Do you think I'm bad?" later in the car, he puts the key into the ignition and responds evasively, "Come, . . . don't let's talk" (IV 121/124). But Sabeth would not stop talking about her life and family as they sat in the car, not driving.

Feeling increasingly trapped by the horrifying possibility that his young lover is his daughter, Faber falls back on reason, mathematics, and probability. Feverishly he calculates dates and time spans in his head, then later checks his figures on paper. Given Sabeth's birthday, he only needs to insert two variables into his mathematical considerations: the date that Hanna told him she was pregnant and the date of his departure from Zurich for his first job in Baghdad. The closer he moves the two dates together and the farther he moves them from the date of Sabeth's birthday minus nine months, leaving a comfortable interval between the two sets of dates, the clearer it becomes to him that his calculations are correct: Sabeth cannot possibly be his child; she has to be Joachim's.

The conclusion of his mathematical acrobatics relieves Faber greatly. Ironically, though characteristically, this man of science has ignored the incalculable factors of human behavior, in this case that Hanna might have changed her mind about the abortion she and Faber agreed to before he left Zurich.

Now that his fear about Sabeth's parentage has been dissipated by his self-deception, Faber is merrier than usual. He buys round after round of drinks for the street musicians who have come into the popular pizzeria where he and Sabeth are spending the evening. Sabeth, enjoying the general merriment and Faber's elated mood, bursts out: "Walter . . . isn't this terrific!" (IV 122).

Neither Sabeth nor Faber is really fooled by the outward gaiety, however. The combination of Faber's earlier moodiness, his evasion of her questions, and now his elation, suggests to

Sabeth that their relationship is threatened. She perceives this threat intuitively, but for the wrong reasons: she blames herself, fearing that Faber thinks ill of her because she has had lovers before him, that he will stop loving her, and that he will leave her. Faber, too, senses something is wrong. After they return to their rooms in the hotel, he has an ominous sense of foreboding. Standing alone in his room, he compares himself to a machine that is broken: it receives information commanding it to act, but it no longer functions.

How close, how deeply emotional their relationship has become during the short time they have been together is illustrated by the incident that follows. Sabeth, attempting to set things right between them, goes to Faber's room in tears, dressed in her pajamas and with her black hooded coat thrown around her; she needs to share her fear with him, needs to be reassured by him. To quiet her, Faber, still dressed, cradles her in his arms on the bed. Eventually she relaxes and falls asleep, her head resting on his shoulder, her hand on his chest, reassured by the warmth of his body and the blanket with which he has covered her, by his care and his love for her—"ein schwarzes Bündel mit heißem Haar und Atem" (IV 123), *"a black bundle with hot hair and breath"* (127), Faber observes.

Outside, an Alfa Romeo keeps circling the block, stopping at the corner (for a light?), revving up in neutral gear, and taking off with a roar that shakes the building. All night long, this car passes under the windows of their hotel, preventing Faber from sleeping.

It is possible to interpret the noisy car circling the hotel all night as a symbolic representation of an Erinys, a modern equivalent in a technological age (Blair 153-54, Butler 113-14, Geulen 1965 71).[8] One may also recall that a similar sound bothered Faber weeks earlier: a plane's engines "roaring, being revved up one after the other" (IV 7/3), ready to start the flight to Mexico City. At that time Faber was eager to escape from a woman; now he is holding a different, sleeping woman in his arms. This time he has no desire to escape but silently endures the physical discomfort Sabeth's relaxed body causes him, not daring to disturb her sleep, not wishing to withdraw from her the comfort and the security she needs.

Walter Faber has changed a little from the person he used to be. Sabeth's love and his love for her have opened a window for him through which he is able to glimpse "das wirkliche Leben." Faber, the man who avoids marriage on principle, now admits: "Ich dachte an Heirat wie noch nie — " (IV 108), *"I thought about marriage as never before"* (111). Sabeth, representing the integration of intuitive feeling balanced by intellect, introduced Faber to the creative and mysterious in human nature and to a world of beauty which has no equivalent in his technological world. Sabeth's intelligent mind can follow him into this technical world with genuine interest, but she does not become absorbed by it.

For the first time in his life, Walter Faber really loves another human being. If earlier, on the ship to France or in Paris, he was puzzled sometimes by similarities in looks and manners between Sabeth and Hanna, they trouble him no longer. As he observes: "Since Avignon it had never occurred to me at all" (IV 115/118). His relationship with Sabeth is not just another in a series; it is unique. Sabeth fills his whole existence with spontaneity, with laughter and love. As a result, Faber's insecurities are beginning to diminish, and so is his problem of accepting himself. At last he has begun to place someone other than himself at the center of his universe. His world is expanding exponentially.

Slowly Faber is learning to appreciate the inexplicable rather than to reject it outright because it can be neither proved nor explained. He is also learning to react perceptively with his feelings, not merely his brain, and to express those feelings at least in part. These are all things Sabeth has taught him.

Faber and Sabeth spend their last night together outside, less than a day from Athens. It becomes a memorable night during which Faber's prosaic, rational attitude toward life and Sabeth's imagination unite in a beautiful synthesis (Butler 95). They are not able to find a room in Corinth and decide to spend the night under a fig tree. Barking dogs, an ominous, chthonian symbol Max Frisch employs here, drive the lovers farther away from civilization, out into the hills.[9] As they walk slowly through the cold June night across the mountains to the beach on the other side, Sabeth invents a delightful game of "twenty-one," a game of associate images that forces them to look at the landscape around them and listen to its sounds. The object is to think of an image that describes the shapes, colors, and sounds they see and hear.

They bat their entries back and forth as if they were playing Ping-Pong, and the most appropriate and succinct image wins a point. For example, the path up which they climb between the rocks to the ridge of the mountain is stony, dusty, and moonlit. Faber says it looks like plaster, Sabeth that it looks like snow; they compromise and settle for yoghurt. No point for either. The wind blowing through the grass sounds to Sabeth like the sound of tearing silk; Faber cannot come up with a more appropriate image. One point for Sabeth. When one of them earns twenty-one points, they start a new game.

In the middle of the night they reach the top of the mountain. By dawn the current game stands at nineteen to nine for Sabeth; Faber, with his more technically focused thinking, has trouble inventing appropriate images. But as they continue the game during the dramatic sunrise, it becomes clear that some of Faber's images and similes are as powerful and original as Sabeth's. For a moment, a balance, however fragile, is achieved between two ways of comprehending the world, the rational and the intuitive.[10] What a contrast to the Walter Faber who, only a few weeks ago, could see nothing beyond the volcanic rocks, sand, moon, and downed plane in the Mexican desert. Now, as he watches from a mountain top in Greece the first rays of sun rising out of the sea, imaginative similes pour out of him. He is exhilarated and moved, as is Sabeth; she falls silent, faced with the spectacle of nature, then breaks into song. Faber writes:

> ich werde nie vergessen: das Meer, das zusehends dunkler wird, blauer, violett, das Meer von Korinth und das andere, das attische Meer, die rote Farbe der Äcker, die Oliven, grünspanig, ihre langen Morgenschatten auf der roten Erde, die erste Wärme und Sabeth, die mich umarmt, als habe ich ihr alles geschenkt, das Meer und die Sonne und alles . . . . (IV 152)

> *I shall never forget the way the sea grew visibly darker, the Gulf of Corinth, and the other sea, the Gulf of Aegina, the red color of the plowed fields, the olives, like verdigris, their long morning shadows on the red earth, the first warmth and Sabeth, who embraced me, as though I had given her all this, the sea and the sun and everything. . . . (157)*

Such happiness cannot last. They come down from the mountain and, tired after their wakeful night, fall asleep on the beach. About noon Faber awakes and goes for a swim; Sabeth sleeps on. When he hears her cry out, he rushes back to shore. While she was asleep, a snake bit her. Startled by the experience and blinded by the sun, she seems frightened by the sight of a large, nude male figure rushing toward her from the sea and steps backward, falling over an embankment.[11] Her fall causes a concussion that leads to her death when a doctor at the hospital in Athens fails to diagnose it.

Nowhere in his report does Faber demonstrate more convincingly what he has learned from Sabeth than in his colorful descriptions of nature and people during a four-day stopover in Cuba on his way from Caracas to Europe after Sabeth's death. He is desolate over her loss and believes he is responsible for her accident. He suspects his own illness, which has become worse, will be terminal. Nevertheless, in Cuba Faber experiences some of the happiest and most moving moments of his life. For those four days transient time seems suspended. Faber seems to be standing outside, or barely interacting with, the colorful life pulsating around him. He accepts by now the transitory nature of living, knows death and recognizes it as an essential part of life. Perhaps it is because of that knowledge that, in Havana, he is suddenly overcome by a lust for looking and seeing. He tries to capture in words the vivid colors and rich beauty of the people and in nature which he so joyously sees around him:

> her pink tongue and her brown face (IV 172/*181*);
>
> her white teeth in the red flower of her lips (IV 172/*181*);
>
> storm clouds over the white town, dark purple clouds, the last rays of sunshine lighting up the tall buildings (IV 173/*182*);
>
> this boy and myself, all around us the Flood (IV 176/*185*);
>
> her earrings, her skin . . . her white laugh (IV180/*190*);

HOMO FABER 167

nothing but beautiful people, I gaze at them admiringly as at strange animals, their white teeth in the dusk, their brown shoulders and arms, [their eyes] — their laughter, because they're glad to be alive, . . . because they are beautiful (IV 177-78/*187*).

These expressions of pleasure culminate in Faber's exultation: "I sing the praises of life!" (IV 181/*191*).

But it is too late for him. Now that he has come to recognize "das wirkliche Leben" and is ready to participate in it, his time is running out. He ends the description of his visit to Cuba with a single word: "Abschied" (IV 182), *"Parting" (192)*. During that visit, although Faber feels vividly alive, sometimes even filled with sexual desire, he recognizes also his life's emptiness and sterility. Both are illustrated movingly by a scene on the beach:

ich zeichne eine Frau in den heißen Sand und lege mich in diese Frau, die nichts als Sand ist, und spreche laut zu ihr — (IV 177)

I draw a woman in the hot sand and lie down inside this woman, who is nothing but sand, and talk aloud to her. (187)

No more vividly can Faber express how much he misses Sabeth, how deeply her death has shaken him. Perhaps remembering their night on the beach in Greece, he is also keenly aware at that moment of his sexual impotence, the "vacuum between the loins" (IV 178/*187*), and his approaching death when he comments: "From time to time I shower my body that is leaving me" (IV 178/*188*). His departure from Cuba is a symbolic farewell to life.

Denouement

At the moment of Sabeth's accident, Faber seems like a true tragic hero. When he needs society's technological achievements to help him deal with this crisis, they fail him miserably: instead of a fast highway, only a "road of gravelled tar" (IV 127-28/*131*) is nearby; instead of a fast car to get to a hospital quickly, only a cart pulled by a donkey, later a slow-moving truck, are available to take them to a hospital in Athens; instead of efficient, modern medical care being dispensed to Sabeth, she dies the next day because of a doctor's human failure.

There can be no question that Faber really loves Sabeth and that her death causes him great anguish. Few scenes in the novel are more explicit in portraying how Faber feels about Sabeth than the scene at the Hencke-Bosch works in Düsseldorf. To show the executives what their plantation in Guatemala looks like, Faber tries to find his Guatemalan film among the many unlabeled reels. As the young engineer assigned to help him starts another reel, there is Sabeth on the screen, life-size. "Sabeth in Avignon" (IV 188/*199*), Faber comments. He lets the entire reel run, even though his assistant comments several times that this film cannot possibly be the right one. Faber pays no attention.

As a result, Sabeth appears to Faber once more, as she was in life. The sketchiness of his remarks as the film runs reveals his grief. Perhaps because there is no sound to divert attention, these pictures are overpowering: Sabeth's face "that will never exist again" (IV 188/*199*); her movements as she feeds pigeons; her laughter, "but silent" (IV 188/*199*); her body . . . her hands, as they caress a mule . . . her healthy teeth . . . her youthful forehead . . . her skipping walk . . . Sabeth picking flowers . . . her fingers, as they break off the bark of a cork tree, which she throws at Faber . . . Sabeth after a swim, combing her wet hair, droplets of water standing on her marble skin, unaware of Faber filming her, talking to him . . . Sabeth afraid of a lobster that is still moving . . . Sabeth sitting on top of a post on a jetty . . . then standing at the end of the jetty, hands in pockets, singing inaudibly (IV 189-91).

Suddenly, without explanation, leaving his films behind, Faber flees the Hencke-Bosch-Haus, walks as if in a trance through the busy city to the railroad station, and takes the next express train south. Looking out of the dining car window, Faber wonders why he still bothers to look at the passing landscape, because his eyes shall never again see Sabeth, the person they crave most to see. Overcome by grief and remorse, he wishes he had never existed, then wonders:

Warum nicht diese zwei Gabeln nehmen, sie aufrichten in meinen Fäusten und mein Gesicht fallen lassen, um die Augen loszuwerden? (IV 192)

Why not take these two forks, hold them upright in my hands and let my head fall, so as to get rid of my eyes? (203)

In self-judgment, Faber would punish his figurative blindness with a literal one.

But Faber is not Oedipus, who from his first moment of suspicion sought almost recklessly to uncover the truth. Faber did not. Furthermore, Oedipus' fate, pronounced by the oracle at Delphi, was determined before his birth by the Morai; he had no chance to escape it. Faber, imprisoned by his technological view of the world that rejects intuitive signals, creates his own fate; he could have escaped it through timely and reasonable choices (Lüthi 33-34). As Frisch himself once stated, "the incest between Walter Faber and his daughter runs counter to the Oedipus story" (Petersen 1978a 135).

Faber continues his journey south, first to Zurich and eventually to Athens, to see Hanna once more. He is completing the last part of his journey, going home.

TRANSGRESSION AND GUILT: FABER AND HANNA

Although Sabeth's love opened Faber's world to allow light and spontaneity into it, one must remember that Hanna, not Sabeth, was the first woman he loved. Faber's love for Sabeth's mother is the most enduring emotion of his life, lasting from his student days until his death. Because they lost contact with each other for twenty years, their relationship may be divided into three phases: Zurich, 1933-1936; reunion in Athens just before and after Sabeth's death; and the few days left to them after Faber's second trip to Caracas, before his operation and death.

It is a tragic and circuitous route that leads Faber back to Hanna for what remains of his life. Both have been successful in their respective careers as engineer and archeologist. Hanna, however, calls her life "verpfutscht" (IV 139), *"botched,"* an adjective equally descriptive of Faber's life.

When they meet again in Faber's hospital room in Athens, he is surprised and impressed by the matter-of-fact way Hanna asks about his relationship with Sabeth. He probably expected her to be emotional, even hysterical. He is equally impressed with how competently she deals with the hospital staff. When they go to Hanna's apartment, Faber is surprised that it looks like that of a scholar—a domain, according to Hanna, that Faber expects to be reserved for men. Books line the walls, and her desk is covered with artifacts of her work, all labeled and identified. The furniture, which Faber had expected to be antique, is modern. Indeed, in their respective disciplines, Hanna and Faber are equals, as Faber admits as he watches Hanna make arrangements for them to go to pick up his and Sabeth's personal belongings from the beach. "Hanna behaved like a manager" (IV 153/*159*), he comments admiringly.

Faber provides many contradictory comments and observations about Hanna throughout his report. Details added by others, like Herbert Hencke and Sabeth, help to round out the picture.

Dr. Hanna Piper, née Landsberg, "from Munich, half Jewish" (IV 28/*26*), the daughter of a professor, is one of those remarkable, strong, well-educated, competent, and fiercely independent women one encounters several times in the novels of Max Frisch—women like Sibylle, Marianne, and Ingeborg. Uncomplicated she is not. At a critical moment—pregnant, but not willing to marry the father of her child, on the eve of World War II, a foreigner living in Switzerland—she takes charge of her life. From that time on she lives as best she can, guided by moral and ethical principles that do not always conform to convention but that she can accept and believe in. Faber comments at one point: "Hanna has always done what she thought best" (IV 139/*144*).

In 1933, Hanna left Germany to escape the Hitler regime and moved to Zurich, where she studied art history and met Walter Faber. He was not interested in art, "but apart from this we understood one another immediately" (IV 45/*45*), he comments. A little later he adds: "our interests weren't always the same"

(IV 47/46), which seems to modify the earlier statement somewhat. He called her "a dreamer and an art fairy"; she called him "Homo Faber" (IV 47/46), technical man. Their names for each other, although meant as terms of endearment, suggest the fundamental difference between them. Intuition and form dominate Hanna's life; facts, data, and the intellect, Faber's. He sees himself as "a man who has both feet on the ground" (IV 47/46), while he observes about her:

> Hanna hatte einerseits einen Hang zum Kommunistischen . . . andereseits zum Mystischen, um nicht zu sagen: zum Hysterischen. (IV 47)

> *On the one hand Hanna had Communist leanings. . . and on the other a tendency to mysticism, or to put it less kindly, hysteria. (46)*

Faber's comment seems contradictory. Perhaps the same description should apply to Hanna's political orientation as Frisch once applied to Stiller's: "a very naive Communist, more exactly: a romantic Socialist" (III 592/*Stiller* 212).

When Faber and Hanna meet again twenty years later at the hospital in Athens, this "dreamer and art fairy" has become a respected archeologist. In addition, she earned her academic credentials in philology and art history and trained as a laboratory assistant to help Joachim, then her husband, in his medical practice—particularly if they moved to Canada or Australia, as Joachim had planned. In 1938 she emigrated with Sabeth to Paris, where she worked for a publishing house; and then, when the Nazis occupied France, she moved to England, working in London as an announcer in German for the BBC. She became a British citizen, which she has remained, and married Piper, a self-proclaimed Communist but, according to Hanna, actually an opportunist. They eventually moved to Berlin, where she left him in June 1953,[12] because he was weak and unprincipled or, as Hanna explains it: "He was willing to serve under any flag, as long as he could make his films" (IV 144/*148*).

Although Hanna and Faber became lovers in the 1930s, they never married, for reasons Faber reports and tries to justify many times. First, they were too young. Second, his parents were worried about the effect his marrying a half-Jew would have on his career. Third, their financial situation was precarious: Hanna was still a student, and Faber earned a paltry three hundred Swiss francs a month as an assistant at the Technische Hochschule in Zurich while writing his dissertation. Another factor at the time was the unstable political climate in Europe, which did not promise a peaceful future, especially not for Hanna. The uncertainty of her future in Switzerland, however, was *the* factor, according to Faber, that caused him to resolve firmly to marry her, come what may, "if ever her residence permit [in Switzerland] were withdrawn" (IV 46/46). Even Faber's resolve has a safety catch, "if . . .," although he reports that they really loved each other.

Then an important professional reason militated against marriage. Faber was offered his first job as an engineer by Escher-Wyss, "a chance in a million for a young engineer" (IV 47/47). But this meant he had to move to Baghdad as soon as possible, leaving Hanna in Zurich. As the political situation worsened and Hanna became pregnant, they decided to marry before he left. At the last moment on their wedding day, however, Hanna refused to go through with the ceremony, claiming, Faber reports: "I was only marrying her to prove I wasn't an anti-Semite" (IV 57/57).

Hanna may not have been completely wrong about Faber's real motivation for marrying her, even though he may have seen it as a point of honor to keep a promise to himself: to marry Hanna if her stay in Switzerland should become legally impossible. Evidently that point was reached "when the Jewish passports were withdrawn" (IV 56/56). Faber considered it now his moral duty to marry her, not only to protect her legally but also because she was pregnant with their child. Even if the marriage were to end in divorce, he reasoned, Hanna would remain a Swiss citizen. Hanna may have had even more basic reasons than the one she gave Faber for refusing to marry him. At the time, she may not have dared or even been able to express her intuitive feeling that, by nature, temperament, and personality they were just not suited to each other and would probably fail at marriage because of their differences. Yet one cannot escape the impression that, at the time, these two meant more to each other than they knew or cared to admit, in spite of their different natures.

When they meet again twenty years later, Hanna still believes that a marriage between them would have been "a disaster" (IV 135/*139*), for these differences have not disappeared. If Hanna could not precisely pinpoint them twenty years earlier, she can identify them now. First, their attitudes toward life are basically different: Faber believes that man, through technology, can conquer and control nature, while Hanna believes that nature will never be conquered or controlled. Second, Faber regards life as a continuous repetition of experiences and events in an additive process, while Hanna sees life as unique, consisting of a series of individual experiences and events flowing into each other, and that each person, each life, is an example of that uniqueness. Third, Faber believes in the laws of probability, according to which the likelihood of any event's occurrence can be calculated in advance and, if the probability is low, its actual occurrence can be treated as a chance event. Hanna, on the other side, believes in the unpredictability of human nature and, moreover, in the viable, incalculable forces of fate that can break into man's life and destroy him and his rational world at any moment. The fourth and perhaps most important difference between the two is Faber's view that life is matter, to be treated as the sum of additions, not limited by time, and therefore controllable—a grievously wrong view, Hanna believes, but one that allows Faber to explain all his actions, including his incestuous relationship with his daughter. For Hanna, life is *Gestalt*, form, subject to and limited by transient time, thus not repeatable at any point on the human continuum from birth to death. This last point Hanna states most succinctly when she tells Faber: "Life goes with the children.... That's the way things are ... we can't marry again through our children" (IV 139/*143*).

As Faber reports, Hanna also tells him:

Mein Irrtum mit Sabeth: Repetition, ich habe mich so verhalten, als gebe es kein Alter, daher widernatürlich. Wir können nicht das Alter aufheben, indem wir weiter addieren, indem wir unsere eigenen Kinder heiraten. (IV 170)

My mistake with Sabeth lay in repetition. I behaved as though age did not exist, and hence contrary to nature. We cannot do away with age by continuing to add up, by marrying our children. (179)

This is exactly what Faber tried to do in an effort to cancel an error he made earlier in his life by not marrying Hanna. He will make the same mistake once again when, after Sabeth's death, he again resolves to marry Hanna. But transient time cannot be turned back for them, either.

When Faber and Hanna meet again in Athens, they do not pick up their relationship of more than twenty years ago, which would be unthinkable; nor do they establish a completely new one, because they know each other's strengths and weaknesses too well. It is fairly easy for them to bridge the many years of separation, as neither has filled the intervening years with much significant experience; very little has changed in their lives, except that Faber has recently become more flexible in his outlook on life. But their lives are again closely intertwined through Sabeth's life and death. Instead of picking up their old relationship, they transform it into one of genuine friendship, purged of sensual desire, purified by the acceptance of individual guilt and by mutual forgiveness. The most telling evidence of this transformation is Faber's joyous exclamation, after a brief period of believing that he and Hanna could share the rest of their lives in marriage:[13] "I am not alone, Hanna is my friend, and I am not alone" (IV 198/210).

In this instance Faber is not deceiving himself, as he so often does throughout his report, for Hanna's actions demonstrate her genuine friendship. She neither accuses nor reproaches him, but silently conveys remarkable understanding and a fundamental acceptance of the events that occurred. She does not find Faber's sexual relationship with Sabeth inconceivable, explaining to him that love between a father and his child is something he has never known, so that he misinterpreted his feelings for Sabeth and persuaded himself that he loved her as a woman, not as the daughter he never knew existed. Furthermore, Hanna is sensitive to Faber's feelings when he returns to the hospital, after his second trip to Caracas, for tests and an operation; she changes from her black mourning clothes into white ones that make her look like a bride, Faber tells her, because, he surmises, she does not want to look like a scarecrow when she comes to visit him, or like one of the Guatemalan *Zopiloten* (black birds of prey) he describes for her while she sits by his bed.

Like the faithful friend she is, Hanna visits Faber every day at the hospital, brings whatever he asks for, and listens to him, while Faber wonders how, after all that has happened, she can bear being near him. Afraid of what the results of the operation may reveal, suspecting the truth—incurable stomach cancer—and afraid to die, Faber clings to life as never before: "and if it [is] only another year . . . a quarter of a year, two months . . . " (IV 198/210). More clearly than at any other time, Faber demonstrates here that he has changed, that he has learned to accept the transience of time and the reality of death, which can define the life span and give it meaning.

How much Faber has changed, how differently he views life now, is illustrated by his heightened perceptions in Cuba and by an experience in New York. There he rejects the sterile "American way of life" by leaving the obligatory Saturday-night party at the home of his boss and then experiences an acute identity crisis: having lost the key to his apartment, he calls his own telephone number and is answered by another man who has never heard of Walter Faber.

This dramatic change is the result of Sabeth's influence on Faber. However, during the short two months (May 27-July 25)[14] he and Hanna renew their relationship, Hanna changes too. Her appearance, which Faber could only guess at during his travels with Sabeth, is not that of an old woman, although she has aged and changed enough for him not to recognize her at once when she returns to the taxi in which she left him briefly to pick something up at her institute. Only her hands are markedly different, Faber notes, "older than the rest of Hanna . . . human flesh with veins under the skin, which looked like crumpled tissue-paper" (IV 141/146). Faber provides a lengthy description of Hanna's hand, which—rather than Hanna herself—he seems to feel he is addressing. With this clever device, Frisch illustrates the emotional strain and disorientation Faber suffers at the moment Sabeth is in mortal danger in the hospital and he is sitting beside her mother and his ex-fiancée.

Hanna asks Faber five times about the nature of his relationship with Sabeth, but when Faber in turn asks her whether Joachim was Sabeth's father, Hanna either does not answer or denies, twice, that Faber is the father. Hanna feels compelled to withhold the truth from Faber until she knows the true nature of his relationship with Sabeth. To be able to assess accurately what card fate has dealt her, she must know the whole truth, she believes. She knows she is strong enough to accept the truth if the relationship between her daughter and Faber has been incestuous, but only when she knows does she confirm his growing awareness of his fatherhood. Why she has always concealed this knowledge from him is a question she never answers.

Both Hanna and Faber are guilty of acts of omission. Faber's omission is not having asked obvious questions of Sabeth when he had the opportunity to ask them, before Avignon; instead, he chose to ignore them. Hanna is guilty of two omissions: she never told Faber that, contrary to their agreement at the time he left for Baghdad, she bore their child (strangely enough, Faber's mother knew about the child but never told her son [IV 183-84]); and she never told Sabeth about her biological father, allowing her to grow up believing it is Joachim. When Faber and Hanna decided, before he left for Baghdad, that she would have an abortion, they also decided that Faber's friend Joachim, then a medical student, would perform it. Instead, Hanna carried the baby to full term and married Joachim, whom she trusted to be father to her child. Throughout their marriage Joachim asked only one thing of her: the opportunity to become a father himself in the true sense of the word.

Once Sabeth was born, Hanna grew so possessive of her daughter that she allowed Joachim to be only a legal father, not to share in raising her or in making decisions about her future. Furthermore, Hanna refused to bear a child for Joachim. Without his knowledge, she underwent a tubal ligation. That willful act caused Joachim, when he learned of it, to terminate their marriage, and it may eventually have precipitated his suicide in the Guatemalan jungle.

Although Hanna essentially brought Sabeth up herself, even taught her herself during difficult times when no school was available, she also denied Sabeth the opportunity to grow up in a family in which she could experience the love and influence of both parents. The political and economic arguments Hanna used against Joachim's desire to have a child are as specious as Faber's justification for not marrying Hanna.

Another element in Faber and Hanna's relationship becomes visible only after Hanna reneged on her agreement to abort the baby: by not carrying out their agreement, Hanna was able to demonstrate her power over Faber, who once had thoughtlessly referred to the unborn baby as "your" child, not "our" child. This careless choice of pronoun triggered in Hanna, unknown to Faber at the time, a set of preconditioned responses, based on a traumatic childhood memory. One day she had lost a fight with her younger brother, who thus demonstrated his superior power. In self-righteous indignation and furor she subsequently founded a secret girls' association dedicated to removing Jehova from his seat of power because he unfairly made boys stronger than girls. If she could not dethrone God, Hanna was willing to settle, grudgingly, for a compromise: at least there had to be a goddess in heaven, too, with equal powers, if young Hanna Landsberg were to continue to believe in heaven. This childhood experience illustrates the fierce determination and independence that were already a part of Hanna's character at a very young age.

Although violent reactions of girls to defeat by boys is normal among siblings, it is unusual for a girl to develop, based on a single incident, a philosophy she still adheres to in adulthood. Hanna expresses this philosophy in her fundamental dislike of men and their real or presumed superiority. Defeating them becomes a lifelong challenge. Hanna reacted to that challenge the moment she realized that Faber's commitment to her and their unborn child was weaker than his commitment to his career. What infuriated her was not so much Faber's substitution of "your" for "our," but that, because he was a man, he could walk away from her and the unborn baby.

According to Hanna, men do not understand women; they see them only as their own mirror. Hanna considers Faber, like Piper, her second husband, "stockblind," *"stone-blind"* (IV 144/149). Her whole life seems to be a continuous effort to demonstrate to the world that she, an intelligent, educated, and capable woman, can get along without men quite nicely and succeed on her own—Dr.phil. Hanna Piper, née Landsberg. But she angrily concedes:

> Solange Gott ein Mann ist, nicht ein Paar, kann das Leben einer Frau . . . nur so bleiben, wie es heute ist, nämlich erbärmlich, die Frau als Proletarier der Schöpfung, wenn auch noch so elegant verkleidet. (IV 140)
>
> *As long as God is a man, not a couple, the life of a woman . . . is bound to remain as it is now, namely wretched, with woman as the proletarian of Creation, however smartly dressed.* (145)

Hanna's accusation has a familiar ring: it sounds like one of those voiced by militant feminists during the 1960s and 1970s. It is interesting that it was written in the mid-1950s by a man, Max Frisch, who thus indicates his familiarity and sympathy with feminist issues before they became dominant social issues in Europe and the United States.

Hanna knows that in at least one area women are stronger than men: women alone have the power to decide whether or not to conceive and to bear children. They, not men, are the rulers of their bodies.

As a girl and later as a woman, Hanna seems to have trusted only one man completely: the blind old Armin whom, as a schoolgirl in Munich, she met regularly in the English Garden. He introduced her to the world of ancient Greece and, over the years, nurtured her interest in and love for antiquity. Hanna enjoyed the attention of this old, blind man and the interest he took in her schoolwork; she was excited by his knowledge and experience, and she willingly shared with him the little knowledge she possessed. "The girl had to read to him out of her school books, so that he could learn it by heart" (IV 184/194), Faber reports. Hanna considered their relationship and the games they played fun, interesting, and safe; she had the upper hand and enjoyed the freedom of not being seen by Armin. Faber, however, considers Armin's desire to share her growing knowledge by having her read to him from her schoolbooks to be "his way of raping her" (IV 184/194). Their plan to visit Greece together some day never materialized; Armin knew it was only a game. For Hanna, however, their game turned real; her interest in antiquity continued and became a way of earning a living for herself and Sabeth.

Although Hanna deprecatingly refers to her present work at the archeological institute in Athens as "Scherbenarbeit" (IV 139), *"work with broken pieces,"* and describes her specific task there with the words, "I glue the past together" (IV 139), she is thoroughly familiar with Greek history and mythology. She, better than Faber, knows about the Erinyes, the Furies who avenge man's transgressions against natural order. Unlike Faber, she believes in fate, not chance. She also knows about hubris, the exaggerated pride or self-confidence that, the Greeks knew, leads to a fall, to retribution.

Hanna is proud, not so much of what she has achieved in life, but that she has managed to achieve it independently, without the help of any man. Her pride, therefore, is one of self-sufficiency, somewhat like Faber's pride before he met and loved Sabeth. And Hanna's accomplishments are many: she survived a war with terrible hardships and changes of fortune; she built a successful career, in fact, several; and most of all, she insisted that she alone be the one to teach, train, and guide Sabeth. Hanna made Sabeth the center of her life. At the age of forty, for example, she again took up the violin in order to play duets with her daughter, who played the flute. Faber comments: "Nothing was too much for Hanna, where the child was concerned" (IV 202/214).

Hanna knew that some day she would have to let go the daughter whom she still preferred to think of as a child; some day Sabeth would have to leave home to live her own life. She encouraged Sabeth to attend Yale University for a semester, although it had been difficult for her, especially to let her daughter travel alone. But Hanna managed, as she always did; she did not want to deny Sabeth the independence she herself craved. She also wanted her daughter to love and be loved. Soon after she and Faber met in Athens, Hanna wistfully wonders aloud, "Do you think she has already been with a man?" and then adds quickly, "I wish her that, . . . I wish her that" (IV 141/146).

Hanna could not have known, of course, that on her trip home from six months at Yale Sabeth was to meet, by chance, her real father "who would destroy everything" (IV 203/214). Nevertheless, because Hanna believes in the forces of fate, she might have remembered the Erinyes as well as her own acts of hubris. For her transgressions, the gods mete out their most cruel punishment: the death of her daughter. Her first reaction after Sabeth's death is to lash out furiously at Faber, screaming at him and pounding his forehead with her fists, a response he thoroughly understands.

Although Faber does not know as much about mythology as Hanna, he too feels the forces of fate gathering about him. While he takes a bath in Hanna's apartment, he suddenly likens the tub to a sarcophagus he saw in Rome and his body, submerged in water, to that of a mummy he saw at the Vatican. Next, he thinks of suicide because, at that moment, he prefers never to have lived. Suddenly, lying in the bathtub, eyes closed so he will not have to look at his aged body, an unusual thought occurs to him: "Hanna . . . could easily come in and kill me from behind with an axe" (IV 136/*140-41*). The obvious reference here is to Clytemnestra, Agamemnon's wife, who, upon her husband's return from Troy, killed him with the help of her lover, Aegisthus, and thus avenged the death of her daughter Iphigenia, whom the girl's father sacrificed to appease the angry gods and secure for his fleet a safe passage to Troy.[15] Hanna, too, seems to have cause to avenge a father's sacrifice of his daughter. Hanna does not kill Faber. Instead, he is killed by the destructive force of cancer, which even modern medicine cannot stop.

The day before Faber's operation, Hanna wants to know why he said "your" child instead of "our" child twenty years ago. Was it meant as an accusation, or was it mere cowardice? Faber is lost; he does not understand her questions, so Hanna explains. Did he know then how right he was? That she wanted the child all to herself, right from the start; that she did not want to share her with anyone, including a father; and that she did not want any other child, for her self-realization as a woman was complete with this one? With Sabeth's death Hanna has lost everything.

A heartrending recognition and admission of guilt is hidden in the few lines of text with which Faber describes this conversation. Then, on her knees and in tears, Hanna begs Faber's forgiveness, kissing his hand. He is now the only member of the trio she has so selfishly sinned against who is still alive. Faber is thoroughly confused; he has never known Hanna in such a state, he claims. Perhaps he has forgotten the night before Sabeth's death, when Hanna shrewdly forced him to tell the extent of his love relationship with Sabeth. That night, from the next bedroom, he was a helpless witness to her anguish as she recognized and faced, alone, her grief, transgressions, and guilt. Her heartbroken sobs disturbed Faber deeply. She refused to answer his questions through the wall separating them; she responded to his offers of comfort by locking her door.

Now as then, with Hanna kneeling by his bedside, Faber feels utterly helpless. Seeing her reach out to him, asking *him* to forgive *her*—she who has so much to forgive him—strengthens his new commitment to her and his resolve that they will stay together in Athens as friends.

Faber dies the next day.

REDEMPTION

Max Frisch once referred to Walter Faber as a "verhinderter Mensch" (Petersen 1978a 133), a person prevented by someone or something from becoming a complete human being. That someone is Faber himself. Early in his life he had the power to decide whether to respond more to the rule of feelings, emotions, intuitions, and the senses or to the rule of reason and intellect. Faber chose the second option. He seems to have paid for that choice in all his subsequent relationships with people, especially women. It becomes evident even to him in the course of his report, which starts as a blatant self-justification and turns gradually more humble and self-inquiring, that he has made the wrong decision, but that the transient time that governs all life does not allow him to go back and correct his mistake.

Faber gains this insight primarily as a result of his relationship with Sabeth. This insight is then reinforced and made concrete during the brief period of his resumed relationship with Hanna. The nature of that relationship can best be expressed by the image, a spiral, that is central to the novel. Frisch makes the spiral image concrete late in Faber's report, when he has Faber, during his last visit to Zurich, sit at a small table in the Café Odéon and trace on the marble tabletop the spiral suggested by a fossilized snail enmeshed in the surface (IV 194). In terms of Faber's relationship with Hanna, the spiral suggests transient time that does not allow them to recover lost opportunities.

Faber and Hanna, each in his own way, ran away from their original relationship, both afraid of any real commitment and a shared, equal love. Faber chose his work as a substitute for meaningful human relationships. Hanna chose her child, whom she wanted to keep to herself.

In one of their conversations, Hanna defines the nature of Faber's work as:

> Technik . . . als Kniff, die Welt so einzurichten, daß wir sie nicht mehr erleben müssen . . . als Kniff, die Welt als Widerstand aus der Welt zu schaffen . . . . (IV 169)
>
> *Technology . . . as the knack of so arranging the world that we don't have to experience it . . . . as the knack of eliminating the world as resistance . . . .* (178)

She is right; this is what Faber attempts to do. And although Hanna does not avoid opposing forces in life, or a certain number of human relationships on her own terms, she too used Sabeth as the substitute for an open, equal, and committed relationship with a man.

The grim picture at the end of the novel makes it clear that both choices were wrong. Sabeth and Joachim are dead, Faber is dying, and Hanna is left very alone. In a moment of panic, trying to flee the city after Sabeth's death, Hanna canceled the lease on her apartment and resigned her job at the institute, which was quickly and irrevocably filled by one of her colleagues. Now, however, she wants to remain in Athens, where she is at present working as a tourist guide and living in a *pension*. She wants to be near Sabeth's grave; soon she will have two graves to care for.

If Hanna represents an attempt to master life by following intuitive feeling and Faber by relying primarily on the powers of the intellect, then Sabeth, their child, represents an integration, a synthesis of the two polar opposites of her parents (Butler 104,120). Even though this synthesis remains embryonic, it forms the basis for Faber's relationship with her and his resulting growth. He finds it easy to love her, as he recognizes the qualities he has always liked in Hanna added to Sabeth's demonstrated interest and ability in following his excursions into technology, something Hanna never did. In turn, and not without difficulties, he gradually develops an interest in the arts.

During their short relationship, Sabeth was able to let Faber, for brief moments, glimpse "das wirkliche Leben." How completely Faber was able to recognize the futility of his life, how well he learned to live in the present, and how well he has come to understand the essence and truth of the lesson Sabeth lived is illustrated vividly by his handwritten entry, his last will and testament, written in the early morning hours of the day he died. First, Faber renounces everything he has ever written— reports, letters, loose-leaf notebooks. All are to be destroyed in case he dies, because "none of it is true" (IV 199/210). Then he leaves his legacy, the insight he has gained into "das wirkliche Leben":

> Auf der Welt sein: im Licht sein. Irgendwo . . . Esel treiben, unser Beruf—aber vor allem: standhalten dem Licht, der Freude (wie unser Kind, als es sang) im Wissen, daß ich erlösche im Licht über Ginster, Asphalt und Meer, standhalten der Zeit, beziehungsweise Ewigkeit im Augenblick. Ewig sein: gewesen sein. (IV 199)

> *To be alive: to be in the light. Driving donkeys around somewhere . . . —that's all our job amounts to! The main thing is to stand up to the light, to joy (like our child) in the knowledge that I shall be extinguished in the light over gorse, asphalt, and sea, to stand up to time, or rather to eternity in the instant. To be eternal means to have existed.* (210)

The irony is that when Faber is ready to begin "das wirkliche Leben," he is forced to leave it. It eludes him, as it eludes Hanna, and as it has eluded other Frisch characters before them. The real tragedy of *Homo faber* is the destruction of Sabeth, whose being hinted that "das wirkliche Leben" exists.

If Walter Faber is not portrayed somewhat harshly by Frisch, he is at best portrayed ironically, as a symbol of contemporary technical man: he is secure in his technical know-how but otherwise insecure, selfish, and self-centered. He is arrogant enough to believe that humans, armed with the secrets of nature, will one day be its master. Not only will humanity make nature its servant, he believes, but humans will eventually even replace themselves and their functions—at least partially—with robots that will be more efficient than humans can ever be.

The aspect of contemporary man Frisch projects through the character of Walter Faber is that of someone who feels terribly insecure, timid, and bewildered about himself and his social and personal relationships. He is ignorant of his own nature and ill at ease with the primary functions of his body. All personal relationships, but especially intimate relationships with women, are painful and confusing for him; he prefers to evade them. Until he falls in love with Sabeth, Faber's life is devoid of anything truly human: it lacks compassion, love, spontaneity, social responsibility, and commitment.

It is an ironic, yet perhaps poetically just, conclusion that all the help of modern medicine and medical technology comes too late to save Walter Faber, the technical man, from an untimely death at the moment he has demonstrated his capacity for growth. Nature thus triumphs over the would-be usurper, who in the name of serving mankind through technology attempted to escape the human aspects of life. Only by interacting with other people, Frisch tells us, and especially in a loving relationship with a woman, can a man dare to expose his vulnerabilities and, in consequence, experience both the pain and joys that make us truly human.

NOTES

[1] Walter Faber, a Swiss, may be unfamiliar with the American comedy films featuring the mischievous Dead-End Kids that were popular during the 1930s, but Ivy knows and apparently identifies with them. Faber, unfamiliar with American idiom, might have thought "dead end" meant "going nowhere," thus ascribing to Ivy's expression a negative connotation that would indeed have been odd.

[2] The night sky figures prominently on three occasions in *Homo faber*: during the Indian moon celebration Faber observes in Palenque (IV 45), during Sabeth and Faber's last night on shipboard (IV 90), and during the lunar eclipse in Avignon (IV 124-25). The mythologic implications of the heavens in *Homo faber* have been investigated by Blair 142-70.

[3] Faber's comment that sharing his life with a woman would drive him to join the Foreign Legion is doubly ironic. First, in a Frisch novel—for example, *Stiller*—an escape to the Foreign Legion is meant to symbolize an escape from a boring routine to a life of excitement. Strict adherence to a routine is already a major characteristic of Faber's life while he is not sharing it with a woman. Second, Faber's belief that life with a woman on a day-to-day basis would indeed be boring only exposes his lack of engagement in his relationships with women.

[4] Frisch frequently uses the figure of Hermes, an extremely versatile Greek god, in his work. Among Hermes' many functions relevant here are his patronage of roads and travelers and his conducting the shades of the dead to Hades (*The Odyssey*). In this context, one might be tempted to view Sabeth's death, preceding Faber to Hades, as a function of her Hermes role. More important, though, is Sabeth's function as Faber's guide and companion during his journey through Italy. See Seyfert 286-88; Graves 63-67.

[5] Blair seems to force her case when she labels as "prophetic" Faber's casual reference to their temporary resting place as "unser Grabhügel" (IV 114), *"our burial mound."* Faber, who is frequently vague in his use of language, is no Cassandra; he merely distinguishes the burial mound he and Sabeth occupy at that

moment at the Via Appia from the others around them. See Blair 155.

⁶This bas-relief is known as the *Ludovian Throne* and described in Baedeker's *Italy from the Alps to Naples* (252) and other books. See also Blair 152, 168.

⁷Since the bas-relief depicting the birth of Venus, the statue of the sleeping Erinys, and the relationship between these two art objects is of symbolic importance to Faber and Sabeth's relationship, the reader may be interested in knowing more about the mythological connection between the Erinyes and Venus.

In Greek mythology the Erinys has two sisters. Their births were directly related to that of Aphrodite/Venus, the goddess of love, and their function, to avenge any transgression against the natural order, was well known. The events that led to their specific functions were the following, according to the sources: Uranus, god of the heavens, the son and husband of Gaea, goddess of the earth, who had borne him the three 100-handed Giants, the three one-eyed Cyclopes, and the twelve Titans—six boys and six girls—banished the Cyclopes to the farthest reaches of the underworld and forbade them ever to see the light of the earth again. To reach the depths of the world, where Uranus kept them hidden, would take a falling anvil nine days. Enraged by their banishment, Gaea enlisted the help of her other children, the Titans, against their father, and the youngest of them, Cronus, unmanned his father, cutting off his penis and testicles with a flint sickle his mother had given him. From the blood that fell upon the earth the Erinyes were born. Uranus' genitals fell into the sea, and out of the foam produced around them the goddess Aphrodite, called Venus by the Romans, arose. She was originally called Aphrogeneia, the foam-born, and is reported to have stepped ashore at Cyprus. The common conception of her as the goddess of love limits her agency to the sphere of human life like that of her sisters, the Erinyes, goddesses of vengeance.

The symbolic aptness between the juxtaposition of these two works of art and the relationship between Faber and Sabeth is heightened when one remembers that Sabeth's death occurs on the Greek shore and that she, like the girl the bas-relief depicts standing next to the goddess of love, is also a flute player (IV

111,149). See Seyfert 38-39, 224-25, 639, 664; Graves 31-33, 37-39.

[8] Geulen was the first to suggest this idea, which Blair then developed, combining all images of cars, dogs, and Erinyes that appear in *Homo faber* into a comprehensive system. See Geulen 1965 101-32.

[9] In Greek mythology, dogs are chthonic animals and associated with the rulers of the underworld, whom they serve. In *Homo faber* they function as guardians of society, chasing away outsiders and vagrants in the dead of night. In that sense, they can be considered in the service of the Erinyes who, like hunting dogs, chase their victims and were said to growl and bark in their sleep. See Seyfert 133; Blair 153.

[10] Faber, perhaps in memory of Sabeth, plays this game once more, by himself, when he flies for the last time over Switzerland, from Zurich to Athens (IV 194-97).

[11] Once again, as with her comments about the Roman burial grounds at the Via Appia (see note 5 above), Blair forces interpretation when she observes that Walter Faber and Pluto, the prince of Hades, have similar functions. Her attempt to show that Faber abducts Sabeth near the sea in the vicinity of Eleusis, where, according to some versions of the Greek myth, Pluto abducted Demeter's daughter Kore, is a spurious argument in defense of her thesis that events in *Homo faber* are directly linked to the Demeter-Kore myth. Walter Faber walks out of the sea where he has gone for a swim, not to abduct but to help Sabeth, whose cries have called him back to shore (IV 157). Although Blair is correct in stating that images of the world of the dead abound in *Homo faber* (IV 11,24,51,54,110,150-51,162,170, etc.), it is doubtful that they can be tied together as neatly as she tries to do. Any attempt to take Frisch's frequent allusions to Greek mythology too seriously, especially in this novel, is fraught with the danger of mis- or overinterpretation. Usually, Frisch uses the mythological references ironically, and they are meant to be understood, not literally, but in opposition to the myth. See Blair 154; Seyfert 263-66; Graves 89-96.

[12]June 17, 1953, was the date of the workers' revolt (*Tag der Einheit*) in the German Democratic Republic (Deutsche Demokratische Republik [DDR]). It was crushed by Russian tanks. This event explains why Hanna left Piper, since he was still willing to live in the DDR afterward.

[13]Faber's idea is, of course, illusory. Hanna is still married to Piper, as she twice reminds Faber, who seems not to hear. For some time, even in Cuba, or perhaps especially there, he clings irrationally to the idea of marrying Hanna.

[14]Bullock's 1959 translation of *Homo faber* contains an error. He translates "übermorgen" in Faber's notebook entry, "Meine Operation auf übermorgen angesetzt" (IV 192), as *"tomorrow"* (203). It means "day after tomorrow." Whether that date is July 25 or July 26 is a question. Frisch's text does not make clear whether Faber's handwritten notes (printed in the text in italics) cover the period July 19-26 or July 19-25. One can assume, perhaps, that each handwritten segment not clearly identified by a time or a "P.S." designation represents one day's entry. I follow here Jurgensen's time frame of July 19-25, reasoning that the two handwritten entries on pages IV 169-70/*178-79* and IV 170-72/*179-81* were written on the same day, July 21. The first deals with Hanna's and Faber's different perceptions of life: life as form and life as matter. The second, longer, one contains Faber's careful description of himself while looking into a mirror the nurse brings him. This time, the third time Faber sees himself in a mirror (the first, Houston, IV 11; the second, Paris, IV 98), he accepts himself and his emaciated appearance. Thematically, both handwritten entries belong together; they are linked by the intervening Caracas entry (IV 170; Jurgensen 1976 176).

[15]In most Greek mythological versions of the death of Agamemnon, Clytemnestra did not kill her husband herself but threw a net over him as he was bathing, incapacitating the old warrior so that her lover, Aegisthus, could kill him. Faber is no scholar of Greek mythology; he is an engineer whose school days, from which he may remember this act of revenge by an aggrieved mother, lie a long time in the past.

Blair is correct in her observation that Hanna is not Clytemnestra and that Faber is not sacrificing Sabeth to the gods, as Agamemnon did Iphigenia. Her idea of linking, by analogy, Agamemnon and Faber with the Erinyes, and the moral blindness of Oedipus and Agamemnon to that of Faber, is ingenious but not productive in interpreting Walter Faber. The only valid comparisons of the Oedipus myth and Sophocles' drama with Faber's situation are that both committed incest and both, if they had made appropriate use of the information they had, could have arrived at the truth earlier than they did. Blair's assertion that the quality of the data available to Oedipus and Faber was analogous is wrong. Faber could have made use of the ample information he was given by Herbert Hencke and Sabeth, directly and indirectly, and thus have avoided his incestuous conduct, whereas Oedipus had already committed the incestuous act because his information about his origin was inadequate, which is the real meaning of the Delphi oracle. Oedipus, in addition, had to pursue the information of a second Delphi oracle before he could arrive at the truth. Blair is knowledgeable, but some of her ingenious interpretive combinations are not persuasive. See Blair 144-45.

CHAPTER FIVE

MEIN NAME SEI GANTENBEIN: A LOOK THROUGH THE PRISM

 Ali, a young Arabian shepherd, wants to marry but has less money than the going price for a wife. Even when he travels to another region where wives cost less, he discovers that his money is inadequate: the lowest price for which he can find a wife is eleven pounds, and he has only ten. On his way back home he encounters a miracle: he sees a beautiful young girl, more beautiful than any of the others, but she is blind. Ali purchases her anyway, for six pounds, calls her Alil, and marries her. With the money left over he pays a miracle doctor to heal her blindness. Now Alil can see, and even though she sees that Ali is far less handsome than other shepherds in the area, she loves him and remains faithful to him, for he has given her the gift of sight. Ali and Alil are the happiest couple at the edge of the desert.
 For a while, that is.
 Through their close contact, Ali's eyes become infected with the same malady that once plagued Alil. He is gradually going blind. The more the illness advances, the less is he able to believe that his beautiful young wife really loves him. Perhaps, now that he is blind, she deceives him with some of the other shepherds. Since he can no longer see where she goes, whence she comes, or how she looks when she returns to their tent, Ali's uncertainty grows and his faith in Alil's love vanishes. Because he distrusts her, he beats her regularly. No longer does Ali reach for Alil in love.
 Time passes. Ali and Alil become the unhappiest couple living at the edge of the desert.

> One day Ali decides to avenge Alil's presumed unfaithfulness by making love to another woman who steals into his tent and then returns to it more and more often. This clandestine relationship does not, of course, improve either Ali's eyesight or his relationship with Alil. When he knows her to be near, he beats her so mercilessly that her cries can be heard outside the tent.
>
> When the miracle doctor hears about the couple's problem, he takes pity on them and comes to heal Ali, even though the shepherd cannot pay. Now Ali can see, but he does not tell Alil, because he wants to watch her. What he discovers is astounding. He can see now how Alil cries when he beats her. Afterwards he sees her leave their tent, wash her face, and slip back into the tent, pretending to be the other woman, only so Ali will embrace her, make love to her. (V 161-63)

This touching parable, one of many stories in *Mein Name sei Gantenbein* (*Let My Name Be Gantenbein*), illustrates the themes of love, marriage, and jealousy central to this novel. It employs, in addition, the predominant metaphor of blindness and sight. Placed in the center of the novel, this parable is also the structural pivot of this, Frisch's fourth major narrative, one even more intricate than its predecessors.

As in *Stiller* and *Homo faber*, the protagonist is the narrator, the I. One day, after a minor but disturbing automobile accident, the protagonist imagines that a man, injured in a car accident, lies in a hospital bed, his face covered with bandages. His senses of hearing and smell are intact, but he cannot see. When the bandages are removed his sight returns. What if, the narrator muses, this man, like Ali in the parable, never told anyone that he could see but tried to live his life as a blind man? What would that life be like? A game of sorts, a difficult one. But might not the freedom this man gained from his secret add a special quality to his life? (V 21). This curiosity is the basis of the metaphor Frisch develops in the novel.[1] The man is called Gantenbein; the woman he marries is Lila, whose name, spelled backward, is Alil.

As this incident and the novel's German title suggest, all events of Gantenbein's story remain in the realm of possibility and invention. They never become reality. The same is true of most of the characters; they, too, exist only in the realm of possibility. None has a distinct biography, a life story of his own; all of their actions remain merely conjecture.[2] Even about the narrator the reader learns next to nothing. He remains, as Frisch intended him to, "[ein] weißer Fleck . . . umrissen durch die Summe der Fiktionen, die dieser Person möglich sind" (V 325, "Ich schreibe für Leser"), *"[a] white spot . . . outlined by the sum of the inventions this person is capable of"* (*"I Write for Readers"*).

Mein Name sei Gantenbein was published in 1964. Its first version, finished in 1963, bore, like several of Frisch's other narratives and dramas, a double title: *Lila oder Ich bin blind (Lila or I Am Blind)*. When the final version went to press, however, its title had been changed to the present one. The novel's initial reception, especially in Europe, was mixed, ranging from violently negative to enthusiastically positive. Since that time it has achieved worldwide attention and recognition as one of the important novels of the twentieth century. The approved English translation, revised by Michael Bullock in 1982, is called *Gantenbein*.[3]

The narrator of the events, again a man, is given no name; he appears only as "I". In some respects, *Mein Name sei Gantenbein* is a direct progression in both form and content from Frisch's two previous narratives, *Stiller* and *Homo faber*, but the differences are striking. In *Stiller*, many important events in the protagonist's life are told to him by other characters, who thus reveal and define his identity. Stiller records their comments in his notebooks but does not want to accept the resulting identity they present; eventually he is forced to. The protagonist in *Homo faber* reveals his own life story in a written report; his self-image and identity originally seem sure and secure, but they gradually disintegrate. The technique changes again in *Mein Name sei Gantenbein*, whose narrator creates three fictitious characters, each representing a significant facet of himself, and each moving through individual experiences; collectively, the three characters illuminate and interpret the total personality of the narrator.

Once again, therefore, Frisch is dealing with the problem of identity. In this novel, however, he examines further a second major topic of recurring interest to him, this time with the most care he has shown to date: the protagonist's social relationships, especially his relationship to the woman he loves. The most direct and intimate of these relationships is marriage.

Near the beginning of the novel, the narrator states his motive for telling the story of Gantenbein:

> Ein Mann hat eine Erfahrung gemacht, jetzt sucht er die Geschichte dazu—man kann nicht leben mit einer Erfahrung, die ohne Geschichte bleibt. (V 11)
>
> *A man has been through an experience, now he is looking for the story to go with it—you can't live with an experience that remains without a story. (11)*

The experience has been fundamental, traumatic, and existential. It has affected the narrator deeply, so deeply that he seems unable to describe it clearly. All he can do at first is to describe its sensation: "wie ein Sturz durch den Spiegel . . . durch alle Spiegel" (V 18), *"like falling through a mirror . . . through all the mirrors there are" (18)*. Afterward, his world pieced itself together again, the narrator asserts, as if nothing had happened. Then he states emphatically: "Es ist auch nichts geschehen" (V 18), *"And nothing has happened" (18)*. This statement is suspect, however, because as it recurs in the course of the novel it is either reaffirmed or placed in doubt by such statements as: "es ist immer etwas geschehen, aber anders" (V 313), *"something has always happened, but differently" (297)*. The last time the narrator refers, tentatively, to this basic experience is at the beginning of the novel's final paragraph: "Alles ist wie nicht geschehen" (V 319), *"Everything as if it had never happened" (303)*. The constant change in tone indicates that the narrator is uncertain about the story he is telling, but also that something did happen.

What happened is closely linked to one of two key episodes the narrator describes near the beginning of the novel (V 18-20).[4] A long-term relationship between a man and a woman, perhaps a marriage and probably the narrator's own, has ended.[5] He makes this clear during his detailed description of an empty apartment, his apartment, to which he has returned. On the table he sees a nearly empty bottle of wine, in which islands of mold are floating, and remnants of bread, hard as a rock. In the refrigerator he finds some curled-up, dried-out ham; a bit of cheese, cracked like the bark of a tree; a bottle of cream that has gone sour; a bowl containing crusty leftover stewed apricots; and a can of goose liver. Provisions for a mummy? the narrator wonders. The carpets are rolled up, the upholstered furniture covered with sheets, and the shutters at the windows closed. Until recently, he can see, the apartment was occupied by a man and a woman; the items they left behind indicate that their departure was hasty and permanent. In the wardrobe are a few woman's blouses, some items of woman's underwear, five man's jackets, some neckties, and on the bottom shelf a row of shoes, his and hers, lined up as if ready for roll call.

The narrator, who has no matches, merely imagines setting fire to the apartment. His attempt to burn it down probably would be unsuccessful, he surmises, as one would need to pour gasoline over everything to be sure that once one lights a match all physical reminders of the past and the relationship that existed here would be destroyed. The destructive urge the narrator experiences at this moment is reminiscent of that of Walter Faber when he was tempted to burn down his New York apartment (IV 62) and of the rampage Stiller went on during the studio visit that brought him face to face with his past (III 721-23). Like Stiller, the narrator here realizes that physical destruction of the past is as much beyond his power as his ability to annul that past. In recognition of this he meekly observes, in response to the ringing doorbell: "Der Herr meines Namens ist verreist" (V 20), *"The gentleman of my name has gone away"* (19).

The importance of this scene is underscored by the fact that the narrator refers to it and repeats details from it twice more, each time to punctuate a significant scene. In the first instance, Gantenbein's jealous reaction to the narrator's invented series of incidents that document Lila's adultery is irrational: he locks his wife and a casual male visitor, whom he believes to be her lover, into the bedroom and leaves the apartment. Lila responds by ending the marriage (V 198). At that moment, the narrator sees himself back in the empty apartment. In the second instance, near the end of the novel, the narrator is being interrogated by "someone whom it doesn't concern" (V 313/*297*). That someone wants to know what really happened in the narrator's life and which one of the three fictional characters of his story he really is. Instead of answering, the narrator closes his eyes and remains silent. When he hears the tip-tap of high-heeled shoes, he opens his eyes and sees the uninhabited apartment once more (V 313-14).

This, then, is the stage on which the narrator's fundamental experience took place for which he must now find a story, so that he can understand and live with it. A suitable story is not easy to find. As the narrator searches for one, he admits: "Ich probiere Geschichten an wie Kleider!" (V 22), "*I try on stories like clothes!*" (V 21).

Since the narrator, the I, is unable to understand the traumatic experience he may have precipitated and in which he certainly participated, he realizes that he must begin by trying to understand *himself* better. To examine his own personality, his foibles and strengths more clearly, he decides to dissect the whole, to divide himself into facets that may be easier to analyze. And so, as a prism catching the rays of the sun causes the white light to fragment into its rainbow of individual colors, the narrator shines the light of inquiry onto his own personality and causes it to fragment into three distinct personalities, each projecting one of his major facets. The three dominant "colors" that emerge are named Enderlin, Svoboda, and Gantenbein. Perhaps the last represents the narrator most completely. At least, after carefully considering various options, he decides: "Mein Name sei Gantenbein" (V 25), "*Let my name be Gantenbein*" (24). He repeats this decision periodically throughout the novel, the last time adding in parentheses: "Aber endgültig" (V 271), "*But finally*" (257).

From the time of his first novel, *Jürg Reinhart: Eine sommerliche Schicksalsfahrt (Jürg Reinhart: A Fateful Summer's Journey)*, published in 1934, Max Frisch's writings have indicated a troubled concern about modern man's relationships to women. In *Mein Name sei Gantenbein* he probes the male psyche more deeply than before, tests male attitudes toward women more relentlessly, examining particularly sexual love, sexual jealousy, and modern marriage. In the process, Frisch's narrator hopes to discover a story that will make bearable an experience he never explains, but one that is closely associated with the collapse of a long-term, loving relationship. In his examination of himself, the narrator reveals his own attitudes and behavior toward women.

All events in this novel are merely conjecture, not biography. The oft-repeated phrase "Ich stelle mir vor," "*I imagine*," serves as the narrator's leitmotif. Combined with "Alles ist wie nicht geschehen . . ." (V 319), "*Everything [is] as if it had never happened* . . ." (303), it keeps the reader alert to the realization that what appears on the pages is not historic fact but merely possibility, limited only by the potential of the narrator's personality.

Before discussing the three fictional men who represent the narrator, it seems necessary to examine the narrator himself and the technique he uses to find the understanding he seeks.

THE NARRATOR: PUPPETEER OF THE SELF

In his first sketchbook (*Tagebuch 1946-1949*), Max Frisch introduces and often returns to the figure of a young village boy, Marion, a puppeteer (II 352-59,364-67,382,384-86,500-01; *Sketch I 6-11,27,30-31*).[6] Marion is important to Frisch as a metaphor, and in his story Frisch tests many of the images that recur in later novels.

Marion loves to entertain the poor people of his village with his marionettes, which he carved himself. He is an unpretentious boy, one without special ambition or ulterior motive. His world is whole: his thoughts, feelings, and actions are in harmony with one another.

A visitor from the city discovers Marion and persuades him to accompany him to the city, where riches and fame await him. Marion finds neither. Instead, he notices that people do not say what they think but what they believe others want to hear; instead of being motivated by an inner impulse, their behavior seems to be set in motion by strings that can be pulled by anyone who wishes to do so. People, it seems to Marion, are like his lifeless marionettes, and soon he sees strings everywhere, even in his nightmares.

One evening Marion hangs himself, because of his bewilderment about people, according to the man who brought Marion from the village to the city. The dichotomy between people's feelings and actions bewildered Marion; he could not reconcile the two. An avoidable error, claims the gentleman from the city.

The "I" in *Mein Name sei Gantenbein* has much in common with Marion, the puppeteer. Like Marion he is bewildered, but about himself, not others. He is aware of the dichotomy between his own feelings and actions, which, in his case, resulted in the end of a relationship that was vital to him. What went wrong? Where and how did he make the wrong choices in his relationship? And what were his options?

In his search for answers the narrator creates three "puppets." Like Marion's puppets, Enderlin, Svoboda, and Gantenbein respond when the narrator places them in situations that challenge them to act, and then he figuratively pulls their strings. He manipulates each of his characters through a series of situations and variations thereof that focus on each one's relationship with Lila. In the process, each man displays a limited set of traits that are part of the narrator's complex personality, each acts within the confines of his own existence, and thus each serves a unique function in the narrator's search for answers about himself. Combined, these three male characters relate the narrator's story, the one he must find in order to explain an experience that is still incomprehensible to him when he visits his former apartment (V 18-20).

The first puppet character is Felix Enderlin, a somewhat neurotic, indecisive intellectual, a scholar and art historian, who represents the narrator's basic insecurity and his fear of sexual inadequacy. Second is Frantisek Svoboda, an athletic and professionally successful architect, who portrays the narrator in a conventional marriage: he is loving, dependent, and somewhat chauvinistic. When he learns that his wife has a lover and that his marriage, which he thought stable, seems to have come to an end, he becomes first angrily jealous and then immobilized. The most complex of the trio is Theo Gantenbein, sometimes self-employed, always the homebound blind husband of Lila, an actress well known in the theater, film, and television. The narrator uses Gantenbein more than the other two characters, especially to explore elements of a marriage one partner began with a false premise (blindness), to examine the cancerous effects of jealousy, and to expose the tricks he himself is potentially capable of using when interacting with a woman.

Lila, the woman the three men love, is essentially the same woman for all three—or, better, a figure representing all women. For the narrator she is a symbol of femininity. Although she interacts differently with each of the three men, her character changes little. She is a gracious hostess, an interesting conversationalist, a lively companion, and a generous lover. Sometimes she is deceptive; never is she on time. In all three relationships she is portrayed as intelligent, attractive, well-educated, and independent, a modern woman who could be, but only in her marriage to Gantenbein is, self-supporting.

With Enderlin, she appears to be the somewhat bored wife of Svoboda and therefore receptive to the adventure offered by a brief and strictly sexual encounter of the kind Enderlin proposes. Mild trickery and deception come naturally to her, and she uses them effectively to get what she wants. Yet, better than Enderlin, she is able to keep within the boundaries of the agreement they make concerning the nature and duration of their liaison.

With Svoboda, Lila is the modern wife of a professionally successful man. She does not have to work for a living and feels no need to do so, even though she thinks of herself as a liberated woman; she is sure she could go out tomorrow and get a job, if she chose to. Although occasionally bored, she is perfectly willing to stay at home—but not because she considers herself by nature better qualified to perform household task than a man. In her marriage to Svoboda, even in critical moments, Lila is thoughtful, considerate, self-assured, and imbued with a desire to be fair to all, herself included. Like Enderlin's and Gantenbein's Lila, she is basically an honest person, despite the little deceptions she is willing to engage in if they serve her purpose. She is honest especially with herself. In this respect, Lila is reminiscent of Sibylle in *Stiller*. Like her, she has a fairly secure self-image and a healthy attitude about herself, allowing her intuition and feelings to guide her actions.

In her marriage to Gantenbein, the man who pretends to be blind, Lila is a skillful professional actress, not merely a somewhat deceptive wife and lover. All women, according to Max Frisch, are by nature more suited to the profession of acting than men. In his first sketchbook he writes:

Das Weib ist schauspielerisch von Natur. Kommt eine Begabung hinzu, die sogar einen Beruf daraus werden läßt, wird das Weib dadurch nicht fragwürdig, nur weiblicher. . . . je weiblicher sie ist, um so voller glaube ich ihr die Schauspielerin. (II 622)

A woman is theatrical by nature. If, in addition, she has a talent that might even allow her to make a profession of acting, a woman does not in consequence become unconvincing, but simply more feminine . . . . the more feminine she is, the more I can believe in her as an actress. (Sketch I 224)

Given this frame of reference, Lila as the wife of Gantenbein is the most feminine of the narrator's three portrayals of a modern woman, here shown as a highly respected professional, a caring lover, and a loving wife who does, however, have some personal shortcomings. With the Lila of Enderlin and Svoboda she shares a tendency to engage in wiles and deceptions, which in her case are more readily suggested, more easily carried out, and more convincingly maintained in public because she is both a well-known actress, thus an artist whom the middle class eternally suspects of having loose morals, and the wife of a blind man, whose lack of sight allows her to be less cautious in his presence than she might be otherwise.

Her marriage to Gantenbein is the most completely developed of the three relationships in which the narrator places Lila. However, since any relationship based on a pretense by one partner, whatever the reason, creates false assumptions in the other partner, it ultimately cannot last. Such a relationship may be convenient for a while, but once the pretense is dropped and the false assumptions unmasked, the relationship is finished: the basic trust of the partners, essential for love, has been irreparably destroyed. As with Marion, the puppeteer, the result of this recognition is confusion and bewilderment. Although the consequences for Lila and Gantenbein are not fatal, as they were for Marion, they are nevertheless deeply traumatic for both.

Lila as a character has even less of an independent existence than most of Frisch's women, because she is merely a projection of each of the three men she associates with. Furthermore, since each of them is only a prismic projection of the narrator, she is really the narrator's projection of *woman*—his composite preconceptions, prejudices, attitudes, and assumptions about what women are like and how they behave in relationships like the three in which he places her. Thus Lila is in essence a *chiffre*, a code name that stands collectively for all that is feminine.

Lila and Svoboda spring from the narrator's pen almost full blown onto the pages of the novel, whereas Enderlin and Gantenbein emerge gradually. The narrator takes great care in selecting the appropriate physical attributes for them, as he tries them in one guise and then another (V 8-11). Eventually he clothes them with the personalities, habits, friends, a past, and hopes for a future that are appropriate to the characters they are to play in his story.

Most scenes and new situations in that story are preceded by the leitmotif: "Ich stelle mir vor," *"I imagine."* What the narrator imagines is an infinite variety of situations for each character, some contradicting and others complementing each other. The narrator has no difficulty imagining two or more different versions of any sequence of events any one of the three men encounters, as he explores possible scenes, stories, and behavior for his prismic manifestations. As a result, this is a novel of variations—not only of imagined experiences and actions, but also of actions omitted that, at the level of pure imagination, are here pursued as possibilities to discover what results they might have yielded. Some alternatives to a given scene or action are presented instantly, others appear later in the novel. The result is an immensely complex structure. Behind each episode and its variant remains hidden the real story of the narrator.

He is fully aware that, however one acts, he has chosen only one of a number of possible options available in a given situation. That is why the narrator states that any life story based on biographical facts is "nur ein Teil meines Lebens, und den andern Teil muß ich mir vorstellen" (V 129), *"only part of my life, and the other part I must imagine"* (123). Awareness of those other options not only expands one's perception of reality but also leads to a fuller understanding of any given situation and, therefore, of oneself. That is the narrator's objective.

In the course of his imaginative manipulation, the narrator employs two structural devices familiar from earlier Frisch novels. Not constrained here by logical chronology, he reveals sequential events in his characters' lives in inverted order and in spatially distant sections of the novel, often returning to them later for examination or revision. In addition, he interjects into the narrative numerous brief, self-contained stories like that of Ali and Alil, some told by the narrator himself, some by his and Enderlin's physician friend Burri, some by a party guest, and many by Gantenbein to his friend and manicurist, Camilla Huber. Each story in some way intensifies the focus on one or more of the topics the narrator is examining—the vicissitudes of love, the destructive power of jealousy, the effects of boredom or deceit in a marriage—and furthers his investigation into the problems between men and the women they love.

As the narrator manipulates the three prismic manifestations of himself through their scenes, he, as the I, remains whole. Although he sometimes interacts with his prismic characters, more often he comments on their actions, attitudes, and thoughts during instant evaluations of their behavior and its results.

A number of minor characters, some of whom reappear frequently, join the narrator, his three manifestations, and Lila. Some interact only with the narrator or with one prismic character, others with all major actors except Lila. The most important of these ancillary characters are Dr. Burri, the narrator's close friend and favorite chess partner, and Camilla Huber, a prostitute who would prefer to have a respectable profession and who serves as private manicurist to the blind Gantenbein. Both further the narrator's investigation into man's relationship with woman—Camilla through the secrets she and Gantenbein share (V 261-63), the role she assumes for him, and her acceptance of *his* role; Burri through the stories he tells and the observations he makes, particularly his perceptive reflections about women that are actually observations about men (V 208-09).

In each of his novels, Max Frisch is concerned about reality in a person's life. Three years after completing *Mein Name sei Gantenbein* he wrote on this topic in his second sketchbook:

> es [das Leben] summiert sich aus Handlungen, die zufällig bleiben, es hätte immer auch anders sein können, und es

gibt keine Handlung und keine Unterlassung, die für die Zukunft nicht Varianten zuließe. (VI 75)

it [life] consists of a series of actions that remain fortuitous—things could always have happened differently, there is no action and no omission that does not provide future alternatives. (Sketch II 64)

This is exactly the situation in *Mein Name sei Gantenbein*, where the narrator presents and explores these alternatives. Frisch explains the logic of using this procedure to get a firm grip on the narrator's reality as follows: "Der einzige Vorfall, der keine Variante mehr zuläßt, ist der Tod" (VI 75), *"The only event that provides no alternative is death!" (Sketch II 64).*

In life, Frisch writes, we may be able to correct a mistake we once made. We cannot cancel it, however; we cannot choose a different behavior for ourselves in connection with a specific action we took in the past. In the realm of imagination, this is no problem at all. The availability of alternatives, which are not restricted by the finite limitations of *time*, makes this possible. The narrator in *Gantenbein*, therefore, is not constrained by historic fact but only by possibility, which is limited merely by the potential of his personality; the result is as much a part of reality as any biography.

Even here, however, at the level of imagined, not lived, reality, there is a limitation. It is impossible to imagine oneself to be three different people *simultaneously*, each with a separate personality and character and able to interact with the others. That is why the narrator in this Frisch novel chooses to look through the prism of his own personality, to create three individual characters—Enderlin, Svoboda, and Gantenbein—and to confront each of them in succession with the same issues of love, marriage, and jealousy. As the narrator, the puppeteer, very deliberately pulls the strings of these three characters, he observes what each, through his action or inaction in a given situation, has to say about himself—and, by extension, about the narrator—as a male, his attitude toward women, and his relationship to them.

ENDERLIN: THE PROBLEMATIC LOVER

Enderlin is a mythologist and an intellectual. He is given birth gradually in a bar during a delightfully ironic scene, one of Frisch's little masterpieces in which he describes a single event from two simultaneous perspectives.

The narrator, a stranger in town, has come to the bar to meet a man he does not know. While he waits, he talks with the barman and has a drink, whiskey. More than an hour later, after he has had several whiskeys and has become slightly intoxicated, an attractive woman, later identified as Lila, arrives to tell him that Svoboda, her husband, has been unexpectedly called to London on business and has sent her to apologize. The narrator, who thinks she might be an actress—perhaps a famous one, which prevents him from verifying his assumption by asking her—invites her for a drink, lights her cigarette, and listens to her talk about her husband as she smokes nervously. While he listens, he decides not to fall in love with this woman, a surprising decision that indicates that the narrator has a weakness for attractive women. However, since one of the narrator's goals in this novel is to discover the tricks he uses in his relationship with women, it is plausible that, when the woman unexpectedly starts talking about Peru, "a strange gentleman" should suddenly appear, the narrator's alter ego in such a situation. As the narrator wonders about what role the woman might play best, the "stranger" responds to her comments and takes over the conversation. The narrator then steps back from, but not out of, the scene. He is aware of the amorous prowess of this strange gentleman—later given the name Enderlin (V 68)—and is often embarrassed by his transparent conversational technique. Nevertheless, as the narrator observes, it is successful.

Nothing illustrates more clearly the close relationship between the narrator and Enderlin than the scene in the hospital the narrator describes near the beginning of the novel (V 12). It is the first of the novel's two key episodes and precedes the scene in the empty apartment. As the narrator awakens, there appears out of the grey morning of the new day, which seems like a solid slab of granite to him, first a soundless cry, then the head of a horse, its eyes wide open, foaming at the mouth, whinnying but not making a sound, attempting to escape from its imprisonment in the granite. Its mane flying, its face filled with the terror of death, the rest of its body still trapped in the granite, the whites of its eyes staring in panic at the narrator, it begs for mercy. Its attempt to free itself fails; silently the animal's head retreats into the granite, which closes noiselessly behind it without leaving a crack. Later in the novel, Enderlin experiences the same vision while in the hospital (V 153-54). The narrator merely observes that he can imagine the scene, then adds in parentheses: "(weil ich es erfahren habe)" (V 153), "(because I have experienced it)" (146).

The experience Enderlin shares with the narrator is "der Riß, der durch seine Person geht, der Riß zwischen mir und ihm" (V 130), "the split that runs through his person, the split between me and him" (124). Enderlin, like the narrator, is torn between struggling for what he wants and, once he has reached his goal, accepting the rewards of his achievements and acknowledging the obligations of the person he has become in the perceptions of others. Enderlin lacks commitment to a role, any role, which is the source of his difficulty in making decisions. "Enderlin kann keine Rolle spielen" (V 118), "Enderlin can't play any role" (113), the narrator claims. In the middle of the novel, however, when he does begin to play a role, the narrator discards him as no longer a viable manifestation of that particular facet of himself (V 160). He can be of no further value in helping the narrator understand his traumatic experience.[7] Until that time, however, Enderlin in his relationship with Lila illustrates attitudes and behavior that reflect upon and illuminate the narrator's own attitude about himself and his relationships with women.

Felix Enderlin, Ph.D., age 41, is an academician and a recognized scholar of mythology. His investigations of and writings about Hermes—the notorious god of thieves and rogues, of merchants, herdsmen, and herds; the bestower of fertility; the messenger of death; and the guide of mortals to the underworld—have been particularly brilliant. As a result, he has been invited to spend a term at Harvard. The lecture he is to deliver there is already written. The press and his friends expect him to accept the offer and to leave for Harvard soon. Enderlin expects so, too, but he never goes. Although he hoped to receive such an invitation in recognition of his work, now that it has been extended and everybody, at home and abroad, seems to know about it, thanks to the press, Enderlin feels like an imposter. After working in the peace and isolation of his study without, until now, being blessed with any special recognition, he is unable to step suddenly into the public forum and accept the professional reward that is rightfully his. The narrator, trying to explain why Enderlin does not go to Harvard, observes:

> Wer, wie Enderlin, sich einmal so entworfen hat, daß er sich durch Leistungen legitimieren muß, wirkt im Grunde nie vertrauenswürdig. . . . Was überzeugt, sind nicht Leistungen, sondern die Rolle, die einer spielt. Das ist's, was Enderlin spürt, was ihn erschreckt. (V 118)

> *Anyone who, like Enderlin, has once designed himself in such a way that he has to legitimate himself by his achievements, never seems fundamentally trustworthy. . . . What convinces is not a person's achievements, but the role he plays. This is what Enderlin feels, what scares him. (113)*

Enderlin is simply incapable of playing a role, or so the narrator believes.

To underscore the point he has just made, the narrator tells the story of an ambassador of an important country whose reaction to the challenge of playing a role is just the opposite of Enderlin's. Although that man recognizes his inadequacies and knows that he is a quite different and far less excellent person than the world takes him for, he does not resign his prestigious position but, fully aware of who he really is, accepts the role the world asks him to play and keeps the truth about himself a secret he takes to his grave.

Enderlin's inability to play a role on demand is paralleled by his indecisiveness, which he expresses professionally in his hesitation to accept the Harvard invitation and privately in his relationship with Lila. They had agreed beforehand that, to preserve the unique experience of their night of love, they would not turn it into an extended affair. However at the airport, when he is about to leave the city, Enderlin first calls Lila and then takes a taxi to her apartment, two actions they promised each other they would not take.

Frisch addressed the problem implied here, Enderlin's flawed relationship to transient time, in his first sketchbook:

> Man fragt sich manchmal, inwiefern eine Gegenwart überhaupt erlebbar ist. Könnte man unser Erleben darstellen, und zwar ohne unser Vorurteil . . . nicht die Ereignisse würden sich darstellen, sondern die Anlässe der Ahnung, die Anlässe der Erinnerung. Die Gegenwart bleibt irgendwie unwirklich, ein Nichts zwischen Ahnung und Erinnerung, welche die eigentlichen Räume unsers Erlebens sind; die Gegenwart als bloßer Durchgang; die bekannte Leere, die man sich ungern zugibt. (II 451-52)

> *At times one wonders to what extent one experiences the present at all. Could one depict experience with complete objectivity . . . not the events themselves would be depicted, but the sources of expectation, the sources of memory. The present moment remains somehow unreal, a nothingness between expectation and memory, these being the true dwelling place of experience; the present is a mere passage; the familiar feeling of emptiness, which one does not care to admit to oneself.* (Sketch I 85)

Enderlin, however, seems certain not only that the present can be lived and fully experienced, but also that it is the only valid experience, at least for him. Except for his studies in antiquity, he focuses his life exclusively on the present. He abhors repeating any experience and struggles against taking any action that commits him to a future course of conduct, even when he feels strongly about an issue or a person.

Enderlin's obsession with the present is reminiscent philosophically of the impractical theory of modern marriage Rolf proposed in *Stiller*. Enderlin advances his notion during his first conversation with Lila in the bar.

In a clever verbal maneuver designed to capture Lila's interest, he talks playfully but frankly about major questions of life, such as: Should a woman who has a profession have a child? Or: What is meant by marriage? Then, in a colorful assortment of images, he casually parades a whole series of semantically loaded words like love, man and woman, friendship, sex, fidelity, bed, jealousy, profession, species, and individual in front of Lila before any of these words can have acquired a personal meaning for the two of them. The narrator, forced to listen to his own views diluted into generalities by Enderlin, is bored. Accordingly, Enderlin spices his general comments with specific examples, to give them and his conversational game immediacy and distinctiveness. For instance, he supposes that two people, like Lila and himself, might agree to sleep with each other just once, without allowing this onetime experience to develop into an affair; they will have agreed beforehand not to see each other afterward, so that the experience cannot be repeated and its uniqueness spoiled. Lila listens quietly, as Enderlin proceeds to invent little dialogues between the two imagined lovers, a clever move that allows him, in German, to introduce the familiar pronoun *du* (you) into his conversation (V 64), adding a level of intimacy to it that cannot be canceled, even when Enderlin ends his conversational game and returns to the more formal *Sie*.

Lila smokes and listens. She knows that Enderlin's remarks are to be understood as enclosed in quotation marks. They are meant merely as an illustration of an imagined situation, but one that constitutes an unspoken, open invitation—perhaps Enderlin's response to her earlier, unmotivated, comments about Peru, where she once traveled with her husband and which Enderlin refers to as the land of his hope. His hope for what, one might ask, only to remember that Peru, for many Europeans, is a faraway, exotic place, synonymous with adventure.[8] Is Lila, who began talking about Peru for no obvious reason, trying subtly to convey to her male companion that the adventure has gone out of her marriage to Svoboda? Details of that marriage, as they appear later in the novel, support this possibility. Furthermore, at this point in the conversation the narrator becomes very sober and leaves it up to "the other gentleman" to continue talking with Lila, as if the narrator suddenly understood the implication of her barely disguised invitation to adventure.

That the narrator stays interested in Lila, in her sensuality, while Enderlin takes over the conversation is clear from the narrator's close observations of her movements and his obviously sexual fascination with her mouth. When, in passing, he suddenly hears Lila tell Enderlin that she is faithful, the narrator claims not to know what has prompted her to make that statement; he has been too absorbed in his own thoughts of her and has not been following the conversation attentively.

Enderlin, meanwhile, has guided the conversation into a playful but very personal game. In the process, he once takes hold of Lila's arm, a gesture she accepts without protest, and he would do so again, the narrator observes, did he not feel watched and intimidated by the narrator. However, before they leave the bar Enderlin touches Lila twice more, a sequence of movements, each more intimate than the previous one, that illustrates the rapid progression of their relationship and Lila's somewhat bewildered, yet gradual, surrender to Enderlin.

In the first of these situations Enderlin, who has changed the topic of the conversation to actors, talks about the charm of homosexual men and their sensitivity to a woman's costume and perfume. Then, although he claims to like her ensemble and admits that if he didn't he would not know how to improve it, he takes hold of her collar to demonstrate how such a man, a homosexual, would change this and that to create a different look, as if by magic. Lila is surprised and perplexed by Enderlin's gradual invasion of her "space," since the head is a person's most vulnerable area and thus most staunchly protected from strangers. Lila's face shows only confusion; she does not protest, either by evasive movement or words. Her lack of negative reaction establishes, directly now, the personal, intimate atmosphere between them that was introduced indirectly by Enderlin's situational word game and his use of the intimate *du*. Furthermore, it allows Enderlin the next and final step in his symbolic conquest of Lila, a seemingly involuntary, gentle stroking of her forehead as they prepare to leave the bar. That Lila lets it happen without protest signals her total surrender to Enderlin.

The narrator, however, protests each progression in the level of intimacy. He does not want a love story, an affair between the two. He feels paralyzed by the fear that his freedom to act, perhaps to restrain Enderlin, may have come to an end, as Enderlin, the character, takes on gradually a more intense life of his own. As Lila rides off in a taxi, the narrator turns on his heel to return to his hotel. Enderlin does not want an affair either, as he made clear in the bar with his conversational game.

He wants a single experience of sexual love with Lila, a unique experience.

Surprisingly, it is the narrator, not Enderlin, who, bored with the prospect of spending an evening alone in a strange city, jokingly dials Lila's apartment, then "passes" the telephone to Enderlin. This telephone scene, in tone an extension of the bar scene, continues the ironic dual perspective. The narrator, lying on the bed with his shoes off, claims that he does not want to see Lila again, although he is the one who dials her number; he protests that operas do not interest him, yet he hears Enderlin tentatively accepting an invitation to attend one that evening, using the ticket of her husband, who is in London; and he watches his dark suit being unpacked and hung up, still protesting that this is not necessary. Shortly after six, dressed in his dark evening suit, the narrator leaves the hotel to avoid Lila's agreed-on phone call to Enderlin between six and seven, walks into the middle of a movie, gets bored, visits a couple of bars; Enderlin then appears at Lila's door to take her to the opera.[9]

Lila and Enderlin never get to the opera, because Lila insists on searching for and showing Enderlin the maps of Peru she mentioned during their afternoon conversation at the bar. After she finds them and carefully unfolds one in the hallway, Enderlin repeats his involuntary, tender gesture of the afternoon, gently stroking her forehead, and thus reestablishes a very intimate atmosphere. After several hours of cautious general conversation during which they learn more about each other, not from what they talk about but from what they do not talk about—a conversation filled with awkward pauses and wordless smiles—they decide to leave the apartment and go out for a drink (V 76). Once again they get no farther than the hallway, where Enderlin for a third time involuntarily strokes Lila's forehead. This time it leads directly to a night of lovemaking.

Early the next morning, Enderlin lets himself out of the apartment and drops Lila's apartment key into the mailbox, hoping for her sake that no one has seen him leave. He walks slowly through the city, still dressed in his dark evening suit, washes his face in a fountain, drinks a cup of coffee in a coffee shop where, surrounded by workmen, he savors the recollection of the previous night of love with Lila. He shall never see her again; they have agreed not to call each other, not to write. For them there shall be only this one intimate experience to be remembered, an experience that took place in the darkness of night, removed from the strictures of continuous time that demands repetition and thus reduces the unique character of feelings and experiences. Enderlin and Lila wanted only to capture the *now*, the present moment.

As Enderlin recalls details of his night with Lila he remembers, smilingly, that "Peru!" was the only name he called out during their passionate embraces. Enderlin got to Peru that night, the country of his hope as he had defined it in the afternoon: he had experienced love with Lila as a onetime event in which the "I" and "you" met each other and merged into the "we." They had kept the world away from them and their island of unique experience by talking little all night, and when they did, they whispered. They alone existed, two parts forming a whole; there was neither a before nor an after for them, only the now. Besides her name—and that is already too much, the narrator adds—Enderlin knows little about Lila: she is married, speaks with a slight accent, probably Alsatian, he thinks, and is about thirty years old and slender.

Enderlin's plane is to leave that evening. This morning he has an 11:30 appointment and probably a business lunch. He and Lila will have no time to talk or to see each other before he leaves town. Besides, they have agreed: there will be no repetition. Repetition is Enderlin's greatest fear, particularly repetition in a relationship with a woman. And yet he is obsessed with women.

At his hotel, to which Enderlin eventually returns after an unscheduled visit to an art museum, he finds a message from Lila. At once he is annoyed: she has broken her promise. This is an infamous act, an act of unfaithfulness, he believes, until he discovers that the message was left the previous evening, before he appeared at her apartment. Now Enderlin feels foolish. But when his telephone rings a moment later, he is willing to break their agreement himself, hopes the call is from her, wants to talk with her, wants to see her. The caller, it turns out, is only his 11:30 appointment, announcing that he is waiting in the lobby.

Much as he wants to, even Enderlin, it seems, cannot experience the present by itself. Frisch claimed that the present is "a nothingness between expectation and memory" (II 452/ *Sketch I* 85), but Enderlin is struggling to prove that the present *is* livable.

In his relationship with Lila, he fails. As one facet of the narrator, he demonstrates a flaw—an untenable concept of time, or reality, and of commitment.

The sympathetic narrator, realizing that Enderlin cannot possibly succeed in his attempted flight from the past and the future, feels compelled to warn him: "Hütet euch vor Namen!" (V 127), "*Beware of names!*" (120). For it is names, both personal and place names, that identify lovers as members of a group, each with social ties to others who, in turn, are familiar to both, each with a past that connects seemingly accidental and distant points of each individual life with the others as if by magic— through a name. As a result, any given experience in the present, divorced from the memory of the past, is an illusion; it is as impossible to realize as is a future in which thoughts, feelings, and actions are never repeated. To sustain any experience in the nameless present is impossible, the narrator reflects. To prove his point he imagines the marriage of Enderlin and Lila ten years hence. He sees a daily routine dominated by the deadening forces of habit and repetition, which have combined to destroy the curiosity of the lovers about each other, about each other's body, leaving them with only a mutual longing beyond themselves (V 133-37), a longing that will never be fulfilled.

Repeating the past would be an equally dismal prospect, or worse. To illustrate it, the narrator imagines that Enderlin had to relive a year of his life "in the full knowledge of what is coming and without the expectation that is alone capable of making life bearable, without the openness, the uncertainty compounded of hope and fear" (V 123/117). That would be hell, the narrator concludes, for it is an existence "ohne Hoffnung, daß es anders kommt" (V 124), "*without hope of things happening differently*" (118). Such an existence, the narrator continues, is synonymous with death, a state in which change is no longer possible and time has lost its transience. Given that choice, the narrator concludes, it is better to choose a future, even if it includes repetition, for it offers the possibility of change, the expectation that those thoughts, feelings, and actions may turn out differently than they did in the past.

Enderlin's unsuccessful attempt to ignore in his relationship with any woman the memory of an individual past and the expectation of a common future in favor of an experience so unique that its repetition would destroy it barely disguises the basic truth that he lacks commitment to either the woman or the relationship. His claim that he wants to experience life and love only in the here and now rings hollow. Is what he experiences in the arms of a woman really love? Is it not merely primeval sexual lust? Is the source of Enderlin's sexual desire not more closely related to Rolf's flesh-colored cloth in *Stiller* than to any true feelings of love for the women with whom he has intercourse? Events in the novel suggest that to be the case.

Early in the novel, seriously ill and in the hospital, the narrator imagines himself as the patient standing before the night nurse, nude, reaching out for her, taking off her nurse's cap to free her tawny hair, chanting "I'm Adam and you're Eve," until he frightens her (V 12-13/12-13). Later in the story, when Enderlin, in turn, is in the hospital, erroneously believing he has only a year to live, he too thinks about women. He can see them only in the plural: hordes of women. In an attempt to escape responsibility for his purely sexual, lustful thoughts, his male psyche depersonalizes women, reducing them to mere objects of sexual gratification. The narrator, who is recording Enderlin's thoughts, observes:

> er denkt an ihren Schoß nur, in ihren Schoß; er denkt an keine, die er kennt, aber an alle, die er versäumt hat; Schöße, Münder und seine Zunge in ihren Mündern; wenn ihre Gesichter einander zum Verwechseln gleichen; dazu Wörter, die er nie ausgesprochen hat und deren Obszönität ihn seltsam befriedigt, indem sie Unbefriedigtheit erzeugt; Schöße, Lippen, Schenkel, Haare, Brüste, Augen, die ganz schmal werden dabei, und Schöße, Schöße, alle Schöße—
> (V 149)

> *he only thinks of their sex, into their sex; he doesn't think of any woman he knows, but of all those he has missed; sexes; mouths and his tongue in their mouths; even if their faces are indistinguishably alike; and words he has never uttered and whose obscenity satisfies him strangely by arousing dissatisfaction; sexes, lips, thighs, hair, breasts, eyes that narrow, and sexes, sexes, all sexes—* (142)[10]

Obviously Enderlin is obsessed with sex and driven by primeval feelings of lust. Compulsively, he seems to seek relationships that do not commit him to a future with a single woman but allow him to satisfy his elemental craving to share a sexual experience with a still quite unknown partner. He does not want to become involved in a woman's life, but only wants to be her sexual lover.

The source of this obsession is Enderlin's sexual insecurity, which he shares with other Frisch male characters such as Anatol Ludwig Stiller and Walter Faber. Enderlin reveals this secret after his night of lovemaking with Lila, while he is back in his hotel taking a shower:

> Noch jede Frau, dachte er, jede, die er umarmt hatte, fühlte sich geliebt; jede aber, die er wirklich zu lieben begann, sagte ihm früher oder später, daß er . . . von Liebe keine Ahnung habe. (V 81)
>
> *Every woman, he thought, every one he had made love to, had felt herself loved; but every one he was really beginning to love had told him sooner or later that . . . he didn't know the first thing about love. (77)*

This admission illustrates why Enderlin so urgently wants to avoid repetition of his sexual experience with Lila, why he wants to know as little as possible about her and her past, and why he does not want them ever to meet again after their night of love. He fears less the repetition of the experience than his partner's ultimate verdict—when the mystery of the unfamiliar has worn off, he has fallen in love with her, and they have become used to each other as sexual partners—that he is a poor lover.

Enderlin's attitude toward women is not healthy, his image of them not positive. He considers them to be tricksters and clever manipulators who are by nature unfaithful and who cover the tracks of their infidelities with devious schemes. Two incidents of his night with Lila seem to support his opinion. In the first, while he and Lila are in bed together, she calls her husband in London to make sure that he is still there; her free right hand rests on Enderlin's bare chest while she casually chats with her husband (V 71). The other incident is more elaborate. In an alternative version the narrator tells of their night of love, Lila is the mother of a preschool child. To prepare an alibi for herself with her husband, she awakens the child at three in the morning to tell him or her the story of the opera she has supposedly attended that evening. Before Lila returns to bed and Enderlin, she gives the child a drink and waits until he or she has gone back to sleep. The ruse works. When the father returns from London that evening, the child tells him the story of the opera that Mommy went to see the previous evening (V 265-66).

However, Felix Enderlin, who ironically chose Hermes as his primary topic of scholarly investigation, is as much a devious character as he perceives women to be; his deviousness is merely of a different nature, as his elaborate conversation with Lila at the bar shows. Enderlin's close association with Hermes is no accident. Hermes was himself a master of deceit and cunning. Furthermore his original symbol, the herm, has the shape of a phallus, symbolizing his dominant sexuality. Hermes was also known as the bringer of unexpected luck and opportunity, and equally well as a great misleader of men. Enderlin seizes opportunity and capitalizes on luck during his afternoon and evening with Lila. When he first earns and then does not accept the reward for his scholarly achievements, the invitation to Harvard, his behavior is misleading. The improbable and the capricious are closely associated with Hermes, as are the incalculable in human life and the sinister amidst frivolity, all of which Enderlin reflects to varying degrees.

During his hospital stay, after Enderlin misreads a medical prognosis that was actually another patient's and believes he has only a year to live, he suddenly changes: he evaluates his options and begins planning his final year. He could give up, waste away, hide, or kill himself. He decides not to believe the prediction and to live as if he has a future. For the first time he willingly accepts conventional social roles: he becomes the editor of a new journal and the owner of a house with a garden and swimming pool. He plans and gives a party one year after his hospital stay at which the guests, especially Burri, the doctor whose prognosis he misread, do not know what he is celebrating. His tacit acceptance of the future is illustrated by the narrator's projection of Enderlin at various stages in the process of aging: Enderlin at fifty, at sixty, at seventy (V 158-59). The tension between memory and expectation, an integral part of Enderlin's character and one he has wanted to escape in his relationship with Lila, is what makes him such a useful figure in the narrator's investigation of himself. It is, in essence, the creative tension between being and becoming. Never is Enderlin's inner tension more visible than on the evening after his night with Lila. His plane is delayed, but he repeatedly resists the temptation to break the agreement he made with Lila not to call, not to see each other again, not to repeat their experience. Eventually the plane is announced, and Enderlin suddenly finds himself dialing Lila's number. He will be leaving in a few minutes—not much time to talk. The narrator, aware of Enderlin's tension, is not surprised. Enderlin walks to the gate and waits there to board his plane. The narrator wonders whether he will really leave the city. Enderlin's luggage is already aboard. But Enderlin changes his mind at the last moment and makes his way by taxi back to the city where he searches for Lila's apartment in a neighborhood he barely remembers.

Enderlin's indecision between whether to remain faithful to his principles and fly back home, leaving behind the unfulfilled demands of a new love, or to stay and meet those demands, accepting his role as Lila's lover, dramatizes the creative tension that has intrigued the narrator. When Enderlin decides to stay with Lila, to take an action that commits him to a past and a future, to memory and expectation, repetition and habit, the narrator exercises the other option: *he* flies back home in Enderlin's place. One of them had to stay behind, the other had to fly, the narrator observes. It seems to make little difference who does what, because:

> Der nämlich bleibt, stellt sich vor, er wäre geflogen, und der nämlich fliegt, stellt sich vor, er wäre geblieben, und was er wirklich erlebt, so oder so, ist der Riß, der durch seine Person geht, der Riß zwischen ihm und mir. (V 130)

> *The one who stays imagines how it would have been if he had flown, and the one who flies imagines how it would have been*

if he had stayed, and what he really experiences, either way, is the split that runs through his person, the split between me and him. (123-24)

The total reality of existence, the narrator implies here, consists of lived *and* imagined reality. Together they create that pregnant tension between memory and expectation that is an integral part of the present, perhaps its most salient feature. What we really experience, the narrator points out, is the "Riß," the split, that runs through our being, caused by the actions we have taken and those we did not take but merely imagined taking, actions that were possible for us.

Once Enderlin accepts a role with a future—as editor of the new journal, something he had successfully forestalled until he was hospitalized, and as Lila's lover (their affair lasted at least several months, long enough for her to tell Svoboda, her husband, "I am very fond of someone" [V 225/213])—he is well on his way to becoming a functional part of society. As such, he ceases to be of any further interest to the narrator.

In his relationship with Lila, Enderlin was only useful as a problematic lover, one who woos and wins and then, once he has consummated his love, gives up his beloved. That usefulness ceases when he decides to return to Lila. How much he has become an average member of society, who now buys jewelry for his lover, is illustrated by his startled discovery in the jewelry store that it is mostly elderly men who make presents of jewelry to their loved ones. Enderlin's actions have become predictable, like those expected of other men. That is why the narrator gives him up as a character. Indirectly, he explains his action in a long, parenthetical statement about people he can never give up, because

es bleibt ihnen der Spielraum meiner Erwartung. Solche Leute kann ich nicht aufgeben. Ich brauche sie, und auch wenn sie mich übel behandelt haben. . . . Sie fesseln mich lebenslänglich, durch meine Vorstellung, daß sie, einmal in meine Lage versetzt, anders empfänden und anders handelten und anders daraus hervorgingen als ich, der ich mich selbst nicht aufgeben kann. (V 160)

> *they still have the scope afforded by my expectation. Such people I can't give up. I need them, even if they have treated me badly. . . . They grip me all my life long through my idea that they, if placed in my position, would feel differently and act differently and come out differently from me, who cannot give up myself.* (153)

Enderlin, however, the narrator can and does give up when his conduct comes to resemble too closely the narrator's own.

SVOBODA: THE DECEIVED HUSBAND

Frantisek Svoboda is first mentioned by name early in the novel. He is Lila's husband, the man who was called to London on business and asked his wife to keep his appointment with the narrator in a bar. Svoboda does not assume an identity of his own, however, until the final third of the novel. When he does, he is introduced as a successful professional, an architect who has his own business and employs at least two draftsmen. Unlike Enderlin, whose opposite in character he is, Svoboda is a fairly uncomplicated man. His character is clearly defined: he is used to controlling his environment through decisive, unambiguous action. Like Walter Faber, he performs a socially useful role; like Faber, too, he accepts, naively, appearance as reality. As a lover, Svoboda is involved in his relationship with a woman, unlike Enderlin, the erstwhile detached lover.

Svoboda and Lila have a comfortable marriage and live in a pleasantly furnished apartment. They have season tickets to the opera, and Svoboda has bought his wife her own car, which she enjoys because without it she would not feel independent. Earlier in their marriage they traveled to exciting places like Peru, of which the statue of an Inca dog and an Inca mug in their apartment are silent reminders. They have a small child, at least in one version of the story the narrator imagines, who is the primary reason why Lila was unable to accompany her husband to London.

To judge by his name, the narrator comments, Svoboda is a Bohemian, a tall, broad-shouldered, athletic man who speaks gently and always feels a bit more sure of himself when the top button of his shirt is open and his tie loosened. He is a kind man, but his kindness is of the sort that sometimes tyrannizes people, something he would never be able to understand, the narrator points out, if anyone ever told him. As a character Svoboda could, in some respects, be related to Rolf, Sibylle's husband in *Stiller*. They react alike when they discover that their wives love someone else: both initially appear calm but lose their composure after they learn their wives have slept with the other man. In response, both leave town for a while to give their wives time to think things over; both expect their wives to make the final decision about the future of their marriage and they await the decisions anxiously; both are plagued by terrible, paralyzing jealousy.

In *Stiller*, Rolf confides to Stiller/White the jealousy he suffered after fleeing from Zurich to avoid seeing Sibylle. Rolf was in a Genoa hotel room at the time, Stiller/White recalls in his notebook:

> Es war eine Strapaze. In Kleidern auf seinem eisernen Bett liegend, wobei er rauchte, quälte er sich mit schamlosgenauen Vorstellungen, wie seine Gattin sich dem andern hingibt; das war nicht die Strapaze, sondern die Entspannung, die er sich gönnte. Die Strapaze war die Einsicht, das unfreiwillige Eingeständnis, daß er sich über das Niveau seiner Gefühle bisher doch sehr getäuscht hatte, über seine Reife. (III 560)

> *It was an ordeal.*
> *Lying fully dressed on his iron bed smoking, he tormented himself with shamelessly precise imaginings of his wife giving herself to the other man. This was not the ordeal, but the relaxation he allowed himself. The ordeal was the realization, the involuntary admission, that up till then he had been very much mistaken about the level of his emotions, about his maturity.* (*I'm Not Stiller* 183)

Svoboda's experience, once he knows that Lila has a lover and that they have slept together, is similar. Like Rolf, he has to admit suddenly that what he has taken for his life, his marriage, his reality has been an error of judgment; the truth of his existence does not lie in the visible reality of appearances he has believed in up to that moment, one in which he has played the role of a successful professional and a contented husband. It never occurred to him that his wife might love another man some day. How can that have happened? Confronted with the facts, his immediate reaction is jealousy, once defined by Frisch in his essay on the subject "as the fear of comparisons" (II 713; *Sketch I 268*). In that essay Frisch traces at length the perceptions and faulty logic the jealous person frequently employs—perceptions and thoughts that evoke the violent, wrenchingly painful, and destructive emotions that plague the jealous lover. Frisch writes:

> Obschon du es aus Erfahrung weißt, wie auswechselbar der Liebespartner ist, bestürzt es dich. . . . es bestürzt dich ein Verdacht, alles Gewesene betreffend, ein höhnisches Gefühl von Einsamkeit, so als wäre sie . . . niemals bei dir gewesen, nur bei deinem Haar, bei deinem Geschlecht. . . und als hätte sie dich, sooft sie deinen Namen nannte, jedesmal betrogen . . .
> Andererseits weißt du genau:
> Auch sie ist nicht die einzigmögliche Partnerin deiner Liebe. Wäre sie nicht gewesen, hättest du deine Liebe an einer anderen erfahren . . . . vielleicht . . . ist es gar nicht jenes Auswechselbare, was im Augenblick, da ihre Hand in das andere Haar greift, einen so satanischen Stich gibt, im Gegenteil, es ist die Angst, daß es für ihre Hand vielleicht doch einen Unterschied macht. Keine Rede davon: Ihr seid nicht auswechselbar, du und er. Das Geschlecht, das allen gemeinsame, hat viele Provinzen, und du bist eine davon. Du kannst nicht über deine Grenzen hinaus, aber sie. Auch sie kann nicht über die ihren hinaus, gewiß, aber über deine; wie du über die ihren. Hast du nicht gewußt, daß wir alle begrenzt sind? Dieses Bewußtsein ist bitter im stillen, schon unter zwei Augen. Nun hast du das Gefühl . . . daß sie dich an den Pranger stellt. Daher bleibt es nicht bei der Trauer, hinzu kommt die Wut, die Wut der Scham, die den Eifersüchtigen oft gemein macht, rachsüchtig und dumm, die Angst, minderwertig zu sein. Plötzlich . . . kannst du es selber nicht mehr glauben, daß sie dich wirklich geliebt habe. Sie hat

dich aber wirklich geliebt. Dich!—aber du, wie gesagt, bist nicht alles, was in der Liebe möglich ist . . .
    Auch er nicht!
    Auch sie nicht!
    Niemand! (II 718-19)

Although you know from your own experience how interchangeable the love partner is, you are appalled. . . . What appalls you is a suspicion concerning all that had been, a mocking sense of loneliness: it is as if it had never been you with whom she had lain . . . but only your hair, your sex. . . . It is as if every time she uttered your name, she had betrayed you. . . .
    On the other hand you know exactly:
    Neither is she the only possible partner of your love. If she had never come along, you would have found love with another. . . . Perhaps . . . it is not this interchangeability that gives you such a devilish jab at the moment her hand grasps that other head of hair but, on the contrary, the fear that for her hand there may indeed be a difference. There is no question of it: you are not interchangeable, you and he. Sex, which is common to all, has many provinces, and you are one of them. You cannot go beyond your limits, but she can. She certainly cannot go beyond her limits either, but beyond yours she can go; as you can go beyond hers. Surely you knew that we are all limited? It is a bitter recognition, even when unspoken, kept to oneself. Now you have the feeling . . . that she has put you in the pillory. Thus it is not only grief that remains, but also rage, the anger of shame which often makes a jealous man mean, revengeful, and stupid, the fear of being inferior. All of a sudden you yourself no longer believe that she ever really loved you. But she really did love you. You! It is just that you are not, as I have already said, all that is possible in love. . . .
    But nor is he!
    Nor is she!
    Nobody is! (Sketch I 272-73)

Jürg Reinhart in *Die Schwierigen*, Rolf in *Stiller*, and Frantisek Svoboda in *Mein Name sei Gantenbein* could benefit from Frisch's perceptive comments when they discover that their lovers are unfaithful; instead, they suffer anguish and heartache as jealousy takes possession of their thoughts and actions.

Svoboda first notices an almost imperceptible change in his wife during a party they give a month after his return from London. The guests' conversation turns to opera, especially the one Lila missed the evening she spent in their apartment with Enderlin. So she will not have to say anything about that performance, Lila changes the topic slightly and advances a point of view about opera in general—not really her own opinion, the narrator observes—that rouses at least her husband to object. Never stating what that view is, the narrator explains parenthetically that it actually applies to modern opera, not Mozart. In any case, it is Mozart's *Don Giovanni* that Svoboda puts on the record player, hoping to disprove Lila's presumably heretical opinion. Along with their guests, however, Lila delights in the music and the marvelous singing of Dietrich Fischer-Dieskau. She is especially intrigued by Zerlina who, in her opinion, is the only character in the opera who is "right" in her response to Don Giovanni: she does not make a tragedy of his numerous amorous conquests, "because she has nature on her side" (V 221/210).

In the opera Masetto, Zerlina's fiancé, is plagued by jealousy. He also suffers from a recent beating at the hands of Leporello. Bitterly he complains about his dual burden and the sudden change in his relationship with his beloved. Zerlina comforts him tenderly. Zerlina is the only person who is relaxed and sure of herself throughout the opera, Lila maintains, because she is the only person who possesses the inner freedom to act naturally. Mozart's music, Lila claims, supports her opinion. Svoboda apparently does not respond, and the conversation moves on.

In the middle of the night Svoboda awakens, rouses Lila, and tells her that he thinks she has to leave him. Suddenly, as in a dream, Svoboda suspects Lila to be wearing a mask in his presence for a reason that must lie somewhere in him. Lila tells him to take a sleeping pill and go back to sleep. As he is about to fall asleep again, Lila tells him that she wrote a letter to him while he was in London but never mailed it. If he wants to, he can read it in the morning.

Not until evening, however, in the midst of a meal in a restaurant, does she give Svoboda the letter. Casually, he begins to read it. For the most part it is an affectionate letter, the sort any wife might write to her absent husband, filled with good wishes for a successful trip, concern for his nervous stomach, and a few newsy items, except for two sentences:

> Ich habe Dich sehr lieb wie immer, auch möchte ich nur, daß Du zu mir bist wie immer, auch wenn in mir noch ein anders Gefühl ist. . . . Kein Grund zur Beunruhigung: Das würde ich Dir schon sagen, wenn sich zwischen uns etwas ändert. (V 223)

> *I'm very fond of you as always, all I want is that you should feel the same towards me as always, even if another feeling has arisen in me. . . . No cause for alarm: I would tell you if anything had changed between us.* (212)

For the moment, Svoboda asks no questions, makes no comment. Lila is relieved.

When they get home Svoboda finally asks what this is all about. Lila admits matter-of-factly that she has been seeing someone else, tells her husband his name, Enderlin, and when he presses her, admits that they have slept together. Svoboda still remains outwardly calm. He does not know this Enderlin but remembers that he was to meet someone the day he suddenly had to go to London and that he sent Lila to keep the appointment for him.

After telling Svoboda all there is to tell about her relationship with Enderlin, Lila wants to go to bed; she is tired. Svoboda has fallen silent, assuming a pose of deep thought: elbows resting on his knees, "his glass of lukewarm whisky in both hands" (V 227/216). Unable to reach out to him, Lila fusses with minor chores in an effort to change the mood and end their conversation. She even hangs up his coat, something she never does, which startles Svoboda. He interprets it as a sure sign of her confusion: she no longer seems to know what is customary in their marriage. He watches her intently. Lila tries small talk to diffuse the situation; she mentions a whole series of nonurgent topics, such as his father's birthday, details from their social calendar for the next few days, the dog license that needs to be renewed. Svoboda keeps silent and wonders if and when he should have noticed a change in his wife.

He remembers that Lila has been looking splendid since his return from London; that her migraine has miraculously disappeared; that she has lately been in high spirits, especially at parties; that she once mentioned briefly, without comment, that she had met someone at a bar, as he had requested; that she has a new hairstyle and shows an unusual interest in a new magazine; that she has begun to neglect the family in little ways and has seemed unusually indecisive about family plans; and that lately she has shown little interest in knowing what people he is meeting professionally and no more than a sisterly interest in his work. Once, he remembers, he found her studying international airline schedules, and on particular weekdays she has displayed a nervous punctuality that is unusual for her. In retrospect, Svoboda realizes, the signs were all there for him to notice. For example, those funny and frank comments about men and women that Lila has been making lately. Or her enthusiasm for that daring scene in a movie in which a woman was kissing her husband while caressing another man with her foot. Then there was her pity for the captive animals in the zoo and her comments about the swans who always swim together so virtuously. No, Lila has not been hiding her sudden joie de vivre, the narrator concludes; Svoboda just has failed to notice—or maybe he has, but believed himself to be its cause, certainly not another man. For Svoboda, too, these past few weeks since his return from London have been happy ones in his marriage to Lila.

Svoboda is determined to remain calm and rational. He agrees with Lila, who seems to think her revelation should not be too shattering for him to accept, that she should go to bed because she is very tired. Paradoxically, though, he continues to renew and prolong their earlier conversation. Hours later they are still talking. All evening and through most of the night Svoboda has been able to control his reaction to the knowledge that Lila is no longer interested in his feelings, his thoughts, his plans, and especially in his magnanimity. By around five in the morning, however, he is somewhat drunk. Suddenly his whiskey glass, thrown with force, crashes in the fireplace. The gesture is one familiar to Frisch's male characters when they feel frustrated beyond endurance and can no longer communicate effectively with the women they love.

Their final row starts when, after a long silence, Svoboda insists that Lila say something. Outside, the birds are beginning to sing. Lila has nothing more to say, she tells him, because she can see and hear that he is unable to change his perspective. "Du siehst mich bloß als Frau" (V 232), she tells him, *"You see me solely as a woman"* (220).

As the first rays of sun fall into the room, Svoboda repeats Lila's accusation slowly and cynically, apologizes to her, then hurls the empty whiskey bottle into the fireplace and apologizes again. The intensity of his furor becomes visible: he is trembling. He finds Lila's accusation monstrous. After she has told him she loves and has slept with another man, for which he has not reproached her, she has the audacity to reproach him for seeing her "only" as a woman! The breakdown of communication between them is complete: there is nothing more to be said, and they finally agree to go to bed.

From this time on, jealousy has a growing effect on Svoboda's life. The narrator sees this facet of himself tortured by a jealous imagination. As Svoboda, the deceived husband, he will not, cannot share the woman he loves with another man. But he must find some way to respond to his sudden marital crisis.

Confronted with his wife's infidelity, Svoboda undergoes an experience similar to one the narrator had when he nearly drowned at the seashore, or so he believed at the time: the sudden panic that grips him as he loses his footing; his desperate struggle against the waves that threaten to crush him; and, after he regains his footing and walks back onto the beach crowded with sunbathers unaware of the existential experience he has just survived, the feelings of relief and sheepishness that overcome him as he returns to solid ground.

The collapse of Svoboda's marriage opens before him an abyss into which his known world suddenly threatens to disappear (Butler 146). As a man of action, given to pragmatic solutions and partial to either-or decisions, Svoboda, as the narrator sees him, has only a few choices in responding to this crisis: He can kill himself; adopt a wait-and-see posture (as Rolf does in *Stiller*); drown his sorrows in a life of night-clubbing; start an affair of his own; throw himself into his work, maintaining his nerve and dignity by operating "business as usual," ignoring his personal life and carrying on as best he can until a decision about his marriage is reached (another option Rolf exercises); or he can temporarily flee from the scene of his threatened marriage (as Rolf does) until Lila's affair wears itself out and she comes to her senses again or decides to end their marriage.

Svoboda exercises the last option. The morning after the long night of the smashed bottle and whiskey glass, Svoboda leaves on a three-week trip to somewhere: Salamanca, for example, where three times a day he checks anxiously at the post office for mail from Lila; or Arles, where he writes to her and repeats his daily visits to the post office. It could be Agrigent, Siena, Brindisi, or Cadiz; the place does not really matter. Lila will know where he is, the narrator observes, and wherever that is, Svoboda's days, one after the other, will be filled with the same monotonous activities: sitting in a café, looking at his watch, getting his shoes polished, checking his watch again; going to the post office, waiting for a letter from Lila.

Why has he gone away? To give Lila time, he claims. She was surprised when he told her that, surprised that he is taking the whole matter more seriously than she. She has not sent him away to drive endless roads for three long, lonely, angry, tortured weeks. Unable to live with uncertainty, Svoboda insists that she must choose between him and Enderlin, something Lila did not suggest at all. In his letters to her he pressures her into a decision that, if nothing else, is premature.

One day a telegram arrives from Lila announcing that in two days he will receive a reply to his letters, which have been dignified, bold, sober, and free of reproach. Then a second telegram arrives, telling him that she has mailed the promised letter to Barcelona, cautioning him to drive carefully after he has read the letter, and requesting that he tell her when he expects to arrive home. Svoboda races recklessly, like a Neapolitan, the narrator comments, to Barcelona. The letter awaiting him there is as dignified, as bold in its insights, as sober and intelligent as his letters to Lila have been, but it does not contain a decision about the future of their marriage. It only says that Lila is carefully considering all aspects of the situation before she decides with which of the two men, her husband or Enderlin, she wants to spend the future—or if she wants to spend it alone. The reasons why she can no longer live with Svoboda are intelligent, the narrator observes; they are not new to Svoboda, although they have never before been stated in writing. Why she thinks she could live with Enderlin Lila does not specify.

Although Lila has made no decision yet, Svoboda has the feeling that something has happened and is both confused and relieved as a result. Life is no longer standing still for him. Suddenly unshackled from his doubts and jealousy, he believes he perceives this moment of his life correctly: it is the end of a past—his life with Lila—that no longer flows into a present from which a future together evolves. Like a bystander, he knows that for those two people, Svoboda and Lila, divorce is the only solution, and as quickly as possible. Relieved, he relaxes and drives at a leisurely sixty miles an hour toward home.

Svoboda gained an important insight during those three weeks away: that the belief one cannot live without someone is a self-delusion. He now knows "there is no person without whom one cannot live" (V 236/224). His sense of the continuity of life has not deserted him. Having momentarily stood dangerously close to the edge of the abyss, Svoboda recovers quickly from his bout of vertigo and returns to a world whose solidity he, unlike the narrator, never seriously doubted (Butler 146).

When Svoboda arrives back home, tanned and at peace with himself after three weeks in an open car, a bit leaner, his face looking younger, Lila hardly recognizes him. In good spirits, since he now has nothing more to lose, he unintentionally rekindles Lila's feelings for him. Lila, the narrator tells us with a grin, "betrays" Enderlin with Svoboda, her husband, within the hour of his arrival home, happy to be with him as long as he does not demand any rights. But after only a few days of bliss, days that seem like a honeymoon to them, Svoboda is his old self again: he wants to know where he stands. Shackled once again by possessive feelings, Svoboda loses the perspective and sovereignty of action he gained while away.

Life continues for Svoboda and Lila, but Svoboda now seems to be hiding behind a wall while Lila escapes into social activity. They are civil in public, overly sensitive and critical in private. Instead of facing their problems, they decide to go on vacation at the sea, "family style." Neither admits it to the other, but the vacation demonstrates to them that their marriage is at an end.

Both wait to see which will have the courage to take the final step and what incident will provoke it.

Meanwhile, Svoboda insists on meeting Enderlin, his competitor for Lila's love who, it seems, has won her. Lila feels uncomfortable about Svoboda's request but understands its motivation: Svoboda cannot live with the ghost of Enderlin; he whose life is built on certainties and facts needs to face his opponent in person at least once, even at this late stage in their rivalry when the contest between them is all but over and Svoboda's divorce from Lila is almost certain.

After Svoboda's and Lila's long night of conversation, the narrator had concluded that he "shouldn't like to be Svoboda" (V 233/221). After their effort to resume their marriage fails, the narrator imagines what he would do if he *were* Svoboda: he would go on a rampage in their apartment—like Stiller in his destructive outburst at the studio—to try to annul the visible remains of a failed relationship. "But," the narrator asserts, "I am not Svoboda" (V 261/248). As the reader recalls from the narrator's description of his old apartment at the beginning of the novel (V 18-20), he would not be violent but would only consider the possibility of violence, because he knows the past cannot be annulled.

Although Svoboda returned to Lila with inner freedom and serenity regained, his behavior regresses. To the narrator Svoboda's life seems synonymous with a living death. Obviously it offers little possibility for individual growth. Perhaps he has adopted Dr. Burri's theory that man is fundamentally inferior to woman. In his excursus on the topic, Burri focuses attention on the psychological difference—expressed in social behavior—and the biological difference between men and women. In both arenas, Burri concludes, man is shown to be vastly inferior. In the sexual act, Burri claims, men reveal their individual limitations, whereas women reveal their individual freedom; because of their biological and psychological nature, women are able to remain an infinite enigma. Specifically, Burri continues, the sexual act enables the woman, biologically, to be a whore: she "can be together with ten men in one night, a man can't be together with ten women; he has to have desire, she can let it happen even without desire; for this reason the whore is possible, but not the male counterpart"

(V 208-09/198). This possibility, according to Burri, grants women, biologically, permanent superiority.

Svoboda, who seems to have absorbed Burri's ideas well, expands on them in commenting on an episode in which the narrator's object of attention is actually Lila (V 284-85). On an ocean voyage from Italy to the United States, the narrator meets a woman who at least physically resembles Lila. One might label the ensuing series of events "Lila from outside," because during these events the narrator attempts to gain some objectivity about her (V 279-89). The woman, married, carries on over several days a subtle-not-so-subtle flirtation with a recently married passenger that eventually leads to adultery. The narrator concludes his report of the incident with the startled question, "Am I Svoboda?" (V 289/274).

As he watches the flirtation develop, the narrator imagines how Svoboda would react to this woman's behavior. Svoboda becomes uncharacteristically philosophical in his comments. A natural difference between men and women, he observes, is that in lovemaking the man is always the one who acts, consequently the one who always remains himself (V 284). He is the constant, and the woman knows it, or at least is able to guess it, Svoboda decides. The man, in contrast, has no idea how the woman he has made love to acts in the arms of another man. He cannot even guess, for a woman's ability to adapt to different situations and people, especially men, seems limitless. She is much like a chameleon, Svoboda contends, or at least she is a born actress. She has to feign interest a lot more often than a man. When she is with a different man or when she comes from him, Svoboda observes, a woman is never the same. Not merely her intellectual interests but her opinions, attitudes, and judgments have changed. This is especially so, Svoboda notes, when that new relationship with a man continues for some time. The reason is that a woman, when she is with another man, has to go farther away, figuratively, from the first relationship than does a man in the reverse situation, and she therefore has a greater readjustment to make when she returns to the first relationship. In a love triangle, Svoboda continues, a man wants to know from the woman things about the "other" man and their relationship that are none of his business. A tactful woman, Svoboda observes, never reveals these details, but in the reverse situation a man will bore a woman with them, as if he could be different when he makes love to the "other" woman from when he is with her.

Unfortunately for Svoboda, these hard-won insights cannot save his marriage. Was it really Lila's infidelity that destroyed this marriage, the narrator seems to ask, or was some other factor in their relationship responsible for her infidelity?

When Lila first met Enderlin in the bar, she told him that she is faithful. This could mean that her ensuing affair with him is her first during her marriage to Svoboda. Or did Lila mean faithfulness to herself? That might explain her unexpected reference to Peru in that first conversation with Enderlin, if "Peru" symbolizes the exotic and romantic, an element she craves but that has waned in her marriage. Consequently, Lila is receptive to Enderlin's advances, and he, the problematic lover who offers her no future, wins her without much difficulty. Does she really love him, the deceiver, or is she merely in love with the excitement and adventure he offers her?

Whatever the answer, it is clear that Svoboda is the deceived husband. As such, he is unable to rekindle a lasting love relationship with his wife. Svoboda's male possessiveness, his sexual jealousy, and his inability to understand his wife may be as responsible for the breakup of the marriage as Lila's adultery.

When the narrator mentions Svoboda again, he refers to him as Lila's ex-husband (V 167). Lila, by then, is married to Gantenbein. Since Svoboda is a facet of the narrator, however, his experience in his marriage to Lila helps the narrator piece his own story together. Svoboda's behavior, combined with the narrator's view of it, illuminates the nature of the narrator's own complex relationship to the woman he loved and apparently lost. The narrator may not wish to be Svoboda because of what he has seen of Svoboda as a man, but of course he *is* Svoboda, at least part of him is.

GANTENBEIN: THE SEEING BLIND HUSBAND

Setting the Stage

Of the three characters the narrator creates in the process of looking through the prism of his own personality, Theo Gantenbein is the most captivating. The narrator obviously has great interest in this character, especially in his behavior and judgments. With Enderlin, Theo Gantenbein shares an intellectual bent; with Svoboda, the jealousy of a deceived husband.

A marriage—Gantenbein's marriage to Lila, this time a well-known actress rather than the housewife she was in her marriage to Svoboda—is the focus of the novel's Gantenbein story. It is divided in the middle by the parable of Ali and Alil. In the first part, as the blind husband who is not blind, Gantenbein explores the advantages and limitations of that role. In the second part, Gantenbein at first drops the ruse of blindness, only to turn into a jealous husband like Svoboda. When he then resumes the blind-husband role, this time adding the role of blind father to Beatrice, who is presumed to be his and Lila's daughter, he discovers that the pleasures of fatherhood do not sufficiently curb the destructive powers of jealousy.

The narrator is fascinated with the character of Gantenbein. Unlike his ultimate reaction to Enderlin, whom he abandons in the middle of the novel, or to Svoboda, whom he claims he neither wants to be nor is, he returns time and again to Gantenbein. The reason is obvious: as a seeing blind man, Gantenbein offers the narrator a much wider choice of situations and many more behavioral possibilities in his marriage to Lila than could either of the other characters. The narrator hopes that Gantenbein will help him comprehend the fundamental experience that lies behind the empty apartment.

When Lila and Gantenbein first appear together in the novel they are already married. The narrator reports society's stunned reaction to a great actress's marrying a blind man. When they appear together for the last time, Gantenbein has just disclosed his secret to Lila: he is not and never has been blind. For Lila this startling disclosure ends their marriage. She regards Gantenbein's role-playing as a deception that invaded her privacy, violated her trust, and demonstrated that Gantenbein never loved her. On that last point Lila is wrong.

The story of Gantenbein's marriage to Lila is told in many episodes and their variants. It is the most completely developed of the narrator's three investigations into his personality. By showing what happens in this marriage, the narrator hopes to illustrate basic aspects, both strengths and weaknesses, of marriage in general. His purpose, as always, is to illuminate the possible cause or causes for the traumatic event, the collapse of his own relationship, that initially motivated his search for an appropriate story.

Gantenbein's name is mentioned for the first time at the beginning of the novel, as the narrator thinks about the sudden death of a friend; could that be Gantenbein's end? More likely Enderlin's, he muses. Later, the narrator imagines a man after an automobile accident:

> Schnittwunden im Gesicht, es besteht keine Lebensgefahr, nur die Gefahr, daß er sein Augenlicht verliert. Er weiß das. Er liegt im Hospital mit verbundenen Augen lange Zeit. . . . Eines Morgens wird der Verband gelöst, und er sieht, daß er sieht, aber schweigt; er sagt es nicht, daß er sieht, niemand und nie.
> Ich stelle mir vor:
> Sein Leben fortan, indem er den Blinden spielt auch unter vier Augen, sein Umgang mit Menschen, die nicht wissen, daß er sie sieht, seine gesellschaftlichen Möglichkeiten, seine beruflichen Möglichkeiten dadurch, daß er nie sagt, was er sieht, ein Leben als Spiel, seine Freiheit kraft eines Geheimnisses usw.
> Sein Name sei Gantenbein. (V 21)

his face is cut, his life is not in danger, the only danger is that he might lose his sight. He knows that. He lies in hospital with bandaged eyes for a long time. . . . One morning the bandage is removed and he sees that he sees, but he keeps quiet about it; he doesn't tell anyone he can see, doesn't tell anyone ever.
I imagine:
His life henceforth, as he plays the blind man with his tongue in his cheek, his dealings with people who don't know that he can see, his social possibilities, his professional possibilities due to the fact that he never says what he sees, his life as a game, his freedom by virtue of a secret and so on.
Let his name be Gantenbein. (20-21)[11]

The man now has a name and a role to play—the beginning of a story—but his identity is still separate from the narrator's. A few pages later, however, the narrator signals his acceptance of Gantenbein as a feasible role for him to adopt, a valid character to represent important facets of himself, by stating clearly:

Mein Name sei Gantenbein. (V 25)

Let my name be Gantenbein. (24)

The narrator has thus identified himself with a man who has chosen to pretend that he is blind but in reality is able to see and observe everything. Now the narrator's search for a suitable story for this character can begin in earnest.

Throughout the novel there are times the narrator seems tempted to discard the character of Gantenbein, but he keeps returning to it. Twice he reaffirms his earlier decision: "Mein Name sei Gantenbein" (V 81,261), *"Let my name be Gantenbein"* (78,248). Twice more he states his resolve to maintain the role he has chosen: "Ich bleibe Gantenbein" (V 199,201), *"I remain Gantenbein"* (189,191). Finally, only forty-five pages from the end of the novel, the narrator is sure that his identification with Gantenbein is complete. In unmistakable resolve he exclaims:

Mein Name sei Gantenbein!
(Aber endgültig.) (V 271)

Let my name be Gantenbein!
(But finally.) (257)

Until the narrator makes this final, definitive statement, Gantenbein's viability as a character representing the narrator has periodically been in doubt.

However, after the narrator first creates this seeing-blind man, names him Gantenbein, and links his own identity to him, Gantenbein quickly establishes himself as an independent character like Enderlin and Svoboda. He buys a pair of dark glasses the blind wear and a black walking stick, then becomes legitimate by acquiring a pass for the sightless and a yellow arm band.

But before he presents himself to the authorities to become officially certified as a blind person, Gantenbein practices his blind-man's role in a section of Zurich he knows well, wearing his dark glasses that make the world "outside" and the people in it look ashen with a tint of violet, and tapping the curb from time to time with his cane.

During one of these outings Gantenbein accidentally walks out in front of a car. He is not hurt and only loses his cane temporarily. The driver, a blonde woman who is more upset than Gantenbein about the incident, drives him to her apartment since, as they discover, they live in the same neighborhood. They introduce themselves formally (she pulls out her business card as if Gantenbein were able to read it), then announces "Camilla Huber," omitting her profession, "Manicurist," which Gantenbein sees printed on the card (V32/31).

Witnesses to the near-accident told Gantenbein that the driver of the car that had almost bumped him was "eine Kokotte" (V 30), "a tart" (27). In her apartment he can see the suggestions of her trade—an unmade sofa bed, two cognac glasses, full ashtrays, a brassiere, a pair of discarded stockings. But Gantenbein is quite willing to accept her in her role of independent, socially acceptable businesswoman, as long as she accepts him as a blind man. This mutual acceptance is the secret they tacitly share during many meetings together, in which Camilla serves as Gantenbein's private (and unpracticed) manicurist and he encourages her hope that miracles really do happen by telling her stories, for Camilla "believes in true stories, she is crazy about true stories, she is gripped by everything that she believes really happened . . . but it must have really happened" (V 114/108). Only at their last meeting, when Camilla is able to give up her dual role of prostitute-manicurist to live her own story, now socially accepted as the bride-to-be of a dentist, does she assure Gantenbein:

> Ich werde niemand sagen, . . . daß Sie nicht blind sind, verlassen Sie sich darauf, und auch Sie sagen niemand, was Sie gesehen haben. (V 263)

> *I shall never tell anyone . . . that you're not blind, you can rely on that, and don't you tell anyone what you have seen. (249)*

That is their pact.

Gantenbein is sad that he will not see Camilla again. They have become friends; their friendship is based on mutual trust, mutual acceptance, and a nonjudgmental attitude. Gantenbein is even sadder when he learns that, on the eve of her wedding, Camilla has been murdered, probably by a jealous client who could not allow her to abandon her established role.

Camilla's reasons for printing "Manicurist" rather than "Prostitute" on her business card are understandable, especially since she would really like to change her actual profession to one socially more acceptable. Gantenbein has understandable reasons for playing his blind-man's role, too, as the narrator explains:

> Die kleine Begegnung mit Camilla Huber neulich bestärkt ihn in seiner Hoffnung, die Menschen etwas freier zu machen, frei von der Angst, daß man ihre Lügen sehe. Vor allem aber, so hofft Gantenbein, werden die Leute sich vor einem Blinden wenig tarnen, so daß man sie besser kennenlernt, und es entsteht ein wirklicheres Verhältnis, indem man auch ihre Lügen gelten läßt, ein vertrauensvolleres Verhältnis— (V 44)

> *His recent brief meeting with Camilla Huber reinforces his hope of making people freer, free from the fear that one sees their lies. Above all, however, Gantenbein hopes, people won't camouflage themselves much against a blind man, so that one will get to know them better, and a more real relationship will come into being as a result of granting validity to their lies, a more trusting relationship— (42)*

This is the basis, the modus operandi, for the "blind" Gantenbein's marriage to Lila.

The first of the narrator's two basic versions of this marriage illustrates the benefits and advantages, but also the limitations, that arise in a marriage in which one of the partners, in this case the husband, brings to it an ostensible blindness to his partner's shortcomings. The presumed *physical* blindness makes it possible for him to distance himself from any unpleasant or petty incident that may occur in the marriage as a result of such shortcomings in the partner. Lila and Gantenbein thus manage to avoid in this first version of their marriage the accumulation of minor irritations and tensions that can eventually destroy a marriage, and Gantenbein, the narrator believes, participates reasonably well in the marriage.

In time, however, Gantenbein tires of the repetitive artificiality of his blind-man's role. The narrator's second version of Gantenbein's marriage to Lila illustrates, therefore, what happens to the marriage when Gantenbein drops his pretense of blindness. He immediately falls victim to the destructive feelings of jealousy that produce in him a *spiritual* blindness that eventually destroys his marriage (V 163-98).

An alternate version, in which the blind Gantenbein brings up his and Lila's daughter in a reversal of traditional roles, turns out equally unsatisfactorily: it cannot satisfy Gantenbein's need to drop his blind-husband role, of which he has become thoroughly tired, and to reveal himself to his wife as he really is. When he finally takes this crucial step, Lila sends him away and ends the marriage.

Two stories, that of a jealous baker (V 111-14) and that of Ali and Alil, thematically bridge the two versions of Gantenbein and Lila's marriage. The stories' common theme is jealousy, which in the first story is dealt with violently, in the second ironically, as the wronged party (Ali) takes revenge on the presumed guilty party (Alil). The question of whether the marriage continues is left open.

Version 1: A Tolerable Marriage

Right from the start of his marriage to Lila, Gantenbein knows she is deceiving him. Because she is an accomplished actress and much in demand, she travels frequently. Gantenbein always goes to the airport to welcome her home, which delights her. Therefore he always notices the man accompanying her: the man carries her coat, and she slips her arm through his as they walk from the plane to the terminal and disappear from view in the Customs area. Lila never mentions this stranger, for she believes completely in Gantenbein's blindness. She may discover her husband among the waiting crowd, but she has no idea he can pick her out in a crowd, too, and that he notes the sign of recognition on her face when she sees him. His most difficult problem at that moment is to maintain his role and not to wave his arms in joyous recognition.

Gantenbein's situation on such an occasion is somewhat like that of a supernumerary on a stage: he springs into action only as required by the plot, in Gantenbein's case by Lila's kiss of welcome, her first interaction with her blind husband. Otherwise, his role permits him only to watch the action unfold and to imagine the feelings of the participants while he remains divorced from the scene, stands outside it, and is thus free of its emotional content; hence, he is able to remain unperturbed and relaxed. Thus Gantenbein can impassively watch Lila's travel companion pass ahead of her without giving him a sign of recognition and watch Lila come to greet him, then observe her confusion when she cannot find her passport and leaves him briefly, ostensibly to buy a newspaper, to ask her travel mate if he has the passport, and finally see her relief to discover the errant document in her purse. Gantenbein does not even feel obliged to question her about the newspaper when she returns to him without it.

Lila shows her joy in being home again, back with her husband, when they are finally together in the arrival hall. Her joy is genuine every time, as Gantenbein recognizes with a shock the last time he meets her at the airport; that time she arrives alone, unaccompanied by any stranger, and the narrator, also surprised, observes: "Lila betrügt ihn nicht" (V 311), *"Lila isn't deceiving him"* (296). Until then, both of them play a similar game, Gantenbein acting the part of the blind husband, Lila the part of the faithful wife. Her deception is, of course, made possible only by his deception.

These mutual deceptions do not seem to endanger Lila and Gantenbein's marriage. Instead, by faithfully maintaining his deception, Gantenbein can stay detached from the routine encounters of a married couple that often lead to tension, annoyance, and misunderstandings.

Lila is not the most orderly person. When she comes home from a trip or from shopping, the apartment immediately looks as if a whirlwind has struck. It would stay that way if Gantenbein did not secretly straighten it up, reinforcing Lila's delighted belief in pixies who come around periodically and tidy up the place.

Dirty dishes, which lead to annoyance and tension in many a marriage, nearly cause a problem in Lila's and Gantenbein's, too—*not* because neither of them wants to wash the dishes but because Gantenbein washes them all and cleans up the entire kitchen while Lila is at the theater for a rehearsal or performance. Lila reacts with hurt, as if Gantenbein is accusing her of being a poor housekeeper. Thus Gantenbein learns to employ subterfuge: he never again cleans the entire kitchen at once, but only a section at a time, and secretly washes only enough plates, cups, glasses, and tableware so that, miraculously, they never run out of clean ones, while Lila can plainly see dirty ones always stacked in the sink. Finding her husband sitting at leisure in his rocking chair, smoking a cigar, when she comes home pleases Lila. She is relieved to notice that he no longer pays attention to the state of the kitchen.

Gantenbein discovers that blindness, when it is merely a role and is played consistently, has other advantages in a marriage. He can, for example, help his wife find lost objects without saying a word by quietly placing them in her path. He can also help them avoid irritating discussions of money. Lila is the sole wage earner; she handles all the money and gives Gantenbein an allowance. She enjoys the role reversal. Gantenbein neither knows nor asks what she earns and is uncomplainingly ready to reduce expenses, at any time, if she thinks it necessary. Nonetheless, Gantenbein, who has a sizable bank account of his own that Lila is unaware of, does not need to bother her about periodic expenses she may forget, such as the dog's license, a parking ticket, or an oil change for the car.

Gantenbein is aware that Lila receives letters regularly from a foreign gentleman and lets them lie about in the apartment, letters that would destroy the marriage should Gantenbein read them, or at best could lead to questions about the sender. Gantenbein, hiding behind his blindness, ignores them. Similarly, when Lila announces she has to go to the hairdresser's and returns home hours later with her hair looking the same as before, the blind husband accepts that she has been where she says she has, accepts the little gossip items she allegedly heard at the beauty shop, and does not confront her with the knowledge that, wherever she has been, it was not the hairdresser's. When Lila is obviously in a bad mood, Gantenbein does not ask her about the cause, does not pursue her with questions or wonder aloud if he has done something to upset her. Because of Gantenbein's blindness they can both avoid those nasty scenes that begin with his asking what is the matter, go on to her denial that anything is wrong, and end with both thoroughly irritated without ever identifying the source of the initial annoyance. Instead Gantenbein, presumably unable to read Lila's facial expression, remains silent until she tells him voluntarily what has upset her.

Gantenbein and Lila love each other, as numerous comments by Gantenbein and the narrator make clear. Once the narrator has identified himself with the character he has created, he imagines:

> mein Leben mit einer großen Schauspielerin, die ich liebe und daher glauben lasse, ich sei blind; unser Glück infolgedessen.
> Ihr Name sei Lila. (V 81)
>
> *my life with a great actress, whom I love and hence cause to believe that I am blind; our happiness in consequence.*
> *Let her name be Lila.* (78)

Waiting for Lila at the airport he admits that his heart is pounding, and as they drive home, Gantenbein knows "daß ich der glücklichste Liebhaber bin" (V 84), *"that I am the happiest of lovers"* (80).

Gantenbein loves to have flowers waiting for Lila when she returns from a trip. One day, as he arranges a bouquet of them in their apartment, his random thoughts expose his excitement about and his love for her. At the conclusion of that scene, Gantenbein admits: "Ich glaube, ich liebe sie wirklich" (V 110), *"I believe I really love her"* (105). In the love letters he wrote to her before they were married, his special term of endearment for her was "Lilalil." At one point the narrator comments that Gantenbein may not be equal to the magnitude of his love for Lila (V 103), at another he tells him point-blank: "du liebst sie! Alles andere ist Unsinn" (V 192), *"you love her! Everything else is nonsense"* (183). Gantenbein, by his own admission, is happier with Lila than he has ever been with a woman, and Lila, too, is happier in their marriage than she has ever been (V 104). At times Gantenbein wonders whether she knows that he only pretends to be blind and reasons that she may perhaps allow him to continue in that role because she loves him. Nothing is visibly more persuasive that Lila loves Gantenbein than the joy with which she greets him when she returns from a trip.

The marriage of Lila and Gantenbein is very happy. Lila feels freed from hypocrisy because she knows that Gantenbein does not spy on her, is not suspicious of her. She would not want to live with any other man, she tells him, and Gantenbein believes her. No wonder, for Gantenbein observes:

Was ich sehe und was ich nicht sehe, ist eine Frage des Takts. Vielleicht ist die Ehe überhaupt nur eine Frage des Takts. (V 105)

What I see and what I don't see is a question of tact. Perhaps marriage is altogether only a question of tact. (100)

Everyone can see that Lila is beautiful except her husband, she believes. Therefore when he tells her, in intimate moments, that she is pretty, she is especially happy, for she knows her blind husband does not compare her beauty with that of other women; he believes his tactile sense, his skin.

Occasionally Gantenbein needs to escape the accumulated inner tension of his role. At those times he either goes to visit his manicurist, Camilla Huber, or he takes their dog Patsch to the woods, away from prying eyes. At the Grunewald in Berlin, for example, he can continue to train Patch as a Seeing-Eye dog, which he is not. Sometimes Gantenbein throws pine cones far out into the lake for Patsch to retrieve, and both enjoy their unusual version of baseball: Gantenbein tosses a pine cone into the air and hits at it with his cane; Patsch races through the sand to retrieve the cones. In the forest, with no one around, Gantenbein enjoys a brief respite from the burden of his blindness. He needs this relief, he claims, as a Catholic needs confession to unburden his soul:

> eine großartige Einrichtung; er kniet und bricht sein Schweigen, ohne sich den Menschen auszuliefern, und nachher erhebt er sich, tritt wieder seine Rolle unter den Menschen an, erlöst von dem unseligen Verlangen, von Menschen erkannt zu werden. (V 99)

> *a splendid arrangement; he kneels and breaks his silence, without giving himself into the hands of men, and afterwards he gets up and enters into his role among men again, redeemed from the unfortunate desire to be recognized by men. (95)*

When he and the dog are ready to return to civilization, Gantenbein tosses his paperback book into a wastepaper basket, and he and Patsch take each other on the leash again.

Not only in the woods, but also in a garden nursery, does Gantenbein find relaxation from his role. He loves the multitudinous colors of flowers. With his arm band and his eyeglasses stowed safely in his pockets, he strolls among the flower beds as he selects a large bouquet to welcome Lila home from a series of out-of-town performances. At home he carefully arranges the flowers in a vase. Fearful that Lila might return earlier and surprise him in the act of arranging her welcome, he holds his dark glasses between his teeth, ready to turn back into a blind husband if he hears her key in the lock.

In his periodic visits to Camilla Huber Gantenbein has another escape that serves as a substitute for the confessional. As he invents "true" stories for her, trying to satisfy her yearning for miracles, Gantenbein sorts out those inner tensions that threaten chaos, the disintegration of the "real" Theo Gantenbein. For the man who is able to see, the crucial test of his role is not in society or with Camilla, but in his marriage to Lila (Butler 137).

As he once again watches Lila arrive at the airport, sees her male companion carrying her belongings to the Customs area, sees Lila say farewell to him a mere fifteen feet from where Gantenbein stands holding Patsch, who whines and pulls at the leash as if he were objecting to Lila's and the stranger's farewells, Gantenbein expresses a wish and a fear when he says: "Hoffentlich werde ich nie eifersüchtig" (V 110), "*I hope I shall never get jealous*" (105).

This prayerful wish ends the first version of the story of Lila and Gantenbein's marriage. It has illustrated the benefits their relationship derives from Gantenbein's assumed blindness; it has also reflected Gantenbein's doubts that he can keep his secret or maintain his role indefinitely. He is still not completely sure of himself in the role and continues to hope he will never do anything to give himself away. He knows that "if Lila knew that I can see, she would doubt my love, and it would be hell, a man and a woman, but not a couple." He adds the surprising observation that "it is the secret that a man and a woman keep from each other that makes them a couple" (V 103-04/99). The ending of the narrator's second version of Gantenbein's marriage to Lila seems to confirm the validity of this observation.

Version 2: An Intolerable Marriage

After telling the story of Ali and Alil, whose marriage was plagued by blindness and jealousy, the narrator returns to Gantenbein and Lila and questions the purpose of Gantenbein's continuing to play the role of a blind man any longer. The temptation for him to give it up is growing continually stronger. If Gantenbein yields, however, he will have to face two overwhelming problems. Lila believes in his blindness. How will she react if she learns he has deceived her? And second, can a sighted Gantenbein avoid the destructive jealousy normal for a husband whose wife is deceiving him?

One night, after their party guests have gone home, Gantenbein and Lila are relaxing over a drink. Lila, who is reading the paper while Gantenbein watches her, suddenly asks if he has read the front-page story about a murder.[12] The question is really rhetorical, since she knows Gantenbein is blind; it is a question asked without thinking by a person able to see. Gantenbein, however, seizes the opportunity to step out of his role. He replies: "Ja . . . habe ich gelesen" (V 164), *"Yes . . . I've read it"* (156). Lila seems not to hear him. He repeats his answer. Still no response from her, so he eventually calls her attention to what he said and repeats it again. This time Lila responds, but not to what he said; she is referring to the ghastly murder when she asks: "Don't you think it's horrible?" (V 165/157).

Gantenbein's situation at this moment is similar to that of the actor who has to play a man with a limp. Once his role is clearly established, as Gantenbein observed earlier, he no longer has to limp all the time on stage, only at crucial moments (V 102). The audience, thus reminded of his limp, continues to accept him in his role, even if, for a while, he walks across the stage without limping.[13] The same is true for Gantenbein. His role as a blind man is by now so firmly established in the minds of all who know him that any action of his to the contrary is ignored and goes unregistered by the people around him, especially by Lila who lives with him. Only people who meet Gantenbein for the first time, particularly at a party at their home, might doubt that he is really blind if they watch him carefully.

The first exchange about the newspaper story occurs at midnight. Gantenbein does not insist that Lila respond to his comment. Instead, the narrator takes over and in a sequence of scenes imagines, first, what would happen if Gantenbein got angry, even violent, in attempting to persuade Lila that he is not blind, and then what his life, his marriage, might be like if he were not pretending to be blind. Gantenbein recalls that he answered Lila's question about the murder being horrible with a simple "Yes. . . I've read it" (V 164/156). Then he fell silent for a long time, while the narrator let his own imagination run overtime. At the end of that long pause the narrator resolves: "Ich bleibe Gantenbein" (V 199), *"I remain Gantenbein" (189).* The narrator has seen clearly that if Gantenbein were to abandon his blindness, one consequence would be a devastating jealousy. Jealousy is the common theme in all the imagined scenes that follow, a jealousy so overwhelming that it eventually drives Lila away and destroys their marriage.

In the first of these imagined sequences (V 165-66), Gantenbein stages a violent confrontation with Lila to convince her that he can see. He throws his whiskey glass into the fireplace, kicks the furniture about the room, and breaks Lila's necklace, leaving the pearls rolling around on the floor, then grabs her and shakes her until she cries. Gantenbein fails to persuade Lila; for her he remains blind. For him, however, now that he is no longer playing the blind husband, a totally new life begins.

The next long scene (V 166-73) introduces Lila's new admirer, a man she met in Hamburg. According to Lila he is a beautiful specimen of a man, though very arrogant. Lila is completely under his spell, which does not stop her, however, from referring to him as a nasty fellow, but handsome. He may be a student or a dancer and wants to take Lila away to Uruguay or Paraguay— wherever. That she is already married does not seem to trouble either of them; they are seeking something absolute, not an ordinary, conventional marriage. Gantenbein briefly considers slapping Lila's face to bring her back to her senses. He refrains.

Next morning a wire arrives, signed "Einhorn" ("*Unicorn*"), announcing the young man's arrival the following day.[14] Together, Lila and Gantenbein draw up various versions of possible responses. The final one, which reads "PLEASE DON'T PLEASE" (V 171/*163*), is sent. When the young man's wired reply arrives the following morning, Lila immediately tears it into shreds and later flushes it down the toilet.[15] Gantenbein assumes Einhorn is coming anyway. Suddenly, as their relationship seems seriously threatened from without, Lila and Gantenbein feel closer to each other than ever. To savor their emotional unity, they decide to leave their present environment for a while. Lila cancels the only rehearsal scheduled for the coming week, and they escape to the sea, where they dream of growing old together peacefully, like Philemon and Baucis.[16]

The reference is ironic—not, as Butler suggests, "another obfuscation," its purpose "to sound out a possible conclusion to the Ali/Alil fairy-tale" (Butler 141). On the contrary, Frisch (*not* the narrator) smiles in irony at the characters of Lila and Gantenbein when he baptizes them with the names of the couple who symbolize a tranquil old age illuminated by love and loyalty. As is true for Frisch's references to antiquity and mythology in previous novels, especially in *Homo faber*, this allusion is meant to be understood in the opposite way. The imagined events in the life of Gantenbein and Lila illustrate that its course is anything but tranquil and the allusion to the mythical couple does not brighten it with love and loyalty. Thus the names of Philemon and Baucis, which the narrator uses interchangeably with the characters' "real" names until the end of this sequence (V 199), are meant to be understood ironically, as Gantenbein's modern version of the ancient couple's story, which he tells to Camilla, makes clear (V 233-34).

If Einhorn, Lila's admirer, ever arrives, he misses Lila and her husband. But Gantenbein is unable to forget him. During the next five imagined scenes, Gantenbein becomes obsessed with Einhorn.

Since Gantenbein in this whole sequence of scenes has normal eyesight, he sees the many typewritten letters that arrive for Lila bearing Danish stamps. Of course Lila is a popular, well-known actress who also appears on television, thus Gantenbein is not surprised that she receives fan mail. But all of it coming from one small country, all of it written on the same typewriter? While some letters that come for Lila lie around for weeks, these letters always disappear after he hands them to her, and she never talks about them. Gantenbein believes his suspicions that Lila has a lover are well founded.

Perhaps Lila hides the letters in the drawer she always keeps locked and from which she removes objects occasionally. Only she has a key to its antique lock, and she hides it carefully, thus making clear that the drawer's contents are none of Gantenbein's business. He is tempted to break it open but rejects the idea. Instead, he tries to control his growing jealousy—nourished continually by the arrival of two or three letters a week from Denmark—by betraying Lila with another woman. The effect is temporary. Lila does not seem to notice his infidelity; she is merely pleased that he is once again in good spirits. But the letters keep coming, and their frequency indicates that Lila must send at least one a week, if not two, up north.

For a week Gantenbein intercepts the three letters that arrive for Lila from Denmark. Soon it bothers him to carry them in his pocket, since Lila does not ask about them as he expected. If she had, he could have claimed absentmindedness and given them to her. One day a special-delivery letter arrives for Lila, which she herself accepts and signs for. She never talks about it and never mentions the missing letters.

Gantenbein considers dropping the three confiscated letters into a mailbox to have them redelivered, but abandons that solution because the post office will probably add a current Swiss postmark. That would be synonymous with an indictment for his misdeed. He can think of only one way to rid himself of the letters: burn them. One rainy morning, driven by jealousy and guilt, he drives up into the woods and attempts that remedy. He fails, however, because of the rain, which soaks the still-unopened letters and prevents their burning properly. Gantenbein fears that readable portions may remain for curious eyes. He makes a brief attempt to bury the letters, but fails in that, too, because he has no shovel; the wooden sticks with which he tries to dig a hole break in the hard ground. Frustrated and angry, Gantenbein tears open the remains of the three letters, determined at last to read them. He hesitates—and puts them away again.

All Gantenbein has to show for his efforts are a dirty car, which will have to be washed before he gets home, a ruined pair of muddy shoes that must be replaced by new ones before he returns to the apartment, and a dent in the car that will have to be fixed some day (V 180-81). Lila is pleased with the clean car and the new shoes; Gantenbein tells her the dent is an old one. Later that day, as he and Lila are on their way to a movie, he throws the three letters into the sewer. Lila makes no comment. She assumes he can throw away anything of his that he wants to.

Instead of confronting Lila and forcing her to confess her infidelity, Gantenbein lives with his agonizing suspicions and painful jealousy as if nothing were wrong in their marriage. One day, while he is waiting in a Munich hotel lobby to meet Lila and drive her home to Zurich, he suspects that the young dandy he observes paying his hotel bill in the lobby might be Einhorn, Nils, Olaf, or whatever his real name is. When Lila arrives, Gantenbein asks her so often whether she has paid her hotel bill that she becomes annoyed. Some time later Lila is taken slightly ill with a cold, accompanied by fever and headache. Looking for aspirin, which she tells him is in her purse, Gantenbein comes across a Munich hotel bill for a single room, marked paid. He also finds a recent, opened letter addressed to "General Delivery" and bearing Danish stamps. Although sorely tempted, he does not read it.

One night, while Lila is sleeping, Gantenbein is driven by his irrational jealousy and suspicion to break open the lock on Lila's little drawer. It is full of letters, as he suspected. Pure hatred for Lila surges through him as, standing barefoot and in pajamas at three o'clock in the morning, he begins to read the letters addressed to Lila. They are, he discovers, his own love letters and ecstatic telegrams, sent to her while she was still married to Svoboda. With typical Frisch irony, Gantenbein's suspicion of Lila's infidelity has proved correct, it seems, except that then *he* was its beneficiary. Is it someone else now? Gantenbein still is not sure.

Except for a single letter from Lila's ex-husband, Svoboda, which is still in its envelope and is, as Gantenbein has to admit, a beautiful letter, unemotional and to the point, Gantenbein finds in the drawer no incriminating letters besides his own. His suspicions do not subside, however, and the torment of his jealousy does not cease, because he is now positive that Lila must have another hiding place for her letters from Einhorn or Nils or Olaf. Back in the bedroom Gantenbein looks thoughtfully at the sleeping Lila. Involuntarily, his lips whisper the special term of endearment he once used in the letters: Lilalil. Lest Gantenbein fail to understand the significance of this, the narrator interprets: You love her.

To restore the damaged trust in their marriage, Gantenbein confesses his infidelity with a secretary. Lila was unaware of it, does not want to know about it, and asks not to be informed of such brief affairs of his in the future, if they should recur. About the broken lock on the drawer Lila is deeply hurt; Gantenbein confesses the deed to avoid having their cleaning woman unjustly fired. He asks to be forgiven for breaking the lock to read his own love letters to her, but Lila, pale and speechless, mourns inwardly as true love does in such a monstrous situation.

Gantenbein's unabated jealousy is like a disease. Now that he has dropped the guise of a blind man and is, as everyone knows, able to see, he has become spiritually blind. He is a living example of the pitifully jealous person who can no longer help himself, tormented as he is by the destructive feeling that Frisch described so vividly in his *Tagebuch* essay on jealousy (II 713-16; *Sketch I* 268-71). And Gantenbein's trials are not yet over. He and Lila have planned a trip to Hamburg, but Gantenbein, in a fit of false generosity, insists that she go alone. He wants to give her and her lover some latitude, some time to themselves, he rationalizes, his motives born of jealousy. Lila is disappointed.

Finally, Gantenbein's obsession with Lila's nameless lover bears macabre results. Early one morning, when Gantenbein answers the doorbell, he confronts a young man who asks to see Lila. Taking the young man to be Einhorn, Nils, Olaf, or whoever, Gantenbein leads him into the bedroom where Lila is still sleeping, wakes her, then leaves the room and locks the door with the presumed lovers inside, puts the key in his pocket, and goes for a drive. Casually, like Svoboda on his way back to Zurich from Barcelona, Gantenbein drives slowly through the countryside in his open car, whistling, the wind blowing his hair, his left arm hanging outside, one hand on the steering wheel. Then a second thought occurs to him. Perhaps the stranger isn't Einhorn, whom he has never met, but someone else wanting to see Lila? That could be the reason she screamed when he brought the man into the bedroom. Hurriedly, Gantenbein turns around and drives back to the city. At home, he finds the bedroom door broken open. Lila and the stranger, who has come to ask Lila's advice about changing careers and becoming an actor, are in the living room, talking.

When the young visitor has left, Lila has but two words for her husband: "I'm leaving." He understands the reason: "She can't live with a madman" (V 198/*188*).

After this sequence of imagined scenes, the narrator has a single comment: "Was hilft Sehen!" (V 198), "*What help is it to see!*" (*188*). He resolves that Gantenbein is to remain blind, at least for now. The cost of jealousy, the price Gantenbein would have to pay if he abandoned his blindness, is too great; Gantenbein cannot take that risk with his marriage to Lila.

Once he has experienced them, however, if only in his imagination, Gantenbein cannot rid himself of his suspicion and jealousy. To find out what people are saying when he is not present—both in general and specifically about him—he buys a tape recorder, installs it in their apartment, and when he and Lila have guests, secretly turns it on as he leaves the room. He wants to find out who he really is or, at least, who others think he is. He also wants to find out who *they* really are.

The recordings do not yield any of the expected results, and Gantenbein gives up the enterprise. The narrator, however, understands Gantenbein's agony. In a reflective commentary he defines jealousy as

[ein] wirklicher Schmerz darüber, daß ein Wesen, das uns ausfüllt, zugleich außen ist. Ein Traumschreck bei hellichtem Tag. Eifersucht hat mit der Liebe der Geschlechter weniger zu tun, als es scheint; es ist die Kluft zwischen der Welt und dem Wahn, die Eifersucht im engeren Sinn nur eine Fußnote dazu, Schock: die Welt deckt sich mit dem Partner, nicht mit mir, die Liebe hat mich nur mit meinem Wahn vereint. (V 270-71)

[a] real pain that a being who fills us completely is at the same time outside. A dream-terror in broad daylight. Jealousy has far less to do with the love of the sexes than appears; it is the chasm between the world and madness, jealousy in the narrower sense is only a footnote to this, a shock: the world is identical with my partner, not with me, love has merely made me one with my madness. (256)

Now that Gantenbein has once experienced the full force of jealousy in his relationship with Lila, even though only in his imagination, he will never be able to discard it completely.

Eventually the narrator realizes he has never let the blind Gantenbein appear in the role of a father. Accordingly, Gantenbein is placed into a new series of scenes (V 292-308). Periodically, Gantenbein doubts that he has fathered the child Lila gives birth to; nevertheless, in another reversal of traditional roles, he rather than Lila is the one who brings up their daughter, Beatrice. He is the one who cares for her daily, feeds her, bathes her, plays with her; he is the one who has to deal with her childish lies when she has helped herself to a cookie without permission. The trouble is that Gantenbein has a difficult time knowing how to deal with such a situation. How can he, the blind daddy, comment on the crumbs or remnants of marmalade on her face or dress without arousing her suspicion about his inability to see? He worries that she may intuitively discover his secret and expose him as a fraud. Once again, Gantenbein is trapped by his role.

Usually, as Beatrice grows up, their family life is normal. Gantenbein and Lila are not even spared the fear that all parents have of possibly losing their beloved child: Beatrice, at ten, falls off her bicycle and suffers a cerebral hemorrhage. She recovers, and develops into a normal teenager and a young lady who shows as little respect for and interest in the accumulated wisdom and experience of her elders as any other youngster. Quite naturally, however, she expects and trusts those same elders to help her out of difficulties, assured of their willingness and their continued, unquestioned interest in her welfare.

Bringing up their daughter, Gantenbein learns some important lessons that affect his relationship with her and with his wife, though not fundamentally: first, that it is impossible to teach a child anything that her mother opposes, and second, that in spite of the child's many minor deceptions about trifles one has to remain a good father, resisting the constant desire to educate, to be ready to help, and to rush to his daughter's aid when life itself tries to discipline her. Like all men, Gantenbein learns these lessons slowly, but learn them he does.

Gantenbein now plays both his roles well—those of blind husband and blind father. It appears as if, in this alternate version of their marriage, he and Lila could indeed grow old together contentedly like Philemon and Baucis. They do not. Although the child for a time forms a special bond between the parents, she cannot bridge the gap between Lila and Gantenbein's perceptions of the state of their marriage, which is not helped by Gantenbein's continued suspicion and jealousy. Living through their daughter, especially in Gantenbein's case, merely allows Lila and Gantenbein to avoid each other and avoid facing the basic problem of their marriage: mutual deception. Once the daughter has grown up, the surrogate life Gantenbein has tried to live through her proves an illusion; more than ever, Gantenbein sees himself forced out to the periphery of Lila's life, except when she is at home.

Indeed, Gantenbein's blind-husband role has been a curse in disguise. Even though his blindness permits him and Lila a personal freedom not usually attainable in a marriage, that freedom has a limit, which is prescribed by the intensity of love and the degree of commitment each has to the other.

From the first awkward meeting, years ago, between the great actress and the blind man in Lila's dressing room, a story she never tires of telling, real love has grown and matured between

Gantenbein and Lila. Their love is unusual, because it allows for other, lesser loves in Lila's life, as long as Gantenbein maintains his assumed blindness. Both Lila and Gantenbein realize that he alone is the man Lila chose for her husband, the one to whom she always returns. The narrator states specifically: "sie liebte ihn um seiner Blindnis willen" (V 298), *"she loved him for his blindness"* (283). It is this nonexistent blindness of Gantenbein's in which Lila believes that enables her to engage in her various clandestine affairs, always, however, returning to her husband, which compels the narrator to observe:

> Erst das Geheimnis, das sie voreinander hüten, macht sie zum Paar. (V 106)

> *It is only the secret which they keep from each other that makes them a couple. (102)*

Gantenbein made the same observation a little earlier (V 103-04/99). Both he and the narrator know that Gantenbein and Lila are trapped in their respective interdependent roles.

When, for the last time as the blind husband, Gantenbein waits at the airport for Lila's arrival, he realizes she is carrying her own coat and making her way through Customs unassisted by any strange man. She greets him as enthusiastically and joyfully as she always has, glad to be home again. The narrator comments:

> Lila betrügt ihn nicht.
> Dafür hat er keine Rolle. (V 311)

> *Lila isn't deceiving him.*
> *For these circumstances he has no role. (296)*

Gantenbein is at a loss. He cannot respond to her happy chatter as she drives them home. At home, when she sits on his knee as she always does after returning from a trip, he does not respond as usual by stroking her hair. Instead, he gets up to get a drink of water. Lila senses that something is different today about this oft-repeated reunion ritual between them. When Gantenbein begins to speak she interrupts him, alarmed; she wants to know what is the matter. He takes off his glasses with a gesture of finality. She does not understand what is happening, does not grasp the importance of the moment, and repeats her question, confused, because he does not replace the glasses over his eyes as usual.

Slowly Gantenbein explains his charade, holding the glasses, now a superfluous prop, in his hand. This time Lila is the one rendered speechless. While Gantenbein believes he is declaring his love with the disclosure of his secret, Lila feels humiliated and utterly betrayed. Hurt and angry, she tells him three times to go away, the last time screaming it at him (V 312). Ironically, Gantenbein discloses his secret at a time Lila is not—perhaps no longer?—involved with another man. Was her infidelity only a figment of his blinded imagination?

The dilemma of Lila and Gantenbein and the breakup of their marriage illustrates once more, this time with a twist, one of Frisch's dicta about human relationships, especially between a man and a woman: "Du sollst dir kein Bildnis machen" (II 369-71), *"Thou shalt not make unto thee any graven image"* (*Sketch I* 16-18). Both Lila and Gantenbein created fixed images of each other. Gantenbein bears the greater share of guilt because he deliberately deceived Lila, forcing her to form an invalid image of the man she married. Once she knows the truth about him, Lila is unable, even though she loves Gantenbein, to accept him in his new role as the husband who is not blind.

Gantenbein formed an image of his wife, too: one of a woman who engages in extramarital affairs, but always returns to him. He is baffled when he discovers that she is *not* deceiving him; Lila, however, feels only humiliated after learning the truth about her husband. She has no other choice, she believes, but to send him away, for there can be no future for her in a marriage that from the outset was based on a false premise.

Because the images Lila and Gantenbein formed of each other do not allow them to change, they deprive their partners of the possibility of growth. Only Lila, it seems, is willing to accept the consequences of her error by ending the relationship; Gantenbein, although he walks away from their marriage as Lila requests, cannot comprehend what has happened.

THE NARRATOR: END OF A LONG JOURNEY

A traumatic experience, the death of a long-standing, intimate relationship, set the narrator off on his search for a story that would make the experience comprehensible. Not concerned primarily with death in its literal sense, the narrator here considers it more figuratively, a potential yet unalterable force that may break into a person's life at any moment, changing lives and relationships forever.

The description of the minor car accident at the beginning of the novel illustrates this point: the narrator not only nearly caused his own death, but involved eleven children in the near-tragedy as well. However, as the scene in the empty apartment illustrates, the narrator's more immediate concern is with a kind of death that might have been prevented, the death of a relationship. The experience that led to the empty apartment has left the narrator stunned, as stunned as Gantenbein is when Lila sends him away after he discloses his secret. As the narrator surveys the remnants of a shared life, he is reminded of Pompeii: "alles noch vorhanden, bloß die Zeit ist weg" (V 20), *"everything still present, only time has gone away"* (19). Outside, beyond the apartment's closed shutters, life goes on, unconcerned; inside, the narrator, looking at the scene before him as if he were remote from it, tries to understand what has happened and why.

Near the end of the novel, an interrogator, asking the narrator which of his three characters he really is, summarizes what has happened in the narrator's life:

> Ein Mann liebt eine Frau . . . diese Frau liebt einen andern Mann . . . der erste Mann liebt eine andere Frau, die wiederum von einem andern Mann geliebt wird . . . eine durchaus alltägliche Geschichte, die nach allen Seiten auseinandergeht— (V 313)
>
> *A man loves a woman. . . . This woman loves another man. . . . The first man loves another woman, who in turn is loved by another man . . . a very ordinary story that breaks up in all directions—* (297)

This summary illustrates the simultaneous occurrence of the ordinary and the unusual in every life, and also the complexity of the characters' relationships with Lila and each other. While the narrator has Enderlin explore the conflicting pressures of a love relationship in its early stage and Svoboda articulate the experience of a love and marriage that end unexpectedly, he has Gantenbein examine how such a love and marriage might have been kept alive.

To understand a fundamental experience, the narrator not only projects facets of his personality onto the three characters he creates—three dominant colors separated prismically from the white light of his own being—but he also participates actively in the investigation of himself. He contributes to the emerging story with comments and illustrative stories that are stimulated by the process of associative thinking, a technique familiar from earlier Frisch novels. His comments add up to a series of short essays on the major themes of *Mein Name sei Gantenbein*: love (V 161-63,233-34), jealousy (V 111-14,161-63,193-94,270-71), blindness (V 44,111-14,161-63), and especially the problems of marriage (V 133-37,192-93,233-34,266-71,311-14).

The narrator makes no pretense of omniscience and offers no universal verities. Rather, he presents everything that happens in the novel from an exclusively male perspective—the perspective of Enderlin, Svoboda, Gantenbein, or himself. Lila never speaks in her own voice, nor are her thoughts ever described. Her partners or the narrator record only her words and her actions, and sometimes the contents of her letters. What happens inside Lila remains a mystery.

At the end of a scene in which the narrator imagines that Gantenbein confronts and calmly questions Lila about her infidelity and her relationship with Einhorn, Nils, or whatever the name of her lover (V 183-84)—an imagined scene that, like many in this novel, never takes place—Lila readily admits her transgression. Gantenbein responds laconically: "So I was right!" (V 183/174). He will survive, the narrator comments, as is proper—after he apologizes to Lila for having asked her in the first place. Unexpectedly, the narrator then observes:

Ich habe noch keine Frau gekannt, die nicht eine Entschuldigung erwartet, wenn sie bei einem anderen Mann gewesen ist, und sie auch erreicht, nämlich eine Entschuldigung meinerseits, damit der Zukunft nichts im Weg steht. (V 185)

I have never known a woman who didn't expect an apology when she has been with another man, and has also obtained one, that's to say an apology on my part, so that nothing shall stand in the way of the future. (176)

This is one of the few indications in the novel that there is a direct link between the narrator's basic experience and that of Gantenbein. The narrator even offers an explanation, presumably based on personal experience, of why Gantenbein is able to remain calm in the face of Lila's monstrous admission of infidelity:

Es verfeinert sich das Vermögen zu unterscheiden zwischen Gefühlen, die man hat, und solchen, die man schon gehabt hat. Das hat mit Reife nichts zu tun. Ich empfinde den Augenblick wie Erinnerung. Das ist alles. Ich erinnere mich, wie ich vor Jahren auch nicht geschrien habe, weil es auch nicht das erste Mal gewesen ist, und das erste Mal, als ich es gehört habe von einer Frau, daß sie bei einem anderen gewesen ist, habe ich nur geschrien, weil es sich mit meiner Ahnung so vollkommen gedeckt hat, wie es sich seither deckt in meiner Erinnerung an das erste Mal ... (V 184)

The ability to distinguish between feelings one has and feelings one once had improves. This has nothing to do with maturity. I experience the moment like memory. That's all. I remember how years ago I didn't shout, because it wasn't the first time either, and the first time I heard from a woman that she had been with another man, I only shouted because it tallied so exactly with my suspicion, as since then it has tallied with my memory of the first time ... (175)

These comments make clear that a woman's infidelity and the narrator's own jealousy have been recurring problems for him. The narrator seems convinced that any extended relationship, whether or not it includes marriage, invites boredom that threatens the relationship. He illustrates this point with his account of the couple on the beach (V 244-46).

Perhaps these two people are Lila and Svoboda, perhaps they are just any two people who resemble them and are approaching the end of their marriage. The two are visibly bored with each other as they sunbathe in silence and later toss a beach ball back and forth. The moment the woman notices the narrator watching them, however, her face becomes animated and her movements change from awkwardly listless to gracefully awkward, girlish (V 244); her listlessness obviously extends only to her partner. The couple abruptly breaks off the ball play, and as the woman limps back to their spot on the beach and sits down, her expressions and movements make clear that her husband is to blame for her twisted ankle, since it was he who compelled her to play ball. She reacts with annoyance to everything he does to show his sympathy, to be attentive to her. This couple is reminiscent of Julika and Stiller during the first part of their marriage. The relationship lacks not only compassion but also, and primarily, communication.

The couple on the beach is one of many illustrations with which the narrator suggests the inadequacy of marriage as an institution, because the inevitable repetitiveness of daily routine leads to boredom. Repetition, the narrator believes, kills any positive feeling the partners have for each other—an opinion he shares with Enderlin. This is also the narrator's point when he projects a possible marriage between Lila and Enderlin ten years into the future: the routine and repetitiveness of their daily life will have turned them into two lifeless bodies, dead to the excitement and pleasures of love (V 133-37). Perhaps, the narrator seems to suggest, marriage as it is traditionally practiced is inadequate, for it seems to accomplish the opposite of what it hopes to achieve. Maybe another, more satisfactory, arrangement should take its place.

The narrator seems to share Lila's delight with a party guest's account of a different form of permanent relationship between men and women, allegedly practiced in Africa by a remote, obviously male-dominated tribe, the Tohulis (V 192-93). Every male member of the tribe is assigned a woman by lottery. He cares for her for the rest of her life: when she is young and

MEIN NAME SEI GANTENBEIN   257

healthy; when she is bearing children, not necessarily his; when she is ill; and when she is old. She is his responsibility, her care his obligation until she dies. This arrangement is not, however, based on sexual monogamy. On the contrary, the spirit of Eros is common property in this African tribe; men and women are free to choose their sexual partners and to change them as often as they please. Sex and person are separate from property and thus subject to different laws: sex is ruled by the laws of nature, property by the laws of men.

Theft of property is the only recognized crime and is punished with death, the form of execution paralleling the magnitude of the theft. A thief of household utensils is punished simply by cutting the jugular vein; a thief of jewelry is tied between two palm trees until the next storm sways the palms and tears the offender's body in two; a thief of arrows, essential for hunting, is emasculated and then buried alive; a woman who steals is burned to death by her husband. Theft of a woman, however, is impossible, because she is not property.

Jealousy is unknown among the members of this tribe, reportedly one of the most peaceful in Africa. Men do not shoot each other because of a woman, since sexual relationships are free of the possessiveness that marks marital relationships in western society, where right of ownership extends to person as well as property. Max Frisch, in his effort to identify the causes of jealousy in human relationships, makes an important point here, one that is not lost on Lila. For the moment, it seems to have escaped the narrator's attention; he merely observes, in a concluding remark, that nothing happened in Gantenbein's marriage to Lila that could have led him to suspect that Lila led a Tohuli-like marriage (V 193).

The many, frequently outrageous, tales the narrator incorporates into his search for his own story are all exempla, stories with morals that illuminate one of the novel's primary topics. The one about the African tribe illustrates a problem in marriage: possessiveness of person. On the one hand, it restricts personal freedom, the narrator realizes; on the other, when a partner breaks free of the marriage's confinement, it leads to jealousy.

Dr. Burri, the narrator's close friend and favorite chess partner, is another resourceful storyteller and a philosopher of sorts. Burri tells several stories illustrating human relationships (V 111-14) and sometimes comments directly on events in the novel.

Like the narrator, his vision is purely male, but he does not seem to be hampered by jealousy. He is the one who sums up the problems men have with women.

Men have only themselves to blame, in Burri's view, when they claim that women are not easily understood, because men cannot admit that, basically, they despise as much about women as they adore. Feeling guilty about this, they take the least stressful and most unrealistic way out of the dilemma: they glorify women. It is a man's own fault, Burri claims, if he suffers because of a woman: he is enslaved to her by his contempt for her, which he represses—pretending to be blind to his feelings—and replaces with his glorification of her.

If the reality of life forces a man to open his eyes to a woman's faults, what does he do? Burri asks. He leaves the woman he has adored and glorified in his blindness and rushes on to the next one, as if she were not also a woman. The cycle begins anew, because men, according to Burri, are unable to let go of their dream, their ideal of the perfect woman (V 208). With a large dose of cynicism Burri observes:

> Die Frau ist ein Mensch, bevor man sie liebt, manchmal auch nachher; sobald man sie liebt, ist sie ein Wunder, also unhaltbar— (V 209)

> *The woman is a person before one loves her, sometimes afterwards as well; as soon as one loves her she is a miracle and hence untenable—* (198)

For men, the magic of women is created from many particulars, according to Burri: women's insatiable need for love; their special right to feel disappointed; their tendency to be reproachful; their trick of always being the victim; their dreadful ability to be consoled at any moment; their willingness to let the man decide what happens and then, when he wants to know where he stands so he can act appropriately, their craftiness in leaving the question unanswered, insuring that the decision for his action—and thus the guilt for it—is his from the outset; their need for protection and security; and their unfathomable inconstancy (V 208). The more chivalrously a man behaves to a woman, Burri believes, the more contempt he is hiding behind that civil facade.

Svoboda, perhaps more than either Gantenbein or Enderlin, may be at least in part an example of such a man. He obviously loves Lila, his wife, throws himself into his work, becomes professionally successful, and is able to accumulate material wealth. Meanwhile his marriage deteriorates, perhaps because he takes Lila's love for granted, perhaps because the routine of married life extinguishes the magic of their love. Yet none of the three, not Svoboda, not Enderlin with his tendency to avoid commitment, and not Gantenbein with his fundamental deceit of Lila is able to maintain a durable marriage to the woman he loves.

What did the narrator learn from his investigation? Perhaps that for a man to employ a little blindness, if it is not excessive, may be a good thing for a marriage, or for any important relationship. Blindness obviates pettiness and unnecessary criticism, which is useful when the partner is someone like Lila, for example, who always misplaces things, is never on time, seldom unpacks and puts away her belongings when she comes home from a trip, is an untidy housekeeper who is not bothered by unwashed dishes, wilted flowers, and a clutter of unanswered mail. A little blindness allows the partners to feel more free, to act more openly, more naturally, something Gantenbein hoped would happen when he chose the role of a blind man. He suspected that if people were spared his observation and constant judgment, they would be free of the fear that he would see their little lies. They would then not feel compelled to hide and would allow him to get to know them better, to establish a trusting relationship with them. Gantenbein's friendship with Camilla seems to prove his thesis.

A little blindness keeps a marriage focused on important things, such as the partners' love for each other, their enjoyment of each other's company, their happiness in living together. A little blindness can prevent the gradual destruction of happiness by petty criticisms of annoying habits or constant disagreement about unimportant issues. The first version of Gantenbein and Lila's marriage seems to confirm these observations.

This kind of blindness also helps to keep alive the spontaneity of action in a marriage, the narrator has learned. Since Gantenbein pretended literal blindness, however, not the figurative blindness suggested here, his behavior cannot serve the narrator as a model of how a man might build a more successful relationship with a woman—provided that was one of the narrator's objectives. Nevertheless, the narrator might well adopt various aspects of Gantenbein's technique in a future relationship with a woman to avoid its ending unexpectedly, an experience as traumatic as death.

Ominously, the narrator began this novel with someone's death. The incident makes clear from the beginning that the narrator is very conscious of the passing of time. He is no longer young, with hopes and possibilities stretching infinitely before him. He remembers the appealing young woman who, some time ago in Italy, stood close to him on an ancient Roman burial mound (echoes of Walter Faber and Sabeth?) and answered his question, "What can one do with a daydream?" with the spontaneous confidence of youth: "Take it!" (V 138/132). The narrator marvelled at the woman's youth and grace, her intense happiness in the present moment, while he was taut with a tension born of memory and expectation. He did not take the young woman's advice but drove on. Months later he threw away a once-fragrant pine cone and tore up the woman's address, both reminders of that tempting encounter. He is aware of the debilitating effect of transient time; he knows man is not allowed to relive any part of his life. He acknowledges that life is a continuous sequence of choices, choices between acting and not acting. The relentlessness of having to choose provokes him to comment:

> Langsam habe ich es satt, dieses Spiel, das ich nun kenne: handeln oder unterlassen, und in jedem Fall, ich weiß, ist es nur ein Teil meines Lebens, und den anderen Teil muß ich mir vorstellen. (V 129)
>
> *I'm gradually getting tired of this game that I now know: to act or not to act, and in any case I know it is only a part of my life, and the other part I must imagine. (123)*

As the experiences of Enderlin, Svoboda, and Gantenbein in their relationships to Lila have shown, any actions the narrator might or might not have taken in attempting to maintain his relationship with the woman he loves are interchangeable. The important factor in life is not clock time, a specific action or repetition, but transient time, the narrator observes. Transient time moves on, whereas clock time merely repeats itself every twenty-four hours. As man grows older, the past is no longer a mystery and the future becomes merely an anticipation of old age and death, the one experience that is absolute and offers no option.

Time, then, is the master of life, the ultimate conquerer of man, who moves through it toward his predestined goal: destruction and death. Only man's imagination can provide him with an illusory sense of freedom—freedom of action and freedom of choice. This is the fragile and somewhat bleak conclusion one might be tempted to draw from the narrator's elaborate investigation into his own personality and behavior. But this conclusion ignores the fact that in the process of his extensive investigation the narrator gained insights about himself that enabled him to transcend the traumatic, existential experience that was plaguing him when the novel opened and that lies behind the scene in the deserted apartment, filled with lonely symbols of a past that has neither a present nor a future.

Having thus found and told his story, the narrator returns to the present, rejuvenated from his long journey into himself. His most important insight is stated humbly and in a few words near the end of the novel: "Ich bin blind. Ich weiß es nicht immer, aber manchmal" (V 314), "*I am blind. I don't always know it, but sometimes I do*" (298). This recognition strongly suggests that the experience that made the narrator return to the deserted apartment early in the novel now lies behind him, that he has transcended it.

In the final paragraph, the narrator returns to the present after his excursion into the realm of imagination and reflection. This final scene exudes the grace of self-acceptance that had eluded him throughout the novel. On a hot September day, seated outside a roadside inn and shaded by an olive tree somewhere in Italy, he is eating bread and drinking wine, waiting for the arrival of the fish he has ordered. Having accepted himself, the narrator is satisfying three basic human needs: thirst, hunger, and love—for someone is sitting with him at the table. It is safe to assume that it is a woman with whom he shares this moment, for he exclaims: "Leben gefällt mir" (V 320), *"Living pleases me."*

And why should it not? The moment is precious, filled with a present that seems to exist outside the restrictions of continuous time and its polarities, past and future.

NOTES

[1] The story is told in the second of the series of forty-two answers Max Frisch gave in a fictitious interview entitled "Ich schreibe für Leser" (V 323-34), "*I Write for Readers,*" and published (without the questions!) in *Dichten und Trachten* (1964). The story corresponds closely to the events of the novel, except that in the novel two people, Enderlin and Gantenbein, rather than the interviewee alone, are involved in the events resulting from the action.

[2] Readers interested in pursuing the philosophical aspects of the relationship between possibility, reality, and invention in this Frisch novel may want to read Petersen's lucid discussion of this topic in Gerhard P. Knapp (ed.), *Max Frisch: Aspekte des Prosawerks* 131-56.

[3] The first English translation by Michael Bullock (1965) was entitled *A Wilderness of Mirrors.*

[4] The first key episode of the novel, related more to the theme of identity than the second one, consists of the description of two visions: at dawn, a horse unsuccessfully attempts to escape from the confines of a granite wall; subsequently a convoy is seen approaching Jerusalem (V 12).

[5] Although the novel contains numerous incidents that can easily be traced and linked autobiographically to Frisch, it would be a mistake to equate the narrator of *Mein Name sei Gantenbein* with the author, or the narrator's basic, traumatic experience, never explicitly stated, with the breakup of Frisch's relationship with Ingeborg Bachmann. *Mein Name sei Gantenbein* is too complex, its narrative situation too universal, for its scope to be narrowed to the purely biographical, as various interpreters have tried to do.

[6] The English translation of Frisch's *Tagebuch 1946-1949* omits half the Marion entries, specifically II 359, 364-67, and 500-01.

[7] Enderlin's reappearance in three sections of the second half of the novel (V 219-32, 234-47, 263-66) after he has been dropped must be viewed either as an extension and variation of events

described in the first half (as in V 263-66) or as seeing the identical situation (Lila's affair with Enderlin) from a different perspective, in this case Svoboda's, who knows that his wife has a lover (as in V 219-47).

[8]Like Killian in *Bin*, for whom Peking was the symbol of his secret longing, Enderlin seems to think of Peru as a symbolic place where his most fervent longings and desires will be fulfilled.

[9]We note that the moments when the narrator's conscious will has the least control over Enderlin are influenced by his consumption of alcohol. He shares this feature with other Frisch characters, especially Stiller and Walter Faber, both of whom exercise the least control and are most closely in touch with their true nature when inebriated (III 361-68, 432-35, 761-77; IV 81-85, 89-95).

[10]Although the German *Schoß* means "sex" in the most general sense, the meaning here is much more specific and would be better translated as "vagina." The phrase *"Augen, die ganz schmal werden dabei"* could be more appropriately translated as "eyes that grow narrow as a result"—here, as the result of approaching orgasm. Frisch describes this phenomenon similarly in other novels (see *Homo faber* IV 94, *Montauk* VI 703).

[11]This last sentence does not appear in Bullock's 1982 translation, *Gantenbein* (V 21/21), which I take to be an inadvertent omission. This first mention of Gantenbein's name is especially important, because this sentence is repeated almost verbatim a few pages later with one significant change: instead of writing "sein" (*"his"*) before the name "Gantenbein," the narrator of the novel uses "mein" *my"*).

[12]The murder reported in the paper is that of Camilla Huber, as becomes evident later in the novel (V 199, 271-79).

[13]In this context a reference to an important Frisch essay about the theater seems appropriate, as it deals with the themes of a viewer's perception and imagination when watching a play. This essay, written in 1948, includes also a specific reference to Dürrenmatt's play *Der Blinde* (*The Blind One*), which might have provided Frisch with the germ of the idea for Gantenbein's role as Lila's blind husband and must therefore be considered one of

this character's early sources (II 570-76); concerning other possible sources for the figure of Gantenbein see also Butler 123.

[14]The unicorn, a mythical animal of oriental origin—sometimes depicted with the body and head of horse, the hind legs of a stag, and the tail of a lion—bears a single horn in the middle of its forehead. It can only be caught, according to legend, if it flees and rests its head in the lap of a maiden. For that reason, the unicorn is occasionally viewed as a phallic symbol. Traditionally, though, it is a symbol of innocence and purity. In this latter context, Frisch's use of the name here is obviously meant to be ironic (Bulfinch 299-300; Jung 21).

[15]This action of Lila's is reminiscent of Rolf's action in *Stiller*, when he disposes of the troublesome parcel of flesh-colored cloth by flushing it down a public toilet (III 570). The similarity is probably coincidental.

[16]The reader not familiar with the ancient myth may appreciate the following: Philemon and Baucis, an elderly married couple in Greek mythology, are famed for their true love, faithfulness, humility, and hospitality. According to the myth, Zeus and Hermes, temporarily bored by the goings-on on Mount Olympus, have disguised themselves as poor travelers and roam the countryside in human form to test the hospitality of mortals. All the rich mortals on whose doors they knock turn them away rudely, barring the door and refusing their requests for food, drink, and a place to rest. Finally they come to the humble home of an aged couple, Philemon and Baucis, who receive them with kindness and offer hospitality.

In punishment for the people's inhospitality, the gods destroy with floods the neighborhood and the people in it, except for the elderly couple, whom they reward by changing their humble cottage into a magnificent temple. There the two hold priestly office until they die, at which time the gods grant their wish never to be separated, even in death. Gradually they are transformed into an unusual pair of trees, a linden and an oak, growing from a single trunk. For years people come from far and wide to admire the miracle and to hang wreaths of flowers on the trees' branches in honor of the faithful couple (Ovid 234-42; Bulfinch 56-59; Hamilton 111-13; Seyfert 478).

When Gantenbein tells Camilla his modern version of the old couple's story, eulogizing them as *the* couple, Frisch's intent is clearly ironic (V 233-34/*221-22*).

CHAPTER SIX

MONTAUK: LIFE AS A MAN

This is the story of Max, a writer, sixty-three years old. It is a thoughtful story, autobiographical in nature. Its point of departure is a quiet weekend Max and Lynn, his youthful lover, spend together at Montauk Point, a summer resort area at the northeastern tip of Long Island, slightly more than a hundred miles from New York City. Theirs is an accepting kind of love, shared in the immediate present. Their relationship will end in a few days when Max returns to Europe, to a wife from whom he is separated, and to his work, writing.

Max and Lynn's relationship is of recent origin: they have known each other just a month and have been lovers for only a couple of weeks. It has no tangible future, which both recognize and accept. Their different languages—she speaks no German, his English is not fluent—make it difficult for them to talk easily about their thoughts and past experiences. Nevertheless, the resulting silences between them are easy silences. For Max they are also pregnant: he fills them with memories stirred to life in a process of association with his present situation, memories of important relationships shared with other women.

The story of *Montauk*, which was published in 1975, has a basis in fact. In the spring of 1974 Max Frisch, at the invitation of his American publisher Harcourt Brace Jovanovich, came to North America to give a series of lectures throughout the northern United States and eastern Canada to promote his books and plays. The publisher assigned a young woman, the Lynn of *Montauk*, to assist him. On the afternoon of May 10, 1974, the Friday of Frisch's last weekend in the United States, the two drove in a rented car to Montauk Point, where they spent Saturday and part of Sunday before returning to Manhattan. Forty-eight hours later, Frisch flew back to Europe (Hage 104).

As the novel begins, Max and Lynn have stopped their car and climbed out in response to a sign that promised an "overlook," a view of the ocean. Taken literally, this "overlook" never materializes. It proves as elusive, and the overgrown path Max and Lynn follow in hopes of reaching it as misleading, as the figurative "overlook" one might expect from an autobiographical story. However, as the protagonist follows the winding path of his selectively recalled memories, overgrown with quotations from his own literary works and those of others, he discloses a great deal about himself and his relationships with five women, Lynn included, whom he has loved.

To preserve the mood of this weekend—intensely felt, vividly alive, yet peaceful—Max wants to record it, just as it is. As he watches Lynn looking at accessories in a boutique in Amagannsett, a little resort town, he thinks:

> Ich möchte diesen Tag beschreiben . . . unser Wochenende und wie's dazu gekommen ist, wie es weiter verläuft. Ich möchte erzählen können, ohne irgend etwas dabei zu erfinden. Eine einfältige Erzähler-Position. (VI 671)

> *I should like to describe this day . . . our weekend together, how it came about and how it develops. I should like to tell it without inventing anything. In the role of a simple narrator.* (54)

Sunday morning, as he trudges alone along the beach, this wish returns: to describe this weekend with Lynn, "diese dünne Gegenwart" (VI 708), *"this thin present moment"* (94). Later that day, as he and Lynn pass through Amagannsett again on their drive back to Manhattan, the thought recurs—to write down the experience of this weekend:

> autobiographisch, ja, autobiographisch. Ohne Personnagen zu erfinden; ohne Ereignisse zu erfinden, die exemplarischer sind als seine Wirklichkeit; ohne auszuweichen in Erfindungen. (VI 719)

> *in an autobiographical way. Completely autobiographical— without inventing a single character; without inventing happen-*

ings of more significance than his own simple reality; without taking refuge in inventions of any kind. (106)

In some ways Max succeeds well in his self-imposed task. In *Montauk* he does preserve the weekend, selecting from the many quiet events and conversations shared with Lynn those that convey the actions and mood of these few days. But in other ways he fails, because Max cannot live for long in only the present. Thus he not only records the unadorned weekend, the love story of Lynn and himself, but he also allows memories of the past to crowd into his narrative, just as they did into the weekend at Montauk.

The events of the present and the immediate past, those involving Lynn and Max, separate and frame his recollections of the four women most significant in his past: Käte, a foreign student; Constanze, the mother of his children; Ingeborg, a fellow writer; and Marianne, a "Lektorin" (editor).[1] His relationships to these women have not been easy, and each has left a residue of unexpiated guilt. A problem common to all four relationships seems to have been a lack of effective communication between Max and the women, a problem Max shares with other male characters in Frisch's novels.

With Lynn, however, Max's relationship is different. "Lynn wird kein Name für eine Schuld" (VI 742), *"Lynn's name will not become a synonym for guilt" (131)*, he observes confidently toward the end of *Montauk*. This is so partly because of the somewhat superficial nature of their relationship, dictated by the very brief time they spend together and the language barrier that hampers serious verbal communication. In addition, Lynn is unfamiliar with Max's life and the books he has written. These factors create a distance between them that neither can easily overcome. Max gives this distance symbolic expression by referring to Lynn as "the young woman," "the young stranger," or "the strange young woman" and to himself most of the time in the third person as *"er,"* "he"—as if he were an observer standing outside their relationship rather than a participant. In contrast, he consistently uses the first-person pronoun *"ich,"* "I," when referring to his relationships with the other four women. In the course of *Montauk*, Max's recollections reveal the nature of these previous relationships and also the nature of the guilt each has left behind.

Ostensibly, the primary focus of *Montauk* is the immediacy of the present Lynn and Max experience in each other's company, including the silences they share—driving along the coast and exploring little Amagannsett; walking on the beach; sitting in two isolated beach chairs implanted in the sand, looking out over the ocean, each separate from the other and pursuing his own thoughts; or watching the night sky from the balcony of their hotel room while listening to the rhythmic roar of the surf. But Max, no longer young, knows that the present is but an intermediate state, a "Durchgangsstation," between the past and the future. On this point he agrees with the narrator of *Mein Name sei Gantenbein*, who once observes:

> Vergangenheit ist kein Geheimnis mehr, die Gegenwart ist dünn, weil sie abgetragen wird von Tag zu Tag, und die Zukunft heißt Altern . . . (V 137)

> *The past is no secret any longer, the present is thin because it is worn out day by day, and the future means growing old . . . (Gantenbein 130)*

These lines are not bitter. They simply state an observation, an assessment of reality, the truth of which the narrator recognizes and accepts. For Max, too, the past holds no secret: he remembers it vividly in the present, which is thin but filled with the presence of Lynn, and he is fully aware that what the future holds for him is old age and, eventually, death. At the time of the Montauk weekend, Max's state of mind is peaceful and reflective. For the moment, he does not struggle against the flow of transient time.

AUTHOR VERSUS NARRATOR: AN INTIMATE RELATIONSHIP

To assure an accurate reading of *Montauk*, it is necessary to clarify the delicate relationship between the novel's author, Max Frisch, and the narrator-protagonist. Even though both answer to the same name and share much of the same biography, they are at all times separate. This situation has created much confusion among interpreters, particularly since the narrator mentions his (and the author's) full name several times in the course of the novel. How fine is the line that separates one from the other may be illustrated by the use each makes of a quotation from Montaigne. Frisch, the author, places the bulk of the Montaigne quotation as an epigraph on an unnumbered page before the first chapter of the novel:

> ... Denn ich bin es, den ich darstelle. Meine Fehler wird man hier finden, so wie sie sind, und mein unbefangenes Wesen. ... So bin ich selber ... der einzige Inhalt meines Buches. (VI 619)

> ... *For it is myself that I portray. My defects will here be [found the way they are], and also my natural form .... Thus ... I am myself the [only] matter of my book. (v)*

Max, the protagonist, quotes from the epigraph twice (VI 679,747), the second time to precede, in ironic opposition, his implied admission that the account he has given of his life is not entirely truthful, does not divulge everything but contains omissions. Max, the professional writer and narrator of the account called *Montauk*—whose subtitle might well be "My Life as a Man," a phrase that turns into the novel's major leitmotif—exercises his right as an author writing "unter Kunstzwang" (VI 633), under artistic discipline, to select from the material of his life—including dates, names, places—those most appropriate and to arrange them in a sequence suitable to his purpose; Max, the protagonist, is trying to come to terms with his biography. But Frisch, the Swiss novelist, gave his novel *Montauk* its real subtitle, "Eine Erzählung," a story.

Some interpreters take the position that Frisch identifies himself with every word of the Montaigne epigraph. Yet in the first three pages of *Montauk* Frisch makes clear, by his frequent allusions to literary images, especially in his vivid physical description of Lynn without ever mentioning her name, that Max's story takes place in the world of autobiographical fiction, not fact: the young woman Max describes in those first few pages bears a striking resemblance to Sabeth in *Homo faber*, a novel Frisch wrote nearly twenty years earlier.

The relationship between author, narrator, and protagonist is generally complicated in Frisch's novels, but it seems especially obfuscated in *Montauk*. Fortunately, Frisch has given us some clues to unraveling it. In an interview, Horst Bienek, himself a writer, asked Frisch why he chose to write many of his novels in the form of a journal, a *Tagebuch*. In answering, Frisch made an important distinction between the *Tagebuch* as it is commonly thought of and the form he developed for himself. When he uses the word *Tagebuch*, Frisch explained, he does not speak "von dem privaten Tagebuch, das man als junger Mensch einmal geführt und dann vernichtet hat" (Bienek 26), "*of the private journal that one once kept as a young person and then destroyed.*" On the contrary, for Frisch the *Tagebuch* is something

> das über ein Logbuch der Zeitereignisse hinausgeht, das die Wirklichkeit nicht nur in den Fakten sucht, sondern *gleichwertig* in Fiktionen. (Bienek 26; italics mine)
>
> *that goes beyond being a logbook of current events, that seeks reality not only in facts but, equivalently, in fiction.*

This distinction is especially relevant to *Montauk* because the novel "borrows" from and expands on the autobiographical section of *Tagebuch 1946-1949* (II 583-90/*Sketch I 191-97*) in which various facts are stated succinctly as lived reality. Frisch's distinction also makes clear why the English title *Sketchbook*, rather than *Diary* or *Journal*, is appropriate for his *Tagebücher*, since they contain not only carefully selected biographical journal-type entries but also lengthy early drafts of literary works, many of which Frisch later developed fully or incorporated in other works.

In that same conversation with Bienek, Frisch also tried to explain the difference between the "Erzähler-Ich" (*"narrator-I"*) and the "Privat-Ich" (*"private-I"*). The narrator-I is "[der] Verfasser meines Namens" (Bienek 26) *"the author who bears my name,"* whereas Frisch, in his own person, is the private-I, which he sometimes refers to as the "direct I" ("direktes Ich"). Frisch continues: "natürlich ist das Erzähler-Ich nie mein privates Ich. . . ." (Bienek 27), *"of course, the narrator-I is never my private I. . . ."* The private I can, however, assume a number of other roles, Frisch points out; the *author* Max Frisch is only one among all those other Max Frischs—the interviewee, the son, the lover, the father, the husband. Frisch acknowledges that these fine distinctions may be difficult for the layperson and concludes: "perhaps one has to be a writer to know that every *I* that expresses itself is a role. Always. In life, too. Also at this very moment" (Bienek 27).[3]

Frisch employs primarily a narrative I, "ein erzählendes Ich," in *Montauk*. But because the material is autobiographical, the private I, closely linked to the direct I of the *Tagebuch*, is also present. It always appears on those occasions in *Montauk* when the narrator is retelling and expanding incidents from a more distant past that are also recorded in the autobiographical sketch in *Tagebuch 1946-1949* (II 583-90).

Frisch refers again to the differences among author, narrator, and protagonist in *Tagebuch 1966-1971*, which was published three years before *Montauk*. There he distinguishes between the "narrative I," the novelist, and the "direct I," the person who records events in a journal. He writes:

[Der] Unterschied zwischen dem erzählerischen ICH und dem direkten ICH eines Tagebuches: das letztere ist weniger nachzuvollziehen, gerade weil es zu vieles verschweigt von seinen Voraussetzungen. . . . (VI 287)

The difference between the [narrative] "I" and the direct "I" in a journal: the latter can less easily be filled in, for the very reason that it provides too little in the way of background knowledge. . . . (Sketch II 239)

Perhaps it is this "direct I," his "private I," that Frisch had in mind when, self-critically, he seemed to regret having remained silent about so many details Max could have recounted in *Montauk*. During a 1982 conversation with Volker Hage, Frisch commented: "When I read it (*Montauk*) again, it seems to me that too much is concealed, unnecessarily concealed; it is too little direct" (Hage 124).

The lack of directness Frisch feels responsible for may well be the cause for some of the interpretive confusion that surrounds this novel. One misconception involves the identity of the narrator, who Gerhard Knapp, for example, insists is separate from Max.[4] Knapp bases his claim on Max's frequent switching between the pronouns "he" and "I" when he relates events that involve himself. Knapp claims that whenever Frisch refers to Max's relationship with Lynn he uses "er," but whenever he has the narrator talk about anything not related to their relationship he uses "ich." Knapp is mistaken. As early as the novel's fourth page, Max, clearly the speaker, suddenly switches from "er" to "ich" when he describes how he and Lynn met for the first time (VI 624). From there on he occasionally substitutes "ich" for "er" in reference to Max and Lynn, until the two pronouns eventually merge and the "er" is actually replaced by the "ich" at the novel's end. No different identity is involved here. Another factor is operative in the change of pronouns, as I shall demonstrate.

Montauk was not the first work in which Frisch has the narrator switch pronouns, alternating between "er" and "ich." He explored it in some depth eleven years earlier in *Mein Name sei Gantenbein*. Granted, the purpose was different then. In *Gantenbein*, Frisch had the narrator change pronouns to create and maintain entities representative of, but separate from, himself—the characters of Enderlin, Svoboda, and Gantenbein. In *Montauk* the purpose is to identify levels of time, that is, to distinguish *current* experience from events that took place in the more distant past. Max usually uses "er" when he is recounting events in the present and immediate past; he most often uses "ich" when he records his associative memories of the more distant past. The result is a constantly changing perspective in the narrative flow, an outside-inside double vision into the protagonist, until the two eventually merge (VI 752). The process is similar to that of adjusting, individually and in slow motion, the lenses of a pair of binoculars, putting them gradually into focus to yield finally a fused, clear, single picture of the object in view—in this case, Max.

Max also uses the familiar personal pronoun "du" (you) in *Montauk*, but only when he is referring to his relationship with one particular woman, Marianne. All other women are referred to as "sie" (*"she"*). Max's use of the "du" adds a tremendous immediacy and intimacy to his recollections of Marianne, occasionally leaving the reader with the feeling of intruding into a very private sphere.

In his previous novels, especially in *Stiller* and *Homo faber*, Frisch had set for himself much the same task as Max does in *Montauk*: to make visible and comprehensible the life of one man, his protagonist. Furthermore, the mosaic-like structure of *Montauk*, its diary-like style, and Frisch's collage technique of narration are also reminiscent of *Stiller* and *Homo faber*. Common to all three novels is another element: each, in a broad sense, is a report, an account of the protagonist's life through which he comes to terms with himself. What is unusual in *Montauk* is that Frisch places at his protagonist's disposal his own biography, complete with names and dates, without any attempt, or so it seems, to fictionalize details.

This uncommon procedure in a novel by a writer of Frisch's stature may be thought of as indiscreet. It is not; Frisch is too sensitive and tactful a person and too fine a writer to violate the conventions of good taste. Instead, he deliberately employs this unusual procedure in an effort to subject to the toughest test an idea he has pursued in all his previous novels. This idea may be stated as a question: Can a man's life be so described that it becomes visible and comprehensible to others? What better way to test his concept than to use his own life as resource material for his protagonist?

Max chooses relationships, those from the remembered past and the present, as vehicles for examining and sorting out his life. Most significant are the relationships with the five women he has loved.

KÄTE: THE FOREIGN STUDENT

Max and Käte meet in 1933. She is a student in Zurich, he a young journalist. He proposes marriage to her three years later, and she accepts. That same year, 1936, Max begins to study architecture because he does not want to be a "good-for-nothing," and both believe that he should have a "real" profession before they marry (II 587; Hage 28).

Käte's family background is upper-middle class, like that of most of the women Max will later love. Her father is an art historian and a museum official in Berlin; her mother comes from Nuremberg. Käte has little in common with her literary counterpart, Hanna in *Homo faber*: they share only their religion (Jewish), their nationality (German), and their status as students in Zurich.

Käte and Max visit Germany often. What they see there disturbs Max. Once, on a visit to Nuremberg, Käte wants to show him the *Bratwurst-Glöckl*, a famous local restaurant with an especially pleasant atmosphere. As they enter, she does not notice the sign "No Jews Allowed;" Max sees the sign but keeps quiet. Since Käte's features are not easily identifiable as Jewish, nothing happens—except that the incident spoils Max's appetite completely.

The situation in Germany causes both of them to worry about the future. Max wants to marry Käte soon; married to a Swiss, she would be safe. Käte, who prefers to wait until Max is financially more secure, refuses. She tells him: "Du bist bereit mich zu heiraten, nur weil ich Jüdin bin, nicht aus Liebe" (VI 728), "*You are prepared to marry me just because I am Jewish—not for love*" (116). Max protests, urges her to reconsider. In 1938, however, they dissolve their engagement and separate. Käte moves to Basel to continue her studies; Max stays in Zurich to complete his architectural training. Not once in their five-year relationship, Max realizes, did it ever occur to him to be unfaithful to Käte. She was the first woman with whom he had a prolonged relationship. Max is still certain that she was the one who broke the engagement and moved away. Years later she admits she moved only to recover from the pain of separating from Max (Hage 28).

Max and Käte seem to have loved each other; circumstances beyond their control and ability to deal with at the time led to their separation. Earlier in their relationship, however, a serious strain was already noticeable. Käte wanted to have a child. This alarmed Max, as he was not sure he was mature enough to be a father. Besides, at that time he thought of himself as a failure in one profession (journalism) and was only then preparing himself to enter another (architecture); he did not feel able yet to support a wife and child. Käte interpreted the issue differently: Did he not want a child because she was Jewish, she asked? Max was confused; he did not know what he wanted, did not know what to think. When finally, in 1938, he insisted that they marry, Käte was convinced that, although the source of his insistence was a genuine concern for her safety, it was not love. Hence their separation.

Years later, Max's elder daughter meets and falls in love with Käte's eldest son. They do not marry, to Max's regret—perhaps because their parents once were lovers, Max muses, as he waits for Lynn by the ocean at Montauk (VI 652).

Max admits he still thinks of Käte. His memory of her comes alive at odd moments: at the Friedrichstraße railroad station in Berlin, for example, when he has to show his passport to the East German officials and watches the expression on their faces as they size him up. The situation reminds him of an experience in 1937 at the Basel railroad station, where a Nazi official inspected his papers. "Journalist?" he asked, and when Max nodded with youthful pride in his profession, the official added: "And I suppose this Jewess gives you all the atrocity stories" (VI 727/114).

The unexpiated guilt Max still carries with him from his relationship with Käte is related to his behavior when, during that frightening period in Europe, he found himself in love with a young Jewish woman. Later he was unable to explain his behavior to himself, but he believes it contributed significantly to ending the relationship.

CONSTANZE: THE MOTHER OF HIS CHILDREN

Max and Constanze meet in 1941. He now has a "real" profession: he is an architect. Constanze is an architect, too; they work together for the same firm. The first assignment for either of them is to design and build a house. They do it together (II 588).

In 1942 Max wins the design competition for a municipal swimming pool, a large project that establishes his professional reputation and adds three thousand Swiss francs to his bank account. Max and Constanze are now able to marry (II 588; VI 732-33). Max admits that he loved Constanze. So often in Frisch novels, however, one does not learn how the women loved by the protagonists feel about the men; Constanze is no exception. Her parents, wealthy aristocrats, give their daughter an appropriately lavish wedding and an advance of 120,000 Swiss francs on her inheritance. Max, whose background is much more humble, is nevertheless adamant about providing for his family himself. They move into a small but comfortable three-room ground-floor apartment.

Max's income is small: 350 Swiss francs a month to start with, eventually 500 Swiss francs monthly. His financial accounts for the months of August and September 1943 show that Constanze and Max live frugally: going out one evening a month is all they can afford. Even at that, however, their monthly expenses far exceed their monthly income during the two months recorded (VI 732). Fortunately, the money from Max's design award covers the deficit. He abhors using other people's money, even when it is his wife's and is offered willingly. He dreads going into debt even more. When his father died, he left the family a debt that was eventually paid off by Max's brother.

Later that year Max opens his own architectural office in an old house that belongs to an aunt: two rooms, rent-free. Toward the end of the year Max begins to write again, resuming a career he had thought ended in failure several years earlier. His first novel is published in 1943 (II 588). That year their first child, Ursula, is born; a year later a boy, Hans Peter, arrives, and in 1949 their third child, Charlotte, is born (VI 665-69; II 589; Hage 34,40,51). Max admits frankly in *Montauk*:

Als jüngerer Mann habe ich mir Kinder nicht eigentlich gewünscht; die schlichte Nachricht, daß ein Kind gezeugt worden ist, hat mich gefreut: der Frau zuliebe. (VI 689)

As a [younger] man I did not really desire children; the simple news that a child had been conceived gladdened me for the woman's sake. (73)

That attitude changed in later years, Max adds. Twice, he was present at the birth of his children, at his wife's request. When he mentions it briefly, twice, in *Montauk*, he leaves the vague impression that he would have preferred not to have been there (VI 669,688).

During the first few years of his marriage to Constanze, Max is involved in energetically pursuing two careers: that of a young architect whose reputation is growing and who earns the money to pay the bills; and that of a writer who writes his first play in five weeks, his second in three, and sees both performed at the municipal theater in Zurich.

After trying for twelve years to meet the demands of both careers, Max decides in favor of his first love, writing. This change of profession, however, also forces changes in Max's personal life. For logical reasons he had entered a conventional profession; his father had been an architect, too, so Max's choice was not difficult. He had also married "conventionally", choosing a woman who shared his professional interest and was willing to accept his pursuing a second career. When Max actually abandons architecture for writing and a lifestyle different from an eight-to-five working day, however, the marriage is soon in trouble. Eventually he has to send his father-in-law a letter that is painful for him to write, informing him that his and Constanze's marriage has failed. How Constanze feels about the breakup of the marriage and what its actual cause is Max discloses only indirectly in *Montauk* in describing a woman

die sich ihre zehn Finger am Verputz in der Toilette blutig gekratzt hat, nachdem ich meinen Ehebruch gestanden habe. (VI 702) who scratched all her ten fingers bloody on the walls of the lavatory after I had told her of my adultery. (87)

Writing his father-in-law of the failed marriage may have been torture for Max; for Constanze, it seems, the breakup was devastating.

Max's comments about Constanze when they meet accidentally at social functions during the years after their separation make clear that she considers herself the wronged party. He describes Constanze's face as "für immer ein Gesicht voll betroffener Unschuld" (VI 690), *"forever a face of dismayed innocence"* (74-75). He is filled with respect for her, he admits, and with surprise that he is the father of her children.

Frisch dealt creatively with the conflict that Max faces during his first marriage—that of being pulled in two directions—in his early fable *Bin oder Die Reise nach Peking (Bin or The Journey to Peking)* (1945). Kilian, the protagonist of that poetic story, is also an architect. When he feels too confined and restless with job, wife, and child, he sets off on an imaginary journey to Peking, the symbol for the happiness and fulfillment possible in life. Kilian learns, however, that his chosen destination can never be reached, because "our life is short and Peking so far away" (I 649). In this gentle story Kilian expresses an unfulfilled longing to experience "the real life" now, soon, before his life slips past him. It seems always just out of reach; he has already lived half a lifetime and has not yet met his expectations.

Although Max, unlike Kilian, does not have an alter ego, a *Bin*, the similarities between the two are obvious. In spite of his success as an architect, Max shares with Kilian a certain dissatisfaction with his professional achievements, a boredom even, born of the routine of daily professional and married life. Kilian's situation matches that of Max when he observes:

Mag sein, man ist ein Herr geworden.
   Manchmal geschah es, daß ich Bin einfach wieder vergessen hatte, wochenlang, vielleicht auch jahrelang. Wer könnte es wissen, da er die Zeit nicht wirklich lebt? Man

stellt seinen Wecker, man wäscht sich, man schneidet die Fingernägel, man arbeitet, man ißt, man verdient. Es gibt zu vieles, was man immerfort muß, immerfort sollte. . . (I 624)

It's possible one has become a gentleman.
Sometimes it happened that I simply forgot Bin again, for weeks, perhaps even for years. Who could know, since he does not really exist in time? One sets one's alarm clock, one bathes, one trims one's fingernails, one works, one eats, one earns a living. There is too much one always must do, always should do. . .

Routine, Kilian and Max discover, can destroy the pleasure and excitement of any experience; routine may diminish the quality and freshness of each moment, the uniqueness of every new encounter with others, even with oneself.

Max is particularly vulnerable. Early in *Montauk* he confesses: "My greatest fear: Repetition" (VI 628/10). But he realizes that to follow one's yearning for the excitement of a life that is new at every moment without balancing it with the steady routine of daily activities, personal and professional, would result in instability. Kilian, in the end, returns contented to his wife and child. For Max, the conflict leads eventually to separation from his family.

During the early days of his marriage to Constanze, Max has an experience involving a childhood sweetheart that he cannot forget. His behavior puzzles him. The woman, Therese Haller, lives in the apartment above Max and Constanze. She and Max went to school together, and she was his first love. Max and his school friends could find no better way of expressing their affection for this girl than to catch her and pull her blond pigtails. One time, Max remembers, when she was about fourteen, she kissed him on the lips while they were on a school outing. Now, Max learns, she is completely paralyzed, as a result of an injury in childbirth.

Constanze and Frau Haller have become friends, but Max has been strangely reluctant to accept her invitation to stop by. A domestic accident eventually precipitates their meeting. Constanze, pregnant with their second child, is cooking during a thunderstorm when the stove is struck by lightning. In shock, she grabs Ursula, their firstborn, and races to Frau Haller's apartment. Max finds her there after he returns home from work and sees their apartment door standing wide open, an empty, red-hot pan on the electric stove, and no one there.

Constanze is badly frightened by the experience, but she suffers no physical harm, as her doctor later verifies. She has recovered from her shock and is enjoying the company of the paralyzed woman and her housekeeper when Max arrives. For months he has avoided meeting Frau Haller, and now he feels extremely uncomfortable in her presence. To speak to her in a familiar tone is awkward; a more formal one seems more appropriate to Max. He leaves the apartment with his family as soon as he can without appearing rude. He never visits Frau Haller again, although he vaguely promises to do so.

Max never explains whether it was his own feeling of helplessness in the presence of his former friend, the paralyzed Thesy Haller, or another emotion that made him avoid visiting her before the accident, leave her apartment as quickly as possible after he could no longer avoid a meeting, and never see her again during the ten subsequent years he lived in the same house. The guilt of this omission seems to trouble Max as much as the guilt he feels from abandoning his children and Constanze. Even thirty years later Max cannot let the memory go and recalls vividly the details of his onetime visit to Frau Haller's apartment (VI 665-69).

Max's guilt, especially about his children, weighs heavily on him, as this comment shows:

> Was ein Vater, indem er die Familie verlassen hat, seelisch seinen Kindern schuldig geblieben ist, läßt sich nicht wettmachen mit Geld. (VI 664)
>
> *When a father leaves home, what he deprives his children of spiritually cannot be made good with money.* (47)

This guilt does not diminish over time, nor can the failure of a marriage ever be explained to a child. Max observes:

MONTAUK 283

Ich leugne nicht meine Schuld; sie ist mit langen Briefen, die der erwachsenen Tochter meine damalige Scheidung erklären, nicht zu tilgen. (VI 652)

I do not deny that the fault was mine, not to be wiped out with letters to my grown-up daughter explaining why, years before, I had got a divorce. (35)

Then Max adds, cryptically: "Sie wird gebraucht, unsere Schuld, sie rechtfertigt viel im Leben anderer" (VI 652), *"Our guilt has its uses. It justifies much in the lives of others"* (35).
Max and Constanze's marriage was not a bad marriage. Unfortunately, the life they envisioned for themselves when they entered the marriage just did not materialize. Gradually, Max drifted away from both his family and his "real" profession to embrace anew, this time wholeheartedly, the profession and life of a writer. He and Constanze separate in 1955; they divorce four years later, after thirteen years of marriage (VI 734; Hage 42-44,101,135). As Max, the writer, might put it: an ordinary story.

INGEBORG: THE FELLOW WRITER

During a visit to Hamburg in 1958, where he has some business at a radio station, Max hears the latest radio play, "Der gute Gott von Manhattan" (*"The Good God of Manhattan"*), written by a colleague, Ingeborg. He has never met her, but he likes her new play so much that he writes to her spontaneously. He tells her he likes the play, but goes on to say much more: how strongly he agrees that the depiction of men through the eyes of a woman, which she does in her play, is needed; that the need is also great for women to portray other women; and how correct she is to do what she is doing. Her response is brief, and it puzzles him: On her way to Paris she will travel via Zurich, and they can talk.

Their first meeting actually takes place not in Zurich but in Paris, some time later. One of Max's plays is having its premiere, and Ingeborg has come to see it. When they meet in a café before the performance, Max, illogically, persuades her not to attend the play but to join him for dinner instead. Ingeborg, confused at first, becomes gradually intrigued and is pleased by Max's genuine interest in her. He does not seem to know anything personal about her. She likes that and eventually accepts his unorthodox dinner invitation.

On that evening in Paris Max begins a difficult and stormy relationship with a highly intelligent, verbal, sensitive, and creative woman: Ingeborg, a fiercely independent Austrian, fifteen years his junior, and a colleague as successful as he. Their relationship is to last four years. Max is captivated by her. He frankly admits: "In ihrer Nähe gibt es nur sie, in ihrer Nähe beginnt der Wahn" (VI 711), *"Near her I could see only her, but near her, I knew, madness began"* (97).[5]

Max tries to escape the power this woman seems to hold over him: he flees from Paris back to Zurich. Shortly thereafter Ingeborg, distraught, arrives in Zurich. There, as lovers, they spend a happy week together. Then they decide not to see each other again. This is the first of many separations; it lasts exactly four weeks and ends in Naples. That time they stay together for seven months, until Max develops hepatitis and is hospitalized.

Max is not used to hospitals and to the effects of illness. He is afraid he will never recover from his illness and therefore sends Ingeborg away, back to Rome where she was living when they met. Max's recovery is slow, but once he knows he will get well again, begins to regain his strength and to think clearly again, he realizes he does not want to live without Ingeborg. The letters he writes to her remain unanswered, however, and his attempts to reach her by phone are unsuccessful—for an entire day and a long night. Eventually he does reach Ingeborg, and they agree to an experiment: to try living in the same city (Zurich) in separate apartments.

The arrangement is less than satisfactory for Max. Six months after his divorce from Constanze has become final, while on a trip through Italy, he writes Ingeborg a long letter from Siena in which he proposes marriage. Like Svoboda in *Mein Name sei Gantenbein*, who waits for Lila to decide about their future (V 239-42), Max calls anxiously at the post office of every city he visits on his trip, hoping to find an answer from Ingeborg waiting for him (VI 713). Her response is silence.

When he returns to Zurich Max learns that his letter arrived. Ingeborg, however, wants to know what he means by proposing marriage—six months after the belated dissolution of his first one.[6] If Max answers her question, he does not include the answer in *Montauk*. They continue to live in separate apartments.

That fall, Max accompanies Ingeborg on the first of her many trips to Frankfurt, where she delivers a series of lectures. In a way, both pursue their own lives from now on, in large measure independent of each other. Eventually they move to Rome and share an apartment there, but their relationship continues to be difficult. Ingeborg travels a good deal and is sometimes away from the city for weeks. As a consequence, each develops an individual circle of activities and friends and individual domains. Ingeborg, who has several, keeps each strictly separate. Being the fiercely independent person she is, she insists that Max stay out of them.

Three years later, the once passionate relationship between Max and Ingeborg has cooled substantially. During that summer Max meets and falls in love with another woman, Marianne, thirteen years younger than Ingeborg. The two women know each other slightly; Max reports that Ingeborg once talked to Marianne, then still a student, like a "grande dame" (VI 718). Max and Ingeborg's relationship effectively ends that year, although they meet twice more, once in Zurich, the other time in Rome. Sadly, Max observes: "Das Ende haben wir nicht gut bestanden, beide nicht" (VI 717), "*We did not show up well at the end, either of us*" (103).

The reasons their relationship fails are difficult to establish clearly, although Max's report suggests that his jealousy and her secrecy are among them. Primary, however, are two: Max's obsessive emotional dependence on Ingeborg and her fierce independence.

An incident that takes place two months after their first meeting in Paris illustrates Max's troubled awareness of his deepening emotional dependence on Ingeborg. The scene is an Italian coastal road at dawn. Max is walking along it at a quick pace, as if he were trying to escape. For the last hour he has apparently been trying to make a decision, as he sat on the pier in front of a house in which Ingeborg is still asleep. Now and then he looked up at the house, as if hoping the door would open and Ingeborg would come out, looking for him.

Then, ostensibly to ward off the morning chill, as he says, Max walks rapidly down the road to the nearby village. Its stores and cafés are still closed. Not even the market shows any signs of life yet. At the railroad station Max studies the train schedule, checks how much money he has in his pockets, and tries to decide: Should he leave Ingeborg *now*, or should he return to her? Torn between two equally plausible courses of action—to leave, commanded by reason, and to stay, commanded by love—Max in self-mockery throws a coin into the air, leaving the decision to chance. Once before, in his relationship with Käte, when he no longer knew what to do, he used the same diversion (VI 728). Now, as then, the coin toss does not determine the outcome. Two months earlier Max had left Paris to escape the power and "magic spell" Ingeborg's presence seemed to cast over him; this time he decides to stay.

Max's love for Ingeborg is enslaving, not liberating. She, her presence, has an almost hypnotic effect on him. Max recognizes that his relationship with Ingeborg contains for him an element of *Hörigkeit* (bondage). He had a similar experience once before in his life, in his relationship with W., a schoolmate who became his friend and later his benefactor. Max reviews this relationship at length in *Montauk* (VI 636-49); it shows that he has a tendency to become entrapped by people whose personality, character, intellect, and knowledge he admires greatly.

W., unlike Max the son of wealthy parents, opens doors to the worlds of philosophy, music, and painting. An intellectual, W. scorns all superficiality; in his presence Max always feels somewhat inadequate, inferior. Yet he feels pulled, as if by a magical force, to seek the company of his friend time and again. In his relationship with Ingeborg, Max experiences a similar phenomenon; psychologists, not Max, may be able to explain it.[7]

When Ingeborg and W. meet one day, Max does not participate in their conversation, "not wishing to disturb them with my half-knowledge" (VI 648/31). W., who does not know at the time that Ingeborg has written a dissertation on Wittgenstein, is surprised and impressed by her knowledge of philosophy. However, the two most extraordinary people in Max's life do not get along well with each other, Max comments. Perhaps they are too much alike: strong, independent, and somewhat difficult to get to know, even by close friends. Max often feels his relationship with W., to whom he owes much, is confining. It disturbs him more and more as he grows older. Any attempt to break out of it proves to be awkward and as ineffective as his attempts to break out of his relationship with Ingeborg, years later. Even when Max has a brief affair with another woman while he and Ingeborg are living in separate apartments in Zurich, thus in effect betraying Ingeborg, Max cannot free himself from the magic spell her presence casts over him. He craves it like an addict.

When Ingeborg is absent, Max is miserable. Jealousy plagues him, that "fear of comparisons" that is fueled by Ingeborg's independence and her tendency to be secretive about her activities and her associates. At times, overcome by the pain of his jealousy, Max tries to escape by drowning his troubles in alcohol. With embarrassment and shame he recalls one night in Rome when Ingeborg was once again out of town. That night, feeling jealous and lonely, Max got drunk and slept through a mild summer night on the floor of their apartment terrace, his face in his own vomit.

The madness that keeps Max spellbound is a vortex of conflicting emotions: love, jealousy, obsessiveness, dependency, vulnerability, and the fear of losing Ingeborg. He admits that his actions are sometimes foolish, like those of any besotted lover. One day he waits eagerly in his car, parked on the edge of a highway outside Rome, for Ingeborg's blue Volkswagen to appear so he can welcome her home from a trip. When she passes without recognizing him, he pursues her in his car like a police officer and frightens her by forcing her car to stop at the edge of the road. Another time, missing her desperately, Max drives all night without stopping from Rome to Zurich, once nearly driving off the road in thick fog. He arrives in the early morning hours, unannounced, and rouses Ingeborg from sleep. She is startled by his unexpected presence and afraid something terrible has happened. Nothing has; Max only needed to be with her.

Ingeborg's insistence on keeping separate the various spheres of her life is a primary source of strain in the relationship. She refuses to allow personal friends, and especially not her lover, to associate with her professional colleagues, and even keeps personal friends secret from each other. This behavior frequently upsets Max. On one occasion Peter Huchel, a writer who knows Max only by sight, stops to speak to Ingeborg in a restaurant, and Ingeborg talks to him for half an hour without ever introducing Max (VI 714). On the sole occasion when she permits Max to attend a meeting of *Gruppe 47*, an exclusive literary group she belongs to, she ignores him completely—he with whom she is living and who is as well known a writer as she—as if he were an unknown stranger. She allows him to go with her to Frankfurt for the first of her series of university lectures, but asks him to stay behind in Zurich when she goes to deliver the others. She does, however, let him accompany her to her home in Klagenfurt, Austria, and introduces him to her family.

Max recalls another incident in connection with the Frankfurt lectures. Ingeborg is returning to Zurich from one of them, and Max goes to the railroad station to meet her. When she sees him standing on the platform she suddenly stops in her tracks, her face showing complete confusion. Has she expected someone else? Or is her mind elsewhere, leaving her geographically disoriented and surprised to find herself in Zurich, Max's realm, instead of somewhere else? This phenomenon is familiar to people who travel frequently and work intensely while traveling. Max never learns, however, what startled Ingeborg.

Several of the incidents that particularly upset Max, he remembers, occurred while they were living together in Rome. He cannot help overhearing her telephone conversations and is tortured by those with unidentified persons that she never explains. Once she has a long telephone conversation with someone unknown whom she tells happily that she will be in London in a few days, never mentioning that she will be there with Max to attend a performance of one of his plays. Max does not say so, but the implication is clear, and his feelings are hurt. On another occasion she receives a telegram whose content obviously distresses her, but she never tells Max who sent it or what it says.

Behavior like this makes him feel angry, insecure, and jealous, as his actions demonstrate. Once, driven by suspicion and jealousy, he reads all Ingeborg's private correspondence.

Included are letters from a man; the two are considering marriage. When he asks Ingeborg about it she answers him honestly. She also tells him: "Wenn sich zwischen uns etwas ändert, so werde ich es dir sagen" (VI 716), *"If anything changes between us, I shall tell you"* (102). These words are almost identical to those that turn up in a letter from Lila to Svoboda in *Mein Name sei Gantenbein* (V 223). Max, like Svoboda, is not reassured.

Max continues to feel excluded from Ingeborg's life, even while he is sharing it intimately. When he visits her in Naples, she refuses to show him where she lives (with a man, he later learns), and insists they stay at a hotel.[8] A somewhat related experience occurs in Rome: as they are about to walk through one of its small streets, Ingeborg stops abruptly, puts the back of her hand to her forehead, and pleads: "No, please let's not go down that alley, please not!" (VI 714/101). The past and present are about to meet; Ingeborg needs to keep them separate.

This time Max understands and asks no questions; he observes:

Man vergibt sich mit seinen Geheimnissen. Das ist wahr. Eine Versammlung aller, die je in unser Leben hineingespielt haben . . . ist eine schreckliche Vorstellung. . . . (VI 714-15)

One compromises oneself through revealing one's secrets—that is true. A gathering of all the people who have played a role in one's life . . . that is a dreadful thought. (101)

Max's agony increases his longing for the beloved. When she is away, he yearns for her; when she is near, he suspects she might really be somewhere else, with someone else. He lives in a vicious cycle of conflicting feelings from which there seems no escape. Ingeborg's secretiveness, her unpredictability, and her need to be free—not accountable to him—alternately distress and delight him. This fierce independence of hers, Max admits, "was part of her radiance," a radiance he treasured (VI 715/102). But as time goes on these factors destroy their relationship that has lasted four years. Max is thrown out of it and into a different relationship, with Marianne. The year is 1962.

During the year following Max and Ingeborg's separation, they meet twice more, the first time in a clinic in Zurich that Ingeborg has entered. This news startles Max, who at the time is planning another trip to the United States. En route he stops in Zurich to visit her. Is she suffering from depression, a nervous breakdown? Max does not say so, only that he does not quite believe her to be physically ill, although Ingeborg looks pitiable. The doctor's prescription is diet, rest, and no visitors—especially not *him*. Max insists on visiting her. They walk for an hour in the woods, part of the medical regimen. Ingeborg hopes Max will want her to join him in the United States once he comes to his senses; that will speed her recovery. But he only promises to send her his address when he has one.

Max is surprised by all the flowers in Ingeborg's hospital room; probably from an admirer, he surmises. He feels no jealousy; Ingeborg's spell over him has been broken, he notes. Ingeborg's story explaining the flowers is fascinating: the sender is an old man whom she met years ago in Vienna; she does not disclose his name. Although they never talked together then, she and the man had understood each other silently, with a single glance. But Ingeborg fled from him, as if escaping fate. Now, by coincidence, she has met him again at this clinic. They recognized each other and went on a walk together. Every day he sends her flowers: thirty-five roses. The story seems mysterious; Max believes it.

Six months later, when Max returns to Rome, he and Ingeborg meet again in a café. There she admits that she sent the roses to herself every day to make Max jealous and, she hoped, to persuade him to send for her to join him abroad. Max never considered it. Their relationship was finished.

Ingeborg died ten years later in Rome as a result of burns suffered in a fire in her apartment, "der schrecklichsten aller Todesarten" (VI 682), *"the most terrible of all ways of dying"* (66), Max comments. During those ten years Max never talked with her again (VI 717). If he feels any guilt about that, he does not say so. He admits, however, that, looking back at the four years of his relationship with Ingeborg, "I can see, but not recognize myself" (VI 717/104). What he sees is perhaps the figure of the man who walked out of the post office in Siena years earlier "wie ein erwachter Traumwandler" (VI 713), *"like an awakened sleepwalker"* (99), after mailing his long letter proposing marriage to Ingeborg. Obviously Max loved Ingeborg deeply and suffered greatly in his relationship with her, as long as he was under her mysterious spell. Once he escaped it, the pain and suffering, it seems, became Ingeborg's. A sad ending to an unusual and difficult relationship between two intelligent, sensitive, and creative people.

MARIANNE: THE EDITOR

Max meets Marianne in 1962. He recalls, in a brief scene in *Montauk* entitled "Deja Vu" (VI 684), a specific September day when they were together at the Mediterranean shore. The day is special for Max. Was it the day they became lovers? Max does not say.

That the relationship is special, however, Max indicates immediately: of the five women in *Montauk*, Marianne is the only one he addresses directly, using the personal pronoun "du" (you). The effect is startling. The use of the familiar form and direct address conveys vividly their intimacy and the anguish and the closeness Max still feels a year after he and Marianne have separated. The effect is intensified when sections about Marianne are juxtaposed with those about Lynn in which Max creates a deliberate distance between the partners by referring to himself in the third person.

Marianne is still a student when they meet, studying Romanistic and Germanistic (VI 686).[9] She is twenty-three years old, thus twenty-eight years younger than Max. At Montauk, Max remembers especially the way she wore her hair that day: piled high on top of her head, leaving her ears uncovered and her neck bare and youthful. When she removes a clasp, her black hair cascades onto her shoulders. An aesthetically pleasing, sensual image, as Max describes it.

Marianne joins Max in the United States. During a side trip to Mexico, he asks her to live with him. She hesitates, but when they return to Europe she at least moves to Rome, where Max is presently living. After a summer living in separate quarters, they move into an apartment together (VI 686). Max, conscious of his age, hopes they will be able to share two, perhaps three years of their lives together. He comments: "Ich traue mir den Mut zu, Einsicht zu haben, wenn ich zu alt geworden bin für sie" (VI 686), *"I believe I have the courage to know when I [have] become too old for her"* (70). Unlike another Frisch protagonist, Walter Faber, who found himself in a similar situation, Max indicates clearly here that he is fully aware of transient time and that his relationship with Marianne has not only a present but a *limited* future as well. He accepts that restriction from the outset—so it seems—and their relationship lasts nearly eleven years.[10]

Max remembers his delight in setting up housekeeping with Marianne in Berlin, exploring the city with her, making new friends and meeting old ones again. Below the threshhold of his pleasure, however, lies a somewhat strained relationship. The cause may be that Max is overly sensitive to their difference in age, although he gives no indication that this ever bothered Marianne. When they visit a shop run by two students in which Marianne has found chairs they need for their Berlin apartment at a reasonable price, she is delighted not only with the chairs but also with the shop and its bearded owners. As Max inspects the chairs she turns away from him, which makes him feel like a stranger, merely another customer who has nothing to do with the chairs, *her* chairs, even though the store owners treat them as a couple. Whatever the basic problem in their relationship was, Max shows his awareness of it when he comments: "Wenn Du fröhlich bist, vergesse ich für eine Weile wieder Dein Unglück mit mir . . ." (VI 672), *"When you are cheerful I forget for a while your [misfortune] with me . . ."* (56).

Max's memories of their second winter and spring in Berlin include working days filled with books for both of them; an occasional party at home in the company of good friends, and some evenings of dancing; vacations in London and Brittany; the sound of Marianne's bare feet as she walks across the parquet floor through their uncluttered apartment, coming to his study to bid him a good morning.

In their third year together, Max and Marianne buy and remodel a house in Berzona, in the Tessin; they move into it in 1965. This is to be their permanent home, which they furnish together with great care and pleasure; one of their favorite spots is a square granite table in the garden. Three years later, in 1968, Max and Marianne marry, he for the second time, she for the first.

Their relationship before and during the first year of their marriage is, on balance, happy and productive, though not without difficulties. Max is not allowed to write about those happy years, or their marriage, or the problems that gradually intensified. Marianne makes that clear when she tells him: "Ich habe nicht mit dir gelebt als literarisches Material, ich verbiete es, daß du über mich schreibst" (VI 686),[11] "*I have not been living with you to provide literary material. I forbid you to write about me*" (70). Thus Max can only summarize: six years without quarrels, without jealousy, without attrition. They travel together to Prague, Warsaw, Avignon, Paris, Leningrad, Odessa, Venice, London, Jerusalem; they vacation in Greece and Brittany; and they continue to enjoy their house. However, like all the other protagonists of Frisch's novels, Max can narrate only his own memories, from his point of view.

Less than two years after their wedding, while they are temporarily living in New York, Marianne falls in love with another man. He is a mutual friend, and is also married. Marianne believes Max knows about the affair, but he seems to be blind to it. He suggests and plans trips for them, but she keeps finding reasons not to go with him. When he accepts an invitation to lecture in Austin, Texas, he particularly wants Marianne to come along so he can show her different parts of America, Texas and New Orleans. But Marianne stays in New York, using a recurring fear of flying as her excuse. However, after they spend the next summer in Europe, she is so eager to return to New York that she flies back alone, a month before he can join her. Max knows that being in New York is important to Marianne's work as an editor, and that he cannot help her as much as he would like because his English is still fairly limited. Friends in New York, however, are glad to work with her.

His relationship with Ingeborg gave Max a painful familiarity with jealousy. He is determined to remain reasonable and calm this time, to avoid that reaction. Thus, like Gantenbein, he pretends to be blind to Marianne's small daily deceptions. When she leaves the apartment and returns hours later, Max does not ask where she is going or where she has been. He knows she loves him. Why, then, should he be concerned? He also loves her, which bolsters his determination not to spy on her, although the temptation arises periodically. He reasons that if Marianne has really found a new love, she and her lover, his friend, will eventually tell him. Meanwhile, he looks the friend squarely in the eye and allows his suspicions to disappear gradually. He does not acknowledge the secrets he and Marianne keep from each other; keeping silent about them reduces their need to lie to each other. Marianne, however, believes that Max does not want to confront her with his suspicions because he wants to avoid facing the truth.

Max readily acknowledges his failings. One is his oversensitivity when his partner disagrees with him—"the reverse side of self-accusation, which is itself a reverse side of self-righteousness," Max observes (VI 723/109). Another disturbing trait is his occasional tendency to be seized by an all-consuming rage, similar to the fury that beset Gantenbein and Svoboda (*Mein Name sei Gantenbein*, V 165-66,230/157-58,218-19) and Rolf and Stiller (*Stiller*, III 497-99,623/128-29,239-40). Such an attack can be set off by any triviality, is always incomprehensible, and is very unpleasant for the partner. She is in no physical danger, Max points out, although his speech at those times has a lethal quality. During an attack he does not really converse, but delivers a monologue about issues that at the moment he sees clearly. He speaks the truth as he perceives it at the time, and feels absolutely compelled to express it.

When an attack overcomes him, Max recognizes, his partner has little chance to stop him: all Max asks is that she understand what he is unable to put into words and accept it. A paradox, and Max is aware of it: at its root is man's inability to communicate effectively with another human being. As Max comments: "At such moments I would give my life to be able to make myself for once [understood]—nothing more than that" (VI 635/17). In the grip of an attack, Max admits, he is neither reasonable nor is he able to listen to reason. All he is interested in is the truth—as *he* sees it. Such sessions never clarify anything, Max observes. In time they undermine the relationship, as events show.

During the second winter in New York, Max is obviously not happy with his work, his life, or himself. Marianne's affair grows more intense and more complicated. Her lover's young wife has become difficult, so the two couples can no longer meet as a quartet as they used to. In addition, Max is less and less able to persuade Marianne of anything, on any topic. By now she knows that he wants to be ignorant of the true state of their marriage; how can she then believe he is right about anything else, Max wonders. He becomes increasingly unsure of himself—as a writer, as a thinker, but mainly as a man. He now lacks the courage that, eight years ago, he thought he would have "to know when I [have] become too old for her" (VI 686/70).

As Marianne spends less time with Max, he drinks more to escape his loneliness. Max reports a pathetic incident from that period: he stands at the window of their apartment, watching longingly for Marianne's return, hoping she will not be late, hoping he can subdue his suspicions once more. He sees a brown hat in the distance on the street; he feels joyous, then deeply disappointed as the hat and its wearer go off in another direction. On another occasion, when Marianne returns after midnight, she finds Max lying on the carpet, drunk, his arms spread wide and proclaiming blissfully: "[I feel the curvature of the earth] . . . I am embracing the earth" (VI 674/57-58). Marianne does not reproach him, then or later. She takes a bedspread and covers him carefully so he will not catch cold, then lets him spend the rest of the night sleeping on the floor. His ecstacy has been respected, Max observes, and she, finding her husband in this incoherent state, is spared an explanation of where she has been so late.

Two years later, at Montauk, Max insists that he did not know then about Marianne's affair. But other people did. One of them is Jörg, a fellow Swiss and a trusted friend, with whom Max has shared many hours of intimate conversation over the years. Marianne took Jörg into her confidence, Max learns later; thus Jörg knew of her affair, her anguish, and her difficulties with Max. He even kept a bundle of love letters from America for her at his home when asked to. When Max hears this, he feels hurt and jealous, and he is shocked that, while his own vanity compelled him to deceive himself about Marianne's affair, it was no secret to those who knew them both.

Sailing back to Europe at the end of that winter in New York, Max and Marianne are two lonely, troubled people. Max entertains himself for hours playing solitaire chess; Marianne spends her time alone, either lying in a deck chair covered with blankets or sitting in the bar when the wind on deck is too strong. Max wonders: "Was machen wir zusammen falsch?" (VI 725), "What are we doing wrong together?" (112).

Back in Europe, Max's behavior becomes increasingly difficult. On a trip through France with a good friend, Max acts deliberately provocative and insulting. After lunch one day, during which he has been overly sensitive to the friend's courtesy toward Marianne and insensitive to Marianne's silent appeals to him to stop acting peculiar, Max challenges the friend by asking "if he can say why he uses me as his [butler]" (VI 722/109). And back in Berlin, Max is just as eccentric in front of guests in their apartment: having failed to persuade anyone of his side in a discussion, not even himself, he goes to the kitchen and returns with a garbage pail on his head, encouraging his wife and friends: "Keep on talking—don't mind me" (VI 681/65).

In these escapades Max, becoming increasingly insecure, vents his cumulative agitation and frustration on those around him. One day, on their way home from a friend's house, Marianne has had enough and explodes:

> Wenn du die Kinder unserer besten Freunde und ihren kleinen Hund nicht mehr verträgst, so können wir gleich in ein Altersheim einziehen! (VI 727)

> *If you can no longer put up with our best friends' children and their little dog, we might as well go into an old people's home right away. (114)*

At the time, they are driving through Berlin with Max behind the wheel; he runs a red light and drives across the Bundesallee, as he recalls somewhat sheepishly.

Finally, in 1973, while they sit at their favorite spot, the granite table in the garden at Berzona, Marianne tells Max about her affair with the mutual friend in New York. This is the first time, apparently, that the two have looked openly at their troubled marriage and talked constructively about their problems. Without obvious anger, Marianne voices a bitter accusation that Max never forgets: during the ten years of their relationship, he has done nothing to help her develop her potentialities. Max is surprised; it takes him a whole year, he admits, to accept the truth of her accusation. He has adored Marianne, has lavished attention on her. But he now realizes that such behavior is the easiest and the worst way to treat a woman. "I have been acting . . . as if I were . . . at least Adam, from whose rib Woman was made: COME, FOLLOW, AND I WILL LEAD!" (VI 679/63). Max's vice, he states clearly, is male chauvinism. In practicing it he resembles other Frisch characters, like Rolf in *Stiller* or Svoboda in *Mein Name sei Gantenbein*: each of them, more by his attitude than his actions, unintentionally stifles the growth of the woman he loves and thus curtails the full development of her abilities and talents. "What else," Max asks rhetorically, ". . . could have made a sensible woman believe that the development of her potentialities was a matter for her husband—for men at all?" (VI 679/63).

Soon after that conversation, Max and Marianne decide to separate. It was a difficult decision. Max's recollections at Montauk make clear that they cared and still care deeply for each other. They miss each other, as is evident from the tearful long-distance telephone call Max mentions early in the novel (VI 628) and his silent eulogy of Marianne (VI 741) in response to Lynn's question, while she sews a mismatched button onto his jacket, as to whether another unmatched, reddish button was sewn on by his wife. Watching Max move silently in her kitchenette, not answering her, Lynn states what Max already knows: "You love her" (VI 741/129).

Nevertheless, Max's extreme intolerance of others disagreeing with him and his insecurity as an artist and as a man, which cause him to feel that others do not take him seriously enough, and his self-confessed chauvinism are the main reasons why he and Marianne found living together impossible. They remain friends, although Marianne lives in Berlin and Max in Berzona. One of the last gifts Max looks for before he leaves New York to return to Europe is a brown campaign hat, possibly a present for Marianne, to replace the worn and rain-stained Texas hat she has been wearing.

LYNN: UNDINE AND NURSE

Max and Lynn meet for the first time in his New York hotel room while a newspaper reporter is interviewing him. Max first mistakes her for a photographer, then realizes that she must be the person his publisher has assigned to help him in New York. Lynn accidentally leaves her cigarette lighter behind when she and the reporter leave; Max gives it back to her two weeks later when she again comes to his room.

Lynn is the kind of intelligent and independent modern woman Max has always felt attracted to. She is also rather pretty: slender, about as tall as Max; her long red hair, when worn loose, reaches to her hips; her eyes are the color of bright slate under water. She wears glasses, which Max believes are not becoming to her, but she needs them, as she points out when he removes them to look directly into her eyes. Her lips are thin, often mocking, Max finds.

As he works with her, Max is impressed by this attractive, competent woman and her direct manner. He is tempted, one day, to call her on some professional pretense, just to be with her. Perhaps they can have dinner together, he muses, but then feels awkward and observes: "Sowie eine Frau mir gefällt, komme ich mir jetzt als Zumutung vor" (VI 625), *"Now, whenever a woman attracts me, I feel presumptuous"* (7).

"Now" is the key word in this observation. Since his recent separation from Marianne, Max has become even more self-conscious about his age. He will soon be sixty-three; Lynn is only thirty-one, the same age he was when he married Constanze and the age of his eldest daughter, Ursula, now. Instead of dinner, Lynn and Max have lunch together one day at Sweet's, Max's favorite seafood restaurant in New York. It is a business lunch, Lynn believes, and insists she should pay for it; it is a private lunch, Max knows, and pays for the lunch himself, over Lynn's protest.

After completing the first part of his lecture tour, Max returns to New York for the weekend. Lynn invites him to her apartment for a home-cooked meal, partly because he paid for their lunch at Sweet's and partly because she suspects he has probably eaten most of his meals in restaurants since arriving in New York three weeks earlier.

During the three weeks since they met, Max has learned quite a bit about Lynn. He knows that she was born in Florida and that, according to her, her upbringing was puritanical. She went to college in California, where she won competitions as a javelin thrower. She was married briefly to an Australian and lived in Sydney for a while, where she rode horses. During the summer she plans to travel to Greece with her parents—a guided tour, Max adds. Some day Lynn wants to marry again, perhaps have a child. Her current job with the publisher is interesting but also hectic, demanding, and insecure. If the publisher is no longer satisfied with her work or no longer needs her services for any number of internal reasons, she can be let go from one week to the next. Lynn accepts these working conditions as a matter of course, Max comments, but to him, accustomed to European employment conditions, they seem harsh. When, during a subsequent trip to New York, Max asks about Lynn at the publisher's—contrary to the agreement they made not to stay in touch—he is told she no longer works there.

Lynn knows a lot about dolphins, a lot more than he does, Max admits. Although dolphins have the intelligence of humans, Lynn informs him, their lack of arms and hands has rendered them unable to conquer the world; but neither do they destroy the world, Lynn observes. Dolphins never founded a nation, she comments, and yet they appear to be happy. Lynn has talked with the dolphins; she says she does not want a child on land.[12] "Undine and a little bit of nurse," Max muses, looking at her thoughtfully (VI 635); sometimes Lynn is one, sometimes the other[13] (VI 683). As a lover, she is Undine; as his guardian on behalf of the publisher, and when she cooks for him or sews on a missing button, she is nurse.

In *Mein Name sei Gantenbein* the protagonist-narrator recounts an episode when he, no longer a young man, stands on a Roman burial mound with a woman much younger than he (V 137-39). The two are strongly attracted to each other, yet the man's feelings are ambivalent: on the one hand, he thinks of her as a child; on the other, when he looks into her eyes, he knows she is not. "What [does] one do with a daydream?" he asks her (V 138/*Gantenbein* 132). "Take it!" she replies, but the narrator does not. Weeks later, he throws away a pinecone he has kept as a memento of that experience—another missed opportunity to act, to experience life, the present moment, in the company of a woman. "She could be my daughter," the narrator comments about his companion, a young woman with reddish hair (V 137/*Gantenbein* 129).

Max feels similarly ambivalent about Lynn as he watches her prepare dinner in her tiny kitchen during his first visit there. Sensually stimulated by her presence, he resolves that he will not kiss her, will not touch her hips; but before he leaves he grasps his daydream. After dinner he does kiss Lynn, and they eventually make love.

Before Max returns to Europe, he and Lynn spend a peaceful weekend at Montauk, one filled with love and, for Max, many memories. His description of the weekend weaves in and out of his report; it creates an intricate pattern of recollections from the distant and not-so-distant past and the extended present he shares with Lynn.

It was Lynn who casually mentioned, as they sat together in Central Park on a beautiful Sunday, that if they could have driven out of the city (she had to work that day), she knows just the place they could have gone: Montauk Beach, out on the tip of Long Island. She has been there once on a company outing. Max likes the idea and suggests they rent a car and go the following weekend.

Lynn's presence reawakens in Max a strong sense of immediacy, of experiencing the present moment, that has become rare for him, the aging writer, particularly in his encounters with people and literature, he admits. Lynn's presence also reawakens Max's memories and heightens his physical sensations, just as the rays of the warm spring sun falling on the carpet of his hotel room heighten his sensation of the present moment and stir alive his sensual memories of spring, of youth and vitality, of hope and promise, culminating in Max's sudden burst into poetry as he quotes two lines from Mörike's ecstatic love poem, "Er ist's," *"It's He"* (VI 627-28).

Max's detailed description of Lynn at the start of *Montauk*, as they walk, she in front of him, along a narrow, overgrown path in search of an ocean view they never find, illustrates his acute sensual awareness of her. At the same time Frisch suggests, subtly, through obvious similarities in the appearances of Lynn and of Sabeth in *Homo faber*, that Max is slightly uncomfortable about his relationship with a woman so much younger than he.[14] The incest theme of *Homo faber* reechoes gently in *Montauk*, as Max realizes that one of his daughters is exactly Lynn's age. In addition, he shows his self-consciousness about the age discrepancy when he observes that strangers who see them together might think of them either as a couple or as father and daughter.[15]

Max is not in love with Lynn, he points out (VI 681), at least not the intense kind of love he felt for Ingeborg and Marianne. He genuinely enjoys her presence; her uncomplicated, matter-of-fact manner delights him. He enjoys her hearty way of eating, with the appetite of slender people; her laughter, polite in public, a bit shrill and surprised in private; the way she moves, striding confidently along a crowded sidewalk in Manhattan, skipping down the wooden steps of their Montauk hotel, walking along an overgrown path, jogging on the beach; and the way she sits quietly next to him in the car, in an isolated beach chair, or on the balcony of their room. Their physical relationship is as relaxed, unpressured, and accepting as their friendship. Max realizes that Lynn has not had a great deal of experience with men, but she is not timid. Sexuality enlarges the dimensions of their relationship but does not change its character. Although Lynn cannot make love the first night they are intimate with each other, and Max is impotent on their last night together, these occurrences do not disturb their relationship; neither has a sense of having to "perform" for the other. They share each other's bodies with the same gentle acceptance as they share a meal or a conversation.

This uncritical acceptance of each other gives the relationship its special flavor. Max is aware of that. It surprises him that he feels so relaxed, so peaceful in Lynn's company. He is not at all nervous when he has to wait for her, something he has never liked doing. When she corrects him because he is wrong, he does not react as if she has reproached or admonished him, and when she objects to what he says, he does not wince, his enthusiasm for a topic or activity does not suffer because of it, for Max does not take Lynn's comments as censorship.

Her short, direct questions during their weekend at Montauk reflect the practical aspect of her personality and indicate how honest their relationship is. "How did I encourage you?" (VI 623/5), she wants to know, and then goes on to ask: "Do you snore?" (VI 677/61), "Do you want to be buried or cremated?" (VI 679/63), "Max, did you love your mother?" (VI 696/81), "Are you very fond of your children?" (VI 696/81), "What do you think?" (VI 687/71) and "How do you know?" (VI 689/74), and finally, "Max, are you jealous?" (VI 697/82).

Although he is very fond of Lynn, Max knows "daß es sich verbietet, eine jüngere Frau an diese meine Zukunftslosigkeit binden zu wollen" (VI 751), *"it is wrong to attempt to tie a younger woman to this lack of future which is mine" (140)*. Aware of his age, Max believes he is at last ready to accept it. Lynn offers him a chance to feel unencumbered in their relationship not merely because of her age, but also because of their difference in language. Standing back and looking at himself and Lynn as if from a distance, Max observes:

> Vielleicht weil es zwischen Lynn und ihm nur die englische Sprache gibt . . . fällt ihm in ihrer Gegenwart mancherlei ein, was ihm sonst . . . gar nicht einfällt. (VI 688)

> *Perhaps because he and Lynn have only the English language in common . . . matters occur to him, when he is with her, which ordinarily would not occur to him to say. (73)*

And Max continues: "There is a difference between being silent in a foreign language and in one's own" (VI 688/73). Keeping silent in a foreign language he suppresses less, and his memory allows more to sift through. What rises into Max's consciousness are predominantly, but not exclusively, memories of the life he has shared with women.

What Max needs to do in New York, he realizes—in addition to what his American publisher wants him to do—is to come to terms with his past, something that still needs to be done in

Zurich and Berlin as well, he observes (VI 631). On Saturday afternoon at Montauk, Max has the feeling that he has succeeded, that he has accepted his past "once and for all, a look back without anger and without self-pity" (VI 709/95). But he has thought so on earlier occasions, too, he remembers. At Montauk Beach he realizes that the past can only be mastered in the present, a present in which "die Welt entrückt [ist] in ihre Zukunft ohne mich" (VI 709), *"the world [is] withdrawn into its future without me"* (95). Thus forced to focus on itself, the "I", knowing it is excluded from the commonality of a shared future, craves the present.

The extended present of the relationship Max and Lynn share during his stay in New York has no place for a shared future. What remains, Max observes, is "das irre Bedürfnis nach Gegenwart durch eine Frau" (VI 709), *"the mad desire for present identity through a woman"* (95-96). During those few weeks in New York, especially during their weekend at Montauk, Lynn personifies the immediacy Max craves. Yet when he speaks of her as "the young lady called Lynn" (VI 670/53) or refers to her as "this young stranger" or "this strange young woman" (VI 689,703,723,726/74,88,110,113), he is emphasizing the distance between them, which may be a cautionary distance for Max, to prevent him from becoming too absorbed with Lynn. He is only superficially interested in her past and, during a visit to her apartment, comments that he dislikes looking at photographs, a record of the past.

For a few moments Max seriously questions whether he might not be deceiving both of them, whether his feelings are really directed to her or to someone else. He looks at Lynn closely—her hair, her chin, her neck, her lips, her nose, her whole figure, her manner of walking—and compares these details with those of other women he has loved (VI 684). Reassured, he concludes that in moments of intimacy his caresses are meant exclusively for Lynn; his feelings do not confuse her with anyone else; no, he is not using Lynn as a substitute (VI 702-03). He does not pursue what he does not understand about her and shares with her, consciously, only the present. Her presence makes Max glad; it validates his being, his identity. Lynn will not get to know his vices—male chauvinism, his hysterical, compulsive sensitivity to criticism, his susceptibility to irrational behavior and "attacks," or his habit of drinking himself insensitive when he is miserable—because it takes a much longer relationship than theirs for these vices to emerge.

After their return to Manhattan on Sunday afternoon, they have very little time left to themselves before they have to say good-bye. By choice, they part in public; the parting is free of melancholy or drenching emotion. Lynn gives Max a small present: a new tobacco pouch to replace the one he lost at Montauk; he leaves her his typewriter, the only exception to her request for "no presents," because she can really use it.

After a hasty lunch in a crowded French restaurant, they walk to the United Nations Park to watch the river and the sea gulls. They talk quietly. When Lynn's lunch hour is over, they kiss and then hold hands as they run through the traffic across First Avenue. Then, almost casually, they separate. As Max describes it:

> Wir sagten: BYE, kußlos, dann ein zweites Mal mit erhobener Hand: HI. (VI 754)

> *We said: BYE, without a kiss, then a second time, with raised hand: HI.* (143)

As long as he is describing their weekend together, recapturing the extended present of those few days, Max almost exclusively refers to himself in the third person. Only when he is on the plane and heading back to Europe, that is, when his relationship with Lynn has ended and thus become part of his past, does he refer to himself in the first person, as he always does when writing about Käte, Constanze, Ingeborg, or Marianne. This switch from "er" (he) to "ich" (I) occurs prominently twice near the end of *Montauk*: once in Max's description of the last few hours he spends with Lynn before they say good-bye, details of which he recalls as his plane heads out over the Atlantic (VI 752-54), and again when he reports that he tried to visit Lynn at her office on a subsequent trip to New York and learned she no longer worked there (VI 740).

How quickly the past comes about, Max thinks. He remembers his surprise last Sunday, as he and Lynn were driving back to Manhattan, when he suddenly realized: "the figure of that strange young woman on the path through the undergrowth, OVERLOOK—that was yesterday" (VI 726/113). A little later, while Max was driving, he nearly caused an accident when he mistook the car's brake for the clutch and brought their car to an abrupt stop on the busy parkway. Max wonders what might have happened: two traffic fatalities, a young American and an elderly Swiss, "their weekend at the coast would have become public property" (VI 727/114). It does not, until Max writes and publishes his account.

MAX: WOMEN, AGING, AND IMMEDIACY

During the weekend with Lynn at Montauk, Max is able to confront his past and his memories quietly, from a distance. Surprisingly, though, nearly all those memories, especially those of the four women he has loved most intensely, are closely associated with guilt. Guilt runs like a thread through his past experiences and relationships. The immediate cause of this guilt is desertion: of Käte through a lack of decisiveness; of Constanze and his children; of Ingeborg, alone and ill in a clinic; of Marianne, tearfully alone in Berlin; of W., his friend and benefactor; and of his mother, who died alone while Max spent the evening meeting a professional commitment and the night drinking with colleagues and friends. In addition, Max carries the guilt of four abortions, involving three of the women he loved. One of these abortions, especially, Max now believes, was an error.

The weekend at Montauk has demonstrated to him that this process of remembering is a way of finding at least a temporary release from the burden of cumulative guilt. In recording that weekend, Max succeeds in making visible and perhaps more comprehensible to himself his life and his difficult relationships with women.

He has written about women a great deal, even though his mother once admonished him: "You shouldn't write so much about women, for you do not understand them" (VI 688/72). The advice came a little late, when Max was already fifty-five years old. Besides, he believes that he really does understand women, at least some of the time. When he draws a verbal character sketch of one of them, he comments, the woman is pleased at first and is surprised when he sees something in her that other men have not seen. Max admits that he never sees a woman as uncomplicated and simple, but always as full of contradictions. Although he believes in the sketches he makes of women's personalities, he is surprised when later their behavior corresponds to his projection. Max is careful to treat each woman differently, as an individual, he points out; he neither generalizes about them nor does he transfer his experience with one woman to the next. All the same, his important relationships with women have always resulted in pain for him. Thinking about this, Max concludes:

> Es muß an mir liegen, wenn ähnliche Verhaltensweisen wiederkehren, oft sogar haargenau. (VI 695)

> *If similar behavior patterns emerge—and they often do, to a hair—it must be due to something in myself.* (80)

Max describes in detail the process by which he arrives at the completed sketch of a woman; the result is highly subjective, he admits, because he includes every characteristic that fits his own perception of the woman. Since he therefore knows, or believes he knows, everything about her, he feels obliged to tell her, when he sees her suffer, why she is suffering—or he does *not* tell her but is still certain he knows the cause. Self-righteously, as if defending himself against some unspoken accusation, Max asserts:

> Ich sehe es doch, ich höre es doch, und wenn ich nicht dabei bin, so kann ich es mir ungefähr vorstellen. (VI 696)

> *I [see] it . . . I [hear] it. And if I [am not] there, I can visualize more or less how it will be.* (80)

For each of his partners, Max admits, he also invents "a new difficulty in relation to myself—for instance, that she is the stronger character or, alternatively, that I am" (VI 695/80). The women act accordingly, he observes—at least when he is present.

The ironic tone of these self-critical observations suggests that Max is aware of the fallacies in his attitude toward and behavior with the women he loves. At the end of this self-examination, Max admits: "Es sind nicht die Frauen, die mich hinters Licht führen; das tue ich selber" (VI 696), *"It is not the women who make a fool of me. I do that myself" (81).* Thus Max is trying to escape, not women, but himself. Soon he will be sixty-three. He has decided to accept his age, and he realizes the time has come not merely to think about death—his own—but to talk about it, too.

Recently he has been dreaming often about death. Even without a dream he sometimes awakens in alarm: he is sixty-one, sixty-two, sixty-three. "Already so late!" (VI 751). Yet the doctors tell him he is healthy for his age, and he is by now older than his father was when he died. Soon he will reach the average life-expectancy age. His heart, on occasion, feels as if a hand were clutching it, a paw without claws, he tells the doctor. If he is alone at these moments he becomes frightened —not of death, but of being unable to get up from a chair or to perform a normal task in the day's routine.

Max does not wish to become very old. He likes to be around younger people, to share his ideas and experience with them. "Fear of old age is melancholy," Max asserts, "but [the consciousness] of death is something different: [a consciousness even in joy]" (VI 751/140).

Max accepts the passage of transient time, and with it the process of aging. Despite his conscious awareness of this process and his diminishing future, he experiences the present intensely. He learns this at Montauk, and is grateful to Lynn for the opportunity. His situation is similar to that of the crazed woman he watched one day in Manhattan. She seemed to be feeling her way along Fifth Avenue, her fingers lightly touching the stone and metal facades of the buildings as she passed them. Using her fingers as feelers, she seemed to need to make sure that everything was still there. The day seemed to be special for her, a day of fulfillment, Max observes, and she appeared happy. Like that woman, Max at Montauk is experiencing everything very intensely, missing nothing. Huddled close to each other after making love, with the cool night surrounding them and Lynn's head resting comfortably on his shoulder, Max muses, relaxed: "Eine wird die letzte Frau sein . . . " (VI 703), *"one woman will be the last" (88).* He wishes it would be Lynn. She has been able to still, at least temporarily, his "mad desire for present identity through a woman" (VI 709/95-96).

Max shares this craving with other Frisch characters, among them the narrator in *Mein Name sei Gantenbein,* especially in that novel's final paragraph, and Walter Faber, who near the end of his life bursts out in exultation in a hymn to *Being* (IV 199), which Frisch deliberately repeats in *Montauk:*

> Auf der Welt sein: im Licht sein. Irgendwo . . . Esel treiben, unser Beruf!—aber vor allem: standhalten dem Licht, der Freude im Wissen, daß ich erlösche im Licht über Ginster, Asphalt und Meer, standhalten der Zeit, beziehungsweise Ewigkeit im Augenblick. Ewig sein: gewesen sein. (VI 685)

> *To be alive: to be in the light. Driving donkeys around somewhere . . . that's all our job amounts to! The main thing is to stand up to the light, to joy in the knowledge that I shall be extinguished in the light over gorse, asphalt, and sea, to stand up to time, or rather to eternity in the instant. To be eternal means to have existed. (69)*[16]

The intense immediacy of living these lines express, an immediacy that Max experiences at Montauk, is unique and makes that weekend and Max's relationship with Lynn so very special for him.

Frisch's undertaking, using his own biography for a novel about the life and loves of a fictional progatonist called Max, is both courageous and controversial. Courageous, because the educated reader who is familiar with details of Frisch's life may be tempted to equate Max with his creator, Frisch, thus falling victim to an intentional fallacy and doing an injustice to both the novel, a work of art, and the man, its author. Frisch's undertaking is controversial because the nature of the material for the novel forces its author to disclose names, places, dates, and details of his life that belong not only to the private domain of *his* life but also to that of the people he mentions by name, real people whose identity is disguised only barely or not at all.

Montauk illustrates the life and realized potential of the protagonist in five different relationships with women. Max, the protagonist, continues the tradition of his predecessors in earlier Frisch novels: he presents all events and each relationship almost exclusively from his own perspective. None of the women is ever given a chance to state her own views or feelings about her relationship with Max or about a particular incident. Even on the rare occasions when the woman's point of view is heard—as in the case of Marianne, whose statement about her lack of self-realization in their relationship Max quotes directly (VI 678-79)—their ideas are always stated through the mouth of a man.

Just who is the man, in the character of Max, who emerges from the pages of *Montauk*? How successfully does he build relationships with women?

The man has much in common with many of his predecessors in Frisch's novels, from Jürg Reinhart to Theo Gantenbein. Like Stiller, Faber, Enderlin, and Svoboda, he is egocentric yet unable to be without the company of a woman. But women are an enigma to Max. His mother was correct when she told him he did not understand them.

His various relationships with a woman have taken Max to the highest peaks of joy and the deepest valleys of despair. He has reveled in a woman's company and felt intimidated and unsure with her. Women have made him feel inadequate about himself as a man and unsure of his ability to maintain a loving relationship. He has been obsessed with the woman he loved and suffered extreme jealousy because of her. But never has a woman hurt him so severely that he was unable to seek love and companionship from the next woman. Will Lynn be the last? Has he grown more secure and at peace with age?

Max, in this novel, seems to illustrate Frisch's conviction that man cannot live without woman. No matter what the difficulty, pain, and costs may be, he needs her near him. Her existence completes his. Unless he can establish a workable relationship with the woman he loves, at least for a time, Max is the poorer. Frisch seems to state here, more clearly than in any other work, that only in a collaborative relationship with a woman can a man test some of the ideals he holds and realize some of the joy he craves.

In *Montauk*, Max courageously holds his shortcomings, insights, strengths, and achievements up to a mirror for all to see. The frailties and failures exposed are those of any man of the twentieth century, not uniquely Max's. Their universality, however, does not justify their persistence. This may be one of the messages Frisch wants to leave with his readers.

NOTES

[1] Marianne's occupation is never clearly stated in *Montauk*. When I asked Frisch about Marianne's profession, he replied that she worked "als Lektorin beim Funk und bei Verlagen. . . ." (letter from Max Frisch, Nov. 26, 1986), *"as editor for radio and publishing houses. . . ."*

[2] This phrase is the title of a book by Philip Roth (VI 633). Although the extensive use of citations is an important aspect of *Montauk*, it is only peripherally related to this study's focus on modern man in his relationship with women. Readers interested in Frisch's use of citation in *Montauk* see Bänziger 267-84, Knapp "Noch einmal" 285-307, Krättli 428-34.

[3] See also Schröder 29-74 and Kieser 157-71.

[4] Knapp "Noch einmal" 288-97.

[5] I suggest that "In her presence only she exists, in her presence madness begins" may convey the anguished intensity of the German better than the translation Skelton offers. For some reason the translator also changed Frisch's present tense to the past, thus sacrificing the immediacy of Max's admission.

[6] According to the details Max provides, he left Constanze in 1955 (VI 669). Volker Hage comments that Max Frisch actually left his family in 1954 and that his divorce from Constanze did not take place until February 1959 (Hage 55). The discrepancy is minor and of no importance here; however, the 1959 date in *Montauk*, an important one in the novel, corresponds to the biographical facts of Frisch's relationship with Ingeborg Bachmann.

[7] Bänziger asserts that Max experiences real wealth in his relationship with W. and real greatness in his relationship with Ingeborg. Although possibly true, I believe this superficial distinction oversimplifies the complexity of the problems Max experiences in both relationships and avoids addressing the involved psychological issues confronting Max (Bänziger 280).

[8] This may seem odd, but not for those acquainted with Ingeborg Bachmann's life, who know that she shared an apartment with the composer Hans Werner Henze in Naples (Beicken 74,154).

[9] Letter from Max Frisch to me, Nov. 26, 1986; see note 1 above.

[10] Although Marianne speaks of their relationship as lasting for ten years (VI 679), nearly eleven years elapsed between the time in 1962 when she and Max first met and their formal separation in July 1973 (VI 653,684).

[11] Beicken assigns this statement to Ingeborg, not Marianne, and links it to the character Leo Jordan, the psychotherapist in Ingeborg Bachmann's unfinished novel *Der Fall Franza* (*The Case of Franza*), who makes his wife the object of his psychoanalytical obsessions (Bachmann III 339-483).

Beicken is in error on several accounts. First, the statement does not appear in or even close to the primary Ingeborg section, which is fairly self-contained in *Montauk* (VI 710-18/*141-45*). Second, it is not the kind of statement Ingeborg would make. She is a writer of primary literature, that is, she creates literature and thus knows that creative writers, in plying their trade, tend to capitalize on any experience, their own included, no matter how private. If, as a writer herself, she objected to being the subject of a literary production, she would not issue a prohibition but might destroy any preliminary efforts (notes, sketches) she discovered. Ingeborg does just that: during her last meeting with Max in Rome in 1963 she admits that she found Max's *Tagebuch* (literary diary), read it, and burned it (VI 717; Beicken 146-48).

Marianne is also a writer, but primarily of secondary literature, that is, she writes mainly *about* literature. She selects the material she writes about, rejecting whatever she finds inappropriate to her interests or task. Thus, if she did not want to be used as a subject of literature, she would not merely object, but would prohibit it. Max, in *Montauk*, relates an incident that reveals Marianne's attitude. During an interview with a German television reporter in Central Park, New York, the cameraman tried to put Marianne into the picture; she objected and declined. Since the topic of the interview was "the writer's responsibility toward society," she felt it inappropriate for her to be part of the scene (VI 694-95/79). Except for *Montauk*, Frisch has honored "Marianne's" prohibition. As Hage reports, however, after Max Frisch and his second wife, Marianne Oellers, separated in 1973 and before their divorce in 1979, Frisch wrote his still-unpublished *Berliner Journal*. Frisch himself has said that it contains, among observations about fellow writers, notes about his marital crisis. The journal lies sealed in the Zurich Max-Frisch-Archive and will not be published until twenty years after Frisch's death (Hage 104).

[12] Lynn's observations about dolphins and her statement about not wanting to bear a child on land are thinly veiled references to Undine, the water nymph, reminding Max gently of Ingeborg's story "Undine geht" (1973) (Bänziger 277-78).

[13] In the system of the world postulated by the sixteenth-century Swiss alchemist and physician Paracelsus (1494-1541), Undinen are elemental feminine water spirits. They prefer to find a husband among men because they will then receive a soul and their children will be born with one.

[14] Another similarity between Lynn and Sabeth is that both are excellent Ping-Pong players.

[15] To conclude from this tentative observation of Max—as Jurgensen does—that Max is positively and consciously aware that his love for Lynn is incestuous in nature seems to force the argument unnecessarily (Jurgensen 1976 262).

[16] The phrase "Irgendwo . . . Esel treiben, unser Beruf!" might be rendered into English more accurately as "To drive donkeys somewhere, our vocation!" The original translator of these lines is Michael Bullock, not Geoffrey Skelton, *Montauk*'s translator. Bullock's 1959 translation of this important passage from *Homo faber* approaches an interpretation of the German text; its verbatim quotation in the English translation of *Montauk* is unfortunate.

CHAPTER SEVEN

DER MENSCH ERSCHEINT IM HOLOZÄN AND *BLAUBART*: OLD AGE AND THE QUESTION OF GUILT

Although Frisch's two most recent novels, *Der Mensch erscheint im Holozän* (1979), *Man in the Holocene*, and *Blaubart* (1982), *Bluebeard*, may be related only peripherally to the main thesis of this study, they should be investigated to see the direction their author's thinking has taken about the problems modern man is facing. Frisch has already shown that he sees his contemporaries as men suffering from a combination of chauvinism and insecurity, that they have great trouble communicating in a close relationship, especially one with a woman, and that they have difficulty integrating their lives into the inevitable forward movement of transient time. As a result, the male character who is able to maintain a satisfyingly close relationship with a beloved woman is rare in a Frisch novel, even though such a loving relationship is what all the men seem to crave.

Related to and developing along with Frisch's concern with "das wirkliche Leben," usually symbolized by a mutually enriching marriage or love affair, are his concerns with the inevitable process of aging and with guilt, something many of his characters accumulate over their lifetimes. Both these topics are, of course, tied to the concept of time—transient time that carries every life through cycles and phases during which it accumulates the baggage of positive and negative experiences and moves inevitably toward death.

In the first of Frisch's two latest novels he emphasizes the effects of time more than he does the struggle to establish and maintain a relationship with a woman. *Der Mensch erscheint im Holozän* examines time at the end of the protagonist's life, focusing especially on the process of aging and its consequences. In *Blaubart*, however, Frisch is once more concerned with male-female relationships, but this time from a different perspective. He examines the protagonist's repetitive movements through seven marriages, focusing especially on the guilt he accumulates in the process, a guilt that often originates in jealousy.

THE FINAL STAGE OF TRANSIENT TIME:
DER MENSCH ERSCHEINT IM HOLOZÄN

The protagonist in this unusual short novel lives alone and remote from the rest of the world in a small village in the mountainous Tessin, Switzerland. For a few days, because of a natural calamity (torrential rains caused a landslide that blocked the only road leading in and out of the valley and disrupted the telephone lines), the novel's protagonist, Herr Geiser, is literally cut off from the outside world. He is seventy-four years old and retired from a small business in Basel that bears his name; the company is now run by his son-in-law, "who always knows everything" (VII 233/34). Herr Geiser, a widower, has one child, Corinne. She is the mother of three children, something Herr Geiser knows, even if he has trouble remembering the names of all his grandchildren.

About the quality of Herr Geiser's relationship with his deceased wife, Elsbeth, we learn very little, and most of that indirectly. She would not have approved of his current activities, he is sure (VII 236-37/37-39). To have more wall space to tack up his memory-aiding notes, he recently removed an oil painting of her and placed it in the bedroom, behind a wardrobe (VII 260/66-67). The painting "shows a face Geiser never knew, and the eyes do not look at one" (VII 260/66). One gets the impression that the relationship of Herr Geiser and his wife was somewhat analogous to his present relationship with his cat: benevolent tolerance. However, since a cat often has a symbolic function in Frisch's novels, especially in *Stiller*, and mirrors to some extent the protagonist's feelings for the woman he loves, it may be significant that this cat ends up being killed and roasted over a fire because Herr Geiser is nearly starving. Once it is cooked, however, he cannot bring himself to eat his cat but buries her in the garden (VII 287-88/97).

Although this is the account of an old man and his struggle against the gradual dissolution of his existence, it is not gloomy or melancholy, but a narrative full of humor, compassion, and a certain kind of grace. It is also a thoughtful account, filled with such searching questions as: What does man really learn during his life? What does he know? What does he remember of what he knows? Why does he remember it?

Herr Geiser's age-related problems are manifest through his progressive loss of control, both physical and mental. Physically, his energy level has decreased; climbing in the nearby mountains is not as easy as it used to be. Toward the end of the novel, after suffering a stroke, he also experiences loss of control over his limbs and his speech. Mentally, Herr Geiser's greatest problem is progressive loss of memory, both short- and long-term. How does one cope with these frightening aspects of advancing age? That is the novel's central question.

Herr Geiser's solution to his problem of a failing memory is obsessively to construct endless lists of the things he needs to remember *now* and of the many things he has learned or that he once knew. He writes them down by hand, copies them out of reference books, and even cuts individual items, complete with illustrations and diagrams, out of encylopedias. Then he tacks or tapes each item onto the walls of his living room where he can look at it whenever he needs to remember something. His solution to this very real aspect of growing old is, of course, eccentric—but in its exaggeration it points up the seriousness of this problem for Frisch, who has worried about the effects of aging for more than thirty years.

Frisch raised the issue of aging for the first time in *Homo faber*, where it is associated with Walter Faber's problem of discovering who he really is. The extent of Frisch's concern with aging is reflected clearly in the various comments, discussions, and questionnaires contained in the pages of his second *Tagebuch* under the heading "Vereinigung Freitod," "*Voluntary Death Association.*" Mockingly, the author advocates the creation of an organization of aging people whose members voluntarily decide to commit suicide in the interest of humanity and the burgeoning world population when they reach a certain age (VI 79-95,85-92,97-103,107-17,126-31,163-68,173-78,244-46,293-97,389,394-97,402-04; *Sketch II* 68-72,74-77,81-84,87-94,101-06,134-

37,143-46,212-14,244-47,331,336-38). Frisch's observations on the topic in *Tagebuch II* are always sardonic; at times they are also hilarious, especially when their chief proponent, the narrator, reaches the critical age. Those sketchbook entries precede *Der Mensch erscheint im Holozän* by eight to twelve years.

The approach Frisch takes to exploring this most universal human problem, aging and ultimate death, is more detached, less anxious in *Der Mensch erscheint im Holozän* than it was in previous novels. Perhaps Frisch is following the advice of Max, who observed in *Montauk*: "Es wird Zeit, nicht bloß an den Tod zu denken, sondern davon zu reden" (VI 750), *"The time is coming, not only to think of death, but also to talk of it"* (139). In this novel Frisch does not reach conclusions about old age and aging, not even ironically as in *Tagebuch II*. Here he merely explores his subject in characteristic detail, treating it with compassion and understanding. If Herr Geiser, not necessarily Max Frisch, draws any conclusion from his investigation, it is that man forever remains an amateur (VII 255).

However, man does have choices open to him. In Herr Geiser's case he can either live on in the village, waiting for a major landslide to bury his house, his land, his entire village and all its inhabitants, or he can leave it. Herr Geiser does not like the option of remaining where he is and living under the constant threat of a major natural disaster. He chooses to escape the threatening environment by leaving, even though that involves a difficult and dangerous trek across treacherous mountains, especially at his age and with his waning physical strength. One stormy early morning, in the dark, he leaves the village before any of its inhabitants are up and about to see him go. He exercises his existential choice to depart from a place that threatens his existence, giving himself, the existential "I", a chance to rise above a potentially life-threatening calamity. He chooses to begin once more somewhere else, in the civilization that lies beyond the confining, threatening mountains.

Herr Geiser never completes his journey; shortly before reaching his goal, in plain view of the habitation and safety on the other side of the mountains, he makes another existential choice and retraces his steps under worsening weather conditions. He reaches his village, as he left it, in darkness. There he awaits the possible massive landslide, during which the tallest mountain is expected to slide down, burying everything in its path.

This catastrophe never occurs. But when Herr Geiser learns that the threat has passed, a personal disaster of equal proportion has taken place: he has suffered a stroke that ultimately leads to his death.

Closely associated with the problem of aging in *Der Mensch erscheint im Holozän* is the concept of time, both the serial time measured in minutes, hours, days, weeks, months, and seasons that affects day-to-day, hour-by-hour activities and transient time, the cumulative, chronological time that governs life from birth to death. Except for Walter Faber, Herr Geiser is the only Frisch protagonist who has lived through the entire cycle. Although blessed with a robust nature and good health for a man his age, Herr Geiser is acutely aware that transient time governs his life; mounting evidence in the form of his gradually weakening physical condition and his increasingly failing memory indicate that his life is nearing its end. He struggles as valiantly, though ineffectually, against this knowledge and the impending personal disaster it will bring as he struggles against the natural disaster that threatens the life of the village.

In his efforts to shore up his failing memory by assembling "traces of human existence in excerpts of human knowledge" (Schmitz 145), Herr Geiser is documenting not only his own existence, but also that of humanity and the world in which men and women have learned to survive. By recalling, with the aid of reference works, past human development, knowledge, and achievements, he validates his own existence; by tacking onto his living room walls the bits and pieces of knowledge he is still able to recall, he documents that existence, until a sudden loss of brain function, known medically as cerebral hemorrhage or apoplexy, causes it to cease. Apoplexy is a condition "combined usually with paralysis and loss of consciousness, and often accompanied by loss of speech" (VII 298/*109*), as the last note Herr Geiser tacked on the wall of his living room explains; all three symptoms afflict Herr Geiser. As a result of the stroke, Herr Geiser's earthly existence soon comes to an end, and his material body merges with the elements of nature. Herr Geiser knows that nature needs no names and also that "the rocks do not need his memory" (VII 296/107). Human beings alone have that need, as they alone of all living creatures on earth attempt to identify and catalogue the things they discover in nature, and they alone seek to measure time in nature on the scale of millennia.

Der Mensch erscheint im Holozän may be viewed purely as the account of an old man or, in some ways, as the chronology of aging. In the former context, all works of history, geology, biology, and theology that Herr Geiser reads, clips out of his books, and fastens to his walls may be understood as nothing more than bits of knowledge he tries to preserve or recover. That these bits and pieces of paper end up at the conclusion of the novel in "a confused heap that makes no sense" (VII 295/106), because Herr Geiser's daughter Corinne opens the windows to air out the house, is Frisch's ultimate irony. Herr Geiser no longer has any use for these scraps of paper and the bits of knowledge they contain, and neither does anyone else. However, if one looks more closely at the substance of the fragments Herr Geiser has assembled, one notes that much of it is related to life, survival, and the deaths of individual human beings and the planet they inhabit (Probst 171).

The novel's title, *Der Mensch erscheint im Holozän*, literally translated as *Man Appears in the Holocene*, supports both interpretive stances. In the first instance, the title refers to only one of the bits of knowledge Herr Geiser assembles: after the rocks and mountains and streams, man appears in the Holocene, the geological present. This judgment seems to be a personal one of Herr Geiser's, however, as it contradicts another item on his wall, one stating that "according to present views, man first made his appearance in the Pleistocene (*see* Old Stone Age)" (VII 220/19). In the second instance, Herr Geiser's choice of information from the corpus of human knowledge and the way he assembles it make clear that his selection is by no means random but is, instead, related both to his own stage in the aging process and to the natural crisis brought on by excessive rains and the landslide they cause. Thus the novel's title may imply that man appeared and will perish in the Holocene. This interpretation elevates Herr Geiser's personal catastrophe and death onto a more universal plane, where it, too, conforms to the concept expressed in all of Frisch's novels, that human death is the proper goal of transient time.

THE LABYRINTH OF GUILT: *BLAUBART*

Not always does Max Frisch state the question of guilt as clearly as he does in *Homo faber*, where he has Walter Faber ask repeatedly, although rhetorically: "Was ist denn meine Schuld?" (IV 123), *"What did I do wrong?"* (127). This is the question with which Faber begins the important Avignon section of his "report," before he reveals relevant details of his first incestuous night with Sabeth, his daughter. The question is never directly answered in that novel.

Guilt is *Blaubart*'s primary topic, specifically the guilt of its fifty-four-year-old protagonist, Felix Schaad, a physician. Schaad has been falsely accused of the brutal murder of his sixth ex-wife, Rosalinde Zogg; he is currently married to wife number seven, but that marriage, like all previous ones, is headed for divorce. Page one of the novel states that Dr. Felix Schaad has been acquitted of the murder charge for lack of sufficient evidence, and in the final pages we learn that the real murderer has been apprehended and has confessed the crime.

Blaubart can thus be seen as something of a detective story, although not in the conventional sense. It is *not* a logical investigation of events preceding the crime and leading eventually to the identification and pursuit of the real murderer. On the contrary, this novel is an investigation of the guilt, general and specific, that arises out of the relationship of two people, Felix Schaad and Rosalinde Zogg. It proceeds through a selective re-enactment of the trial, taking place only in Schaad's mind, during the three months that follow his acquittal. Schaad has plenty of time to engage in this compulsive mental activity: the patients who once filled his waiting room are staying away, frightened by what they learned of his private life during the well-publicized trial. One cannot blame them: Who would be foolish enough to entrust his life to a doctor accused of murder and merely acquitted for lack of evidence rather than found to be innocent of the charges?

What Schaad asks himself after his acquittal is a question basic to the novel: "Wie lebt einer damit?" (VII 303), *"How does one live with that?"* (8), that is, with the devastating judgment of merely having been "acquitted for lack of proof" (VII 303/8), not found innocent of the crime that one knows, on the basis of the facts, one did not commit?

Schaad's internal reenactment of cross-examinations of the more than sixty witnesses called during his trial and of the prosecution's cross-examination of Schaad himself adds up to the character profile of a man who may, after all, be guilty of the crime for which he has been tried. Testimony by Schaad's five living ex-wives and his current wife is particularly influential in creating the picture of a man who is strongly egocentric, self-righteous, compulsively possessive, overly sensitive, insecure, sexually impotent, extremely jealous, and alcohol addicted. This man, as his own mental reenactment of the trial shows, abuses women with verbal brutality and mental cruelty (VII 330-37). In a variation of the defendant's concluding statement Schaad admits: "Ich bin nicht unschuldig . . ." (VII 343), *"I am not completely free of guilt . . ."* (60), then adds in clarification: "Nur bin ich nicht der Täter . . . . " (VII 344), *"Only I did not do it . . . ."* (62).

This reprise of the trial includes, however, statements from witnesses who could not possibly have appeared in court at the time, such as the defendant's deceased parents and the victim herself (VII 381-84,393-96). By including these people among the witnesses, Frisch explores the labyrinthine nature of guilt in general and the cumulative, personal guilt Schaad has amassed in his seven marriages, especially in his marriage to Rosalinde Zogg.

During his reenacted closing remarks to the court, Schaad wonders at one point about the general nature of guilt, asking: "Was ist Schuld?" (VII 344), *"What is guilt?"* (62). Like Walter Faber, who seemed at least rhetorically concerned about his own guilt as a result of his relationship with Sabeth, Schaad owes us a direct answer to this question. He pursues the question much more fervently than did Faber and eventually accepts the answer his investigation produces. Paradoxically, that answer leads him then to admit publicly that he committed the very murder of which he has already been acquitted and which, as the facts now clearly show, was committed by someone else. His unshakable belief that he *is* guilty of murdering his ex-wife causes him, after his confession is rejected by society (the police), to sentence himself. He carries out that sentence by driving his car at 80 miles an hour against a tree, which results, presumably, in his death a short time later.

Schaad bases his guilt on the sworn statement, which he knows to be true, of a witness at his trial: Pfeifer, a former friend, once heard Schaad—then still married to Rosalinde—exclaim in a drunken fit of jealousy: "er könnte dieses Weib erwürgen" (VII 310), *"he could strangle this woman"* (17). Rosalinde was indeed found strangled in her apartment with one of Schaad's neckties. Since this threat against her life also appears in Schaad's handwriting in his diary, which was submitted to the court as evidence, Pfeifer's assertion gains support (VII 351). To the court's question about how long he and Schaad have been friends, Pfeifer answers with a startling nonsequitur: "Ich habe nie mit seiner Rosalinde geschlafen!" (VII 311), *"I've never slept with his Rosalinde!"* (17), although he stayed overnight at the Schaads' house many times. His unexpected declaration suggests that the thought of making love to Schaad's wife was probably never far from his mind. It suggests also that Schaad's jealousy of Rosalinde during their marriage was perhaps not totally unfounded.

But jealousy, a cancerous, self-destructive feeling, is rooted in "the fear of comparisons," as Frisch wrote in his first sketchbook (II 713/*Sketch I* 268). Unfortunately, this negative, destructive feeling, unlike other emotions such as joy and sorrow, cannot be shared with others. Yet it must be resisted lest it destroy the relationship between two people who care deeply for each other, as Jürg Reinhart, Stiller, Rolf, Walter Faber, Svoboda, Gantenbein, and Max all discovered before Felix Schaad came along. In fact, Schaad never makes that discovery while he is married to Rosalinde; the marriage ends in divorce.

Curiously, after divorcing his sixth wife, Schaad manages to overcome his fierce jealousy finally, albeit too late, with the help of that same ex-wife. How he does this is both bizarre and slightly perverse. The problem's solution is suggested by Rosalinde who, after her divorce from Schaad, becomes a prostitute. She invites her ex-husband to watch—via video-camera transmission from the next room—as she plies her trade with three of her customers in succession. Afterward, Schaad and Rosalinde go to the movies together. The experience of watching Rosalinde make love to three different men cures Schaad forever of his compulsive jealousy.

As Schaad rethinks the trial that ended in his acquittal, a reenactment in which the witnesses' accounts undergo many variations, it becomes evident that he suffers from a guilt he has not yet acknowledged and thus cannot expiate. This becomes clear in the court's sentence that Schaad invents. In this enactment (VII 379-80), contrary to the facts of the actual trial, Schaad is found *guilty* of the murder of Rosalinde Zogg and sentenced to ten years in prison. With a gesture reminiscent of the circus visitor in Kafka's sketch, "Auf der Galerie," the thus-sentenced Schaad "stützt die Hände auf den kleinen Tisch . . . [und] weint . . . mit gesenktem Kopf" (VII 380), *"rests his hands on the little table . . . [and] weeps . . . with [bent] head"* (110)—"offenbar vor Glück" (VII 380), *"apparently for joy"* (110), the narrator comments.

This invented version, which ends with the sentencing, not the acquittal, of the accused, stands in stark contrast to the real event, which the narrator, perhaps to heighten the contrast, places immediately after the invented outcome. In reality, the accused is acquitted, and the court not only releases him from the obligation of paying for the trial but also awards him 178,000 Swiss francs as compensation for the 291 days he spent in jail (VII 380). The paradox of the accused's reacting with sorrow to the acquittal while responding with tears of joy to his prison sentence in the invented version is explained by Schaad's acknowledgment, at least to himself, that he is in principle guilty of the murder because he *thought* of it, not once but several times.

Again, as in *Mein Name sei Gantenbein*, Max Frisch explores and tests in *Blaubart* the limits of reality, which, for him, consists of both *lived* and *imagined* reality—that is, a reality composed of those actions and events that actually happen and those that could happen, based on the potentials of the situation, the participants involved, and the choices open to them. As a consequence, the mere thought of strangling Rosalinde, even though he never acted out that thought, constitutes the real guilt of Dr. Felix Schaad. He acknowledges and accepts it, which leads eventually to his self-judgment, self-sentencing, and self-execution, a suicide that is made to appear an accident.

CONCLUSION

In *Der Mensch erscheint im Holozän*, Max Frisch focuses on the end of a man's life, examining particularly the relationship between transient time and aging. If he offers any new ideas about aging, they are related not so much to the process of individual aging as to the aging of the whole of humanity. Frisch's outlook for the future of humanity is less than optimistic, because according to it the human race is expected to disappear from the planet during the same geological period, the Holocene, in which it appeared. Humanity, Frisch seems to admit grudgingly, has made a lot of progress since its tentative beginnings. Our physical development has been fairly rapid and substantial; we have acquired much knowledge over the centuries and millennia and have learned to apply that knowledge to explore and manipulate our environment; but in the end Frisch tends to agree with Herr Geiser, who observes: "Der Mensch bleibt ein Laie" (VII 255), *"Man remains an amateur"* (60). Therein, Frisch seems to suggest, lies ultimately the source of humanity's eventual extinction.

In *Blaubart*, Frisch presents a contemporary man who has failed in seven attempts to achieve "das wirkliche Leben" in marriage. He has the failings of many earlier protagonists and, like Max in *Montauk*, his residuum is guilt. This novel presents a well-focused illustration of its author's concept of reality, one he developed gradually in previous novels, especially and on a grand scale in *Mein Name sei Gantenbein*. There, Gantenbein observes succinctly: "action and inaction are interchangeable" (V 129/123); together they constitute each person's reality, limited only by the finite number of possibilities for action or inaction open to that person. By presenting one more illustration of his philosophical concept of reality in *Blaubart*, Frisch seems to suggest the need for human beings to create a new code of ethics, one more effective than the one they live by now, an ethical code according to which a man may live in a relationship of peace, harmony, and equality with his neighbor, and especially with the woman he loves.

CHAPTER EIGHT

FINAL CONSIDERATIONS

Max Frisch once answered the question, "What is the domain of literature?" with, "The private realm." He went on to observe:

Was die Soziologie nicht erfaßt: das Einzelwesen, das Ich, nicht mein Ich, aber ein Ich, die Person in allen ihren biologischen und gesellschaftlichen Bedingtheiten . . . . (*Die Zeit*, 22.12.1967)

What sociology does not comprehend: the single individual, the I, not my I, but an I, the person with all his biological and social limitations . . . .

The individual is Frisch's primary concern, specifically the contemporary male. In his novels he portrays characters, both men and women, who wrestle with the kind of issues and confront the kind of complexities of modern life that are familiar to us all.

In each novel, Frisch challenges himself with the same question: Can he describe a man's life in such a manner that it becomes comprehensible to others? In an attempt to answer that question, he creates primary characters whose lives resemble the rich texture of a cloth in which multiple strands of fiction and autobiographical fact are closely interwoven. The most vivid example of this narrative technique occurs in *Montauk*, whose protagonist even shares the author's name. Not only Max, however, but all protagonists in Frisch's novels illustrate the effectiveness of this artistic technique in exposing the substance, aspirations, vulnerabilities, and anguish of any man—from the youthful traveler, Jürg (*Jürg Reinhart*), and the neoromantic seeker of reality, Kilian (*Bin oder Die Reise nach*

Peking), to the lonely old man in a Tessinian mountain village, Herr Geiser (*Der Mensch erscheint im Holozän*), and the accused murderer of his ex-wife, Dr. Felix Schaad (*Blaubart*). In the process of revealing themselves, all of Frisch's major characters illustrate the complexity of human nature.

In his occasional theoretical comments, Frisch has made clear that he views the individual as something more than his or her biography, but rather as the sum of possibilities, "eine nicht unbeschränkte Summe, aber eine Summe, die über Biographie hinausgeht" (V 327), "*not an unlimited sum, but a sum that goes beyond biography.*" According to Frisch, a person's total character includes every possibility that lies within his or her reach. These possibilities indicate what else that person might have become, if he or she had exercised other options available. These possibilities, Frisch insists, are limited only by an individual's potential for realizing them—and the unrealized possibilities of a person's life are as much a part of that life as the realized ones that make up his or her biography. The two combined constitute the *real* person. This original idea Frisch demonstrates and pursues most extensively in *Mein Name sei Gantenbein*, wherein the protagonist, the narrator of the novel, explores his own unrealized possibilities, the actions he never took but could have taken, through three separate characters, each of whom represents one facet of himself.

Once one accepts Frisch's notion that a person is measured not only by the sum of events that occur in his or her biographical life but also by all those events that could have occurred, it is easy to understand why Frisch's major characters—usually the male protagonist—are so multidimensional, so different from each other and yet so strangely similar, and often so very troubling. Each one faces the kind of searching questions familiar to modern man: questions of identity, interpersonal relationships (especially with women), career, and aging. Each copes with his challenges in his own way, limited by what and who he is. None is more successful in solving his particular problems than are other human beings, but by the same token none, with the possible exception of Jürg Reinhart, can be considered a complete failure.

By choosing carefully the situations in which to place his characters, Frisch is able to address in each novel a number of topics that concern him. Many of these run like leitmotifs through all his novels, emerging in the spotlight here, in the background there. However, two concerns seem primary: first, how contemporary man may learn to know and to accept himself and, in so doing, develop his potential for living richly; second, how contemporary man may build and maintain a sharing, caring, and loving relationship with a woman. Frisch seems to believe that men are essentially lonely. Unless they can live in a mutually supportive relationship with a loved and loving woman, they will be unable to realize fully their personal potential and to live a meaningful life, "ein wirkliches Leben."

Frisch's protagonists rarely achieve that kind of relationship with a woman for any length of time. Exceptions might be Kilian, who, after his attempted flight, returns to his wife, at peace with himself and his life; Rolf, who is not a protagonist but, in the postscript of *Stiller*, becomes the narrator; and Gantenbein, who is only an imaginary character, created by the novel's narrator, and whose relationship with Lila is eventually destroyed by jealousy and a basic honesty.

A number of factors always seem to interfere with Frisch's men as they attempt to form and maintain an enduring and loving relationship with a woman. Frequently that relationship is a marriage, although sometimes it is an intensely experienced long-term affair such as that of Max and Ingeborg in *Montauk*, or a pseudomarriage such as that of Jürg and Yvonne in *Die Schwierigen*. The disruptive factors in every relationship, Frisch shows repeatedly, are jealousy, sexual insecurity, the tendency to create a frozen, unchangeable image of one's partner, the dulling effect of repetition, and the absence of communication between the partners. Frisch examines the effects of each of these factors on the men and women he writes about. From these accounts we, the readers, are left to draw our own conclusions about interpersonal relationships, the nature of love, the problem of living with the threat of inexorably passing time, and the possibility of marriage as a viable, realizable, permanent relationship between a man and a woman.

Marriage and its problems are important topics in each of the seven Frisch novels discussed in this study. In *Stiller*, marriage is the dominant topic, since Anatol Stiller's lifelong search for his true self can only be successfully completed in his social role as Julika's husband. At the other extreme, marriage and its problems are merely hinted at in *Der Mensch erscheint im Holozän;* clues come from the portrait of Herr Geiser's deceased wife, his awareness of her attitude about the way he is living, and, most subtly, his relationship with and treatment of the cat, always a creature with symbolic meaning in Frisch's novels. That marriage and its problems take a prominent place in Frisch's novels is not surprising, because marriage, for him, is *the* model of an interpersonal relationship.

Significantly, only the male perspective is presented on any relationship between a man and a woman. Even if the woman's views are considered or expressed, they are always filtered through a male reporter. Thus, to understand what Frisch says about men's relationships with women, it is essential to recognize the behavior and character traits that unite the male characters he has created over the past fifty years. Interestingly, as the protagonists of his novels age, the nature of their problems in a relationship with a woman changes, too—from youthful sexual inexperience to impotence; from feelings of inadequacy in a profession to problems of aging, retirement, and loss of physical strength and memory. Nevertheless, when all major male characters in Frisch's novels are taken as a group, they present a composite image of contemporary man as he relates to women.

FRISCH'S MEN: COMMON CHARACTERISTICS

Frisch's protagonists are typical of the modern intellectual. They are confused about themselves and their role in society. They have lost their inner equilibrium and struggle valiantly against great odds to regain it. In the process, they also discover who they *really* are. Most of them appear as the first-person narrator of the novel. Stiller, for example, writes his own story in seven notebooks while in jail; Faber records his in a final report; the unnamed narrator of *Mein Name sei Gantenbein* relates events from the lives of three imaginary characters he has created from the whole cloth of his own personality; Max describes a quiet weekend at Montauk, filled with the present and recollections of his past; even Dr. Schaad in *Blaubart* is forced by circumstances to review his own life as punctuated by his seven marriages while he wrestles with the guilt of a murder he did not commit.

Isolation

Frisch's contemporary man is essentially a loner, yet paradoxically he suffers from loneliness. None of the protagonists is actively involved with society; all pursue their careers in solitude. They have few if any male friends, their parents are usually dead or far in the background, and they have very scant interaction with any relatives, siblings, or children. They crave the companionship of a woman, and each of them builds at least one loving relationship during the course of his story. However, few of them meet a woman fully compatible sexually, socially, intellectually, and temperamentally—and if they do, they do not seem to know how to interact with her so as to keep the relationship alive, honest, and satisfying for both. Partly because they are so alone, they become heavily dependent on the woman.

Within these generalizations, however, are a number of temporary exceptions. Jürg Reinhart, for example, deliberately gives up his painting and the bohemian, individualistic life-style that went along with it to join productive society and thus position himself more properly as an appropriate husband for Hortense. Unfortunately, by abandoning his art he loses his charm for Hortense; no longer does he represent for her the free, romantic, somewhat irresponsible way of life that attracted her to him in the first place. Through her relationship with Jürg, Hortense has glimpsed what to her seems to be "das wirkliche Leben." She is not nearly as interested in a nine-to-five draftsman as she was in the carefree artist with the unstructured life-style. As for Jürg, once his affair with Hortense ends, he retreats completely from society. He changes his name and becomes a gardener, again a loner who only observes life from the sidelines. Eventually, believing his life to be of no value and he a useless misfit, he commits suicide.

Stiller's outcome is considerably more positive. Like Jürg, he is an artist, a sculptor. Although his profession is a solitary one, he seems to have a circle of male friends. He meets Julika with a group of them, and some of them come to visit him in jail. He even volunteers to fight in the Spanish Civil War, thus indicating his willingness to become a cog serving a social cause. His enlistment is a personal misjudgment, however, and Stiller frequently gives the impression that his friends are not really important to him. The next time he needs to escape social pressures he travels alone, as a stowaway on a freighter, to America.

Stiller makes one significant friendship while he is in jail. Rolf, the prosecuting attorney for his case, becomes perhaps the best friend he has ever had. Their initial conversations are motivated by Rolf's curiosity to meet this Stiller who was once his wife's lover; their friendship, however, grows to be a sincere one, and by the end of the novel Rolf seems to be Stiller's only true friend.

Like Jürg, Stiller attempts to commit suicide at a time when he believes his life is useless. He fails in the attempt and, given an option, chooses to live. He tries for a second time to create a meaningful marriage with Julika, but when she dies without his succeeding, he retreats into the complete solitude of his *ferme vaudoise* in the Swiss mountains (III 733). Unlike Jürg, however, Stiller continues to practice some form of his art and lives at peace with himself.

The civil engineer Walter Faber is also a loner. Although his job with the United Nations requires him to travel to many lands and to interact with a great many diverse people, Faber prefers to avoid all strangers whenever he can. He considers people to be a strain, as he demonstrates repeatedly: first when he tries, unsuccessfully, to escape from Ivy's company at the New York airport; next when he ignores the conversational overtures of his seatmate on the plane; and later when he wants to leave his boss's Saturday night party and return to his own apartment, which now, however, seems to belong to someone else.

Another loner is Felix Enderlin, the scholar, one of the three facets of the narrator of *Mein Name sei Gantenbein*. Enderlin can work creatively by himself but is at a loss when he is expected to accept the laurels he has won and to interact with his peers and with students. Max, the writer (*Montauk*), is another protagonist who practices a lonely profession. He has had a family and friends and continues to think warmly of them, but his memories are filled with losses and failed relationships, and at the time of the novel he is content with a temporary, though not a casual, affair. Herr Geiser, too, in Der Mensch erscheint im Holozän, remembers a fuller life with a wife and daughter, not so much with regret for his present solitude as with acceptance. His chosen isolation from society becomes frighteningly complete, though, as a result of a prolonged mountain storm and a landslide. Finally, Dr. Felix Schaad in Blaubart is also a loner of sorts; he abandons his medical practice in the course of the novel, retreats into psychological isolation, and finally drives into a tree to end his life.

Loneliness

Ironically, the loner life-style chosen by Frisch's protagonists produces in most of them a profound loneliness they seek to escape in a relationship with a woman, almost any woman. With few exceptions, Frisch's men cannot keep their own company for very long. Felix Enderlin before his hospitalization and Walter Faber before he meets Sabeth illustrate this characteristic prominently. Enderlin dreams obsessively of women—not whole women, but merely their genitals. His talent for flirtatiously opening a relationship is demonstrated when he joins the narrator in a conversation with a stranger, Lila, in a bar. The smooth way in which he moves from bar to opera invitation to Lila's bed demonstrates considerable experience. Faber is probably less facile than Enderlin in his seduction of women, because Faber fears sexual involvement almost as much as he craves it. Nevertheless, his near sexual-bondage-type relationship with Ivy symbolizes his unsuccessful lifelong search for meaningful, normal companionship with a woman.

That neither Enderlin's nor Faber's relationships with women have satisfactory outcomes is primarily the result of a lack of commitment on their part, either to their partner or to the relationship. They enter each relationship tentatively, fearing the result of making a total commitment to someone outside themselves. This inability to make a commitment, not only to a woman but to any interpersonal relationship, is a common problem of the modern intellectual. In Frisch's novels, it is the source of Enderlin's indecisiveness and of Faber's detachment from life and people.

Nowhere is the deep loneliness of a protagonist more vividly portrayed than in Faber's description of his solitary life:

> Gefühle . . . sind Ermüdungserscheinungen, nichts weiter, jedenfalls bei mir. Man macht schlapp! Dann hilft es auch nichts, Briefe zu schreiben, um nicht allein zu sein. Es ändert nichts; nachher hört man doch nur seine eigenen Schritte in der leeren Wohnung. Schlimmer noch: diese Radiosprecher, die Hundefutter anpreisen, Backpulver oder was weiß ich, dann plötzlich verstummen: Auf Wiederhören bis morgen früh! Dabei ist es erst zwei Uhr. Dann Gin, obschon ich Gin, einfach so, nicht mag, dazu Stimmen von der Straße, Hupen beziehungsweise das Dröhnen der Subway . . . es ist ja egal. Es kommt vor, daß ich dann einfach einschlafe, die Zeitung auf dem Knie, die Zigarette auf dem Teppich. Ich reiße mich zusammen. Wozu? . . . Dann stehe ich einfach da, Gin im Glas, den ich nicht mag, und trinke; ich stehe, um keine Schritte zu hören in meiner Wohnung, Schritte, die doch nur meine eigenen sind. (IV 92)

> *Feelings . . . are fatigue phenomena, that's all, at any rate in my case. You get run down. Then writing letters doesn't make any difference; afterward you still hear your own footsteps in the empty apartment. The radio announcers promoting dog food, baking powder or what have you, and then suddenly falling silent after wishing you good-by "till tomorrow morning at six o'clock." And now it's only two o'clock. Then gin, although I don't like gin by itself, in the background voices from the street, cars honking or the rumble of the subway trains . . . sounds like that. Sometimes I just fall asleep, the newspaper on my lap and my cigarette on the carpet. I pull myself together. What for? . . . Then I just stand there with the gin, which I don't like, in my glass, drinking; I stand still so as not to hear steps in my apartment, steps that are after all only my own. (Homo Faber 94)*

Max too is lonely, but at Montauk his loneliness is somewhat different from Faber's, although as painful. Loneliness has driven Max at various times in his life to anger, to bitterness, to self-doubt, and to irrational acts like his dangerous nonstop drive from Rome to Zurich through a rainy, foggy night over treacherous mountain roads just to be with his beloved Ingeborg (VI 716-17). Moments of loneliness attack him, even on the peaceful Montauk beach in Lynn's company, when he remembers the women he has loved.

Max has separated from four well-loved women for a variety of reasons—twice related to a change in career and life-style (Käte and Constanze), once because of a temperamental incompatibility that eventually surpassed his tolerance and destroyed his love (Ingeborg), and once perhaps because an age difference and resulting opposing perspectives caused his partner (Marianne) to love someone else. For the present, though, Max is not alone, but finds warmth and comfort in his relationship with Lynn.

The narrator of *Mein Name sei Gantenbein* (and Gantenbein himself when the novel ends) is not so much lonely as baffled. The narrator's aloneness is the motivation for the novel: he wants to find out why he is left alone, why the loving relationship in which he was a partner has been dissolved. Although Frisch never provides a direct answer to that question, the narrator, after he sees Gantenbein's marriage end because Lila cannot live with a lie, seems to have found enough of an answer to satisfy himself. At the end of the novel he, like Max, has begun a new, comfortable relationship with a woman and is content.

Creativity

Frisch seems to see creativity, or at least an aesthetic sensibility, as an important component of contemporary man. Most of his protagonists have in common an essentially creative profession. Jürg and Stiller are artists, Max is a writer. Kilian and, in his youth, Max are architects, a profession Max (and

Jürg) consider less creative and more routine than art, but one that nevertheless requires both creative imagination and engineering skills.

Walter Faber may be the exception in this company. He symbolizes a certain type of contemporary man who distinguishes himself through his predominantly rational relationship to the world. As an engineer, he sees man as the ruler over nature and the complex problems of human existence as merely a raw-material problem. Before his return to Europe—the cradle of art, philosophy, and mythology—from the United States—the land where technology and industry dominate and shape "the American way of life"—Walter Faber lacks any relationship to art. Aesthetic aspects of human existence escape him; they do not fit into his utilitarian view of the world. In Faber's life everything has been reduced, or so he believes, to that which can be measured; his life is run by an appointment calendar; the world becomes for him explainable through perfection and precision (Honsza 74-75). Frisch shows that he disagrees with this sort of contemporary man for, as the novel develops, the aesthetic element enters Faber's life along with Sabeth. Under her tutelage Faber learns that he, too, can be creative; his creative potential is merely undeveloped.

The profession of the narrator of *Gantenbein* is never stated, but his method of investigating his particular problem through three fictional characters demonstrates that he belongs to the creative group. For most of his other male characters, Frisch has selected professions familiar from previous novels. In *Gantenbein*, Svoboda is an architect, Enderlin a scholar and writer, and Gantenbein, if employed, seems to be a writer able to work at home. Rolf, in *Stiller*, is an attorney, and Schaad, in *Blaubart*, is a physician—both occupations that fit the general creative nature of the professions Frisch's male characters practice.

Chauvinism

Frisch's men share one characteristic uniformly: every one of them is a chauvinist—and so are several of the women, on occasion. Chauvinism seems to be widespread in twentieth-

FINAL CONSIDERATIONS   337

century society, as Frisch sees it, and he deplores its presence. Only Max comes to recognize this characteristic in himself clearly, as he shows in his reaction to Marianne's comment that, during the ten years she and Max have lived together, he has done nothing to help her realize her potential (VI 678-79). The basic situation is clear enough: each man behaves from the start of the relationship as if he were "Gottvater oder mindestens Adam, das Weib aus seiner Rippe gemacht: KOMME FOLGE MIR, ICH LEITE DICH!" (VI 679), *"God Almighty, or at least Adam, from whose rib Woman was made: COME, FOLLOW, AND I WILL LEAD!" (Montauk 63).*

But Marianne is not the only woman who speaks up on the subject of chauvinism. Lila, in her all-night discussion with Svoboda about her relationship with Enderlin, also accuses her husband of chauvinism, though more obliquely, when she objects to his seeing her "solely as a woman," not as a partner and a human being who has as much right to self-fulfillment as a man (V 232/*Gantenbein* 220). Implied in Lila's objection is that her marriage fails to offer her the opportunity for self-realization. Hanna voices a similar complaint when she tells Faber, "Der Mann sieht sich als Herr der Welt, die Frau nur als seinen Spiegel" (VI 140), *"The man sees himself as master of the world and the woman only as his mirror" (Homo Faber 144).*

Although none of the other women Frisch writes about addresses the problem of male chauvinism as directly as Hanna, Lila, or Marianne, the problem clearly exists. When Jürg Reinhart, for example, expects Yvonne to write to Hauswirt accepting the money her former employer offered so she and Jürg can extend their vacation in the Tessin, his behavior is not only selfish but also chauvinistic (I 462). Stiller's behavior is chauvinistic when he expects Sibylle to drop everything and accompany him to Paris on short notice (III 632-35) and when he is so preoccupied with preparations for an upcoming exhibition of his sculpture that he is oblivious to Sibylle's need to share important news: she is pregnant with their child (III 629-32). Walter Faber demonstrates chauvinism in his relationship with Ivy: for example, he tries to break off their relationship with a letter typewritten in the desert (IV 30-31) and later deliberately stays away from his apartment rather than face Ivy and her wiles, hoping she will get tired of waiting for him and leave (IV 64-65)—behavior that is cowardly as well. His most cruelly chauvinistic act is leaving for his first job in Baghdad, comfortably assuming that Hanna will follow instructions and abort the child, his child, she is carrying (IV 56-57). Nor is Faber the only male in Homo faber to act like a chauvinist: the Baptist minister does his share when, under the guise of art enthusiast, he uses every opportunity to paw Sabeth (IV 76-78), which infuriates Faber.

To be fair, several of the women, too, take dramatic and high-handed, chauvinistic actions affecting the men. Yvonne decides on her own to abort a child and leave her first husband, assuring him there is nothing more to talk about, actions so devastating to him that he commits suicide. Seeming not to learn from experience, she suddenly leaves Jürg, too, and gives him the same answer—nothing to talk about—although this time she keeps the child but never tells either Jürg or her husband Hauswirt who the father really is. Similarly, Sibylle aborts Stiller's child and only tells him about it years later, while he is in jail. Hanna in Homo faber, like Yvonne in Die Schwierigen, keeps her child, marries a substitute father (who in Hanna's case knows about the pregnancy), but refuses to allow him to become a real father by having herself sterilized—thus destroying the marriage and, quite possibly, the man. Hanna's behavior is basically chauvinistic with all men, none of whom has her respect and all of whom she feels are inferior to her and to her daughter.

From their perspectives, all Frisch's women have their own particular reasons for their chauvinistic attitude. Hanna seems to speak for all of them when she observes:

Solange Gott ein Mann ist, nicht ein Paar, kann das Leben einer Frau . . . nur so bleiben, wie es heute ist, nämlich erbärmlich, die Frau als Proletarier der Schöpfung, wenn auch noch so elegant verkleidet. (V 140)

As long as God is a man, not a couple, the life of a woman . . . is bound to remain as it is now, namely wretched, with woman the proletarian of Creation, however smartly dressed. (Homo Faber 145)

Hanna prophesies a dismal future for true equality between men and women in these lines.

One might assume that the chauvinism of the protagonists in Frisch's novels, like that of the women, reflects their strong confidence in themselves. That is not the case; instead, the men's chauvinism frequently masks their sexual insecurities. This is especially apparent in Stiller and Faber, both of whom have difficulty accepting their own sexuality. This discomfort is reflected in Stiller's dislike of sweating, his feeling of awkwardness and filth when he is with Julika, and his retreat from her when she occasionally reaches out to him in love (III 458-60). Faber's uneasiness is also reflected in his aversion to such normal bodily functions as sweating and growing a beard and in his extreme vulnerability to, and dread of, Ivy's seduction. In addition, both Stiller and Faber are plagued by the irrational fear that they may be unable to satisfy a woman sexually. Enderlin shares that fear; his experience with women has taught him that the longer he knows them and the more he comes to love them, the more readily they tell him that he knows nothing about love.

Behind the sexual fears of Frisch's male characters lies man's ultimate fear of impotence. Only Stiller openly admits this fear to a sexual partner, Sibylle, when they discuss the meaning of his traumatic experience during the Spanish Civil War (III 617); Faber and Max merely record instances of its occurrence (IV 178; VI 661,741). Even Enderlin's obsession with female genitalia may be interpreted as an expression of his excessive fear of sexual inadequacy and impotence (V 148-49).

Agnosticism

None of the protagonists in Frisch's novels ever feels for any length of time really whole, comfortable, and secure about himself in his relationship with the woman he loves. Yet, because they characteristically have no close friend or family, they have no place to turn outside the partnership for comfort and support. One source of strength for such a man could be religion—but only in *Stiller*, during the long conversations between Rolf and Stiller, does Frisch introduce this possibility. Stiller frequently reads the Bible while he is in jail, but on two occasions he admits that he is unable to pray (III 690,772); later, fearing for Julika's life, he specifically asks Rolf to pray for him that she recover from her lung operation (III 777).

Stiller, like all Frisch's protagonists, is an agnostic. He cannot believe in the existence of any superior, supernatural being, any ultimate power or reality beyond himself. Such a power or reality is unknown to him, and he believes it to be probably unknowable. He cannot take the leap of faith that religion requires. Marion, the puppeteer in Frisch's *Tagebuch*, is also unable to take this kind of leap, although the leap to which his "guardian angel" invites him is not a religious leap of faith but an existential leap to himself, his own true being (II 500-01). Stiller, like Marion, is a man whose experience of life is grounded in an empirically verifiable existence. Such a man cannot believe in the existence of an unverifiable God, just as Marion cannot believe that he can walk across water, as his angel bids him to do.

Stiller shares this fundamentally agnostic attitude with the other Frisch protagonists, especially Walter Faber. These men perceive life as existence in an unfathomable universe in which the individual alone assumes ultimate responsibility for his deeds. The deeds are committed as exercises of free will, without the individual ever knowing for certain if any of his acts are right or wrong, good or bad. He has no criterion, no moral yardstick against which to measure his behavior. Like the relationships Frisch's protagonists form, the world they inhabit has no security; neither does it contain values or beliefs on which they can rely. The only thing they can really depend on is their existence in the present.

Nowhere in Frisch's novels is the recognition and acceptance of this state more vividly illustrated than in *Homo faber*. In the process of writing his report, and later in his conversations with Hanna, Faber gropes through memories of his relationship with Sabeth, seeking to come to terms with himself, his guilt, and his life. In remembering the joy that Sabeth lived and shared, symbolized by the beauty of their last sunrise together, he achieves a radiant insight, which he records shortly before his death:

Auf der Welt sein: im Licht sein . . . standhalten dem
Licht, der Freude . . . im Wissen, daß ich erlösche im Licht
. . . standhalten der Zeit . . . [der] Ewigkeit im Augenblick. Ewig sein: gewesen sein. (IV 199)

*To be alive: to be in the light . . . to stand up to the light, to
joy . . . to stand up to time . . . to eternity in the instant. To
be eternal means to have existed. (Homo Faber 210)*

Max, in Montauk, gains a similar insight that he states less
ecstatically: "Fear of old age is melancholy, but the [conscious-
ness] of death is something different: one is [conscious] of it
even in times of [joy]" (VI 751; Montauk 140). That consciousness
enhances the experience of the present moment. The narrator
in *Mein Name sei Gantenbein* expresses the same insight when, at
the conclusion of the torturous analysis of himself, he declares
in the final sentence of that novel: "Leben gefällt mir—" (V
320), "living pleases me—."

The composite picture of modern man that emerges from
Frisch's novels is that of a creative though often lonely intellectual who, because he lacks real commitment to the people and
relationships most important to him, leads for the most part the
life of a loner. He is plagued by fears of sexual insecurity that
he frequently masks with chauvinistic behavior, especially toward the woman he loves. Spiritually, he is an agnostic.

How, then, does this man respond when confronted with
typical twentieth-century situations? Taken separately, each
protagonist is distinctly individual, and the story each tells is
strictly personal. Nevertheless, because each protagonist represents contemporary man as Frisch sees him, their behavior is
often similar.

FRISCH'S MEN: SIMILAR RESPONSES

In all of his novels, Frisch places his major male characters in
a series of interpersonal-relationship situations that provoke

specific attitudes and reactions. Since his primary focus is always on the individual, these situations generally take place in the private realm, sometimes even in the most intimate sphere of a character's life, where he reveals his most personal thoughts and feelings, often completely unguarded. The thoughts and feelings and the characters' resulting behavior are not as individual as one might suspect, given the distinctive nature of each of the Frisch men. This is in part because the situations in which Frisch places them are associated with a cluster of topics and themes that tend to recur and reappear in various ways throughout his oeuvre. Those that recur most prominently in the novels are love and the affiliated concepts of marriage and jealousy, the tendency to form an unchanging image of one's partner, the fear of repetition, and the effect of time on a man's life. Each major theme subsumes associated concepts: for example, figurative blindness and problems in communication are associated with marriage, aging and death are associated with time. In the comments that follow, I shall show to what extent the responses of Frisch's male characters are similar within each of these six recurring thematic clusters.

Love

Jürgen Schröder observes that Frisch's novels portray men in a world in which, despite their best efforts, they repeatedly lose in the game of love (Schröder 58). Insurmountable obstacles are placed in their way, or circumstances force them into impossible situations that seem to be or clearly are beyond their control. Confronted with such difficulties, Frisch's men consistently are unable to establish any lasting, intimate relationship with a beloved woman, no matter how hard they try.

It might be argued that Frisch's novels really are concerned not with love, but with the absence of love—at least of the love that goes beyond *philia*, friendship, and *eros*, sexual love. Most of Frisch's protagonists are searching for a love that includes *agape*, the all-embracing, universal love that allows both partners to realize themselves emotionally and spiritually through the beloved. Most of them find it only briefly, if at all. Of all the protagonists, Stiller exemplifies most completely the struggle to find that love, and in the end he fails. The narrator of *Mein Name sei Gantenbein*—in the figure of the "blind" Gantenbein—pursues a similar goal, although less obsessively. Walter Faber, the *homo technicus*, becomes aware at least subliminally of the existence of *agape* during his brief relationship with Sabeth; and Max in *Montauk* sometimes glimpses it, too, especially in his relationship with Marianne. Only Jürg Reinhart in *Die Schwierigen* does not seem to be aware of this kind of total, all-encompassing love. Until Yvonne unexpectedly leaves him, the love he feels for her remains subordinate to his love of painting landscapes, and his love for Hortense remains constrained by social convention and is eventually overpowered by the couple's irreconcilable differences of birth that extinguish their love for each other.

Jealousy

Factors outside the love relationship may have a dampening effect on it—in Jürg's case even a fatal one. However, factors at the very heart of the relationship may also undermine its vitality and rob it of its spontaneity and joy. Two such factors are jealousy, which fills the lover with terror and doubt, and the propensity to form a rigid image of one's partner, which stifles the relationship. All of Frisch's men suffer from jealousy and tend, along with many of the women they love, to form an inflexible image of their partners.

Jealousy, as Frisch relates it to each of his protagonists, is an expression of their characteristic insecurity and self-doubt. Because they are unsure of themselves, especially in relationships with women, they easily become victims of jealousy. The common sources of this jealousy are two sides of the same coin: fear of comparison with another man on one side and excessive possessiveness of the beloved on the other. In every case the jealousy is detrimental to the behavior of the lover and, in consequence, to the relationship.

Once he is a victim of jealousy, the protagonist often becomes tongue-tied and unable to express his feelings. In reaction to the emotional turmoil raging within him, his behavior becomes either compulsively eccentric or violent. For example Jürg, in the grip of jealousy, sneaks up to Yvonne's apartment where, outside her door, he eavesdrops on her conversation with Hauswirt; he stands for hours in snow and rain in the courtyard, looking up at the lighted windows of her apartment behind which two shadows move; and, since Yvonne has been hanging up the telephone when he calls, he lies in wait for her on a street corner to force a discussion of their situation. Only when she rejects him publicly can he accept that he has lost her forever (I 471-76).

Stiller, in contrast, tries to escape the reality of Julika's affair with a public relations agent by taking a large quantity of a sedative that lets him sleep for days (III 453). When Walter Faber is plagued by jealousy over Sabeth he becomes overbearing, patronizing, or devious. He once coaxes her boyfriend, a graphic artist, to leave her cabin with him and then, to keep him from going back, engages him in a conversation about his profession and his future (IV 81-82). Another time, during an animated conversation between Sabeth and the Baptist minister about art, Faber, just because he is jealous of their knowledge of the subject, insists that the job of an engineer, compared with that of an artist, is truly a man's job, perhaps the only worthwhile job for a man (IV 76-77). He also displays alternately bored and overeager behavior when he believes that Sabeth's youthful enthusiasm for the visual arts exceeds her interest in him (IV 108-12).

Gantenbein expresses jealousy mainly through eccentric behavior. After he decides to abandon his role of blind man and now openly sees Lila's deceit, he first has an affair to get even (V 176) and then embezzles and destroys three letters addressed to his wife that, without ever reading them, he assumes are from her lover (V 176-82). Next he breaks open Lila's private safe where, ironically, he finds only the love letters he himself wrote to her when *he* was the illicit lover and she the wife of Svoboda (V 189-91). Finally he locks Lila and a casual visitor, whom he mistakes for her lover, into their apartment bedroom and leaves the apartment for a drive in the country (V 195-98).

Svoboda's reaction, when he learns his wife has a lover, is equally compulsive. Blinded by his emotions, he keeps Lila up all night in a futile effort to make sense of the situation, then in the early morning hours hurls first his whiskey glass and soon thereafter the whole bottle into the fireplace to vent his frustration and anguish. Then, no longer able to face the reality of his threatened marriage, he drives aimlessly from resort to resort, stopping in every post office in hopes of finding a letter from her. Unable to act sensibly himself, he leaves to Lila the decision about their future (V 238-40).

Of all the protagonists in Frisch's novels, Max seems to suffer from jealousy most deeply, as he reveals in his memories of Ingeborg and Marianne. Because of ravenous jealousy, Max gives way to frustration, anger, and a sense of helplessness. At times he waits for hours for the return of the beloved, either fearfully joyous or hopelessly drunk (VI 674,680,715-16). With Ingeborg he learned that angry accusations drive the beloved away, and so he watches and waits from his New York hotel room, a prisoner of his jealousy yet anxiously expectant, for a sign of Marianne among the crowd of pedestrians passing in the street below (VI 673). His relationship with neither woman survives. His deeply felt love for them cannot transcend the destructive power of his jealousy.

Whether Herr Geiser was afflicted with jealousy we can only surmise from his reaction to his son-in-law, the know-it-all (VII 233). Felix Schaad in *Blaubart* certainly suffered greatly under the malaise of this powerful emotion in his numerous marriages.

A Graven Image

If a relationship is not destroyed by jealousy, Frisch seems to say, it runs the risk of being smothered by the inflexible expectations the partners have for themselves and for each other. This danger is first stated explicitly in *Stiller*. Julika is told, at Davos, that to keep God's second commandment one must not make "a graven image" of another person. She then accuses her husband of having formed such an image of her, seeing her as a physically frail, frigid woman whose sensuality is imprisoned within her and needs to be set free (III 495-500). She does not realize that her behavior and the role she plays offstage have contributed materially to Stiller's image of her, nor does she recognize that she has formed an equally inflexible image of him. Not without reason, she sees him as a man obsessed with the idea of saving her, turning her into a "normal" woman. She fails to convince him that she is quite content with her life.

Both Walter Faber and Hanna, in their youth, formed images of each other that are partially reflected in their pet names for each other: "Kunstfee" and "Homo faber" (IV 47). These images stifle the growth of their relationship and contribute materially to its dissolution. Hanna goes even one step further by forming an image of *all* men as creatures who see themselves as masters of the world and women only as their mirror (IV 139-40). This image may account for her less-than-successful relationship with any man, illustrated by her two unsuccessful marriages. On the surface, one might accuse Walter Faber of a similar fault: forming a less-than-flattering image of all women. His superficial relationship with Ivy, which symbolizes all relationships he has had with women since he left Hanna, would support such a claim. However, a more careful look at Faber produces evidence that his superficial relationship with women is the result more of his lack of self-knowledge and self-acceptance, a problem he shares with all of Frisch's protagonists, than of a fixed image.

The men are not the only culprits who stifle their partners. Yvonne in *Die Schwierigen* forms images of two men: her first husband, Hinkelmann, and Jürg Reinhart. In both instances the "sin" of forming a fixed image contributes substantially to the eventual termination of the relationship. Yvonne considers her first husband a helpless, utterly dependent man. Of Jürg, the father of the child she is carrying, she has formed the image of an irresponsible, carefree man who lives from day to day and only for his art. Although the particulars of Yvonne's image have a basis in fact, its rigidity eventually destroys the relationship—even though Yvonne loves Jürg enough to want to keep and protect his child.

The image Hortense forms of Jürg is one of an artist who experiences life free of the social constraints of tradition and convention that bind her. She sees a man intimately involved in and totally committed to the adventure of life and art, a man in full pursuit of "das wirkliche Leben." The image Jürg ultimately develops of himself, that of a failure and a misfit in the world, differs diametrically from Hortense's and is even less realistic. Its danger, again, lies in its rigidity; it leads Jürg to suicide.

Lila has an unreal image of Gantenbein, but in her case the image is based entirely on Gantenbein's pretended blindness. Gantenbein's image of Lila as the unfaithful wife is equally based on the "role" she plays. When both terminate their roles, the devastating power of their rigidly held images of the other becomes menacingly apparent: Gantenbein reacts with confusion when he realizes that Lila is no longer betraying him; Lila, feeling betrayed and publicly exposed, sends him away when he confesses that he has never been blind. What has been a happy marriage is destroyed when the images prove false; Lila simply cannot live with a *seeing* Gantenbein.

The need to form an image of others, even of God, may be a basic human need. In his novels, however, Frisch demonstrates its inherent danger to any relationship, especially an intimate one. The images partners form and hold of each other stifle the partners' growth and curtail their opportunity to develop fully. Julika's illness, tuberculosis, may in this context be seen as symbolic of the suffocating effect Stiller's image of her has on her life during both parts of their marriage. Thus Stiller/White may not be incorrect when he accuses himself of having killed his wife (III 376-77), even though at the time he "confesses" the deed to Knobel, his jailer, it has not yet become a reality.

The complementary marriage of Rolf and Sibylle suggests, albeit tentatively, that a love consisting of *philia, eros,* and *agape,* however imperfectly the three are developed, can free a couple from their reciprocal images. A couple practicing this kind of love can perceive and accept the richness of life that is possible, because that possibility lies within each of us. Frisch writes in his *Tagebuch*:

So wie das All, wie Gottes unerschöpfliche Geräumigkeit, schrankenlos, alles Möglichen voll, aller Geheimnisse voll, unfaßbar ist der Mensch, den man liebt—
Nur die Liebe erträgt ihn so. (II 369)

> Because the person one loves is as ungraspable as the universe, as God's infinite space, he is boundless, full of possibilities, full of secrets—
> Only when one loves can one bear it. (Sketch I 17)

Religion commands man not to form an image of God; Frisch commands the characters of his novels not to form images of those they love, because for Frisch, who places God inside man, God is "das Lebendige in jedem Menschen, das, was nicht erfaßbar ist" (II 374), "*the living part of every human being, the part that cannot be grasped*" (*Sketch I* 21). Only love, uncompromising and unconditional, is able to accept that which cannot be grasped, that which is unique to an individual and cannot be expressed in words or images without limiting that individual's wealth of realized and still-unrealized possibilities.

Repetition

According to Frisch, another factor inherent in any relationship of some duration is repetition, which can also stifle the relationship. The problem for Frisch's protagonists is not so much repetition per se as their *fear* of repetition—any kind of repetition: of feelings, thoughts, actions, words, experiences, or situations. This existential *Angst* frequently becomes an obsession. Its paralyzing effect on a character may be seen especially in the imaginings of the narrator in *Mein Name sei Gantenbein*, who demonstrates the effect of repetition by projecting Enderlin and Lila's relationship ten years into the future. He sees them as "two bodies dead to love . . . that [hardly ever reach out for each other any more]" (V 133-37/*Gantenbein* 127-30). Everything in their life has become routine. Instead of enthusiasm and spontaneity, only monotony and the dull daily routine of life are left to them—except for an unsatisfied longing Enderlin and Lila share, not for each other, but beyond each other (V 136). This longing is similar to the one Kilian experiences each spring in *Bin oder Die Reise nach Peking*, a longing that can never be satisfied.

Stiller, after his suicide attempt and before his trial, has moments of keen insight that he records in his notebooks.

FINAL CONSIDERATIONS 349

Although he states repeatedly that he fears repetition, he is about to repeat the challenge that destroyed his marriage. For the second time he is falling in love with Julika, and he will once again make the challenge of awakening her to real love the basis of their relationship. He is aware that he is repeating himself, but he knows:

> alles hängt davon ab, ob es gelingt, sein Leben nicht außerhalb der Wiederholung zu erwarten, sondern die Wiederholung, die ausweglose, aus freiem Willen (trotz Zwang) zu seinem Leben zu machen, indem man anerkennt: Das bin ich! . . . (III 421)

> *everything depends on whether one succeeds in ceasing to wait for life outside repetition, and instead, of one's free will (in spite of compulsion), manages to turn repetition, inescapable repetition, into one's life by acknowledging: This is I . . . (I'm Not Stiller 59)*

This view does not alleviate his fear of repetition, but it provides him with a means of accepting it. By placing the repetitive action on the continuum of transient time, he hopes to be able to succeed. Some situations, however, cannot be improved by repetition. Hanna's caution to Walter Faber that one can't live one's life over again could apply as well to Stiller.

Max in *Montauk* is concerned about repetition, too, although his concern is of a different kind. As he begins his brief relationship with Lynn, he expresses the hope that he will not fall into a role, one learned by the repetition of experiences shared in the past with other women. It would diminish the unique experience of his still-embryonic relationship with Lynn (VI 683). But since their relationship will not progress much beyond the embryonic stage, something both know and accept from the start, the experience they share is potentially even more subject to the dangers and dulling effect of repetition, the repetition of similar experiences with other partners, because neither partner makes a total commitment to the other. Like Enderlin, Max attempts instead to capture and savor only the uniqueness of his experience with Lynn, which takes place in an extended present and has no future.

The challenge facing Max—to escape the larger, repetitive pattern—becomes even more trying during the weekend he and Lynn spend at Montauk. There, removed from the hectic routine of a busy day in Manhattan, old memories of situations he has shared with other women break into his consciousness. He is living in a "dünne Gegenwart" (VI 708), a *"thin present moment"* (*Montauk* 94), which, transparent to the past and its memories, functions for Max like a membrane that things long repressed and secret can penetrate to become at last communicable (Stauffacher 59-64).

The memories that surface most often are those of four women whom Max loved deeply and still cares about. In addition to underlining the repetitiveness of his experience with women, Max's memories invite comparison between past and present experiences, even between the partners then and now, thus threatening the uniqueness of each. Max, aware of this danger, looks at his current young lover "to see if his tender feelings are really directed at Lynn" (VI 684/*Montauk* 69). His conclusion is reassuring: "his caresses are meant for Lynn . . . his feelings are not taking her for another . . ." (VI 702-03/*Montauk* 88).

All Frisch's protagonists are as concerned as Max about the deadening effect of their repetitive behavior on the quality of their experience. But repetition is the basis of diurnal (clock) time, an integral part of living and thus of relationships. Frisch suggests that, as an antidote to the dulling effect repetition has on any relationship, the partners keep alive the sense of enthusiasm, joy, and spontaneity that marked the beginning of the relationship. These ideas develop gradually in Frisch's novels. They are more implied than suggested in the first version of *Die Schwierigen* (1942), but appear quite clearly, although still embryonically, only two years later in *Bin oder Die Reise nach Peking*. They are stated more explicitly and explored in much more detail in the later novels.

Marriage

Marriage as an institution, a theoretical concept, and a way of life is investigated repeatedly and at length in Frisch's novels.

FINAL CONSIDERATIONS 351

In *Stiller* and *Mein Name sei Gantenbein* marriage becomes a dominant topic; in *Homo faber, Die Schwierigen,* and *Montauk* it figures less prominently but remains important; in *Der Mensch erscheint im Holozän* and *Blaubart* marriage is only a peripheral topic.

Jürg Reinhart, after Yvonne has left him to marry the businessman Hauswirt, sees in marriage "the greatest adventure that one can enter into . . . [the] commitment to a puzzle that outlasts us" (I 500). Having lost Yvonne, Jürg is willing to enter that great adventure with Hortense. For her, however, the greatest adventure in life is not a conventional marriage with Jürg but a close, unmarried association with him that allows her to participate in what she perceives to be his untraditional, carefree life—her version of "das wirkliche Leben." Years later, when Jürg and Hortense meet again, she admits that her marriage to Ammann, although not unhappy, has not been the great adventure Jürg once perceived marriage to be: it is a continuous series of incidents and events that make constant demands on her time and energy and challenge her consistently to do her duty as a wife and mother as best she can (I 586).

Jürg's concept of marriage as life's greatest adventure must be wrong, if the marriages of Yvonne and Hortense are reliable indicators. Yvonne's eventual opinion of marriage is even less positive than Hortense's and far removed from Jürg's. Yvonne's pragmatic, even somewhat cynical, view resembles the narrator's dismal projection of Enderlin and Lila's future life together as a married couple. As Yvonne describes her life with Hauswirt and her thoughts on marriage in general, the picture that emerges is one of a relationship lacking in love, enthusiasm, and spontaneity:

Man wohnt zusammen, man verträgt sich, und der Mann, der das Geld verdient, setzt sich in den anderen Lehnsessel, raucht, schiebt ein Scheit ins Kamin . . . . Man zerstört sich nicht, das ist der Grund, worauf man geht, man ist nicht verliebt, man ist sich gewogen, man verträgt den Geruch des anderen, und das ist viel. . . . Man kennt sich, seine Ansichten, seine Art zu sehen und zu reden, seine Vorlieben im Essen, seine Manieren, seine Grundsätze, seine Wünsche, seine Wunden und seine Empfindlichkeiten. . . . Sie [die Ehe] ist möglich, sobald man nichts Unmögliches von ihr fordert, sobald man über den Wahn hinauswächst, man könne sich verstehen, müsse sich verstehen . . . sobald man ein Gefühl davon gewinnt, daß die Ehe einfach ein Dienst ist, ein Verfahren fürs tägliche Leben. (I 551)

One lives together, one gets along with the other, and the man, who earns the money, sits down in the other armchair, smokes, shoves a log into the fireplace. . . . One does not destroy the other, that is the basis on which one operates, one isn't in love with the other, one appreciates the other, one tolerates the scent of the other, and that is a lot. . . . One knows the other, his opinions, his way of looking at things and of speaking, his preferences in food, his mannerisms, his principles, his wishes, his wounds and sensitivities. . . . It [marriage] is possible as soon as one does not demand anything impossible of it, as soon as one grows beyond the delusion that one can understand the other, has to understand the other . . . as soon as one accepts the feeling that marriage is simply a service, a procedure for daily life.

No two concepts of marriage could be more dissimilar than the routine Yvonne endures and the adventure anticipated by Jürg.

Max, in *Montauk*, has experienced a little of both extremes in his two marriages—a good marriage but less exciting and adventurous than "das wirkliche Leben" in his conventional marriage to Constanze, after he gave up early attempts at writing in favor of a more secure career in architecture (VI 665-69,731-34), and, in his marriage to Marianne, almost the fulfillment and the great adventure Jürg proposed (VI 742-47). Max was committed to both marriages, as his detailed recollections of scenes and incidents show. He still holds Constanze, his first wife and mother of his three children, in high regard (VI 690) and is concerned about his children (VI 652). He also still cares deeply about Marianne, although they have separated by mutual consent.

After the young Faber and Hanna call off their wedding at the last moment, Walter Faber never again sees any reason to marry, certainly not to escape the fundamental loneliness that is

FINAL CONSIDERATIONS 353

a part of his life—that is, not until he meets and falls in love with Sabeth. Faber has a special problem when he thinks about himself as a married man. His description of the daily breakfast routine shared with a woman is more cynical than amusing (VI 91), although it is less stark than the description of the routine of married life projected for Enderlin and Lila (V 133-37). Nevertheless, in his relationships with Hanna and Sabeth, Faber experiences something so appealing that he, a self-professed bachelor on principle, admits: "I thought about marriage as never before" (IV 108/*Homo Faber* 111). By this time he feels so strongly about marriage that, after Sabeth's death, he transfers his desire to marry from the daughter to the mother in a belated attempt to correct an earlier omission (IV 165).

However Faber, like most of Frisch's male characters, never develops any clearly defined ideas about marriage. Marriage is something Frisch's men either do or don't do. Except for Gantenbein, who really works at making his marriage a success, their behavior illustrates that they are mostly conventional husbands; Rolf is even less than that, since Sibylle can accuse him of being a "married bachelor" (III 639/*I'm Not Stiller* 254).

In *Stiller* and *Mein Name sei Gantenbein*, Frisch explores the possibilities and limitations of marriage in a more deliberate, organized manner. In each novel he contrasts two marriages: in *Stiller*, the marriage of Stiller and Julika with that of Rolf and Sibylle; in *Mein Name sei Gantenbein*, the marriage of Gantenbein and Lila with that of Svoboda and Lila. Each of the four marriages exposes different aspects and problems of marital life.

The basic problem in the marriage of Rolf and Sibylle is that the partners are unable to communicate effectively until it is almost too late to preserve the marriage. Inability to communicate effectively is also the problem in the Stiller-Julika marriage, but unlike Rolf and Sibylle these partners cannot solve it; as a result, they and their needs remain essentially incomprehensible to each other. Admittedly, the nature of the communication problem is different in these two marriages. What Rolf and Sibylle have to do is to admit to themselves and each other that they love and need each other; they must also agree that neither needs a periodic extramarital affair to keep their marriage spontaneous and meaningful. Stiller and Julika, however, have always used each other in their relationship in an attempt to free themselves from their own feelings of inadequacy and insecurity. Whereas Rolf and Sibylle learn to give up the restricting images they have formed and hold of each other, Stiller has great difficulty doing so, and Julika will not even try.

The situations of the two couples in *Mein Name sei Gantenbein* differ greatly from each other and from those of the *Stiller* couples. In the Gantenbein-Lila marriage, the husband has adopted the role of a blind man in hopes of getting to know people, especially his wife, more completely; he believes his deception will free the people with whom he comes in contact from the fear that he may possibly see through their pretensions and petty lies. When the need to mask their expressions and actions is removed, people are less vulnerable and more honest, Gantenbein believes, and he hopes that his blindness will enable him to establish a more real, more trusting, and more lasting relationship with them (V 42).

Gantenbein is only partially right. With Camilla, who recognizes his masquerade from the start and accepts him for what he pretends to be—which gives her the opportunity of pretending to be what she wants to be—the ploy works. In his relationship with Lila, who believes in his blindness and needs it to realize her own potential, it works only as long as her belief in her husband's blindness is unshaken. Once he confronts her with the truth, the basis of their marriage is gone. For her, Gantenbein's admission after many years of married "blindness" that he can and always could see is synonymous with his telling her he never loved her.

In the Svoboda-Lila marriage the primary problem is far more ordinary: the husband has taken his wife and her love for him for granted. He has never realized that his wife craves the adventure that once was part of their marriage, an adventure illustrated by her mentioning Peru to Enderlin (V 62,74-75). Like Max in his marriage to Marianne in *Montauk*, Svoboda seems to have done little "to help her realize her potentialities" (VI 679/*Montauk* 63). It is ironic that Svoboda himself sends Lila into the arms of her lover, just as Stiller introduced Julika to the public relations man with whom she then had a brief affair. When they learn that their wives have taken a lover, both men's egos are deeply injured.

Final Considerations 355

Gantenbein and Svoboda, in their respective marriages to Lila, are both figuratively blind to the truths of their situations. Although the "blind" Gantenbein knows that Lila deceives him, he is unable to see that she really loves him. Even though he knows that she would never continue their marriage if she knew that he is not blind (V 103-04), he feels compelled to drop his blind man's role at least temporarily (V 163-98). Then he promptly falls victim to jealousy, just as Svoboda does when he learns about Lila and Enderlin's relationship. In that state, both men illustrate spiritual blindness toward the women they love. Although Svoboda, who has considered his marriage to Lila to be happy and secure, might share Max's admission, "I am always ignorant of [my] true position" (VI 709/*Montauk* 95), Gantenbein, fully aware of his marital situation, is left with no such excuse.

In *Mein Name sei Gantenbein*, Frisch briefly introduces an alternate concept of marriage that illustrates what is wrong with Svoboda's and Rolf's attitudes: each treats his wife as if she were chattel, his exclusive property. The Tohuli, an African tribe, allegedly hold a different concept of marriage (V 192-93). Unlike European and western men, a Tohuli male does not consider the woman he marries his property. Instead, he is her caretaker, and she his responsibility for life. Their marriage has no sexual component; husband and wife are free to engage in sexual activity wherever they find it, including with each other.

On the whole, though, Frisch in his novels does not seriously question the institution of marriage; he only questions, repeatedly and penetratingly, a man's attitudes and behavior in a marriage to the woman he professes to love. In each instance, the man comes up wanting.

Transient Time

The last major recurring concept that affects the male characters' behavior in these novels is their relationship to time. Associated subtopics are aging and death.

In his various *Tagebuch* entries, Frisch identifies two kinds of time. One is measured by a clock, a month, a season, or a year and could be labelled serial or diurnal time; the other is characterized by a progressive transience that moves us inexorably through life toward death, whether or not we pay attention to it. This latter kind of time, transient time, lies at the basis of all existence. Because of it, nothing in life is repeatable, and every existence is confronted by its eventual nonexistence. Consequently the topic of aging, closely associated with the concept of transient time, figures prominently in most of Frisch's novels. It is inevitably related to the various stages in a man's life, each producing its own concerns and resulting behavior.

Frisch understands time in this context not merely as an additive process, but as "a means of showing us one after another things that are in fact interlocked, forming a whole which we can no more grasp than we can see the separate colors that constitute light, until its rays are broken down and dissected" (II 361/*Sketch I* 12-13). What breaks our life into serial form, Frisch continues, is our consciousness; what restores life to its original whole form are dreams. In this context, Frisch observes, fiction serves a similar function: it, too, tries to restore wholeness to a life experienced on a daily basis as "one thing after another," by attempting to emulate dreams.

He continues:

Wenn es stimmt, daß die Zeit nur scheinbar ist, ein bloßer Behelf für unsere Vorstellung, die in ein Nacheinander zerlegt, was wesentlich eine Allgegenwart ist; wenn alles das stimmt . . . warum erschrickt man über jedem Sichtbarwerden der Zeit?
Als wäre der Tod eine Sache der Zeit. (II 493)

If time is really only illusory, a mere aid to our comprehension, separating into a one-thing-after-another what is in fact an omnipresence; if all these ideas about time . . . are indeed true . . . why is one startled by every manifestation of the passage of time?
As if death were a matter of time. (Sketch I, 111)

But death is not a matter of time, Frisch argues. Transient time only brings the inevitability of death into sharper focus. Implicit in this quotation from Frisch's *Tagebuch* are two basic ideas: that the passage of time, its everlasting flow, is experienced by the individual as the process of aging, and that at the end of that aging process stands death, the ultimate goal of all life. Walter Faber's most grievous error is ignoring the existence of transient time and his own aging. In attempting to correct an omission of his youth—not marrying Hanna—by, years later, wanting to marry his and Hanna's daughter, he is woefully out of step with the flow of transient time.

Elsewhere in his *Tagebuch* Frisch expands on the idea of transient time:

> Auch das Tier spürt seine Vergängnis; sonst hätte es keine Angst. Aber das Tier . . . erschrickt nicht über einer Uhr oder einem Kalender, nicht einmal über einem Kalender der Natur. Es trägt den Tod als zeitloses Ganzes, eben als Allgegenwart: wir leben und sterben jeden Augenblick, beides zugleich . . . und da wir nur leben können, indem wir zugleich sterben, verbrauchen wir es [das Leben], wie eine Sonne ihre Glut verbraucht; . . . erst aus dem Nichtsein, das wir ahnen, begreifen wir für Augenblicke, daß wir leben. (II 499-500)

> *Even an animal is aware of its transience; otherwise it would not feel fear. But an animal . . . is not upset by a clock or a calendar, not even the calendar of Nature. It carries death within it as a timeless entity, as an omnipresence, whereas we live and die every second, both at the same time . . . and since we can only live by at the same time dying, we use up life as a sun uses up its glow; . . . it is only the consciousness of a nonexistence which allows us to realize for moments that we are living.* (Sketch I 116-17)

The protagonists of Frisch's novels are conscious of the uniqueness of their life and their ultimate nonexistence. They express that knowledge in various ways, most directly in their relentless pursuit of "das wirkliche Leben." Walter Faber, for example, who has merely a glimpse of this real life before he dies, expresses his conviction about its uniqueness in the exultant one-paragraph summation whose key phrases are:

Auf der Welt sein: im Licht sein. . . . standhalten dem Licht, der Freude . . . im Wissen, daß ich erlösche im Licht . . . standhalten der Zeit . . . [der] Ewigkeit im Augenblick. Ewig sein: gewesen sein. (IV 199)

To be alive: to be in the light. . . . to stand up to the light, to joy . . . in the knowledge that I shall be extinguished in the light. . . to stand up to time . . . to eternity in the instant. To be eternal means to have existed. (Homo Faber 210)

This statement is so important to Frisch that he has Max repeat it in *Montauk*, thus once again illustrating a certain kinship between these two characters. He also has Max express his fervent desire to experience an extended present in his relationship with Lynn during their weekend at Montauk. The narrator of *Mein Name sei Gantenbein*, too, shares Faber's strong conviction about life; he is equally positive when he asserts at the conclusion of the novel: "Living pleases me—" (V 320). Stiller's resolve, after his attempted suicide, to continue his life—"jetzt aber so, daß ein wirklicher Tod zustande kommt" (III 727), "but this time so that a real death [takes] place" (*Stiller* 334)—must be interpreted similarly.

Only two protagonists do not affirm the singularity of their existence. One is Jürg Reinhart, who first changes his identity to that of Anton, a gardener, and then commits suicide. The other is Felix Schaad (*Blaubart*). He, like Jürg, is defeated by his perception of his position in life and therefore kills himself. However, Kilian (*Bin*) and Herr Geiser (*Der Mensch erscheint im Holozän*), each in his own way, are positive about life and the uniqueness of their being.

To experience "das wirkliche Leben," Frisch believes, one must be aware of and respect the various stages in life and engage in activities appropriate to each. It is impossible, as he demonstrates emphatically in *Homo faber*, to repeat or relive any given moment or any particular stage. The metaphor from his first *Tagebuch*, quoted in Chapter One, makes Frisch's position clear.

Wir leben auf einem laufenden Band, und es gibt keine Hoffnung, daß wir uns selber nachholen und einen Augenblick unseres Lebens verbessern können. Wir sind das

FINAL CONSIDERATIONS 359

Damals, auch wenn wir es verwerfen, nicht minder als das
Heute—
Die Zeit verwandelt uns nicht.
Sie entfaltet uns nur. (II 360-61)

*We live on a conveyer belt and have no hope of ever catching
up with ourselves and improving a moment in our life. We are
Then, even if we spurn it, just as much as Now—
Time does not change us.
It just unfolds us. (Sketch I, 12)*

Frisch wrote these lines in 1946. A decade later, Hanna in *Homo faber* expresses similar ideas when she explains to Faber the cause of his error with Sabeth. Although Faber is not really sure what she means by many of the things she says, he does realize that her views of life differ from his. Attempting to explain Hanna's words to himself in his report, he writes:

Mein Irrtum: daß wir Techniker versuchen, ohne den Tod zu leben. Wörtlich: Du behandelst das Leben nicht als Gestalt, sondern als bloße Addition, daher kein Verhältnis zur Zeit, weil kein Verhältnis zum Tod. Leben sei Gestalt in der Zeit. . . . Leben ist nicht Stoff, nicht mit Technik zu bewältigen. Mein Irrtum mit Sabeth: Repetition, ich habe mich so verhalten, als gebe es kein Alter, daher widernatürlich. (IV 170)

My mistake lay in the fact that we technologists try to live without death. Her own words: "You don't treat life as form, but as a mere sum arrived at by addition, hence you have no relationship to time, because you have no relationship to death." Life is form in time. . . . Life is not matter and cannot be mastered by technology. . . . My mistake with Sabeth lay in repetition. I behaved as though age did not exist, and hence contrary to nature. (Homo Faber 178-79)

This is the kind of error Max tries to avoid in his relationship with Lynn. He realizes that "it is wrong to attempt to tie a younger woman to this lack of future which is mine" (VI 751/*Montauk* 140). Intellectually, Max accepts the restrictions transient time places on him at his age. He is also conscious of the three dimensions transient time encompasses—past-present-future—unlike Walter Faber, who tries to ignore them for most of his life. At Montauk, the past—in the form of resurging memories—once again announces its existence. Most of the time the past torments Max; during the weekend at Montauk, however, he comes to accept it and himself (VI 709). This multiple acceptance of the past, himself, and the restrictions of transient time compel Max to experience the present intensely. It is a "thin present" (VI 685) he seeks and shares, gratefully, with Lynn, one into which the past may intrude at any moment. In the peaceful, sheltered environment of Montauk, Lynn symbolizes for Max the present he craves. He observes:

> Ein langer leichter Nachmittag: die Welt entrückt in ihre Zukunft ohne mich. . . . Es bleibt das irre Bedürfnis nach der Gegenwart durch eine Frau. (VI 709)

> *A long, easy afternoon: the world withdrawn into its future without me . . . . All that remains is the mad desire for present identity through a woman.* (Montauk 95-96)

Max shares with other Frisch protagonists this need to validate his existence in the present by interacting with a woman. One is Stiller, who admits that he cannot be alone but needs the presence of a woman (III 681-87). Another is Faber. A third is the narrator of *Mein Name sei Gantenbein*, in the partially representative figures of himself as Enderlin (V 148-49) and Svoboda (V 237), neither of whom can be without a woman's presence, especially in times of emotional stress. The stress Max experiences, however, does not have one specific cause as it does for Enderlin and Svoboda, but arises from his review of important relationships with women throughout his life, stimulated by his dissolving marriage to Marianne.

Frisch makes clear that he is concerned not only with the "mad desire" for a present shared with a woman, but also with the joy to be derived from this shared experience, as he shows especially through Max (VI 680-81,683-84,689-90), Walter Faber in his relationship with Sabeth (IV 124-25,150-52,188-91), and the *Gantenbein* narrator (V 319-20). In these shared experiences with the woman they love, each protagonist comes closest to "das wirkliche Leben."

In *Montauk*, the intense and private experience of the present is illustrated in another way, through Max's description of the madwoman he observes on a street in Manhattan. As her hands gently touch the stone and metal surfaces of the building facades she passes, she experiences an intense happiness, Max observes (VI 747-48). The present this woman experiences is absolute, as Max knows from his life with Ingeborg; it is not subject to the normal restrictions of transient time. In its pure form, it can be experienced only in the state of ecstatic madness, which blocks out memory.

This woman's ecstacy is an extreme illustration of the nature of the experience Frisch's protagonists are trying to describe when they extoll the beauty and happiness they seek and sometimes experience in the present. None of them can explain why this kind of happiness can be achieved only in a relationship with a beloved woman, although they know from experience that it is attainable. They consider it to be an integral part of "das wirkliche Leben," but they never manage to achieve it permanently. The reason lies mostly in themselves, as one after another demonstrates. Max in *Montauk* may be seen as speaking for all when he observes: "It is not the women who make a fool of me. I do that myself" (VI 696/*Montauk* 81).

EPILOGUE

Over the past fifty years, Max Frisch has written eight major novels and many plays, essays, and at least four literary diaries, of which two have been published so far. The composite image of contemporary man that emerges from his novels is that of a modern intellectual, substantially egocentric, often indecisive, and often confused about himself and his life. He is, as Max in *Montauk* puts it, always ignorant of his true situation (VI 709). Periodically, he suffers from loneliness and a sense of insecurity. When deeply involved with a woman, he loses his emotional equilibrium and becomes unsure about his partner and their relationship. He is generally not inclined, however, to make a firm, long-term commitment to a partner.

In any relationship with a woman, this contemporary man frequently adheres to a conventional, outdated, and stereotyped male role; his behavior is chauvinistic, which he does not realize unless a partner, like Marianne in *Montauk* (VI 679) or Hanna in *Homo faber* (IV 140), points it out to him. Even though he never beats her, never makes a servant of her—he takes out the trash, washes the dishes, and does the shopping—he is incompetent when the woman he loves asks him to help her grow and develop as a person. He feels more comfortable with conventionally accepted views about male-female relationships.

Although he is compulsively possessive and easily roused to fierce jealousy, Frisch's contemporary man is plagued by periodic doubts about his masculinity and adequacy as a lover. Generally he masks his insecurity by obsessively seeking to be with a woman, even though he is sometimes unable to perform sexually.

The man whose composite image emanates from the pages of Frisch's novels seems to suffer unduly, though severely, from the tensions caused by the polarity of the sexes. As a result, he sometimes yearns for a completeness and self-sufficiency of being, including sexual self-sufficiency, which may be expressed most clearly and poignantly in Frisch's play *Don Juan oder Die Liebe zur Geometrie* (1953), *Don Juan or the Love of Geometry*. This wish for self-sufficiency is also strongly expressed in *Homo faber* by both Faber and Hanna: by Faber especially in his relationship with Ivy (IV 58-66), and Hanna, though indirectly, in her speech about men (IV 140).

In Frisch's novels, contemporary man also seems to be plagued by a burden of deep-seated, general guilt about women—all women: mothers, sisters, lovers, wives, and daughters. Zoran Konstantinovic goes too far when accusing Frisch's men of incurring guilt every time they have contact with a woman, whether as a child with his mother, a brother with his sister, or merely as a man with the most casual of lovers (Konstantinovic 146,152). This accusation, which casts contemporary man into the role of a creature pathologically wallowing in a guilt he cannot escape, is too broad. It seems to be born of a too-conventional and one-sided view of contemporary heterosexual relationships. It is not Frisch's view.

However, an element of general guilt vis à vis the women he loves is associated with contemporary man and is personified most clearly by Max in *Montauk*. Max feels guilty about all the women he has loved, including Lynn, although he admits that particular guilt only indirectly when, in violation of their agreement, he tries to see her again. The reason for Max's guilt in every case is desertion. He deserted his mother in her hour of death, when no more than his presence was required of him (VI 690-91); he deserted his fiancée, Käte, his first wife, Constanze, and his family, including two daughters; he deserted Ingeborg when she needed him, and he separated from Marianne; by the end of *Montauk* he deserts Lynn, too. Max and the other men in Frisch's novels have other valid reasons, too, for feeling guilty about the women they have loved, such as their sometimes eccentric behavior, their hypersensitivity to criticism by their partner, and the abortions they necessitated and agreed to.

Perhaps the character of contemporary man as portrayed in Frisch's novels is somewhat related to that of Hermes, a mythological figure the author frequently invokes. The mythological Hermes is not only a benevolent messenger but also a devious trickster. Woman, in her turn, may be characterized as Undine, an elemental water sprite without a soul, which, according to legend, she can obtain only by marrying a mortal man. The kind of man the modern-day Undine meets, however, is a complex Hermes-like character, which explains both the attraction and the tension between them.

Although one must not take such an analogy too far, it illustrates a fundamental basis for the often tension-filled and troubled relationships of contemporary men and women. The tensions are similar to those of a seriously played game in which man is a peristent player, however inadequate his skills may be. In the process of playing the game with a woman, the man exposes his basic attitudes and behavior. Frisch in his oeuvre frequently employs the image of a chess game, which requires of its players great concentration and the ability to anticipate the opponent's next several moves. In the serious game men and women play as they associate with each other, hoping to establish and share a temporary or a more lasting relationship, women may well have the upper hand; they seem to be more able to read their partner and his next moves intuitively. He, in contrast, is more given to employing his powers of reason to advance his position and win the game. This approach does not always serve his cause, since by its nature the game of forming and maintaining personal relationships is governed more by the rules of perception and intuition than those of reason and logic.

Taking the image of the chess game a step further, one might be tempted, as Honsza has observed, to interpret the whole of *Mein Name sei Gantenbein* as an intricately complex chess game the narrator plays, with its key figures—Enderlin, Gantenbein, and Svoboda—grouped around the "queen," Lila (Honsza 77-78). That configuration may be a fitting image for contemporary man, the modern, somewhat uneasy intellectual, as he relates to a woman.

Looking at the novelistic work of Max Frisch spanning almost fifty years, from *Jürg Reinhart* (1934) to *Blaubart* (1982), one can identify a single unifying theme: the protagonist's attempt to realize himself and his potential in an environment and a relationship with a woman that is free of conflict. The notion that this is possible, or even desirable, may in itself be the greatest delusion of Frisch's protagonists. By describing their efforts in pursuit of this idealistic goal, however, Max Frisch exposes important male attitudes and failings that are evident in contemporary man's relationships to women.

WORKS CITED

A. Works by Max Frisch

Frisch, Max. *Bluebeard*. Trans. Geoffrey Skelton. London: Methuen, 1983.
———. *Gantenbein*. Trans. Michael Bullock. London: Methuen, 1982.
———. *Gesammelte Werke in zeitlicher Folge 1931-1985*. 7 vols. Frankfurt/Main: Suhrkamp, 1976-1986.
———. *Homo Faber*. Trans. Michael Bullock. San Diego: Harcourt Brace Jovanovich, 1959.
———. *I'm Not Stiller*. Trans. Michael Bullock. London: Methuen, 1982.
———. *Man in the Holocene*. Trans. Geoffrey Skelton. San Diego: Harcourt Brace Jovanovich, 1980/1981.
———. *Montauk*. Trans. Geoffrey Skelton. New York: Harcourt Brace Jovanovich, 1976.
———. *Sketchbook 1946-1949*. Trans. Geoffrey Skelton. 1977. San Diego: Harcourt Brace Jovanovich, 1983.
———. *Sketchbook 1966-1971*. Trans. Geoffrey Skelton. 1971. San Diego: Harcourt Brace Jovanovich, 1983.

B. Works by Other Authors

Bachmann, Ingeborg. "Der Fall Franza." *Ingeborg Bachmann Werke*. Ed. Christine Koschel, Inge von Weidenbaum, Clemens Münster. Vol. 3. 1978. München: Piper, 1984. 4 vols. 339-483.
Baedeker, Karl. *Griechenland: Handbuch für Reisende*. 5th ed. Leipzig: Baedeker, 1908. 104-06.
Bänziger, Hans. "Leben im Zitat. Zu *Montauk*: Ein Formulierungsproblem und dessen Vorgeschichte." *Max Frisch: Aspekte*

des Prosawerks. Ed. Gerhard P. Knapp. Bern: Lang, 1978. 274-84.
Beicken, Peter. *Ingeborg Bachmann.* München: C. H. Beck, 1988. 142-86,212-14.
Bienek, Horst. *Werkstattgespräche mit Schriftstellern.* 1962. 3rd ed. München: Deutscher Taschenbuch Verlag, 1976. 23-37.
Blair, Rhonda L. "'Homo faber', 'Homo ludens' und das Demeter-Kore-Motiv." *Frischs "Homo faber."* Ed. Walter Schmitz. Frankfurt: Suhrkamp, 1983. 142-70.
Bulfinch, Thomas. *Bulfinch's Mythology of Greece and Rome with Eastern and Norse Legends.* 1962. New York: Macmillan, 1967.
Butler, Michael. *The Novels of Max Frisch.* London: Oswald Wolff, 1976.
Chaucer, Geoffrey. "The Canterbury Tales." *The Works of Geoffrey Chaucer.* Ed. F. N. Robinson. 2nd ed. Boston: Houghton Mifflin, 1957. 17.
Geulen, Hans. *Max Frischs "Homo faber."* Berlin: Walter de Gruyter, 1965.
———. "Max Frischs *Homo faber.*" *Frischs "Homo faber."* Ed. Walter Schmitz. Frankfurt: Suhrkamp, 1983. 101-32.
Graves, Robert. *The Greek Myths.* 2 vols. Baltimore: Penguin, 1955.
Hage, Volker. *Max Frisch.* Hamburg: Rowohlt, 1983.
Hamilton, Edith. *Mythology.* 1940. New York: Mentor Books, 1942.
Honsza, Norbert. "Auf der Suche nach neuer Ich-Erfassung." *Frisch: Kritik-Thesen-Analysen.* Ed. Manfred Jurgensen. Bern: Francke, 1977. 67-80.
Jung, Carl G. *Man and His Symbols.* Ed. C. G. Jung and M.-L. von Franz. Garden City, NY: Doubleday, 1964. 18-103.
Jurgensen, Manfred. *Max Frisch: Die Romane.* 2nd ed. Bern: Francke, 1976.
———, ed. *Frisch: Kritik-Thesen-Analysen.* Bern: Francke, 1977.
Kieser, Rolf. "Das Tagebuch als Idee und Struktur im Werke Max Frischs." *Max Frisch: Aspekte des Prosawerks.* Ed. Gerhard P. Knapp. Bern: Peter Lang, 1978. 157-71.
Knapp, Gerhard P. "Noch einmal: Das Spiel mit der Identität. Zu Max Frischs *Montauk.*" *Max Frisch: Aspekte des Prosawerks.* Ed. Gerhard P. Knapp. Bern: Peter Lang, 1978. 285-307.

Konstantinovic, Zoran. "Die Schuld an der Frau." *Frisch: Kritik-Thesen-Analysen.* Ed. Manfred Jurgensen. Bern: Francke, 1977. 145-55.
Krättli, Anton. "'Leben im Zitat'." *Über Max Frisch II.* Ed. Walter Schmitz. 1976. 2nd ed. Frankfurt: Suhrkamp, 1981. 428-34.
Lüthi, Hans Jürg. *Max Frisch.* München: Francke, 1981.
Merrifield, Doris Fulda. *Das Bild der Frau bei Max Frisch.* Freiburg: Universitätsverlag Becksmann, 1971.
Novalis. *Heinrich von Ofterdingen.* München: Goldmann, 1964.
Ovid. *The Metamorphoses.* Trans. Horace Gregory. New York: Mentor, 1960.
Petersen, Jürgen H. *Max Frisch.* Stuttgart: Metzler, 1978a.
———. "Wirklichkeit, Möglichkeit und Fiktion in Max Frischs Roman *Mein Name sei Gantenbein.*" *Max Frisch: Aspekte des Prosawerks.* Ed. Gerhard P. Knapp. Bern: Peter Lang, 1978b. 131-56.
Probst, Gerhard F. "The Old Man and the Rain: *Man in the Holocene.*" *Perspectives on Max Frisch.* Ed. Gerhard F. Probst and Jay F. Bodine. Lexington, KY: The University Press of Kentucky, 1982. 166-75.
Schmitz, Walter. *Max Frisch: Das Spätwerk (1962-1982).* Tübingen: Francke, 1985.
Schröder, Jürgen. "Spiel mit dem Lebenslauf: Das Drama Max Frischs." *Über Max Frisch II.* Ed. Walter Schmitz. 2nd ed. Frankfurt: Suhrkamp, 1976. 19-74.
Seyfert, Oskar. *Dictionary of Classical Antiquities: Mythology, Religion, Literature, Art.* Trans. and ed. Henry Nettleship and J. E. Sandys. 12th ed. Cleveland: Meridian/World, 1966.
Stauffacher, Werner. "Diese dünne Gegenwart." *Frisch: Kritik-Thesen-Analysen.* Ed. Manfred Jurgensen. Bern: Francke, 1977. 55-66.
Stine, Linda J. "'Ich hätte Lust, Märchen zu schreiben': Frisch's Use of Märchen in *Die Schwierigen* and *Montauk.*" *Perspectives on Max Frisch.* Ed. Gerhard F. Probst and Jay F. Bodine. Lexington, KY: The University Press of Kentucky, 1982. 71-78.
Zimmer, Dieter E. "Noch einmal anfangen können. Ein Gespräch mit Max Frisch." *Die Zeit* 12 Dec. 1967.

INDEX

A

Abdominal pain, 125, 130, 138, 147-48, 175. *See also* Cancer
Abortion, 25, 28, 29, 77, 78, 89, 154-55, 162, 176-77
Adultery, 82, 83-86, 195, 208, 210-11, 215, 217, 223, 225, 229-30, 236-37, 242, 245, 279-80
Age
  differences in, 155, 156, 299-302, 335
  inferiority about, 137, 144-45
  old
    fear of, 301, 307
    Philemon and Baucis, 244
    self-conscious about, 281, 298, 301
Aging
  acceptance of, 14, 270, 302, 307, 309, 341, 359-60
  concern with, 1, 4-5, 14-15, 16, 30, 216, 261, 291-92, 296, 315, 316-21, 325, 328-29, 330, 342 355-56
  ignored, 145, 173-74, 359
Agnostic, 119, 339-43
Alcohol, 69, 81, 106, 118, 132, 150, 204, 223, 224, 264, 287, 295, 304-05, 322, 344. *See also* Drunk
Ali (*Gantenbein*), 191-92, 202, 231, 236, 242, 244
Alil (*Gantenbein*), 191-92, 202, 231, 236, 242, 244
Alternatives, not restricted by time, 203, 215. *See also* Possibility
Ammann (*Schwierigen*), 19-20, 24, 28, 44, 47, 351
Angel, 46, 50, 99, 123, 124, 340
Annemarie (*Schwierigen*), 44, 45, 47
Anton (*Schwierigen*), 45, 358
Architect, 2, 7, 18-20, 38, 44, 82, 87-89, 198, 218, 278-81, 283, 335-36
Armin (*Faber*), 178-79
Art
  Faber and, 137, 139, 157-60, 182, 186-87, 336, 344
  Hanna and, 171, 346
  The Louvre, 139-40, 144, 152
  Sabeth and, 144, 158-60, 186-87
Art historian, 198, 276, 338
Artist
  bohemian lifestyle of, 20, 26, 34-35, 331, 346
  doubts and insecurity of, 30, 37-38, 56, 62, 73, 297
  Hortense, as pupil, 28, 36
  Julika, as ballerina, 54-57, 63-64, 67, 76-78, 98
  Jürg, as painter, 17-21, 24, 26-32, 37-39, 42, 44, 47, 331, 335

relationship to society, 6, 7, 21, 26, 118, 200
Stiller
 as potter, 111, 113, 322
 as sculptor, 52, 54, 56, 58, 61-63, 64, 65, 72, 73, 100, 331, 335
Associative thinking, 127, 151, 254, 267, 275

B

Bachmann, Ingeborg, 263, 312, 367, 368
Bänziger, Hans, 311, 313, 367
Baptist minister (*Faber*), 139-40, 144, 148-49, 338, 344
Baucis (*Gantenbein*), 244-45, 250, 265-66
Beatrice (*Gantenbein*), 231, 249-50
Beicken, Peter, 312, 368
Bienek, Horst, 272-73, 368
Bin oder die Reise nach Peking, xiii, 2-4, 81, 280-81, 327-28, 348, 350
Bin or the Journey to Peking, 2, 280
Blair, Rhonda L., 163, 185-86, 187, 189, 368
Blätter aus dem Brotsack, 17
Blaubart, viii, xvii, xx, 11-12, 15, 315, 321-26, 328, 330-31, 333, 336, 345, 351, 358, 364
Blind
 figuratively: Max, 293
 literally
  Ali-Alil, 191-92
  Armin, 173
 pretended: Gantenbein, 11, 198, 230-44, 248-52, 261, 264, 343, 362

Der Blinde (Dürrenmatt), 264
Blindness
 as metaphor, 11, 126-27, 159, 192-93, 198, 200, 230, 342
 Gantenbein's, 230-44, 248-52, 347
 of men, 177
 of Oedipus, 169, 189
 of protagonists, 15, 21, 29, 65, 126, 258
 spiritual, 247
 value of, in marriage, 259-60
Bluebeard, xiv, 12, 315, 367. See also *Blaubart*
Bohnenblust, Dr. (*Stiller*), 52, 98, 109, 119, 121
Bulfinch, Thomas, 265, 368
Bullock, Michael, xiii-xiv, 123, 193, 263, 264, 313, 367
Burri, Dr. (*Gantenbein*), 202, 215, 228-29, 257-58
Butler, Michael, 26, 27, 47, 52, 118, 121, 123, 145, 163, 164, 182, 225, 227, 241, 244, 265, 368

C

Camilla Huber (*Gantenbein*), 202, 234, 235, 240, 241, 245, 259, 264, 266, 354
Cancer, 5, 7, 125, 175, 181. See also Abdominal pain
Cat, 94, 96-99, 316, 330
Chance, xviii, 26, 130, 136, 145-48, 173, 179, 180, 286, 290. See also Fate
Chauvinism
 female, 25, 28, 337-39
 male, 11, 87, 122, 297, 315, 336-39

INDEX 373

Child, attitude toward
  Gantenbein, 249-50
  Hanna, 155, 170, 172, 176, 180, 182, 338
  Hauswirt, 20, 33
  Herr Geiser, 316, 320
  Julika, 58, 65
  Jürg as bastard, 19, 41, 43
  Käte, 277
  represents longing for "das wirkliche Leben," 3, 4
  Sibylle, 65, 76-77, 337
  signifies success of Rolf and Sibylle's marriage, 52, 94
  Yvonne, 18, 19, 25, 28-32, 50, 346
Children, Max and Constanze's, 269, 278-83, 305, 352
Clock time. See Time, measured
Coincidence. See Chance
Colonel (Schwierigen), 17, 18, 36, 40-42, 43-44, 46, 49
Commitment
  essential for successful relationship, 28, 32, 35, 39, 91, 94, 108, 250, 351
  Faber to Hanna, 181
  Jürg withdraws from, 45
  to art, 18
  to a role, 205
  to a significant deed, 6
Commitment, lack of
  to partner, xix, 47, 58, 78, 91, 128, 155, 177, 182, 184, 213, 333, 341, 349, 361
  to relationship, xix, 26, 47, 58, 86, 91, 213-14, 259, 333, 341
Communication between partners
  effective, 118
  lack of, 29, 31, 225, 256, 315, 329, 342

Max, 269, 284-85, 287-90, 293-96
Rolf, 77, 90-92
Stiller, 64, 66, 68, 107-09, 110, 113-16, 353
Constanze (Montauk), 20, 269, 278-83, 284, 298, 304, 305, 311, 335, 352, 363
Control
  affected by alcohol, 264
  Frisch's men lack, 81, 84-87, 89, 130, 224-25, 245, 294
  loss of, with aging, 317, 319-20
  of nature, 127-30, 145, 173, 316, 318-19
  of one's life, 11, 25, 28, 77, 87, 92, 342
Corinne (Holozän), 316, 320
Creativity, 335-36

D

Death
  end of transient time, 13-15, 111-12, 156-67, 166-68, 173, 175, 260-61, 270, 307, 315, 319-21, 340-42, 355-59
  Enderlin and, 215
  euthanasia, 5
  Faber's, 125, 157, 169, 180-81, 182, 184, 348
  annul with technology, 144-45, 148
  compared to Agamemnon's, 188
  fear of, 116, 118, 175, 205
  Frisch preoccupied with, 16, 34, 203, 212, 232, 317-18
  Hinkelmann's, 25
  in life, 228
  in nature, 129, 135, 144
  Ingeborg's, 290

Jesuit's, 68
Joachim's, 129, 132, 147, 182
Julika's, 52, 102, 111, 120-22
Jürg's, 21, 45-47
Max dreams about, 307
of relationship, 253
Philemon and Baucis', 265
Rosalinde's, 321-23
Sabeth's, 125, 157, 166, 168, 174, 180-02, 185-86, 353
Schaad and, 323
Stiller's attempt, 124, 199, 358
Tohuli punishments, 256-57
Dick (*Faber*), 132, 175
Difficult Ones, The, 6. See also *Die Schwierigen*
Don Juan oder Die Liebe zur Geometrie, xiii, 362
Don Juan or the Love of Geometry, 362
Drunk, 42, 112, 118, 132, 152, 224, 287, 295, 344-45. See also Alcohol
Dürrenmatt, Friedrich, 264

E

Einhorn (*Gantenbein*), 244-48, 254
Enderlin, Felix (*Gantenbein*)
 as facet of narrator, 196, 198-201, 203, 218, 231-33, 254, 256, 263-64, 274, 309, 332, 336, 339, 360, 364
 ignores time, 14, 349, 351, 353
 and Lila, 204-17, 222-23, 226-28, 230, 259, 260, 263-64, 333-34, 337, 348, 354

F

Faber, Walter (*Homo faber*)
 and the arts, 139, 152-53, 158-60, 336
 belief in technology over nature, 125, 128-30, 135, 143-46, 151, 154-55, 167-68, 173, 182, 184, 264, 336, 343, 359
 engineer, 125, 153, 155, 170, 218, 330, 332, 336
 and fate, 160, 163, 180
 and Hanna, 127, 147, 154, 158-59, 161-62, 169-83, 337-38, 346, 349, 352-53, 362
 and Ivy, 127-33, 332, 346, 362
 jealous, 136-39, 145, 158, 323, 344
 lonely, 135, 149-50, 332-33
 and love, 156-57, 162-64, 167-69, 171-72, 184
 and marriage, 128, 136, 152, 171-73, 352-53
 and probability, 136, 162, 173
 and Sabeth, 34, 127, 133-69, 174-75, 181-84, 260, 272, 301, 321, 336, 340, 343, 344, 352-53, 359
 and sexuality, 128-31, 148, 151-52, 156-57, 161, 214, 333-34, 339
 toward "das wirkliche Leben," xvii, 4, 7, 14, 156-57, 164-65, 175, 183-84, 195, 308, 340-41, 357-58
 and transient time, 14, 145, 173-74, 181, 292, 317, 319, 322, 349, 356-59
Der Fall Franza (Bachmann), 312, 367
Fate, 4, 5, 75, 90, 169, 173, 176,

177-80
marriage, for Sibylle, 90
vs. technology, 154, 167-68
Feminism, 177-78, 199
Florence (*Stiller*), 95-97, 99
Future, 3, 62, 303, 360. See also Transient time, Past, Present
absence of
  in marriage based on deception, 252
  Max and Lynn, 267, 303, 340
  Svoboda-Lila marriage, 227
  Enderlin and, 14, 207, 211, 212-17, 230
  Jürg and, 29, 42
  limited: Max and Marianne, 292
  offers alternatives, 203

G

Gantenbein, xiv, 7, 203, 264, 336, 367
Gantenbein, Theo (*Gantenbein*)
  as father, 231, 236, 249-50
  blind, 11, 198, 233-34. See also marriage (below)
  end of role, 251-52, 253, 335, 354-55
  essential for marriage, 242, 251, 293
  and Camilla, 202, 234-35, 240-41, 245, 266
  facet of narrator, 196, 198, 203, 230, 231, 233, 254, 260, 299-300, 309, 323, 325, 328, 330, 335
  fury of, 294
  jealous, 198, 236, 242, 243, 247-48, 344

marriage
  based on pretense, 199-200, 252, 347
  benefits of blindness in, 235-240, 241-42
  graven image in, 252
  loving, 250, 252, 254
  possibilities of blindness in, 231, 232, 234-35, 343, 353-54
  result of sight, 242-52, 254-56
  and transient time, 270
  and Patsch, 240-41
Geiser (*Holozän*), 316-20, 325, 328, 330, 333, 345, 358
Gerda (*Schwierigen*), 40, 42, 43, 45
Geulen, Hans, 163, 187, 368
Graphic artist (*Faber*), 134, 136-39, 162, 344
Graven image, 10-11, 31-32, 44, 60, 67, 69-71, 79, 115, 252, 345-58
Graves, Robert, 183, 185, 187, 368
Grégoire de Tours, 49
Guilt
  common to Frisch men, 15, 258-59, 315-16, 362-63
  Faber
    after sex, 128, 130, 132
    and Hanna, 174, 176
    re abortion, 154
    re incest, 156, 321-22, 340
  Gantenbein, of deception, 233-42, 245-46
  Hanna
    of ignoring fate, 179-80
    of possessiveness, 176-77, 180
  Lila, of deception, 236-39
  Max's residue of
    re abandonment, 277, 282-83, 305

376 LIFE AS A MAN

re abortions, 305
toward beloved women, 269-70, 305
of forming graven image, 59-61, 252
Schaad, 12, 321-25, 330-31
Stiller
   re Julika, 54-55, 58, 66, 69-70
   re Little Grey/Julika, 96-98
   "we *are* the guilt," 120-21
Yvonne, re abortion, 29
Guilt not felt, 269, 290

H

Hage, Volker, 268, 273-74, 276, 277, 283, 311, 313, 368
Haller, Frau Therese (*Montauk*), 281-82
Hamilton, Edith, 265, 368
Hanna (*Faber*), 169-184
   aborted abortion plans, 154-55, 338
   archeologist, 158, 161, 169-70
   believes in fate, 160
   counterpart of Käte, 276
   Faber's lover, 125-28, 136, 150, 157, 161-62, 169, 352, 355
   feminist, 337-39, 346, 362
   independent, 20, 71, 170
   married Joachim, 147-48
   Sabeth's mother, 158-59, 161, 164
   understands transient time, 349, 359
Hannes (*Stiller*), 72, 76, 89-90, 92
Hanswalter (*Schwierigen*), 47
Hauswirt (*Schwierigen*), 18-20, 28, 30-33, 35, 47, 50, 79, 337, 338, 351-52
Heinrich von Ofterdingen (Novalis), 16, 369
Henze, Hans Werner, 312
Herbert Hencke (*Faber*), 144, 145, 148, 171, 190
Hermes, 145, 157, 185, 205, 215, 265, 363
Hilde (*Jürg Reinhart*), 5
Hinkelmann (*Schwierigen*), 19-20, 22, 24-25, 28, 31, 33, 49, 346
Homo faber, vii, xiii, xvii, xviii, xx, 4, 7, 13, 15, 20, 34, 71, 192, 125-89, 193, 244, 275, 276, 301, 313, 317, 321, 340, 350-51, 358-59, 368
Homo Faber, xiv, 125-89, 367. *See also* Faber, Walter, *Homo faber*
Honza, Norbert, 336, 364, 368
Hortense (*Schwierigen*), 6, 17-20, 28, 35-47, 49, 74, 331, 343, 346, 351
hubris, 145, 179-80
Huchel, Peter (*Montauk*), 288

I

"I imagine." *See* "Ich stlle mir vor," Imagination
"Ich stelle mir vor," 197, 201, 232. *See also* Imagination
I'm Not Stiller, xiv, 123, 219, 349, 353, 367. *See also* Stiller
Image, graven. *See* Graven image
Imagination
   as device: "I imagine," 197, 201, 232
   and creativity, 336
   presents alternatives, 243-49, 260
   and reality, 7, 34, 37, 164, 201,

INDEX   377

203, 205, 225, 232, 237,
    252, 261, 264
Incest, 6, 69, 89, 126, 156, 169,
    173, 176, 189, 301, 313,
    321
Inge (*Jürg Reinhart*), 5, 6
Ingeborg (*Montauk*)
  and Ingeborg Bachmann, 311-12
  longterm relationship with
    Max, 20, 170, 269, 283-91,
    293, 311-12, 329, 345, 361-
    62
Insecurity
  common to all Frisch men, xix-
    xx, 20, 315, 329, 341, 343,
    361
  of Faber, 138, 139-40, 148, 157-
    58, 184
  of *Gantenbein* narrator, 198, 214
  of Julika, 59, 353
  of Max, 288, 296, 297
  of Rolf, 122
  of Schaad, 322
  of Stiller, 58-59, 61, 100, 122,
    353
  sexual, 58-59, 214, 329, 341
Intuition. *See also* Rational
  balanced with reason: Sabeth,
    163-64, 165, 182
  Faber and, 132, 135, 145, 169
  Stiller and, 79
  women more attuned to, 48,
    72, 75, 171-72, 182, 199,
    363
Isolation of characters, 46-47, 52,
    116, 121, 128, 206, 328,
    331-33. *See also* Loneli-
    ness
Ivy (*Faber*), 127-33, 136, 151, 185,
    332-33, 337, 339, 346, 362

J

Jealousy
  Ali-Alil, 192, 236, 242
  based on fear of comparison,
    138-39, 220, 323, 343
  common to Frisch men, 15, 21,
    196, 329, 342, 343-45, 362
  Faber, 136-40, 145, 148, 149,
    158, 324, 344
  Gantenbein, 198, 231, 236, 242-
    50
  Gantenbein narrator, 196, 202,
    203, 208, 254-55
  Hortense, 37
  Jürg, 32, 34, 221-22, 324, 343-44
  Max, 285, 287-90, 293, 295, 309,
    324, 345
  Rolf, 87-88, 219, 221-22, 325
  Schaad, 316, 323-24, 345
  sexual, 196, 230
  Stiller, 64, 324, 344
  Svoboda, 198, 219-22, 225, 227,
    230-31, 324, 344-45, 355
  Tohulis have none, 257
Jenny (*Schwierigen*), 44-45
Joachim Hencke (*Faber*), 129, 130,
    132-33, 148, 152-54, 161-62,
    171, 176, 182
Julika (*Stiller*)
  affair, 71, 344
  cannot accept Stiller's new
    identity, 51-52
  death, 51-52, 102, 121-22
  dependent, 72
  dislikes sexual intercourse, 128,
    339
  marriage not successful, 51-53,
    54-71, 74, 99, 256, 329-30
  Davos, 75, 76-77, 79, 97
  effect of graven image, 10-
    11, 78, 122, 345-47

378 LIFE AS A MAN

lack of communication, 52, 353-54
resumed, 110-122
self-supporting, 20, 332
second courtship, 100-110, 349
symbolized by Little Grey, 98
Jung, Carl G., 265, 368
Jürg Reinhart (*Jürg Reinhart*), 5-6, 15, 17, 309, 327-28
Jürg Reinhart (*Schwierigen*), 6-7, 17-50, 221, 323, 329, 331, 337-38, 343-44, 346-47, 351-52, 358
  as artist, 6, 26-29, 31-32, 34-38, 44, 47
  and Hortense, 35-50, 331, 346-47
  jealous, 32, 34
  and marriage, 6, 27-31, 39-40, 46, 351-52
  suicide, 6, 19, 45, 47, 49, 358
  and Yvonne, 21-35, 49-50, 329, 337-38, 343-44, 346
Jürg Reinhart: Eine sommerliche Schicksalsfahrt, xiii, 5, 17, 22
Jürg Reinhart: A Fateful Summer's Journey, 5, 15, 17, 196, 364
Jurgensen, Manfred, 7, 22, 188, 313, 368, 369

K

Kafka, Franz, xviii, 50, 324
Käte (*Montauk*), 269, 276-77, 286, 304, 335, 363
Keller, Gottfried, 21
Kieser, Rolf, 311, 368
Kilian (*Bin*), 2-4, 81, 280-81, 327, 329, 335, 348, 358
Kleist, Heinrich von, 37

Knapp, Gerhard P., 263, 274, 311, 367, 368, 369
Knobel (*Stiller*), 94, 95, 101, 109, 124, 347
Konstantinovic, Zoran, 362, 368
Krättli, Anton, 311, 369

L

Leaves from the Haversack, 17
Lajser Lewin (*Faber*), 140, 149, 152
Lila (*Gantenbein*)
  Gantenbein's wife, 11, 192, 195, 198-200, 231, 253
  narrator's use of, 253-56, 259-60, 335, 348, 353
  represents all women, 199-201, 202, 363
  self-supporting, 20
  Svoboda's wife, 199, 218-19, 222-30, 259, 264, 284, 289, 337, 344-45, 354-55
  with Enderlin, 199, 204-12, 214-18, 333, 348, 353
Little Grey (*Stiller*), 94, 96-99
Loneliness. See also Isolation
  as human condition, 221, 329
  common to Frisch men, 331-35, 341, 361
  Enderlin, 332
  Faber, 128, 135, 149-50, 332, 352
  Gantenbein narrator, 261
  Herr Geiser, 328
  Max, 287, 295, 332-33
  Stiller, 62, 112, 121
  Svoboda, 226
  in marriage, 10
  Julika, 115
  Sibylle, 77, 92, 93
Love. See also Marriage, Nonlove

Ali-Alil, 191-92
and blindness, 259
can be killed, 256, 343
Enderlin, 210-11, 214-17, 230
enslaving, 286-87
Faber
   and Hanna, 125, 169-72
   and Sabeth, 4, 7, 126, 151-69
   for painting, 343
   for writing, 7, 279
Gantenbein and Lila, 231, 237, 239-40, 242, 244, 247, 251-52, 354, 355
and graven image, 345-48
in Stiller-Julika marriage, 10, 64
"J'adore ce qui me brûle," 17-19, 37, 41
and jealousy, 249, 343-45
Ivy and, 131
Jürg-Hortense, 20, 36-37, 39-40, 43, 45, 46
Jürg-Inge, 5-6
Jürg-Yvonne, 18, 20, 28-31, 34, 35, 45
Lynn and Max, 267, 269, 301-04, 350
and madness, 249, 287, 291
Max's first, 281
men in, 21, 229-30
Philemon and Baucis, 244, 265
philia, eros, agape, 342, 347
repetition can stifle, 259, 348
Sabeth's boyfriend, 137, 149
sexual, 5, 24, 57, 72, 157, 196
Sibylle and Rolf's, 75, 80-92, 93-94, 118
Stiller's
   for Anja, 73
   for Florence, 95-96
   and Julika, 55-56, 68-69, 105-09, 114-17, 118-21, 124
   and Sibylle, 53, 71-79, 89, 90

Svoboda, 219-21, 230, 259, 354
trust in, 200
ungraspable, 348
and Venus, 159-61, 186
women in, 229-30, 258
Yvonne craves, 22-24, 26-27
Loving relationship with a woman
equals "das wirkliche Leben," 316, 361
every protagonist seeks, xix, xx, 3, 4, 6-8, 10-11, 15, 18, 21, 24, 45, 47, 51, 87, 89, 90, 92, 93, 108, 151-66, 167-69, 181-83, 194-97, 206-07, 209-12, 224-25, 254, 261, 267-69, 275, 276-80, 283-93, 300-04, 309-10, 315, 325-26, 329, 331, 335, 339, 342-45, 350, 352-53, 360, 364
Frisch questions man's behavior in, 355
guilt from, 263
men glorify women in, 258
Schaad fails in, 315
Lüthi, Hans Jürg, 148, 169, 369
Lynn (*Montauk*), xvii, 11, 20, 267-72, 274, 277, 291, 297-98, 305, 307-08, 309, 313, 335, 349-50, 358, 359-60, 363

M

Magic spell, Ingeborg over Max, 286, 287. See also Obsession
Man in the Holocene, xiv, 4, 16, 315, 367, 369. See also *Der Mensch erscheint im Holozän*
Mann, Thomas, 21

380 LIFE AS A MAN

Marianne (*Montauk*)
  accusation of chauvinism, 11, 309, 337, 354, 362
  as lover, 285, 290, 291-93
  as wife, 293-98, 304, 311-13, 335, 352, 360
  independent, 20, 71, 170
  and jealousy, 354
  significant to Max, 269, 275, 301, 343
Marion (*Tagebuch I*), 50, 124, 197-98, 200, 263, 340
Marriage
  Ali-Alil, 191
  as central theme, 1, 9, 21, 47, 51-53, 122, 191-92, 194, 196, 315, 329-30, 342, 351-55
  as an institution, 9-11, 51-53
  as compromise
    Hortense, 18, 20-21, 44, 47, 351
    Yvonne, 9-10, 20-21, 32-34, 47, 50, 351-52
  blindness in, 259-60
  boredom in routine, 3, 212, 256
  conflict with art, 6, 17
  inappropriate, 18, 43, 45
  life's greatest adventure, 39-40, 42-44, 46, 351
  Faber
    against, 127-28, 150, 352-53
    compared to Oedipus, 161
    and Hanna, 150, 154, 170-74, 177, 188, 353
    and Sabeth, 136, 150-52, 164, 353
  failure in, 325
  Gantenbein and Lila, 198-200, 230-53, 254, 257, 259, 347, 354-55
  Gantenbein narrator, 4, 194-96, 198, 202-03, 254, 256-57, 259, 335
  Hanna and Joachim, 176, 336
  Jürg and Yvonne, 27, 45
  Max, 276-85, 291, 293-97, 298, 352, 354, 360
  Rolf and Sibylle, 10, 77, 80-94, 207, 347, 353
  Schaad, 324-25
  Stiller and Julika, 54-71, 79, 98, 104, 107-10, 110-22, 332, 349, 353-54
  Stiller and Sibylle, 75
  Tohuli style, 355
  and transient time, 14
  Yvonne and Hinkelmann, 20, 23, 25, 49
Max (*Montauk*)
  as protagonist-narrator, 270-72, 273-75, 307, 308-10, 330, 332-33, 335-36
  at peace with transient time, 14, 307-08, 341, 350, 358, 359-61
  chauvinist, 11, 337
  and impotence, 339
  jealous, 34, 323, 345
  search for "das wirkliche Leben," 4, 343, 352, 358
  self-acceptance, 8
  and women he has loved, 269, 275-307, 363
    Constanze, 278-83, 305, 311
    Ingeborg, 283-91, 305, 311-12, 313, 329, 352
    Käte, 275-77, 305
    Lynn, xvii, 267-70, 298-305, 307-08, 313, 349
    Marianne, 291-98, 305, 311-13, 352, 354
  Meaningful life. *See* "Das wirkliche Leben"

Mein Name sei Gantenbein, viii, xiii, xviii, xix, xx, 7, 11, 14, 15, 20, 191-266, 274, 284, 289, 294, 297, 308, 324, 325, 332, 341, 343, 348, 350, 353-55, 358, 360, 364, 369
Der Mensch erscheint im Holozän, viii, xiii, xx, 4-5, 15, 16, 315-21, 325, 328, 330, 351, 358
Merline (*Schwierigen*), 26, 32
Merrifield, Doris Fulda, xvii, 24, 369
Montaigne, 271
Montauk, viii, xiii, xiv, xvii, xx, 4, 8, 11, 14, 15, 20, 34, 71, 139, 264, 267-313, 318, 325, 327, 329, 332, 341, 349-50, 352, 354, 355, 358-62, 367-69
Mysticism, 144, 145, 171. *See also* Intuition, Mythology
Mythology
  part of mysticism, 145, 179-80
  Greek, 159-61, 163, 169, 180, 185-89, 244, 265, 336
  Enderlin scholar of, 205

N

Narrator, role of
  as commentator: *Schwierigen*, 25, 27-29, 33, 36, 37, 49
  as protagonist, 1, 330
  in *Gantenbein*, 192-206, 208-13, 215-19, 222, 225-33, 235-37, 239-40, 242-44, 247-49, 253-64, 270, 274, 299, 308
  fragments self into three characters, 193, 328, 329, 332, 333, 343, 360
  independent character, 192, 335, 336, 341, 348, 351, 358, 364
  protagonist, xix, 7, 11, 192, 318
  in *Montauk*
    relationship to author, 270-75
    "simple narrator," 268
  in *Tagebuch II*, 318
  unreliable
  Rolf, 110, 117, 329
  Stiller/White, 53
Natural
  disaster, 316, 318-20
  drive (sexuality), 86, 128
  form (Montaigne), 271
  order, 13, 41, 145, 148, 160, 179, 186
  phenomena make Faber uneasy, 126
  physical functions, 128, 144
Nature
  age and time part of, 359
  colorful, in Cuba, 155
  controllable by technology, 125-26, 129, 145, 154-55, 173, 184, 336
  cycle of, 131, 357
  eclipse, 156
  Greek sunrise, 165
  human, 13, 56, 75, 89, 118, 164, 172, 214-15, 264, 319, 328, 342
  protagonists investigate their own, xix, 4, 48, 63, 184
  women's differ from men's, 9, 199-200, 228-29
  Zerlina's, 222
Night sky, 149, 156, 185, 270
Nonlove. *See also* Love
  factors that contribute to, 329

Frisch's novels concern, 342
graven image equal to, 60-61, 70
of characters, 19-20, 22, 24-25, 33, 351-52

O

Obsession, xix, 30, 34, 46, 142, 207, 214, 245, 248, 339, 348. *See also* Magic spell
Oedipus, 161, 169, 189
Oellers, Marianne, 313

P

Past. *See also* Transient time, Present, Future
cannot be annulled, 203, 228
catches up with Faber, 4, 125, 130, 133, 144, 147
Enderlin and, 14, 207, 212, 214, 216
Gantenbein narrator, 261-62
Jürg, 29, 42
Max comes to terms with, 11, 269, 273-74, 275, 300, 303, 330, 350, 360
Max's experience with Lynn changes from present to, 304-05
no longer a mystery, 261, 270
part of transient time, 3, 262, 360
Sabeth interested in, 158
Stiller wants to leave behind, 62, 112, 117
Peking, xiii, 2-4, 16, 81, 264, 280, 327-28, 348, 350
Peru, 204, 208, 210, 211, 218, 230, 264, 354
Peter (*Schwierigen*), 44, 45
Petersen, Jürgen H., 16, 18, 21, 51, 119, 120, 121, 136, 169, 181, 263, 369
Pfeifer (*Blaubart*), 323
Philemon (*Gantenbein*), 244-45, 250, 265-66
Ping-Pong, 134, 138, 149, 165, 313
Piper, Mr. (*Faber*), 143, 161, 171, 188
Possibility. *See also* Imagination
everything is, in Jürg's life, 37
limited only by narrator's potential, in *Gantenbein*, 192-93, 197, 201, 203, 217, 221, 228, 232, 256, 263
love leaves open for change, 70
of becoming a whore, 228-29
of blindness, 236
of "das wirkliche Leben," 36, 46, 126, 280, 347-48, 364
of death, 212
of deception, 237
of a future, 212
of growth, 252
of marriage, 47, 53, 329, 352
of religious faith, 339-40
of Schaad's guilt, 324-25
sum of all, constitutes a person, 328, 347-48
that narrator (Stiller/White) distorts, 53
that Sabeth is Faber's daughter, 148, 162
Pregnancy
Constanze, 281
governess, 41
Hanna, 162, 170, 172, 338
Sabeth, 161
Sibylle, 76, 91, 337
Yvonne, 18, 25, 28, 31, 32, 49,

50
Present. *See also* Transient time, Past, Future
  agnostics can only be sure of, 340
  Enderlin wants to live *only* in, 14, 207, 210-11
  Faber learns to live intensely in, 125, 157, 183, 341
  Gantenbein narrator finally can return to, 261-62
  hangs between expectation and memory
  as nothingness, 211, 217, 260
  creative tension between past and future, 3, 270
  remains unreal, hard to experience, 207, 211
  is thin, 268, 270, 350, 360
  Jürg lives in, 27, 29
  mad desire to experience
  on burial mound, 260
  through a woman, 303, 308, 360
  Max
    cannot live long only in, 269
    deals with past in, 303
    describes, in *Montauk*, 270, 274, 275, 300, 303, 304, 307, 330
    experienced with Marianne, 292
    experiences intensely at Montauk, 308, 361
    and Lynn's love in, 267, 349
  Sabeth lives in, 158
  and Stiller, 62, 106, 112, 117, 119
  Svoboda's marriage: past no longer flows into, 227
Probability, law of
  Faber relies on, 130-31, 136, 145-48, 162, 173
  includes improbability, 145-48, 162
Probst, Gerhard F., 320, 369
Der Prozess (Kafka), xviii
Providence. *See* Fate

R

Rapunzel (*Bin*), 3
Rational. *See also* Intuition
  balances with intuition, 165
  fate can destroy (Hanna), 173
  in "attack," Max is not, 294
  Jürg's perception of himself is not, 47
  supremacy of, for Faber, 125-26, 128, 164, 173, 336
  Svoboda attempts to remain, 224
  vs. intuitive, 132, 134, 181, 364
  vs. love (Max), 286
Reality
  improbable can become, 148
  includes lived *and* imagined alternatives, 213, 215, 217, 272, 324-25, 328, 347
  major concern of Frisch, 202
  Max's goal in *Montauk*, 168-69, 270
  no language to describe (Stiller/White), 95, 107
  of death (Faber), 175
  of limitless human soul, 27
  of time and nature, Faber ignores, 145
  painter experiences through eyes, 29
  protagonists' concepts of differ, 2, 22, 26, 34, 35, 38, 127, 212

Stiller escapes, with sedative, 344
Svoboda can't face, 345
vs. appearance, 218, 219
vs. graven image, 61, 109, 346-47
vs. imagination, 7, 192, 201, 203, 216-18, 233, 258, 263, 324
Real life, xvii-xix, 1-2, 44, 120, 280. *See also* "Das wirkliche Leben"
Reinhart. *See* Jürg
Relationship. *See* Love, Loving relationship with a woman, Marriage
Repetition
better than death, 212
and concept of time, 216
description of Julika: Stiller/White and Rolf, 102
destroys unique experience, 212-14, 156, 281
Enderlin, Lila, agree to have none, 211
Faber's mistakes, 173-74, 359
fear of, xx, 105, 211-14, 281, 342, 348-50
impossible in transient time, 14
inherent in clock time, 13, 261, 350
related to past and future, 216
stifles a relationship, 2-3, 81, 207, 256, 329, 348
Stiller's, in again accepting challenge of Julika, 105
Robots, 135-36, 140, 144-45, 184
Role
Camilla, 202, 234-35
Enderlin, 205, 216, 217
Faber, uncomfortable with, 144
Frisch: every "I" is a role, 273

Gantenbein
blind father, 236, 249-50
blind husband, 231, 233-38, 240-43, 250, 259, 264, 354, 355
gives up blindness, 242, 251-52, 344
needs escape from, 240-41
trapped in, 251, 347
Gantenbein narrator: Enderlin, Gantenbein, Svoboda are valid roles, 232
Julika, 59, 345
Jürg, 10, 22, 45
Lila, 251, 252, 347
Max, 268, 349
of actor with limp, 243
of confession, to Catholic, 241
of Hermes, 185
of protagonists, xvii, 6, 206, 330
of time, in life, 14
reversal of: Gantenbein and Lila, 236, 238
Sibylle, of injured party in marriage, 90
Stiller, 54, 73, 74
Svoboda, 218, 220
Yvonne, 25
Rolf (*Stiller*), 236, 294, 297
and marriage theory, 10, 209
graven image in, 71, 355
tested by Sibylle's affair, 34, 74-78, 80-94, 123, 213, 219, 221, 225-26, 265, 323, 353
narrator of postscript, 52, 102, 110-22, 329
resumed marriage succeeds, 11, 52, 122, 347
and Stiller, 99, 109, 110-22, 332, 339-40
Rosalinde Zogg (*Blaubart*), 321-25

INDEX 385

S

Sabeth (*Faber*)
  competent woman, 71
  Hanna's daughter, 170, 174, 176, 179-82
  leads Faber to "das wirkliche Leben," xvii, 4, 7, 169, 175, 181, 183-84, 333, 340-41, 357-58, 360-61
  relationship with Faber, 126-27, 133-45, 148-69, 173-74, 185-87, 189, 260, 321, 322, 336, 338, 343, 344, 353, 359
  similarity to Lynn, 271-72, 301, 313
  synthesis of intuition and intellect, 182
Schaad, Dr. Felix (*Blaubart*), 12, 321-25, 328, 330-31, 333, 336, 345, 358
Schmitz, Walter, 319, 368, 369
"Schnäuzchen-Freund," 137. See *also* Graphic artist
Schröder, Jürgen, 311, 342, 369
Die Schwierigen, vii, xiii, xviii, xx, 4, 6-7, 9-10, 15, 17-50, 64, 74, 78, 86, 118, 128, 139, 221-22, 329, 338, 343, 346-47, 350-52, 369
Sex
  Enderlin obsessed with, 208, 214, 333
  Julika dreams about, 67
  protagonists and, 51, 361
  ruled by laws of nature: Tohulis, 257
  synonym for genitalia, 221
  female, 213, 364
  male, 221
Sexual
  act
    Julika dislikes, 58
    reveals man's limitation, woman's freedom, 228
    advances, Isidor's, rejected by wife, 103
  adventure
    basis of Rolf's marriage theory, 86
    one-time experience, Enderlin's goal, 199, 210, 214
    component enlarges Max and Lynn's relationship, 301
    customs of Tohulis, 257, 355
    demands bother Julika, 10
    fascination, 208
    gratification, women are objects for, 87
    impotence, fear of, common to many Frisch men, 167, 330, 339
    insecurity, problem for all protagonists, 57, 61, 65, 71, 198, 214, 329, 339, 341, 362
    jealousy, 137, 196, 230, 339
    Jesuit seminarian asexual, 67
    love, 5, 196, 342
    lust, 213
    maladjustment, 128-29, 131
    overtones, Yvonne with Merline, 26
    relationships
      Faber and Sabeth, 156-57, 174
      Yvonne's, 22, 25
    self-sufficiency, some protagonists crave, 362
    symbolism, 69, 86
    tension between Stiller and Julika, 55
Sexuality

difficulty in accepting (Faber and Stiller), 128, 339
Faber
  and arousal, with Ivy, 128, 132
  and copulation, 152
  craves intercourse, 128
  drive instinctual, 151
  fears involvement, 333
  feelings intensify, 137, 141, 148
  feels desire, in Cuba, 167
  reactions confused, 148
  and Sabeth, 156-67, 174
  Hermes, symbol of, 215
  rampant in jungle, 129
  Stiller defensive about, 58
Seyfert, Oskar, 185, 187, 265, 369
Sibylle (*Stiller*)
  affair with Stiller, 53, 61, 63, 65, 69, 71-93, 98, 337, 338, 339
  as friend of Stiller and Julika, 111-12, 117, 121
  independent, 20, 34, 71-72, 170, 199
  and marriage
    problems in, 10, 72, 75-77, 80-93, 219, 353
    successful, 11, 52, 93-94, 110-11, 116, 118, 119, 122, 347
Skelton, Geoffrey, xiii-xiv, 311, 313, 367
Sketchbook 1946-1949 (I), xiv, 8, 9, 10, 12-13, 50, 53, 60-61, 125, 139, 145, 146-47, 197, 199-200, 207, 211, 220-21, 247, 252, 263, 272-73, 323, 340, 347-48, 355-59, 367
Sketchbook 1966-1971 (II), xiv, 9, 203, 273, 317-18, 367
Society

artist and, 7, 13, 17, 21, 26, 34, 35-36, 73
chauvinism in, 336-37
Colonel (*Schwierigen*) a pillar of, 18
individual and, 1, 7, 39, 43, 44, 45, 51-52, 109, 123, 155, 167-68, 217, 323
  in mythology, 160, 187
  protagonists' roles in, 6, 19, 330, 331-333
  stunned by Lila's marriage to Gantenbein, 231
  western, and marriage, 257
Stauffacher, Werner, 350, 369
Stifter, Adalbert, 24
Stiller, xiii, xvii, xviii, 4, 7, 10, 20, 34, 40, 50, 51-125, 127, 185, 192, 193, 199, 207, 213, 219, 221, 225, 265, 275, 294, 297, 316, 329, 336, 339, 345, 351, 353
Stiller, Anatol Ludwig (*Stiller*)
  affair with Sibylle, 71-80, 219, 338
  agnostic, 339-40
  and alcohol, 132, 264
  artist, 335
  fury of, 294
  hypersensitive to sweating, 128, 339
  and jealousy, 34, 323, 344
  and marriage to Julika
    affected by graven image, 10, 11, 345-46, 354
    lack of communication in, 256, 353-54
    tries to make meaningful, 329-32, 342-43
  needs to be with a woman, 309, 360
  resists former identity, 193, 195

romantic socialist, 171
sexually insecure, 128, 214, 339
suicide and rebirth, 7, 332, 348-49, 358
understands transient time, 14, 348-49
Stiller/White (*Stiller*)
  claims he killed his wife, 107, 347
  loses struggle for new identity, 52
  not necessarily a reliable narrator, 53, 110
  victim of "graven image," 105
  wants to live in the present, 106
  writes seven notebooks in prison, 52, 53, 110, 117, 123
  adventures of Jim White, 94-100
  his dreams, 59, 121
  Rolf and Sibylle's marriage, 80-81, 84, 90, 94, 219
  second courtship of Julika, 62, 100-110, 122
  Stiller and Sibylle's affair, 74-75
  Stiller's original courtship and marriage, 54, 56-57, 61-62, 66, 80, 124
Stine, Linda J., 7, 369
Sturzenegger (*Stiller*), 54, 72, 78, 82, 87-89, 92
Suicide
  emotional, 86
  Faber considers, 180
  Hinkelmann, 19, 25, 338
  Joachim, 129, 153, 176
  Jürg, 6, 17, 19, 34, 45, 49, 331, 347
  Jürg's mother, 41
  Schaad, 325

Stiller
  attempts, 7, 99, 118, 124, 332, 348, 358
  second attempt impossible, 122
Svoboda, Frantisek (*Gantenbein*)
  architect, 336
  chauvinist, 297, 337
  facet of narrator, 196, 198, 201, 203, 231, 233, 248, 254, 260, 274, 360, 364
  fury of, 294
  husband of Lila, 198-200, 204, 208, 217, 218-19, 221-30, 231, 247, 256, 259, 264, 284, 289, 353-55
  and jealousy, 231, 309, 323, 344-45, 355

T

Tagebuch 1946-1949 (I), xiii, 8, 10, 12-13, 50, 53, 60, 78, 124, 125, 138-39, 145-47, 197, 199-200, 207, 211, 220-21, 247, 252, 263, 272-73, 323, 340, 347-48, 355-59
Tagebuch 1966-1971 (II), xiii, 16, 273, 317-18
Tagebücher, 9, 272, 312, 355, 368
Technological
  expertise, 125
  profession, 128
  society, 7, 155
Technology
  can control nature, 145, 154, 173, 184
  can control world of phenomena, 135-36, 182
  can't save Faber, 184
  Faber limited by, 184, 336

not available for Sabeth, 167-68
places Faber beyond time,
   aging, death, 144, 359
Sabeth interested in, 183
vs. the creative, mysterious,
   beautiful, 139, 164
vs. mysticism, intuition, 144,
   169
Time. *See also* Transient time,
   Past, Present, Future
alternative possibilities not subject to, 203
characters challenged to come to terms with, 15, 253
concept of, 12-13, 53, 212, 315
measured (clock), xx
basis is repetition, 13, 261, 350
defined, 13
Faber lives by, 14, 173
Tohulis (*Gantenbein*), 256, 257, 355
Transcience, 13, 14, 212, 355, 357. *See also* Transient time
Transcient time, xx, 355-361
aging, death are associated with, 13-14, 212, 341
concept difficult for Frisch men, 315, 342
Enderlin's relationship to, flawed, 207, 211
Faber accepts, 14, 175, 183
Faber ignores, 144, 145, 148
Max accepts, 14, 270, 292, 307
Stiller finally accepts, 14
unimportant to Jürg, 27
defined, 13-14
embraces repetition, 14, 349
Hanna sees it as basis of life, 173-74
Holozän shows final stage of, 316-21, 325

is suspended, in Cuba, 166
master of life, 261
offers possibility of change,
   174, 181-82, 212, 260
robots exist outside, 144-45

U

"Undine geht" (Bachmann), 313
Unicorn, 244, 265. *See also* Einhorn
Ursula (*Montauk*), 277, 278, 282, 283, 298
Das Urteil (Kafka), xviii

V

Die Verwandlung (Kafka), xviii
Vulnerable
   area: head, 209
Frisch's men, in love relationship, 8, 15, 21, 130, 144, 156, 184, 287, 339
less, with blind man, 354
to repetition, 281

W

W. (*Montauk*), 286-87, 305, 311
Whiskey, 106, 107, 132, 204, 224-26, 243, 344-45
White, James Larkin (Jim) (*Stiller*), 51, 52, 94-95, 100, 101, 107-10, 123
Williams (*Faber*), 153, 162
"Das wirkliche Leben"
   Faber gradually approaches, 125-26, 156, 164, 167, 183
Hortense seeks, 36, 331, 351

Jürg possesses and abandons, 27, 36, 44, 46-48, 346
Kilian and, 280
Max comes close to, 352
protagonists seek through loving relationship, xvii-xix, 1-4, 7-8, 14-15, 315, 357, 358, 361
"real men" seek, 24
Rolf lives *his* version of, 87
Schaad failed to achieve, 325
Stiller aware of, 109, 117, 119-122

Yvonne relinquishes search for, 32-33

Y, Z

Yvonne (*Schwierigen*), 9-10, 17-38, 43-50, 78, 86, 329, 337, 338, 343, 346, 350-52
Zimmer, Dieter E., 369
Zollinger, Albin, 21
Zufall, 130, 145-48. *See* Chance